SOUTH ASIAN CULTURAL STUDIES

A BIBLIOGRAPHY

SOUTH ASIAN CULTURAL STUDIES

A BIBLIOGRAPHY

VINAY LAL

MANOHAR
1996

ISBN 81-7304-134-2

First Published 1996

Published by
Ajay Kumar Jain
Manohar Publishers & Distributors
2/6, Ansari Road, Daryaganj
New Delhi - 110002

Lasertypeset by
A J Software Publishing Co. Pvt. Ltd.
305, Durga Chambers,
1333, D.B. Gupta Road,
Karol Bagh, New Delhi - 110005

Printed at
Rajkamal Electric Press
G.T. Karnal Road
Delhi

CONTENTS

ACKNOWLEDGMENTS

It was in December of 1991 that I was approached, by the Committee on Southern Asian Studies at the University of Chicago, where I was then about to complete my Ph.D., with the idea of preparing a bibliography of Contemporary South Asian Cultural Studies. I have more to say about the parameters of such a study in the short essay that accompanies this bibliography, but suffice to say that the general feeling, among the more keen supporters of this study in any case, was that 'contemporary' could be interpreted as meaning '1980 and thereafter', since 1980 was about the time that 'cultural studies', as it is now understood, began to occupy an important place in the study of South Asia and particularly India.

The initial funding for this study came from the Committee on Southern Asian Studies, and I am grateful to it, and in particular to its chairperson, Professor Clinton Seely, for supporting me in such an innovative fashion at a time when the usual sources of funding upon which I could rely had been quite exhausted. I can only hope that the committee will feel that its investment has been suitably, if not unexpectedly, rewarded. Professors Sheldon Pollock, Ronald Inden, and Bernard S. Cohn always displayed the most avid interest in this project, and I am grateful to them for their support. The project was intended to last for about six months, and a fairly comprehensive bibliography was submitted to the committee before my departure for Columbia University in August 1992. At that point, although I had fulfilled my obligation to the committee, it appeared to me that it would serve a very great purpose to continue with the project and transform it into a book-length manuscript.

Numerous persons brought books, articles, and other material of interest to my attention. This bibliography would have been more complete than it is at present, but for the fact that nearly thirty individuals to whom I wrote did not favor me with a reply. I am grateful to Professors Nicholas Dirks, Wimal Dissanayake, D. P. Pattanayak, Gyan Prakash, and R. Radhakrishnan for responding at length to my queries and alerting me to the considerations that they thought were of most significance in compiling such a bibliography, and to Professors Richard Schechner and Kumkum Sangari for responding to my request for a list of their publications. Ashis Nandy has, as always, been generous with his time and friendship, and I am quite certain that I have as complete a set of his scattered writings as is to be found anywhere. Philip

Bohlman gave me a good deal of his time to talk to me about developments in the scholarship on Indian music. Gauri Viswanathan shared many of her articles with me, and we had a number of conversations on the state of Indian studies, the politics of knowledge, and the conditions for a radical praxis that could draw upon the insights of 'cultural studies'.

I would like to thank my father, Kishori Lal, for procuring catalogs on my behalf from Indian publishers. Professor Anju Relan of California State University, Hayward, besides being a good friend, also gave me the benefit of her technical expertise, and as a consequence saved me from squandering a large chunk of time which I undoubtedly would have spent in repeatedly sifting through the general alphabetical listing of the bibliography to compile separate subject or thematic bibliographies. I cannot adequately thank my friends, Paul Gonsalves of EQUATIONS, Bangalore, and Henry Ranjeet of Kolam Travels, Madras, for their assistance with this project. They have been a considerable part of my 'data bank': the hundreds of clippings they have sent to me from Indian newspapers, including reviews of recent works, have not only kept me informed of recent Indian scholarship and developments in the Indian publishing industry, but also pointed to the myriad ways in which 'cultural studies' has entered the popular media and public consciousness. One cannot ask for more loyal friends. My greatest obligation, however, is to my brother Anil, who as manager of the New World Resource Center on Irving Park Road in Chicago (a left-wing bookstore, despite all appearances to the contrary), not merely alerted me to to recent publications of relevance to the project, but brought them to my front door. He has, besides, always been my best conversationalist.

Los Angeles, June 1994 Vinay Lal

ABBREVIATIONS

The following abbreviations have been used in the bibliography:

BCAS	*Bulletin of Concerned Asian Scholars*
CCCS	Centre for Contemporary Cultural Studies, Birmingham
CIS	*Contributions to Indian Sociology*
CSS	Centre for Social Studies, Surat
CSSH	*Comparative Studies in Society and History*
CSSS	Centre for Studies in Social Sciences, Calcutta
EPW	*Economic and Political Weekly*
IESHR	*Indian Economic and Social History Review*
IICQ	*India International Centre Quarterly*
J.	Journal
JAOS	*Journal of the American Oriental Society*
JAS	*Journal of Asian Studies*
Jrl.	Journal
MAS	*Modern Asian Studies*
NMML	Nehru Memorial Museum and Library, New Delhi
PPST	People and Patriotic-Oriented Science and Technology Bulletin
Univ.	University
UP	University Press

INTRODUCING CULTURAL STUDIES

The Location of Cultural Studies

In 1972 there appeared, under the auspices of the Centre for Contemporary Cultural Studies (CSSS) in Birmingham, the first issue of *Working Papers in Cultural Studies*. Nearly all the contributors to this issue were members of the Centre; as Stuart Hall, Director of the Centre between 1968 and 1979 has put it, the journal aimed "to define and to occupy a space", "to put Cultural Studies on the intellectual map" (Hall et al 1980:15).[1] The Centre itself was established in 1964 at the initiative of Richard Hoggart, then Professor of Modern English Literature at the University of Birmingham, and author of *The Uses of Literacy* (1958). Raymond Williams' *Culture and Society* also appeared in 1958, and was followed by his *The Long Revolution* (1961, rev. ed. 1965) and E. P. Thompson's *The Making of the English Working Class* (1963). Together these works appeared to constitute the foundational texts of what was to emerge as 'Cultural Studies'; however, writing many years later, Stuart Hall could ask, "What was the bibliography of a cultural studies thesis?" and go on to state, "Nobody knew".[2] The problem, at the present moment, is not one of how a bibliography of cultural studies might be constituted, but rather how one would prevent it from getting out of hand.

The parameters of British Cultural Studies have been set out in numerous works (Brantlinger 1990; Easthope 1988 and 1991; Turner 1990; and various essays in Grossberg, Nelson, and Treichler 1992), and this obviates the need for any detailed consideration of how Cultural Studies in Britain has developed since the establishment of CSSS, a task which is in any case well outside the scope of this brief essay. By the late 1970s, Cultural Studies had begun to make its presence felt in the United States, and in more recent years departments or programs going under the name of "cultural studies" have sprung up at numerous universities in Britain, Australia, and the United States. Where such programs do not exist, some other similar institutional apparatus may be found: thus the History of Consciousness Program at the University of California, Santa Cruz, and the Center for Twentieth-Century Studies at the University of Wisconsin-Milwaukee, to speak only of the United States. These programs owe their existence largely to the intellectual ferment in the humanities and (some of the) social sciences, encapsulated in such philosophical and political movements, intellectual practices, and modes of inquiry as feminism, post-modernism, Marxism, post-structuralism, psychoanalysis (particularly of the Lacanian variety), deconstruction, critical theory, dialogism, post-structuralism, New Historicism, and discourse analysis. These modes of inquiry all fall under the rubric of "Cultural Studies".

If Cultural Studies appears to encompass everything that is vital and living in scholarship today, it is an indication of the difficulty of providing cultural studies with an unambiguous definition and clear narrative. While cultural studies undoubtedly did not originate in a fit of absent-mindedness (although the British Empire in India did so, according to one famous imperialist historian), the precariousness of the enterprise, marked not only by brilliant successes and conspicuous political interventions but also by false starts, detours, uncertainties, and constant adjustments, has always been visibly present. Much of the work of the people associated with the center in Birmingham had revolved around subcultures — the culture of the working class and punks, for instance — before moving to an engagement with the work of Gramsci. Feminism provided the next nodal point of intervention, leading to more vigorous thinking on questions pertaining to gender, cultural and sexual politics, and subjectivity; and similarly Cultural Studies found itself engaging in questions of race, ethnicity, and identity in the post-colonial world. Motivated by a critique of disciplinary formations, Cultural Studies could scarcely become a discipline; in the words of Stuart Hall, "Cultural studies is not one thing, it has never been one thing."[3] Migrating from Britain to America, predictably Cultural Studies was divested of its political roots and, some would say, emancipatory possibilities. While Cultural Studies was to witness an unprecedented explosion in the United States, and lead to work on an enormously diverse array of subjects with an emphasis on what Stuart Hall has termed "theoretical fluency", it appeared to substitute "intellectual work for politics", something of an inevitability in the "highly rarified and enormously elaborated and well-funded professional world of American academic life".[4] It is no accident at all that in the years of the Republican ascendancy, the years in which the world was subjected to an orchestrated campaign of pacification under two bandits camouflaging as presidents, and when American cities were allowed to putrefy while the military establishment could display avuncular affection, Cultural Studies was allowed to triumph in the universities, as though to trumpet its powerlessness before the world.

What, then, is Cultural Studies? A number of vital, and what were until the advent of Cultural Studies largely ignored, questions have now come to the forefront. To pose crudely a few of these questions, one might ask: How are texts constituted? Who speaks for whom, with with right, and with what consequences? What are the ways in which power inheres in knowledge? If the so-called "linguistic turn", or the turn toward textuality, led to certain questions about the politics of representation, so did the work of Foucault, who was able to render subjectivities, which traditional scholarship had construed as given, into objects of inquiry. How are subjects constituted, and how are 'others' deprived of agency? What are the exclusionary practices of the state and dominant groups? How does one recuperate the voice of the Other? Cultural Studies also recognizes the inescapable influence of colonialism, and it is not even certain that there is an adequate vocabulary to speak of the pre-colonial past, in view of the epistemological transformation of indigenous spaces wrought by the colonizers (see Mitchell 1989; Carter 1987). These questions are, of course, keenly debated, for if the power of colonialism is construed as totalizing, then where is the space for resistance? One body of work suggests the importance of notions of hybridity, and of those interstitial spaces in which power is negated, negotiated, imitated, parodied, and usurped; another body of work reminds us that calamitous as colonialism may have been for the colonized, it may have been more catastrophic still for the colonizers. In the post-colonial world of shifting boundaries, moving commodities, the infusion of capital, and transnational culture, how is one to conceptualize identity? Into these debates, feminists have injected a number of other concerns. How are discourses gendered? If one speaks of 'woman', it is at the risk of essentializing; and if one does not do so, then how can the discourses of feminism become epistemologically and politically empowering? In pursuance of these queries and many others, questions of race, gender, class, identity, and colonialism have of late assumed an altogether unprecedented importance, constituting a domain that is encapsulated by the term Cultural Studies.

There is, in any body of knowledge, something that is taken for granted, and it is precisely that which Cultural Studies has sought to interrogate. What is at issue are questions not only about Otherness, but also about the place of discursive formations in the constitution of ideologies, the nature and location of power, the relation of politics to aesthetics, and the relation of global or late capitalism to certain discursive practices. Although Cultural Studies obviously brings together a number of positions marked by political and theoretical differences, at least one critic has insisted that these widely divergent positions nonetheless "share a commitment to examining cultural practices from the point of view of their intrication with, and within, relations of power."[5] If Cultural Studies has been successful in altering the contours of knowledge, it is just as certain that we have scarcely developed forms of politics that would alter the political landscape and the positions of those whose agency remains attenuated.

If Cultural Studies signals a reconfiguration of knowledge, has South Asian studies been similarly affected? This is the question that, in the first instance, led to the inauguration of this bibliography. One can point to the emergence — in India, Britain, and the U.S. — of powerful Indian voices of feminism, to bodies of scholars congregated at research centers and institutions like the Nehru Museum and the Centre for the Study of Developing Societies in Delhi, the Centre for Studies in Social Sciences at Calcutta, and the Central Languages Institute in Hyderabad, and to comparatively new organs of expression like *Subaltern Studies*, *Deep Focus*, and the *Journal of Arts and Ideas*. Subaltern Studies has been a phenomenon unto itself, and there are as many articles on it as the number of articles appearing in the eight volumes of *Subaltern Studies* published so far. Subaltern Studies takes us beyond India, and reminds us that any account of 'South Asian Cultural Studies' must reflect the contributions of significant South Asian voices entrenched in American universities and elsewhere. There may be, as has been recently suggested, an intricate relationship between subaltern studies and post-colonial theory (Dirlik 1994). Numerous practitioners of the English novel in India — Allan Sealy, Shashi Tharoor, Upamanyu Chatterjee — have provoked searching questions about the Indianness of English, the transformation of the novel, and the assimilation of Indian texts and traditions to post-modern forms of 'narration', while similar figures belonging to the South Asian diaspora, represented by Salman Rushdie, Amitav Ghosh, Vikram Seth, and Anita Desai, have in addition opened up questions about identity, nationalism, boundaries, and transnational culture. In taking up this bibliographic project, the question remained: does South Asian Cultural Studies remain the preserve of a few individuals of post-structuralist and post-colonial fame, or has its impact on the scholarship on South Asia, in India and elsewhere, been more far-reaching?

South Asian Cultural Studies

South Asian studies, particularly in the United States, has been handicapped until recently by the shortcomings that are common to "language and area studies" programs in general. Throughout the decades following World War II and preceding the 1980s, 'modernization' theory prevailed; among those studying religion, philosophy, literature — in short, the culture of India — the dominant paradigm was provided by the Indologist. India could be encompassed within a few magic words which unlocked all doors: there was Hinduism, and something called caste. Sanskrit, the language of antiquity, was the only Indian language worthy of study; occasionally the presence of Hindi, which had been proclaimed the national language of India, was acknowledged. Too many words need not be expended on South Asian area studies programs; as Ronald Inden has written about the pretensions of American experts on India, "Backed by government funds, disseminated by universities, supported by the ACLS [American Council of Learned Societies] and the SSRC [Social Science Research Council], endowed by the Ford Foundation, and given space in the *New York Review of Books*, the knowledge of the orientalist, known nowadays as an 'area studies' specialist, appears as rational, logical, scientific, realistic, and objective" (Inden 1990:37).

Notwithstanding the legacy of area studies programs, and the constraints of disciplinary formations at universities in India and elsewhere, South Asian Studies has become the focal point for many of the questions with which Cultural Studies seeks to engage itself, and most certainly for the discourses that interrogate the forms of knowledge by means of which the West — in the jargon of the day — "kidnapped" the non-West and held it "captive". The trajectories that led to an awareness of the politics of knowledge and of the shifting nature of entities hitherto assumed to be foundational if not stable, and the emergence of powerful critiques of modernity, can only be traced in a far lengthier and more ambitious essay than the present one. The publication of Said's *Orientalism* in 1978 has often been described as the point of departure for new investigations into colonial discourse; in India itself, such works as Jit Singh Uberoi's *Science and Culture* (1978) and Ashis Nandy's *Alternative Sciences* (1980), had a quiet but influential part to play in the interrogation of the culture of science. Some of the best work in India, I may note parenthetically, has been on the culture and sociology of science, and notable contributions have also been made by Claude Alvares, Deepak Kumar, and Shiv Viswanathan.

The investigations into science initiated a wide-ranging critique of modernity. In the meantime, that is by the early 1980s, *Subaltern Studies* had made its appearance, and it has gone to exert such an influence in the West that it is often taken to be the South Asian form of Cultural Studies, something in the manner in which caste was considered to be the form in which class appeared in a highly stratified and prodigiously 'religious' society like India. Such a view of Subaltern Studies, engaged in the twin task of the deconstruction of the colonial historiography of India and the constitution of new 'subjects', is fundamentally erroneous, considering both its intellectual genealogies and its similarities with new forms of cultural history, in particular 'history from below'. Subaltern Studies has not received, as is sometimes imagined, the endorsement of all Indian historians, and as is well known to students of Indian history in any case, its supposed repudiation of class as a foundational category has caused much grievance to certain Marxist historians and scholars. Like postcolonial criticism, Subaltern Studies "seeks to undo the Eurocentrism produced by the institution of the west's trajectory, its appropriation of the other as History."[6]

Besides Subaltern Studies, which has received a disproportionate share of attention, particularly from scholars in the West, owing to the success with which it has been able to market itself as a transnational scholarly commodity, a number of distinct developments — around which feminism stands as an overarching intervention and achievement — have taken place in India. First, and foremost, a sustained critique of modernity, and of the pathologies of rationality and science, has emanated from a number of different circles in India. Loosely speaking, we can speak of 'critiques of knowledge'. There is the work, for example, of scholars and activists associated with the Patriotic People's Science and Technology Group, and though it has a critical edge, it does not have the theoretical sophistication of a number of other people congregated in Delhi, such as Jit Singh Uberoi, Veena Das, Shiv Viswanathan, and Ashis Nandy, or the work of more or less independent scholars such as Claude Alvares. A recent manifesto issued by Ashis Nandy, Claude Alvares, Ziauddin Sardar (a Pakistani scholar), and Meryl Wyn Davies (a Welsh anthropologist), states that their ambition is "to recover our plural pasts, and through them our plural futures; to resume our numerous histories, metahistories and mythographies, all diverse and equally valid ways of reconstructing the past . . ." The authors state, quite unabashedly, that in the 500 years since the commencement of European voyages to the 'New World', "the generally unhappy features of the European native, his disturbed thinking, his distorted perception and his spiritually barren cultural objectives have been replicated and duplicated mindlessly in all those places and within all those people on whom he sought to impose himself."[7] It is from the stranglehold of a knowledge with an instrumental notion of rationality that the Indian critics of 'knowledge' seek to emancipate not only the formerly colonized world but the West as well. The Delhi-based Committee for Cultural Choices and Global Futures, chaired by Ashis Nandy, describes itself as being "guided by the belief that all knowledge is political intervention", its activities informed by three basis concerns: "an intellectual concern for the ecology of plural knowledge, a normative concern with cultural survival, and a political concern with the search for humane features for the 'victims of history'".[8] Characterizing modernity as "monolithic and cognitively coercive", and seeking to put the Enlightenment concept of progress, now deprived of much of its creative potential, into a "pluralistic encounter with the possibilities it has suppressed", the Committee seeks to generate knowledge that is not the product of the managerial, scientific, and secular nation-state. To this extent the 'critiques of knowledge' emanating from India can be described as sharing the Committee's political positions and epistemological views.

There is, as some of Ashis Nandy's other work suggests, a demonstrable need to turn to studies of cinema, television, and the media in South Asia. To some extent this shift has already taken place. 'Cultural Studies' approaches to the subculture of film stars can be expected; and there is already a small body of work on the manner in which state-sponsored television has aided the cause of Hindu 'fundamentalism' by offering homogenized versions of the Indian epics, the *Ramayana* and the *Mahabharata*, for public consumption when these works have always survived in pluralistic forms. Quite good as some of the recent scholarship is already, we are at a far remove from an understanding of the complex intersections between film and other cultural forms, and the particular ways in which the media does the work of hegemony. The culture of India's popular cinema; the constituency of Hindi films; the place of the Hindi film in the Indian diaspora; the Indian movie hall as a 'masculine' space; the film hoarding as the nexus between popular cinema and street culture; the association of the cinema in North and South India with electoral politics and the politics of the hoodlums; the use of the modern Hindi film to promote national integration and isolate the nation's 'enemies', a task that takes on more salience with the advent of terrorism in the Punjab in the early 1980s and in Kashmir in the late 1980s — all these and a great many other topics will require exploration if we are to understand the ubiquitous and unique place of film in the formation of 'modern' India. If cinema has been the twentieth-century's pre-eminent art form, responsible for ushering in modernity into the 'less developed' parts of the world, it would be hugely ironical if the Hindi film turned out to be the last bastion of a world-view that is not so much anti-modern as non-modern.[9]

In the last years of this century, as other forms of media have emerged, the cinema itself seems to be on the point of being eclipsed. Perhaps there was already a premonition of that in the United States, where the grand movie halls of the thirties and forties had almost altogether disappeared by the early seventies, paving the way for cinemas screening multiple films simultaneously in smaller theatres; and with the advent of video in the late seventies and early eighties, the complete demise of the movie theatre was being spoken of as a fact of life. In India, as well, the corner video store was to become as common as the *pan* shop, and indeed certain neighborhoods were completely dominated by video stores. The place of the video store in Indian social life, and in the public sphere, has never been examined, and neither has anyone probed whether the video store became, at least for a certain class of people, an alternative *adda* in the manner of the *pan* shop, the *chai* shop, or the cafe. As every Indian middle-class family would recognize, the fortunes of these video stores were tied to school schedules, and here again an extraordinary and wide-ranging phenomenon has evaded scrutiny. In the last few years, with the inauguration of satellite television, video stores have in turn been largely wiped out, though now the revolution implies more than the mere substitution of one technology for another. Satellite television is a global, trans-national form, but India may perhaps yet show that MTV is altogether compatible with large-scale versions of Indian epics. In short, it is not only cinema studies that one is speaking of, but also studies of video culture, television, satellite broadcasting, the world of trans-national teenager music shows, advertising, and so on. Studies of Indian cinema, which are now poised to acquire a significant place in Indian intellectual production, may inspire studies of media in general.

Along with 'critiques' of knowledge' and studies of media, two other developments have significantly informed South Asian Cultural Studies. Although in his lifetime Gandhi may not have been recognized as a 'green' leader, today his memory is cherished and invoked by women and men who are at the helm of ecological movements, and it is most certainly Gandhian thinking, along with strands of folk wisdom, the experience of deforestation, the loss of ancestral lands, and other deprivations induced by unthinking 'development', which has contributed to the Chipko movement in the Garhwal Hills, the *Narmada Bachao Andolan* [Save the Narmada Movement], and other notable attempts to reclaim a less exploitative relationship between humans, animals, and nature. While India's ecological movements are more impressive, and of more enduring significance, than the scholarly writings that have accompanied these movements, the pages of this bibliography provide an ample testimony to the manner in which environmental and ecological histories have successfully contested the dominant pathologies of knowledge. As the celebrated (though scarcely unproblematic) work of Vandana Shiva suggests, it is a belief in 'deep ecology' which allows us to speak both of green movements in which peasants and villagers have been the driving force and the 'critiques of knowledge' systems as important aspects of cultural studies. The forest provides a living, besides clean air, water, and fodder, for millions of people, and ecological struggles are thus contestations over civil, social, political, and cultural rights; at the same time, the forest has been, particularly in India, a metaphor for norms of civility and civilization, a retreat for philosophers, a haven of the wise and the good, a resting place for the aged — in short, an expression of pluralistic and humane ways of being and living. Writings under the 'environment and ecology' section of the bibliography show a keen awareness, without always being nativist or 'romantic' (a charge often levied against Vandana Shiva), of the fallacies of presuming that India must be committed to the same discourse on development and progress that the West has so assiduously sought to perpetuate as the universal discourse of our times.

If writings on ecology show one kind of political awareness, English studies in India represent another important and emergent strand in South Asian Cultural Studies. English Studies itself has several dimensions. Indian post-colonial critics, whether in India or located in the academy in English-speaking countries (principally the United States), provide South Asian Cultural Studies with one evident link to the Western academy. Enough has been written about post-coloniality in this connection elsewhere, thus obviating the need for any discussion here, and in any case some other questions posed by practitioners of English studies compel more attention. As a number of writers and scholars have asked, what is to be the pedagogical and institutional place of English in India? These interrogations of the hallowed place of English in India need not be confused with the clumsy and patriotic attempts by government officials in Hindi-dominated states like Madhya Pradesh and Uttar Pradesh to undermine the place of English in government and educational institutions. But pertinent questions remain: to what extent will one ever be able to speak of English as a language 'of the people'? How does English exist politically in relation to Indian languages? What associations does English have with structures of class and caste? How does English do the work of hegemony in India? It is in English studies, in particular, that we see the manner in which Gramsci has been woven into Indian interrogations of the paradigms of knowledge, a phenomenon that takes on greater meaning given the absence of post-structuralism in Indian intellectual circles. More disturbing is the fact that whereas in countries where English is the mother tongue, English is (as most languages must be, except when a difference is theorized between the 'classical' and the 'vernacular', and the 'classical' rendered into the language of oppression alone) the language of both dominant and dissenting modes of knowledge, in India English is seen to have an intimate association with the worldview of development, science, the ethos of 'progress', and the modern nation-state. In India, in other words, English appears to be irrevocably harnessed to those very pathologies that cultural studies lays bare for dissection: modernity, science, and instrumental and bureaucratic notions of rationality. Indians (and other colonized peoples) may not be Macaulay's only progeny, but they are certainly among the most faithful. As the recent work of Tejaswini Niranjana, Susie Tharu, Rajeswari Sunder Rajan, and a number of other scholars of English in Delhi, Calcutta, and Hyderabad suggests, these questions are now unavoidable and must be seriously entertained if English studies are to provide us with emancipatory possibilities. Their work shows, too, that interpretations of English literature, particularly as it has been traditionally construed, are no longer to be left to scholars in the West, and indeed it is arguable that the interpretation of the West can no longer be safely left to the West. The most enduring contribution of South Asian Cultural Studies, after all, might be to conscientize the West to interpretations of itself that it could not arrive at, and for this reason the bibliography includes, by way of a mere sampling, some of the more arresting interpretations of canonical European and American works of philosophy and religion, such as Mukund Lath's paper on Aristotle, even when the works bear no relation to the study of Indian history, society, or culture.

Finally, intersecting with all these developments in South Asian Cultural Studies, and constituting an arch around them, is feminism. Gender has emerged as the most important subject-position from which to question given identities, and in every respect feminism has opened up hitherto closed spaces of knowledge. Writings in the area of environmental and ecological studies, for example, have alerted us to the particular manner in which the oppression of elites in some geographic terrains affects women, while scholars of English have established how the voices of women were sought to be suppressed by those very men who were forging a new literature in the name of the nation and in the spirit of anti-imperialism. Feminism, as I point out elsewhere, has been the single most important factor in the reconstitution (howsoever incomplete) of the academy in the West, and it is feminist voices that have most persuasively and effectively contested the institutionalized forms of knowledge by means of which the world is sought to be comprehended and chained. Perhaps in India feminism has not played so paramount a role, but it is nonetheless the case that feminism has provided, and will continue to do so, the link between diverse strands of Cultural Studies; and it is quite likely that, as in the West, sexuality and not only gender will become an important determinant in the constitution of identity.

Having indicated some of the significant though by no means fully developed trends in South Asian Cultural Studies, I wish only to consider very briefly the future of Cultural Studies in India. If Cultural Studies in India is not to go the way of the West, where the institutionalization of Cultural Studies has been fully achieved, as though to honor the old American way of disempowering any intellectual tradition that poses even the slightest check to reigning orthodoxies, intellectual production in India will have to retain close ties with folk forms of knowledge and with the traditions of marginalized peoples. In India, unlike in America, the left has some standing outside the academy, and so-called grassroots movements are not entirely dissociated from the world of intellectuals. But it would be quite foolish to suppose that a greater public space for the left necessarily entails a more hospitable future for Cultural Studies; quite to the contrary, many of those whose names are linked with Cultural Studies in India (but not in the diaspora) have no association with either the old left or with 'cultural Marxism'. By far the greatest hope that South Asian Cultural Studies will not be consumed by the Anglo-American model is the fact that there remain available to Indian thinkers and writers certain idioms for imagining, conceptualizing, and re-shaping the world no longer available to Western intellectuals. One can still admire Indian civilization while despising the Indian nation. No such distinction is possible when it comes to the West. Indian civilization has always displayed an inherent respect for plural forms of knowledge and South Asian Cultural Studies must take upon itself the agenda of building upon, and engendering, post-modern and nonmodern alternatives to the dominant official discourse of the scientific, managerial, modern nation-state.[10]

Parameters of the Present Essay

I have worked on this bibliography single-handedly for slightly over two years, and could not systematically survey nearly two hundred journals in which material on South Asia (or the South Asian diaspora) reflecting a 'cultural studies' approach appears on a more or less frequent basis. An exhaustive search of the *Economic and Political Weekly* and *Social Scientist*, for example, would have perhaps yielded another 100-150 entries, but I think it is safe to say that the bilbiography includes most of the important pieces published in these two and other like journals. Even articles published in the early part of 1994 appear in the bibliography, but for the most part my survey of periodical literature terminated in the second half of 1993. A list of the 246 journals in which one or more articles appear is included as Appendix One; if there should be a second edition of this bibliography, it is proposed to include the place of publication of each journal, and possibly the address and full details of publication and frequency. For some journals, the place of publication has been indicated.

Needless to say, I have not read every book and article listed in the bibliography, although I have, at the very least, a cursory familiarity with the vast majority of the entries. That much was needed, in order to determine whether the piece warranted inclusion in the bibliography. With respect to certain areas, such as recent works in Indian historiography, including the contributions of the 'Subaltern School', post-colonial theory, film studies, and literary criticism, I have an intimate acquaintance with the literature. The intellectual considerations that helped me to determine the fate, as it were, of each piece are discussed in the introductory essay. I attempted to verify personally the existence of each item in the bibliography, and was largely successful; the handful of items that I could not locate, but for which I had a firm citation, are preceded by an asterisk. For all other items, except unpublished pieces, I am prepared to take the responsibility of accurate citation. Unpublished and "forthcoming" works have not, in general, been included in the bibliography, except in those instances where it appeared quite certain that the piece would appear in the near future: in such cases, the name of the press or the journal has been provided. In a few instances, where the piece is described as forthcoming in 1993, I was unable to ascertain whether the piece had in fact appeared. In a number of other instances, the items have been in my possession for ten years or even longer, and the citation taken at that time may not have been complete; nonetheless, enough information has been furnished for each item to make possible its location.

With a very few exceptions, everything included in this bibliography was written in English. That is a shortcoming which must be acknowledged and which perhaps others may wish to redress. To have surveyed books and periodicals in the numerous Indian languages — and my competency extends only to Hindi, and to a limited extent to Bengali — would have been to extend the bounds of this study immeasurably. It would have entailed a collaborative effort, which in the circumstances was not possible, and for which there were no provisions. In some respects, it would have been more important to include material from the Indian languages, for only then would we be in a position to ascertain how far the 'cultural studies' approach has permeated Indian academia, the publishing world, and the world of the public intellectual. A number of Indian writers and intellectuals well-known among English speakers write mainly in their mother tongue; a case in point is Gautam Bhadra, who may be familiar to historians of India and readers of the several volumes of Subaltern Studies, but who in Calcutta is said to be known in very wide circles. It is quite possible that many of his writings would fall under the rubric of 'cultural studies'. Certain other intellectuals, such as Partha Chatterjee and Asok Sen, write in English as well as an Indian language (in this case, too, Bengali), and wherever I have encountered citations to their work in Indian languages, I have included them in the bibliography. We can expect that certain important works in English will be rendered into Indian languages: Ashis Nandy's *The Intimate Enemy*: *Loss and Recovery of Self under Colonialism*, is already available in Hindi and Gujarati, and one hopes this will set a trend for some other works as well.

In India, unlike the United States, the 'newspaper culture' still flourishes. No middle-class home will be found without a newspaper, and the politics of various newspapers is always a matter of keen discussion and intense speculation. Indian intellectuals write for newspapers, and many vital debates have been conducted in the pages of the *Times of India*, *The Indian Express*, *The Statesman*, *The Hindu*, and other dailies, to speak only of English-language newspapers. The dispute over the Babri Masjid in Ayodhya, the conflagration over the decision of the Government of India to improve the representation of backward classes in government offices and educational institutions by implementing the recommendations of the Mandal Commission, and the 'aspersions' cast on the name of Mahatma Gandhi, 'Father of the Nation', by certain leaders of the Bahujan Samajwadi Party, which claims to speak on behalf of the lower castes, are all instances of subjects on which intellectuals waged intense debates through newspapers. The attempt by the Hindu right-wing to capture the Indian Historical Congress was a matter of considerable discussion in Indian newspapers, and it is doubtful that a comparable phenomenon would have received that kind of attention in American newspapers. Any bibliographic guide which seeks to understand how 'cultural studies' has manifested itself in the Indian arena must undoubtedly pay close attention to the place of newspapers in Indian intellectual life. Here, once again, I can only point to the limitations of working alone, entirely from private funds after the period of initial funding, and to the severe constraints of time. Curiously, the practitioners of cultural studies have failed to recognize the place of newspapers in the political and social life of India, and no one has written on the life of journalism in India, the ethos of the tribe of newspapermen, the manner in which the newspaper mediates between the worlds of literacy and orality, and on the recent attempts to stifle the independence of Indian newspapers by introducing an American-style management.

Many of the books and monographs in this bibliography originated as Ph.D. dissertations. While dissertations are in the public domain, they are not easily accessible except to scholars, and a good many of them, including some very fine ones, remain unpublished. A systematic search of Ph.D. dissertations, much less of M.Phil. theses, was not attempted, but a few about whose existence I was aware of, or which had been brought to my attention, are included in the bibliography. Along these lines, many institutions in India publish series of occasional papers, and these are for the most part inaccessible, often not subject to cataloging, and encountered purely by chance; in other cases, these occasional papers are largely for internal use, and available only in stencilled form. I have included a great many of these occasional papers published by the Nehru Memorial Museum and Library (Delhi), Centre for Social Studies (Surat), and the Centre for Studies in Social Sciences (Calcutta), three important centers of learning in India.

These are not the only limitations of the bibliography, and I need to say a bit more about certain omissions, and the inclusion of certain items that scarcely appear to fall under the rubric of 'cultural studies', lest the selection of the entries appear to be excessively arbitrary. As a certain faculty member at the University of Chicago had observed, various other computer banks and bibliographic guides attest to the fact that each year, well over 10,000 articles in the realm of South Asian "women's studies", or pertaining to the position, rights, and sufferings of women in India, are published each year in periodicals all over the world. What criteria, I was asked, had led me to omit those articles from the bibliography? While not an altogether straightforward affair, it appears to me that I could, without much difficulty, offer justifiable criteria to explain how I came to select certain items as worthy of inclusion. As in most other areas of scholarship, the vast number of articles in the realm of "women's studies" appearing in Indian journals and magazines are largely descriptive, and in many of them the methodological work is largely empirical, based on various spurious models, oral interviews, and other data. Consider, for example, the question of how far women in rural areas have access to reliable post-natal care of the sort that is offered in modern hospitals, and how far they avail themselves of the regimen of inoculations to which Western medicine is sworn. Where the article merely discusses the ratio of doctors to women patients, and the number of beds available to women who have just given birth, its inclusion in the bibliography would scarcely be justified; nor would its inclusion be warranted if the discussion had moved to a slightly more sophisticated level, and considered the level of literacy among women, their awareness of the importance of post-natal care, and the extent of involvement of husbands and other family members. But, supposing that the article showed that structures of patriarchy impeded rather than encouraged women in resorting to such care, or that a number of women in a certain village had decided that they were not prepared to be bound by modern medicine's world-view, and as a consequence they were prepared to renounce the facilities of modern hospitals in the interest of preserving a certain bodily integrity, then it appears that such an article may well warrant inclusion. With the aid of certain strategies of reading and interpretation, it is always possible to ask whether the book or article in question shows an awareness of the conditions under which knowledge is gained and disseminated, and where any piece was shown to evince a sense of the "politics of knowledge", it generally found its way into the bibliography. The politics of knowledge has, in recent times, been structured around notions of race, gender, class, sexual orientation, and the numerous forms in which subalternity appears, not to mention such foundational categories as nation, capital, and community, but as the bibliography itself shows, anti-foundational critiques are also central to 'cultural studies'. In the event, once one has made the transition to the politics of knowledge, and to a cultural politics, the mass of 10,000 articles dwindles down to a few hundred and often no more than a mere handful.

In the arena of Indian history, where subaltern studies has left an ineradicable impress, not just on the scholarship of India but in wide areas of historical and political studies, and in literary and critical theory, where South Asian theorists of post-coloniality — Gayatri Chakravorty Spivak, Homi Bhabha, Sara Suleri, R. Radhakrishnan, Rajeswari Sunder Rajan, among many others — have assumed an important and (in some cases) a disturbingly reverential place in academia, the criteria for inclusion were applied with greater rigor. Many articles that showed an extensive acquaintance with certain traditions of historiography, or with traditional modes of literary criticism, and might otherwise be deemed as significant contributions to scholarship, were excluded unless they displayed some familiarity with Marxist theory, feminism, post-structuralism, post-colonial theory, deconstruction, psychoanalysis, or with some aspect of the theoretical work of recent years. There was no other way to keep the bibliography within bounds. In most other areas of scholarship, however, the picture is exceedingly bleak, and many items were included in the bibliography for no better reason than the fact that the scholarly work within those areas remains impoverished; as a consequence, any piece that even remotely suggested the possibility of an enhanced understanding of cultural politics, the politics of knowledge, the determinative influence of colonialism and orientalism,, or indeed any other question to which 'cultural studies' has devoted its labors, was included. Very little work has been done, for instance, in the domains of art history, cinema studies, dance, and performance studies, and a good deal of what exists has emanated from the scholars associated with the "Journal of Arts and Ideas", published from Delhi.[11] Although India has the largest film industry in the world, and Hindi and Tamil films occupy an ubiquitous place in the lives of Indians and the public spaces which they inhabit and around which they congregate, the popular film has remained a pariah to the mental world of the scholar and public intellectual. The commercial Hindi film had a long and marvelously complicated run in the former USSR, but there is scarcely an article on this intriguing phenomenon. More works have been devoted to Satyajit Ray than to the popular Hindi film; and the Marxists remain fixated upon the films of Ritwik Ghatak, undoubtedly a master of the cinema but one whose oeuvre remains unknown to non-Bengalis and all but the most serious aficionados of cinema. Given the paucity of material on Indian cinema, I thought it best to include the work of Chidananda Dasgupta, which while exceedingly readable and informed displays no familiarity with theoretical literature; nor do his readings display a political awareness. Such compromises were made elsewhere as well. The criteria for inclusion were, thus, relaxed in numerous instances, and nowhere more so than in the areas of art history, folklore, theatre, and dance, as the two papers on folklore by Joyce Flueckiger so amply suggest. In other areas, the pickings were even slimmer; if there is no category for law, legal studies, and jurisprudence, it is precisely because critical and discursive investigations of judicial discourse, and even more emphatically of the manner in which law inflects our understanding of culture, society, and politics, have not been undertaken. The most notable exception is the few pieces devoted to judicial discourse in the seven volumes of *Subaltern Studies*,[12] though one cannot but agree with Upendra Baxi, one of India's most respected legal scholars, that "the law is fugitively present in *Subaltern Studies*, although the nature of colonial law recurs as a central element in structuring subalternity."[13] Every second Hindi film has a courtroom scene, but surprisingly no one has thought that worthy of analysis. Perhaps the Hindi film, more so than the structures of the state, or the legal machinery (elaborate in its pretensions, meagre in the promises it is able to keep), is a telling reminder of the considerable extent to which the colonial rhetoric of the 'rule of law' has left its impress upon Indians.

The paucity of literature reflecting a cultural studies approach pertaining to Bangladesh, Pakistan, Nepal, and Sri Lanka, which has also been listed separately to facilitate access, will strike every reader. Although South Asia area studies programs at American universities make the pretense of covering the entirety of the Indian sub-continent, the study of Indian literature and history dominates those programs. In their earlier incarnation, when modernization theory reigned supreme, these programs dwelled on the purportedly secular nation-state presided over by Nehru. My endeavor was to make this bibliography truly "South Asian", but I found that to be a forbidding task. Take, for example, the work of B. K. Jahangir on Bangladesh. Though his books make use of Foucault (among other European thinkers), they are poorly written and quite unreadable; and a great deal in them belongs to the realm of political science, a discipline from which one can only expect absence of theoretical rigor, little imagination, and even less good. Nonetheless some of these pieces have been included, for lack of anything better. It is possible that, in the case of these countries, a survey of the literature in indigenous languages may be all the more necessary. Often a journal or work that had been brought to my attention was not easy of access, a case in point being the *Thatched Patio*, an important periodical published from Colombo. The literature on colonial Sri Lanka in recent years constitutes something of an exception, and an increasingly large number of dissertations everywhere are being written on Sri Lanka; there is also good work on Sri Lankan cinema, though I know of nothing comparable on the film industries (such as they are) of Pakistan and Bangladesh, which admittedly are parasitic on the film industry of their gigantic neighbor, though that would not preclude the possibility of work on the film culture of these countries.

Works of poetry are not included in this bibliography, with a few exceptions, though works of fiction are.[14] The selection will appear to be wholly arbitrary, for readers will note the inclusion of the works of Amitav Ghosh and Salman Rushdie, but not the novels or travelogues of V. S. Naipaul, who scarcely needs an introduction. The novels of Naipaul, particularly such early ones as *The House of Mr. Biswas* and *The Mimic Men*, are memorable works, and students with an interest in the Indian diaspora, or questions of identity, may well find the novels of sociological significance. But it has been many years since Naipaul wrote a novel, and while his mastery of style is enviable, both Ghosh and Rushdie appear to have contributed in a larger measure to the transformation of the novel. Indeed, it would not be too much to say that *The Circle of Reason*, *The Shadow Lines*, and the *Satanic Verses* owe a great deal to post-modernism, which in turn has been more than adequately 'serviced' by them. Naipaul himself has had no use for the theoretical gains and critical interventions of the last fifteen years, and indeed a few years ago had, much to the delight of conservative academics and the political establishment in the U.S. and U.K., declared that Western civilization has now become "our universal civilization". Of course, all the terms in that phrase, 'our', 'universal', and 'civilization', are precisely what proponents of cultural studies would interrogate, asking: who is it who speaks? with what authority? on whose behalf? how does the 'our' get constituted? what are the lines of inclusion and exclusion? Are we, moreover, agreed on what 'civilization' means — and if we are, by what evaluative scale are we to decide that certain civilizations are "universal", while others are merely parochial? The writings of Naipaul, thus, could not warrant inclusion, and besides that the selection of fiction is aimed at being suggestive, highlighting both significant works of recent years as well as works that remain relatively obscure. The two novels of Sunetra Gupta, for instance, suggest what kind of literature is emerging from England, while the two volumes by Amarjit Chandan alert us to the literature of the Punjabi, and particularly Sikh, community in the United Kingdom. This is no mean matter, for twenty percent of all Sikhs now live outside India, and the identity of Sikhs and the contours of the Sikh faith will, in years to come, be constituted as much by the members of the Sikh diaspora as it will be by Sikhs living in India.

A number of other considerations were also important in deciding which works of fiction to include in the bibliography. In the past few years alone, a number of Indian publishers, such as Penguin, Rupa, Kali for Women, Sterling, and Orient Longman (through their imprint "Disha"), have taken a special initiative in bringing works of fiction by Indian writers before the public. A few hundred volumes have been published, and of these a few were chosen for inclusion, mainly those by women. A number of anthologies of short stories released by the Delhi-based Kali for Women, such as *Truth Tales*, *Inner Spaces*, and *In Other Worlds*, show the influence of feminism, just as they point to the peculiar difficulties faced by women in India. Feminism has unquestionably been the single most important force in the academy since the 1970s, and far more so than post-modernism or deconstruction, feminist theory resonates outside the university, shaping the ways in which relations between women and men unfold, the manner in which women forge common political interests, and the quest for equality at home and in the workplace. In this respect, a work such as Rukhsana Ahmad's *Beyond Belief*: *Contemporary Feminist Urdu Poetry*, must have a place in the bibliography which a hundred anthologies of Urdu poetry, howsoever good they may be, could not claim. No Pakistani poet has exerted a greater influence in our times than Faiz Ahmed Faiz, and though his writings are marked by a political sensitivity, commitment, and urgency that is just as extraordinary as the cadences of his verse, his writings do not, in that sense, fall under the rubric of 'cultural studies'. Besides, his work is already exceedingly well-known, available to English readers in a number of excellent translations. On the other hand, analyses of the annual Faiz mela, which is surely one of the great cultural and political events staged in Pakistan, are sorely needed. Such work may well point to the manner in which the Pakistani establishment has sought to negotiate their desire to encompass him within their fold while recognizing that as a great renegade poet he undermined those cherished beliefs and institutions by means of which they harnessed and exerted their power.

The work of a number of very prominent Indian intellectuals and Western scholars writing on India is conspicuous by its virtual absence from this bibliography. I have in mind, for instance, the writings of the late Indian philosopher, Bimal Krishna Matilal, and the Indian economist, Amartya Sen (known to others as A.K. Sen). Matilal's work on *nyaya* philosophy and logic holds an honorable place in recent critical work on Indian philosophy; and similarly Sen's work on famine and entitlements, which effects a significant intervention in the debate on rights and distributive justice, is already recognized as being of enduring importance. But the grounds for excluding their writings are equally obvious. The same considerations applied to the works of noted political commentators in India like Asghar Ali Engineer and Rajni Kothari. No doubt, it was Rajni Kothari who first directed sustained attention towards grass roots movements, and the hazards of relying on state policies for the amelioration of public grievances, and to this extent he can be considered a source of inspiration for many political movements, particularly those in which the intelligentsia has partaken. Kothari founded the Centre for the Study of Developing Societies in Delhi, where sustained work was done for many years on Indian politics and electoral behavior, and where over the last fifteen years a number of intellectuals — Ashis Nandy, Shiv Viswanathan, among others — have been instrumental in breathing new life into the study of Indian political culture, the sociology of Indian science, and the appropriation by the state of public spaces and discourses. But Kothari himself is at a considerable remove from 'cultural studies', and indeed his work belongs rather with that of political scientists. As for Asghar Ali Engineer, while he has been vociferously diligent in documenting the course of Hindu-Muslim riots, and developments touching upon the Muslim population of India, his work does not have a critical edge; in fact, it remains firmly within the parameters of social science discourse. The same could be said for numerous other intellectuals, political commentators, and scholars: one thinks of Bharat Dogra, who has fought valiantly for the rights of minorities and women through dozens of publications, each of which bears the stamp of utter predictability. In each case I have exercised my own judgment, the basis for which will certainly not be evident to everyone. The name of the historian Bipan Chandra, for instance, appears thrice. Although his work does not show the sophistication to be found in the writings of some of the subaltern historians, he represents an important strand of left historiography, which in India has played an instrumental role by virtue of its opposition to official discourse and its commitment to a practical politics. His book on *Communalism in Modern India*, though it stands superseded in certain respects by Gyanendra Pandey's *Construction of Communalism in Colonial North India*, paved the way for the study of communalism. Many of the recent writings on the Babri Masjid, now no longer extant, share a trajectory that stemmed in part from Bipan Chandra's work.

Various other omissions will strike this or that reader, but I can offer no further justifications for the manner in which the bibliography was composed. In such a work, the shortcomings must invariably be innumerable; and as a matter of fact, when the work was initially undertaken, my knowledge both of computers and library data-bases was at such a primitive level that I could not make use of the facilities that major American libraries offer. Nonetheless, I am certain that users of the bibliography will find that this work has not been done before, and my labors would have been amply rewarded if everyone finds even a few hitherto unknown citations, and more significantly finds her or his work moving in new directions. My own predilections may not be clear to everyone, and accordingly I have taken the liberty of citing, not only under my name, but elsewhere in the bibliography, a substantial number of long reviews and review-articles that I have written over the last five years.

A few words may be mentioned about the form in which citations appear. Diacritical marks have not been used for Indian names, even though they may have appeared in the original citation. *The Chicago Manual of Style* has been followed, except that the form "11, 5" has been used in place of "11, no. 5" in designating the volume and number, respectively, of the journal in which the article appeared. In the general alphabetical listing, where two or more works by one author were included, the listing is chronological, with the most recent work appearing last; in the thematic or subject listings, by way of contrast, two or more works from the same hand appear in strict alphabetical order. (Pieces beginning with the indefinite or definite article will be found under 'a' or 't'.) An entire year's issues of the *Economic and Political Weekly* are numbered consecutively, and a single year's issue may run to 4,000 pages. Every so often the magazine has a special issue, entitled "Review of Women's Studies", "Review of Management", and so forth, and in the supplement the pages are numbered separately. Thus, for example, an article by Jasodhara Bagchi, entitled "Representing Nationalism", appeared in the 25 Oct. 1990 issue of the *Economic and Political Weekly*, and the page numbers, WS65-71, show that the reference is to the pages in the supplement on "Women's Studies" (WS) that appeared in the magazine that day. At least two well-known Indian journals, *Social Scientist* and *Indian Literature*, simultaneously employ two sets of figures for numbering their journals. Vol. 21, nos. 5-6 of the *Social Scientist* (May-June 1993), for instance, was also assigned the numbers 240-41; in the bibliography, the latter form of citation has been used, though there may be a number of inconsistencies owing to the large time-span over which the entries were recorded.

NOTES

1. Citations are, except where a footnote indicates otherwise, to works listed in the bibliography, or (in the case of works not pertaining to South Asia), in Appendix Two, "Select Bibliography of Cultural Studies in General."
2. Stuart Hall, "The Emergence of Cultural Studies and the Crisis of the Humanities", *October*, no. 53 (1990), p. 17.
3. Ibid., p. 11.
4. Stuart Hall, "Cultural Studies and its theoretical legacies", in Grossberg, Nelson, and Treichler (1992), p. 286.
5. Tony Bennett, "Putting Policy into Cultural Studies", in Grossberg, Nelson, and Treichler (1992), p. 33. My own position is adumbrated at greater length in "The Third Orientalism: Problems of Multiculturalism and Post-coloniality in the American Academy", paper presented at a conference on "Politics, Theory and the Place of the American Academy", University of Southern California, 11-13 March 1994.

6. Gyan Prakash, "Postcolonial Criticism and Indian Historiography", *Social Text*, nos. 31-32 (1992):8-19.
7. Ziauddin Sardar, Ashis Nandy, Merryl Wyn Davies, and Claude Alvares, *The Blinded Eye: 500 Years of Christopher Columbus* (Goa: The Other India Press; New York: The Apex Press; London: Zed Books, 1993), pp. 2, 90. See also my review of this monograph, "A Credo for the Post-Columbian World", *Economic and Political Weekly* 29, no. 33 (13 August 1994):2142-44.
8. Untitled pamphlet introducing the "Committee for Cultural Choices and Global Futures", Delhi, [1987].
9. This is an argument I have hinted at in an unpublished paper, entitled "The (Near) Impossibility of the Outsider in the Modern Hindi Film" (1994), as a contribution to a two-volume work on Indian cinema being edited by Ashis Nandy.
10. The most forceful and engaging writings in this respect are those of Ashis Nandy, whose work is truly *sui generis*. There is scarcely a subject to which Nandy has not applied his extraordinarily fecund imagination, and it is my regret that an extended interpretation of his work was not possible within the scope of the present essay. However, I have discussed his work in a long essay entitled "Freedom for those Who do not Speak the Language of Freedom: A Guide to Ashis Nandy's Manifesto of Liberation in the Post-Partitioned World", forthcoming in *Emergences* (1995). Also, for a remarkable homage to the pluralistic nature of Indian civilization, see Ramachandra Gandhi, *Sita's Kitchen: A Testimony of Faith and Inquiry* (Delhi: Penguin Books, 1992), and my review, "Advaita's Waterloo", *The Social Scientist*, nos. 240-41 (May-June 1993):82-89, reprinted in *The Hindu Sunday Magazine* (17 July 1994), p. VI, and in *The Book Review* 18, 7 (July 1994):6-8.
11. A new publication, *Seagull Theatre Quarterly*, brought out by the people who manage Seagull Books in Calutta, promises to fill some gaps. Two issues appeared in 1994.
12. I myself have been moving in the direction of working at the intersection of law and history, and have had occasion to use the work of Foucault and Gramsci in formulating an understanding of the relation between colonial discursive formations and legal discourse, and the place of cultural politics in that intersection. At the annual meeting of the Law and Society Association of the United States in Phoenix, Arizona, 16-19 June 1994, I read a paper entitled "Everyday Crime and the Psychology of 'Native Criminality' in Colonial India". At the same meeting, I also read a paper on "Anti-terrorist Legislation in Democracies and the 'Normalisation' of Repression: A Comparative Study of India, the United Kingdom, and Sri Lanka", now published as "Anti-terrorist Legislation: A Comparative Study of India, UK and Sri Lanka", *Lokayan Bulletin* 11, no. 1 (July-August 1994):5-24.
13. Baxi, "'The State's Emissary'" (1992), p. 247.
14. By an unaccountable oversight, a number of novels were omitted from the bibliography, and I take this opportunity to make amends. I have in mind *English, August: An Indian Story*, by Upamanyu Chatterjee (New Delhi: Rupa & Co., 1989), Allan Sealy's *The Trotter-Nama: a Chronicle* (New York: Knopf, 1988; Delhi: Penguin, 1989), and Shashi Tharoor's *The Great Indian Novel* (New York & London: Viking, 1989). See also my review of *English, August* in *Indian Literature*, no. 137 (May-June 199), pp. 155-162.

BIBLIOGRAPHY OF CONTEMPORARY SOUTH ASIAN CULTURAL STUDIES, ARRANGED ALPHABETICALLY

Abu-Lughod, Janet L. *Before European Hegemony: The World System A.D. 1250-1350*. New York: Oxford UP, 1989. Ch. 8, "The Indian Subcontinent: On the Way to Everywhere."

Adarkar, Neera. "In Seach of Women in History of Marathi Theatre 1843 to 1933." *EPW* 26, 43 (26 Oct. 1991):WS-87 ff.

Adas, Michael. "South Asian Resistance in Comparative Perspective." In *Contesting Power: Resistance and Everyday Social Relations in South Asia*, pp. 290-316. Edited by Douglas Haynes and Gyan Prakash. Delhi: Oxford UP, 1991.

Aden, Michael and Mukherjee, S. N., eds. *Women in India and Nepal*. ANU Monographs on South Asia, No. 8. Canberra: Australian National University, 1982.

Advani, Rukun. "Indian History From Above and Below: Two Academic Parodies." Delhi: Don't Press, 1990.

Afshari, Reza. "Ali-Mazrui or Salman Rushdie: The Satanic Verses and Islamist Practices." *Alternatives* 16, 1 (Winter 1991):107-14.

Agarwal, Anil. "Human-Nature Interactions in a Third World Country." *The Environmentalist* 6, 2 (1986).

Agarwal, Anil and Narain, Sunita. *Towards a Green World: Should Global Environmental Management Be Built on Legal Conventions or Human Rights?* New Delhi: Centre for Science and Environment, 1992.

Agarwal, Bina. *Cold Hearths and Barren Slopes: The Woodfuel Crisis in the Third World*. London: Zed Books, 1986.

________. "Women, Poverty, and Agricultural Growth in India." *Jrl. of Peasant Studies* 13 (July 1986):165-220.

________. "Under the Cooking Pot: The Political Economy of the Domestic Fuel Crisis in Rural South Asia." *IDS Bulletin* 18, 1 (1987):11-22.

________. "Who Sows? Who Reaps? Women and Land Rights in India." *Jrl. of Peasant Studies* 15, 4 (1988):531-81. Reprinted as booklet by the Institute of Economic Growth, University Enclave, Delhi.

________. "Social Security and the Family: Coping with Seasonality and Calamity in Rural India." *Jrl. of Peasant Studies* 17 (April 1990): 341-412.

Agarwal, Bina. "Engendering the Environment Debate: Lessons from the Indian Subcontinent." CASID Distinguished Speaker Series, Discussion Paper No. 8. Michigan State University Press, 1991.

________. "The Gender and Environment Debate: Lessons from India." *Feminist Studies* 18, 1 (Spring 1992):119-59.

Agarwal, Bina, ed. *State, Community and Household in Modernizing Asia.* Delhi: Kali for Women, 1988.

Agarwal, Bina and Afshar, Haleh, eds. *Women, Poverty, and Ideology: Contradictory Pressures, Uneasy Solutions.* London: Macmillan, 1989.

Agrawal, Binod C. "Indianness of the Indian Cinema." In *Continuity and Change in Communication Systems: An Asian Perspective*, pp. 181-91. Edited by Georgette Wang, Wimal Dissanayake, and Emile G. McAnany. Norwood, New Jersey: Ablex, 1984.

Ahmad, Aijaz. "Jameson's Rhetoric of Otherness and the 'National Allegory.'" *Social Text* , no. 17 (1985):3-25.

________. "'Third World Literature' and the Nationalist Ideology." *Journal of Arts and Ideas*, nos. 17-18 (June, 1987):117-35.

________. "Some Reflections on Urdu." *Seminar*, no. 359 (July 1989):23-29.

________. "Between Orientalism and Historicism: Anthropological Knowledge of India." *Studies in History* (New Series) 7, 1 (Jan.-June 1991):135-63.

________. "Rushdie's Shame: Postmodernism, Migrancy and the Representation of Women." *EPW* 26, 24 (15 June 1991):1461-71.

________. "Can Marxism Be 'Dialogic'?" *Seminar*, no. 394 (June 1992):35-40.

________. *In Theory: Nations, Classes, Literatures.* London: Verso, 1992. [Reviewed by Benita Parry, "A Critique Mishandled", *Social Text*, no. 35 (1993):121-33. Almost an entire issue of *Public Culture* (6, 1 [Fall 1993]), with contributions by Michael Sprinker, Talal Asad, Vivek Dhareshwar, Partha Chatterjee, Nivedita Menon, Peter van der Veer, Marjorie Howes, Marjorie Levinson, and Andrew Parker, and a response by Aijaz Ahmad, is devoted to the discussion of *In Theory.*]

________. "Orientalism and After: Ambivalence and Cosmopolitan Location in the Work of Edward Said." *EPW* 27, 30 (25 July 1992):PE98-116.

Ahmad, Karuna. "Gandhi, Women's Roles, and the Freedom Movement." Occasional Papers on History and Society, no. 19. New Delhi: NMML, 1988.

Ahmad, Rukhsana, ed. *Right of Way: Prose and Poetry.* Asian Women Writers' Workshop. London: Women's Press, 1988.

________, trans. *Beyond Belief: Contemporary Feminist Urdu Poetry.* Lahore: ASR Publications, 1990.

Ahmed, Akbar S. *Postmodernism and Islam*. London: Routledge, 1992. [Reviews in *Indian Express*, 5 July 1992, p. 6; *Guardian* (London), 25 June 1992, p. 29.]

Ahmed, Rafiuddin, ed. *Bangladesh: Society Religion and Politics*. Chittagong: South Asia Studies Group, Univ. of Chittagong, 1985.

________, ed. *Religion, Nationalism and Politics in Bangladesh*. Delhi: South Asian Publishers, 1990.

Ahmed, Rehnuma. "Women's Movement in Bangladesh and the Left's Understanding of the Women Question." *Jrl. of Social Studies*, no. 30 (1985):27-56.

Akshara, K. V. "Western Responses to Traditional Indian Theatre." *Journal of Arts and Ideas*, no. 8 (July-September 1984):43-55.

Al-Azm, Sadik J. "The Importance of Being Earnest About Salman Rushdie." *South Asia Bulletin* 11, 1-2 (1991):1-20.

Alexander, Meena. "The Poem's Second Life: Writing and Self Identity." *Toronto South Asian Review* (Fall-Winter 1987-88):77-85.

________. *Fault Lines: A Memoir*. The Cross-Cultural Memoir Series. New York: The Feminist Press at the City U. of New York, 1993.

Ali, Tariq. *Can Pakistan Survive? The Death of a State*. Harmondsworth: Penguin Books; London: Verso Books, 1983.

Alvares, Claude. *Homo Faber: Technology and Culture in India, China and the West: 1500 to the Present Day*. New Delhi: Allied Publishers, 1979; Hague: Martinus Nijhoff, 1980. *Reprinted as Decolonizing History: Technology and Culture in India, China and the West: 1492 to the Present Day*. New York: Apex Press and Mapusa, Goa: The Other India Press, 1991.

________. "Gandhi's Second Assassination." *Indian Express* (Sunday Magazine), 29 January 1984, p. 1.

________. "Science, Colonialism and Violence: A Luddite View." In *Science, Hegemony and Violence: A Requiem for Modernity*, pp. 68-112. Edited by Ashis Nandy. Tokyo: United Nations Univ., 1988; Delhi: Oxford UP, 1990.

Amin, Shahid. "Gandhi as Mahatma." In *Subaltern Studies III*, pp. 1-61. Edited by Ranajit Guha. Delhi: Oxford UP, 1984.

________. "Approver's Testimony, Judicial Discourse: The Case of Chauri Chaura." In *Subaltern Studies V*, pp. 166-202. Edited by Ranajit Guha. Delhi: Oxford UP, 1987.

________. "Every Day Signs." *The Times Magazine* [The Times of India Sesquicentennial], no. 1: *Culture* (October 1988):17, 19.

________. Introduction to *A Glossary of North Indian Peasant Life*, by

William Crooke. Edited by Shahid Amin. Delhi: Oxford UP, 1989.

Amos, Valerie and Parmar, Pratibha. "Resistance and Responses: The Experiences of Black Girls in Britain." In *Feminism for Girls: An Adventure Story*. Edited by Angela McRobbie et al. Boston and London: Routledge & Kegan Paul, 1981.

________. "Challenging Imperial Feminism." *Feminist Review* 17 (1984):3-19.

Amur, G. S. and Desai, S. K., eds. *Colonial Consciousness in Commonwealth Literature*. Bombay, Madras and New Delhi: Somanja Publications, 1984.

Anagol, Padma J. "Literature as Ideology: Rudyard Kipling's Creative World." *Studies in History* 3, 1 (1987):75-96.

Anandhi, S. "Representing Devadasis: 'Dasigal Mosavalai' as a Radical Text." *EPW* (Annual Number) 26, 11-12 (March 1991):739-46.

________. "Women's Question in the Dravidian Movement c. 1925-1948." *Social Scientist*, nos. 216-17 (May-June 1991):24-41.

Anantha Murthy, U. R. "Why Not Worship in the Nude?" *Bahuvachan: An Occasional of the Arts and Ideas*, no. 1 (1988):95-117.

Anniah Gowda, H. H., ed. *The Colonial and the Neo-Colonial Encounters in Commonwealth Literature*. Mysore: Prasaragana University, 1983.

"Another India." Issue of *Daedalus* (Fall 1989), being Volume 118, No. 4 of the *Proceedings of the American Academy of Arts and Sciences*. [Review by Vinay Lal, "Representing India", *New Quest*, no. 86 (March-April, 1991):119-22.]

Ansari, Nasim. "Blasphemy and Religious Criticism." *EPW* 27, 27 (4 July 1992):1383-85.

An Anthology of Twentieth Century Sri Lankan Writing. UNESCO, 1989.

Appadurai, Arjun. "Gastro-Politics in Hindu South Asia." *American Ethnologist* 8:3 (August 1981):494-511.

________. "The Past as a Scarce Resource." *Man* (New Series) 16 (1983): 201-19.

________. "Gratitude as a Social Mode in South India." *Ethos* 13, 3 (Fall 1985):236-45.

________. "Center and Periphery in Anthropological Theory." *CSSH* 28, 2 (1986):356-61.

________. "Commodities and the Politics of Value." In *The Social Life of Things*, pp. 3-63. Edited by A. Appadurai. New York: Cambridge UP, 1986.

________. Is Homo Hierarchicus — A Review Essay." *American Ethnologist* 13, 4 (1986):745-61.

________. "Street Culture." *The India Magazine* 8, 1 (December 1987):3-23.

Appadurai, Arjun. "How to Make a National Cuisine: Cookbooks in Contemporary India." *CSSH* 30, 1 (January 1988):3-24.

________. "Disjuncture and Difference in the Global Cultural Economy." *Public Culture* 2, 2 (1990):1-24.

________. "Technology and the Reproduction of Values in Rural Western India." In *Dominating Knowledges: Development, Culture, and Resistance*, pp. 185-216. Edited by Frederique Apffel Marglin and Stephen A. Marglin. Oxford: Clarendon Press, 1990.

________. "Topographies of the Self: Praise and Emotion in Hindu India." In *Language and the Politics of Emotion*. Edited by Catherine A. Lutz and Lila Abu-Lughod. Cambridge: Cambridge UP, 1990.

________. "Global Ethnoscapes: Notes and Queries for a Transnational Anthropology." In *Recapturing Anthropology: Working in the Present*. Edited by Richard G. Fox. Santa Fe: School of American Research, 1991.

________. "Father Britto." *Polygraph*, no. 5 (1992):248-50.

________. "Patriotism and Its Futures." *Public Culture* 5 (Spring 1993):1-19.

________. "The Heart of Whiteness." *Callaloo* 16, 4 (Fall 1993):796-807.

________. "Consumption, Duration, and History." Forthcoming in *Stanford Literary Review* (1993).

________. "Playing with Modernity: The Decolonization of Indian Cricket." Forthcoming in *Alternative Modernities: Making Public Culture in India*. Edited by Carol Breckenridge. Minneapolis: U. of Minnesota Press.

________, ed. *The Social Life of Things: Commodities in Cultural Perspective*. Cambridge: Cambridge UP, 1986.

Appadurai, Arjun and Breckernridge, Carol. "Why Public Culture?" *Public Culture* 1 (Fall 1988): 5-11.

________. "Public Culture in Late Twentieth Century India." *Items, Newsletter of the Social Science Research Council* 44, 4 (Dec. 1990).

Appadurai, Arjun; Korom, Frank J.; and Mills, Margaret A., eds. *Gender, Genre, and Power in South Asian Expressive Traditions*. South Asia Seminar Series. Philadelphia: University of Pennslyvania Press, 1991.

Appignanesi, Lisa and Maitland, Sara. *The Rushdie File*. Syracuse, New York: Syracuse UP, 1990.

Araeen, Rasheed. *Making Myself Visible*. London: Kala Press, 1985.

________. *The Other Story: Afro-Asian Artists in Post-War Britain.* London: South Bank Centre, 1989.

Araeen, Rasheed; Cottell, Fran; and Schoettle, Marian. *Conceptual Clothing*. Birmingham: Ikon Gallery, 1986.

Aranha, Celine; Fernando, Peter; and Mahale, Prabha. *Beyond the Fire Line: Perceptions of Eight Tribal Women*. New Delhi: Indian Social Institute, 1991.

Aravamudan, Srinivas. "'Being God's Postman Is No Fun, Yaar': Salman Rushdie's *The Satanic Verses*." *Diacritics* 19, 2 (1989): 3-20.

Architectural Review. Special issue on "Indian Identity." Vol. 182, No. 1086 (August 1987).

Armes, Roy. *Third World Film Making and the West*. Berkeley: Univ. of California Press, 1987.

Arnold, David. "Gramsci and Peasant Subalternity in India." *Jrl. of Peasant Studies* 11 (1984).

________. "Cholera and Colonialism in British India." *Past and Present*, no. 113 (1986):118-51.

________. *Police Power and Colonial Rule: Madras 1859-1947*. Delhi: Oxford UP, 1986.

________. "Touching the Body: Perspectives on the Indian Plague, 1896-1900." In *Subaltern Studies V*, pp. 55-90. Edited by Ranajit Guha. Delhi: Oxford UP, 1987.

________. *Famine: Social Crisis and Historical Change*. New Perspectives on the Past. Oxford: Basil Blackwell, 1988. [For a brief article based on the book, see Amit Mitra, "Colonial perceptions of hunger", *Down to Earth* (31 May 1992):50-51.]

________, ed. *Imperial Medicine and Indigenous Societies*. New York: Manchester UP, 1989.

Arnold, Alison. "Popular Film Song in India: A Case of Mass-Market Musical Eclecticism." *Popular Music* 7, 2 (May 1988):177-88.

Arora, V. N. "Popular Songs in Hindi Films." *Journal of Popular Culture* 20, 2 (Fall 1986):143-66.

Asad, Talal. "Ethnography, Literature, and Politics: Some Readings and Uses of Salman Rushdie's *The Satanic Verses*." *Cultural Anthropology* 5, 3 (1990):239-290.

________. "Multiculturalism and British Identity in the Wake of the Rushdie Affair." *Politics and Society* 18, 4 (December 1990):455-80.

Ashcroft, Bill and Tiffin, Helen. *The Empire Writes Back: Theory and Practice in Post-Colonial Literature*. London: Routledge, 1989.

Ashley, Wayne and Regina Holloman. "From Ritual to Theater in Kerala." *The Drama Review* 26, 2 (Summer 1982):59-72.

Aymard, Maurice and Mukhia, Harbans, eds. *French Studies in History*. 2 vols. New Delhi: Orient Longman, 1988.

Babb, Lawrence A. "Glancing: Visual Interaction in Hinduism." *Jrl. of Anthropological Research* 37 (1981):387-401.

________. "Amnesia and Remembrance in a Hindu Theory of History." *Asian Folklore* Studies 41 (1982):49-66.

________. "The Physiology of Redemption." *History of Religions* 22 (1983): 298-312.

________. "Sathya Sai Baba's Magic." *Anthropological Quarterly* 56 (1983): 116-24.

________. Indigenous Feminism in a Modern Hindu Sect." *Signs* 9, 3 (1984): 399-416.

________. *Redemptive Encounters: Three Modern Styles in the Hindu Tradition.* Berkeley: University of California Press, 1986.

Bagchi, Jasodhara. "Representing Nationalism: Ideology of Motherhood in Colonial Bengal." *EPW* 25, 42-43 (25 Oct. 1990):WS65-71.

Bailey, G. M. "On the De-construction of Culture in Indian Literature: A Tentative Response to Vijay Mishra's Article." *South Asia* (New Series) 12, 1 (1989):85-102.

Bajaj, Jatinder K. "Green Revolution: A Historical Perspective." *PPST Bulletin* 2 (1982):87-112.

________. "The Bhopal Tragedy: The Responsibility of the Scientific Community." *PPST Bulletin* 5 (1985):6-14.

________. "Francis Bacon, the First Philosopher of Modern Science: A Non-Western View." In *Science, Hegemony and Violence: A Requiem for Modernity*. Edited by Ashis Nandy. Delhi: Oxford UP, 1992 [1988].

Bala, Poonam. *Imperialism and Medicine in Bengal: A Socio-Historical Perspective*. Delhi: Sage Publications, 1991.

Balagopal, K. "Perception and Presentation: A Telugu Film on Naxalites." *EPW* 26, 29 (20 July 1991):1727-31.

Balasubrahmanyan, Vimal. *Mirror Image: The Media and the Women's Question*. Bombay: Centre for Education and Documentation, 1988.

Bald, Suresht Renjen. "From 'Satyartha Prakash' to 'Manushi': An Overview of the Women's Movement in India." *Univ. of Michigan Working Paper*, no. 23 (April 1983).

Ballhatchet, K. *Race, Sex, and Class Under the Raj*. New York: St. Martin's Press, 1980.

Bandopadhyay, Sibaji, Chatterjee, Ratnabali and Bagchi, Joasodhara. *Femininity Redefined: Politics of Home and the World in Colonial Bengal*. New Delhi: Kali for Women, forthcoming 1993.

Bandyopadhyay, Sekhar. "Caste in the Perception of the Raj: A Note on the

Evolution of Colonial Sociology of Bengal." *Bengal Past and Present* 104, Pts. 1- 2 Nos. 198-99 (Jan.-Dec. 1985):56-80.

Banerjee, Nirmala. "Modernization and Marginalization." *Social Scientist* 13, 10-11 (Oct.-Nov. 1985):48-71; also published in modified form as "Working Women in Colonial Bengal: Modernization and Marginalization", in Sangari and Vaid, *Recasting Women*, pp. 269-301.

Banerjee, Sumanta. *In the Wake of Naxalbari: A History of the Naxalite Movement in India*. Calcutta: Subarnarekha, 1980. Republished as *India's Simmering Revolution: The Naxalite Uprising*. London: Zed Books, 1984.

________. "Having the Last Laugh: Women in the Nineteenth Century Bengali Farces." *Manushi*, no. 59 (July-August 1990):15-20.

________. *The Parlour and the Streets: Elite and Popular Culture in Nineteenth Century Calcutta*. Calcutta: Seagull Books, 1990. [Review by Santo Datta, "A Collision of Class Cultures", *Jrl. of Arts and Ideas*, no. 22 (April 1992):57-63.]

________. "Laughter as Subversion in Nineteenth Century Calcutta." In *The Calcutta Psyche*, pp. 187-208. Edited by Geeti Sen. New Delhi: Rupa & Co. and India International Centre, 1990-91.

________. "'Hindutva'—Ideology and Social Psychology." *EPW* 26, 3 (19 Jan. 1991):97-103.

________. "'La Guerre Est Fine'?" *Polygraph*, no. 5 (1992):242-47.

________. "Towards a Critique of Language Imperialism." *EPW* 27, 28 (11 July 1992):1473-75.

Banerji, Himani. *Representation and Class Politics in the Theatre of Utpal Dutt*. Occasional Paper, no. 106. Calcutta: CSSS, 1990.

________. "Fashioning a Self: Educational Proposals for and by Women in Popular Magazines in Colonial Bengal." *EPW* 26, 43 (26 Oct. 1991):WS 50 ff.

Banuri, Tariq. "Development and the Politics of Knowledge: A Critical Interpretation of the Social Role of Modernization." In *Dominating Knowledge: Development, Culture, and Resistance*, pp. 29-72. Edited by Frederique Apffel Marglin and Stephen A. Marglin. Oxford: Clarendon Press, 1990.

________. "Modernization and Its Discontents: A Cultural Perspective on Theories of Development." In *Dominating Knowledge: Development, Culture, and Resistance*, pp. 73-101. Edited by Frederique Apffel Marglin and Stephen A. Marglin. Oxford: Clarendon Press, 1990.

Bardhan, Kalpana. "Women, Work, Welfare and Status: Forces of Tradition and Change in India". *South Asia Bulletin* 6, 1(Spring 1986):3-16.

Bardhan, Kalpana. "Being a Woman in South Asia." *Jrl. of Women's History* 2, 1 (Spring 1990):200-19.

Bardhan, Pranab. *The Political Economy of Development in India.* Oxford: Basil Blackwell, 1984.

Barik, Rahakanta. "Primordial Loyalty in Subaltern Politics: A Problem of Understanding the Unrecognised Intelligentsia in Orissa." Occasional Papers on History and Society, no. 39. New Delhi: NMML, 1987.

Barz, R. K. "The Cultural Significance of Hindi in Mauritius." *South Asia* 3, 1 (1973):1-13.

Barz, Richard K. and Seigel, Jeff, eds. *Language Transplanted: The Development of Overseas Hindi.* Wiesbaden: Harrassowitz, 1988.

Baskaran, S. Theodore. "Music for the Masses: Film Songs of Tamil Nadu." *EPW* (Annual Number) 26, 11-12 (March 1991):755-58.

Basu, Amrita. "Grass roots movements and the state: Reflections on radical change in India." *Theory and Society* 16 (1987):647-74.

________. "The Challenge of Difference in the Women's Movement in India." *Feminist Studies* 16 (1990).

Basu, Asoke. "Knowledge and Power: The Case of India's Ethnic Intellectuals." *New Quest*, no. 86 (March-April 1991):99-104.

Basu, Tapan; Datta, Pradip; Sarkar, Sumit; Sarkar, Tanika; and Sen, Sambuddha. *Khaki Shorts and Saffron Flags: A Critique of the Hindu Right.* Tracts for the Times, no. 1. Delhi: Orient Longman, 1993.

Baucon, Ian. "Narrating the Nation." *Transition*, no. 55 (1992):144-53. [on Bhabha, ed. 1990]

Baxi, Upendra. *Inconvenient Forum and Convenient Catastrophe: the Bhopal Case.* Bombay: N. M. Tripathi, 1986.

________. *Towards a Sociology of Indian Law.* New Delhi: Satvahan, 1986.

________.* "Discipline, Repression and Legal Pluralism." In *Legal Pluralism: Proceedings of Canberra Law Workshop VII*, pp. 51-62. Edited by P. Sack and E. Minchin.

________. "Complicity and Struggle: Theory and Society." *Social Scientist*, nos. 221-22 (Oct.-Nov. 1991):19-26.

________.* *Marx, Law and Justice: Some Indian Perspectives.* Bombay, 1992.

________. "The State's Emissary': The Place of Law in Subaltern Studies." In *Subaltern Studies VII: Writings on South Asian History and Society*, pp. 247-64. Edited by Gyanendra Pandey and Dipesh Chakrabarty. Delhi: Oxford UP, 1992.

Baxi, Upendra; Sen, Geeti; and Fernandes, Jeanette, eds. *The Right to Be Human.* New Delhi: Lancer International, 1987.

Bayly, C. A. "Rallying around the subaltern." *Journal of Peasant Studies* 16, 1 (1988):110-20.

________. "Knowing the Country: Empire and Information in India." *MAS* 27, 1 (Feb. 1993):3-43.

Bayly, C. A., General Editor. *The Raj: India and the British 1600-1947*. London: National Portrait Gallery Publications, 1990. [Reviewed by Vinay Lal, "Imperialist Nostalgia", *EPW* (17-24 July 1993):1511-13.]

Behal, Rana Pratap. "Forms of Labour Protests in the Assam Valley Tea Plantations, 1900-1947." Occasional Papers on History and Society, no. 11. New Delhi: NMML, 1986.

Behal, Rana Pratap and Mohapatra, Prabhu P. "'Tea and Money versus Human Life': The Rise and Fall of the Indenture System in the Assam Tea Plantations 1840-1908." *Jrl. of Peasant Studies* 19, 3-4 (April-July 1992):142-72.

Bell, L. "Artists and Empire: Victorian Representations of Subject People." *Art History* (March 1982):73-86.

Beneria, Lourdes and Sen, Gita. "Accumulation, Reproduction and Women's Role in Economic Development: Boserup Revisited", *Signs* 7, 2 (1982): 279-98.

Bernal, Martin. *Black Athena: The Afroasiatic Roots of Classical Civilization*. Volume One: *The Fabrication of Ancient Greece 1785-1985*. New Brunswick, New Jersey: Rutgers UP, 1987. Ch. V, "Romantic Linguistics: The Rise of India and the Fall of Egypt, 1740-1880", pp. 224-80.

Beteille, Andre. "Some Observations on the Comparative Method." *EPW* 25, 40 (6 Oct. 1990):2255-63.

________. "Religion as a Subject for Sociology." *EPW* 27, 35 (29 August 1992):1865-70.

Bhabha, Homi. "The Other Question — The Stereotype and Colonial Discourse." *Screen* 24, 6 (1983):18-36.

________. "The Other question: difference, discrimination and the discourse of colonialism." In *Literature, Politics and Theory: Papers from the Essex Conference 1976-84*. Edited by Francis Barker *et al.* London: Methuen, 1986.

________. "Of Mimicry and Man: The Ambivalence of Colonial Discourse." *October* 28 (Spring 1984):125-33.

________. "Representation and the Colonial Text: A Critical Exploration of Some Forms of Mimeticism." In *The Theory of Reading*, pp. 123-46. Edited by Frank Gloversmith. New Jersey: Barnes and Noble; Sussex: Harvester, 1984.

Bhabha, Homi. "Sly Civility." *October* 34 (Fall 1985):71-80.

________. "Signs Taken as Wonder: Questions of Ambivalence and Authority Under a Tree Outside Delhi, May 1817." *Critical Inquiry* 12, 1 (Autumn 1985):144-65; also reprinted in *Europe and Its Others*, ed. Francis Barker *et al.* Volume I. Colchester: Univ. of Essex, 1985, and in *Race, Writing and Difference*, ed. Henry Louis Gates, Jr. Chicago: Univ. of Chicago Press, 1986.

________. "Remembering Fanon." Introduction to Frantz Fanon, *Black Skins White Masks*. London: Pluto Press/Zwan, 1986. Reprinted in *Remaking History*, pp. 131-48. Dia Art Foundation, Discussions in Contemporary Culture, no. 4. Edited by Barbara Kruger and Phil Mariani. Seattle: Bay Press, 1989.

________. "The Commitment to Theory." *New Formations* No. 5 (Summer 1988): 5-23; also in *Questions of Third Cinema*, ed. Jim Pines and Paul Willemen (London: BFI Publishing, 1989), pp. 111-32.

________. "Location, Intervention, Incommensurability: A Conversation with Homi Bhabha", *Emergences* 1 (Fall 1989):63-88.

________. "DissemiNation: time, narrative, and the margins of the modern nation." In *Nation and Narration*, pp. 291-322. Edited by Homi Bhabha. N.Y. & London: Routledge, 1990.

________. "Simultaneous Translation: Modernity and the Inter-National." In *Expanding Internationalism, A Conference on International Exhibitions*. Venice: Arts International, 1990.

________. "Interrogating Identity." *Identity Documents* [Institute for Contemporary Arts, London] 6 (1991), pp. 5-11. Also published as "Interrogating Identity: The Postcolonial Prerogative." In *Anatomy of Racism*, pp. 183-209. Edited by David Theo Goldberg. Minneapolis: Univ. of Minnesota Press, 1990.

________. "The Postcolonial Critic: Homi Bhabha Interviewed by David Bennett and Terry Collits." *Arena* 96 (Spring 1991):47-63.

________. "Bombay Mix. BBC Radio 4: Southern Voices." *Emergences*, nos. 3-4 (Fall 1992):163-69.

________. "'Race', Time, and the Revision of Modernity." *Oxford Literary Review* 13 (1991):193-219.

________. "Postcolonial Authority and Postmodern Guilt." In *Cultural Studies*, pp. 56-68. Edited by Lawrence Grossberg, Cary Nelson, and Paula Treichler. New York & London: Routledge, 1992.

________. "Race and the Humanities: The 'Ends' of Modernity?" *Public Culture* 4, 2 (Spring 1992):81-85.

Bhabha, Homi. "The World and the Home." *Social Text*, nos. 31/32 (1992): 141-53.

________. "Postcolonial Criticism." In *Redrawing the Boundaries: The Transformation of English and American Literary Studies*. Edited by Stephen Greenblatt and Giles Gunn. New York: Modern Language Association, 1992.

________. "Interview: Homi Bhabha." *Stanford Humanties Review* 3, 1 (Winter 1993):1-6.

________. *The Location of Culture*. London: Routledge, 1993.

________, ed. *Nation and Narration*. London & N.Y.: Routledge, 1990.

Bhabha, J., *et al. Worlds Apart: Women under Immigration and Nationality Law*. London: Pluto Press, 1985.

Bhachu, Parminder. *Twice Migrants: East African Sikh Settlers in Britain*. London & New York: Tavistock Publications, 1985.

Bhachu, Parminder and Light, Ivan, eds. *Immigration and Entrepreneurship: Culture, Capital, and Ethnic Networks*. New Brunswick, N.J.: Transaction Books, 1993.

Bhachu, Parminder and Westwood, Sallie, eds. *Enterprising Women: Home, Work, and Minority Cultures in Britain*. London & New York: Routledge, 1988.

Bhadra, Gautam. "The Mentality of Subalternity: Kantanama or Rajdharma." In *Subaltern Studies VI*, pp. 54-91. Edited by Ranajit Guha. New Delhi: Oxford UP, 1989. Also published as Occasional Paper, no. 104, Calcutta: CSSS, 1990.

Bhagwat, Vidyut. "Man-Woman Relations in the Writings of the Saint Poetesses." *New Quest*, no. 82 (July-August 1990):223-32.

Bhalla, Alok. "A Historical Map for a World of Fables: Notes, hypotheses, reflections on a cinematic phenomenon." *J. of Arts and Ideas*, nos. 10-11 (Jan.-June 1985):99-131.

________. "A Plea Against Revenge Histories: Some Reflections on Orientalism and the Age of Empire." *New Quest*, no. 83 (Sept.-Oct. 1990):271-77.

________. *Politics of Atrocity and Lust: The Vampire Tale as a Nightmare History of England in the Nineteenth Century*. New Delhi: Sterling, 1988.

________, ed. *Garcia Marquez and Latin America*. New Delhi: Sterling, 1987.

Bhalla, Alok and Chandra, Sudhir, eds. *Indian Responses to Colonialism in the Nineteenth Century*. New Delhi: Sterling, 1993.

Bhargava, Rajeev. "The Right to Culture." *Social Scientist*, no. 209 (Oct. 1990):50-57.

Bhargava, Rajeev. "Socialism, Democracy and the Problem of Common Meanings." *Social Scientist*, nos. 226-27 (March-April 1992):23-34.

Bharucha, Rustom. *Rehearsals of Revolution: The Political Theatre of Bengal*. Calcutta: Seagull Books, 1983.

________. "David Lean's 'Boom.'" *Splice*, no. 1 (Jan.-March 1982):19-23.

________. "A Collision of Cultues: Some Western Interpretations of the Indian Theatre." *IICQ* 11, 3 (Sept. 1984):287-307.

________. "Forster's Friends." *Raritan* 5, 4 (Spring 1986):105-22.

________. *Theatre and the World: Essays on Theatre and Politics of Culture*. Delhi: Manohar, 1990.

________. "Politics of Indigenous Theatre: Kanhailal in Manipur." *EPW* (Annual Number) 26, 11-12 (March 1991):747-54.

________. "Around Ayodhya: Aberrations, Engimas, and Moments of Violence." *Third Text*, no. 24 (Autumn 1993):45-58.

________. *Questions of Faith*. Tracts for the Times, no. 3. Delhi: Orient Longmans, 1993.

Bhasin, Kamla. *What is Patriarchy?* New Delhi: Kali for Women, forthcoming.

Bhasin, Kamla and Khan, Nighat Said. *Some Questions on Feminism and Its Relevance in South Asia*. New Delhi: Kali for Women, 1986.

Bhatnagar, Rashmi. "Genre and gender: a reading of Tagore's *The Broken Nest* and R. K. Narayan's *The Dark Room*." In *Woman/Image/Text: Feminist Readings of Literary Texts*, pp. 172-87. Edited by Lola Chatterjee. New Delhi: Trianka, 1986.

________. "A Reading of Pope's *The Rape of the Lock*." In *Woman/Image/Text*, pp. 40-53. Edited by Lola Chatterjee. New Delhi: Trianka, 1986.

________. "Uses and limits of Foucault: a study of the theme of origins in Edward Said's *Orientalism*." *Social Scientist*, no. 158 (July 1986).

Bhatt, Vikram and Scriver, Peter. *After the Masters: Contemporary Indian Architecture*. Ahmedabad: Mapin Publishing, 1991.

Bhattacharjee, Anannya. "The Habit of Ex-Nomination: Nation, Woman, and the Indian Immigrant Bourgeoisie." *Public Culture* 5, 1 (Fall 1992): 19-44.

Bhattacharji, Sukumari. "Motherhood in Ancient India." *EPW* 25, 2-43 (20-27 Oct. 1990):WS50-57.

________. "Sita in the TV Uttararamayana." *Social Scientist*, nos. 200-1 (Jan.-Feb. 1990):66-71.

Bhattacharya, Malini. "Utilitarianism and the Concept of Authorial Autonomy in Early Nineteenth-Century England." *EPW* 17, 31 (31 July 1982): 49-57.

Bhattacharya, Nandini. "Ethnopolitical Dynamics and the Language of Gendering in Dryden's *Aureng-Zebe*." *boundary* 2 20, 2 (Summer 1993):153-76.

Bhattacharya, Rimli. "'Public Women': Early Actresses of the Bengali Stage — Role and Reality." In *The Calcutta Psyche*, pp. 143-69. Edited by Geeti Sen. New Delhi: Rupa & Co. and India International Centre, 1990-91.

Bhattacharya, Rinki.* "Feminism and the Cinema of Racism." *Women, Take One* 1 (1986).

Bhattacharya, Sabyasachi. "Paradigms Lost: Notes on Social History in India." *EPW* 17, 14-16 (Annual Number 1982):689-96.

________. "Colonial Power and Micro-Social Interactions: Nineteenth Century India." *EPW* (1-8 June 1991):1399-1403.

Bhattacharya, Sabyasachi and Redondi, Pietro, eds. *Techniques to Technology: A French Historiography of Technology*. New Delhi: Orient Longman, 1990.

Bhattacharyya, Gargi. "Cultural Education in Britain." *Oxford Literary Review*, no. 13 (1991):4-19.

Bhattacharyya, Sibajiban. "Some Philosophical Problems Concerning Culture and Rationality." *Journal of Indian Council of Philosophical Research* 9, 2 (January-April 1992):5-24.

Bhave, Sumitra. *Pan on Fire*: *Eight Dalit Women Tell Their Story*. Translated by Gauri Deshpande. Delhi: Indian Social Institute, 1988.

Bhavni, Kum Kum and Coulson, Margaret. "Transforming socialist-feminism: the challenge of racism." *Feminist Review*, no. 23 (Summer 1986).

Bhayani, Harivallabh. *Bhavan-Vibhavan*: *Collection of Papers and Articles on Literary Theory and Criticism*. Ahmedabad: Parshva Prakashan, 1991.

Bhushan, Madhu. "Vimochana: Women's Struggles, Nonviolent Militancy and Direct Action in the Indian Context." *Women's Studies International Forum* 12, 1 (1989):25-33.

Bilgrami, Akeel. "Rushdie and the Reform of Islam." *Grand Street* 8 (Summer 1989):170-84.

________. "Rushdie, Islam and Postcolonial Defensiveness." *Yale Jrl. of Criticism* 4 (Fall 1990):301-11.

________. "Cry the Beloved Subcontinent." Review of *India: A Million Mutinies Now*, by V. S. Naipaul. *New Republic* (10 June 1991):30-34; also published as "Nation, Community and Naipaul's India", *EPW* 26, 33 (17 August 1991):1907-9.

________."What Is a Muslim? Fundmental Commitment and Cultural Identity." *Critical Inquiry* 18, 4 (Summer 1992):821-42; also published in *EPW* 27, 20-21 (16-23 May 1992):1071-78.

Bilimoria, Purusottama. "The Jaina Spirit in Salman Rushdie." *South Asia Bulletin* 9, 2 (1989):57-64.

Binford, Mira Reym. "The New Cinema of India." *Quarterly Review of Film Studies* 8, 4 (Fall 1983): 47-67.

________, ed. *Quarterly Review of Film and Video:* [Special issue on] *Indian Cinema.* 11, 3 (1989):1-108.

Birbalsingh, Frank. "Indo-Caribbean Test Cricketers." *The Toronto South Asian Review* 5, 1 (1986):105-17.

________. *Passion and Exile: Essays on Caribbean Literature.* London: Hausib, 1988.

________, ed. *Indenture and Exile: The Indo-Caribbean Experience.* Toronto: The South Asian Review, 1989.

Biswas, Liny. "Evolution of Hindu Temples in Calcutta." *Journal of Cultural Geography* 4, 2 (1984):73-85.

Blair, Harry W. "Ideology, Foreign Aid and Rural Poverty in Bangladesh: Emergence of the Like-Minded Group." *Jrl. of Social Studies* 34 (1986):1-27.

Blake, Stephen. *Shahjahanabad: The Sovereign City in Mughal India, 1639-1739.* Cambridge: Cambridge UP, 1991.

Blanchet, Therese. *Meanings and Rituals of Birth in Rural Bangladesh.* Dhaka: Univ. Press Ltd., 1984.

Blum, Stephen, Bohlman, Philip V., and Neuman, Danield M., eds. *Ethnomuscicology and Modern Music History.* Chicago: Univ. of Illinois Press, 1991.

Bohlman, Philip. *The Study of Folk Music in the Modern World.* Bloomington, Indiana: Indiana UP, 1988.

Borthwick, Meredith. *The Changing Role of Women in Bengal, 1849-1905.* Princeton, New Jersey: Princeton UP, 1984.

Boyce, James K. "National Security and the Future of Asian Studies." *BCAS* 24, 2 (April-June 1992):85-88.

Breckenridge, Carol A. "The Politics and Aesthetics of Colonial Collecting: India at World Fairs." *CSSH* 31, 2 (1988):195-216.

Breckenridge, Carol A. and Peter van der Veer, eds. *Orientalism and the Postcolonial Predicament.* Philadelphia: Univ. of Pennsylvania Press, 1993.

Brennan, Timothy. "India, Nationalism, and Other Failures." *South Atlantic Quarterly* 87, 1 (Winter 1988).

________. *Salman Rushdie and the Third World: Myths of the Nation.* London: Macmillan, 1989.

Brennan, Timothy. "Rushdie, Islam, and Postcolonial Criticism." *Social Text*, nos. 31/32 (1992):271-76.

Brow, James. "Nationalist Rhetoric and Local Practice: The Fate of the Village Community in Kukulewa." In *Sri Lanka: History and the Roots of Conflict*. Edited by Jonathan Spence. London: Routledge, 1990.

Burman, Chila. "There Have Always Been Great Blackwomen Artists." In *Visibly Female, Feminism and Art: An Anthology*, pp. 195-99. Edited by Hilary Robinson. London: Camden Press, 1987.

________. "Ask How I Feel/ Automatic Rap/ My New Work." *Third Text*, no. 19 (Summer 1992):79-86.

________, interviewed by Errol Lloyd. *Artrage*, no. 11 (1986).

Burra, Rani, ed. *Indian Cinema 1980-85*. New Delhi: Directorate of Film Festivals, 1986.

Burton, Antoinette M. "The White Woman's Burden: British Feminists and the Indian Woman, 1865-1915." *Women's Studies International Forum* 13, 4 (Winter 1990).

Butalia, Urvashi. "English textbook, Indian publisher." *Media, Culture and Society* 15, 2 (April 1993):217-32.

Butalia, Urvashi and Menon, Ritu, eds. *In Other Worlds: New Writing by Indian Women*. New Delhi: Kali for Women, 1992.

Caplan, Lionel. "'Bravest of the Brave': Representations of 'The Gurkha' in British Military Writings." *MAS* 25, 3 (1991):571-97.

Capwell, Charles. "Musical Life in Nineteenth-Century Calcutta." *Asian Music* 18, 1 (Fall/Winter 1986).

Caro, Francis A. de and Jordan, Rosan A. "The Wrong Topi: Personal Narratives, Ritual, and the Sun Helmet as a Symbol." *Western Folklore* 43, 4 (Oct. 1984):233-48.

Carrithers, Michael. "Passions of Nation and Community in the Bahubali Affair." *Modern Asian Studies* 22, 4 (1988):815-44.

Carrol, Lucy. "Law, Custom and Statutory Social Reform: The Hindu Women's Remarriage Act." *IESHR* 20, 4 (Oct.-Dec. 1983):363-89.

Center for Psychosocial Studies, Chicago. "Center Forum Group: Televising the Discovery of India: A Discussion with Film-Maker Shyam Benegal." *Working Papers and Proceedings of the Center for Psychosocial Studies* No. 38 (1990).

Chaki-Sircar, Manjusri. *Feminism in a Traditional Society: Women of the Manipur Valley*. New Delhi: Shakti Books, 1984.

Chakrabarti, Kunal. "Psychoanalytic Approaches to the Study of Ancient Indian Myths." In *Situating Indian History — for Sarvepalli Gopal*, pp. 384-402. Edited by Sabyasachi Bhattacharya and Romila Thapar. Delhi: Oxford UP, 1986.

Chakrabarty, Dipesh. "Trade Unions in a Hierarchical Culture: The Jute Workers of Calcutta, 1920-50." In *Subaltern Studies III*, pp. 153-96. Edited by Ranajit Guha. Delhi: Oxford UP, 1984.

________. "Class Consciousness and the Indian Working Class: Dilemmas of Marxist Historiography." *Jrl. of Asian and African Studies* 23, 1-2 (1988):21-31.

________. "Sarir, samaj, o rashtra: Oupanibeshik bharate mahamari o janasangskriti." *Anustup*, 1988. [In Bengali.]

________. *Rethinking Working-Class History: Bengal, 1890-1940.* Delhi: Oxford UP, 1989.

________. "History as Critique and Critique(s) of History." *Economic and Political Weekly* 26, 37 (14 Sept. 1991):2162-66. Also published as "Subaltern Studies and Critique of History", *Arena* (Melbourne), no. 96 (Spring 1991):105-20.

________. "Open Space/Public Space: Garbage, Modernity and India." *South Asia* (New Series) 14, 1 (1991):15-32. Also published as "Of Garbage, Modernity and the Citizen's Gaze." *EPW* 27, 10-11 (7-14 March 1992):541-47.

________. "Rethinking Working-Class History." *EPW* 26, 17 (27 April 1991):1117-19.

________. "The Death of History? Historical Consciousness and the Culture of Late Capitalism." *Public Culture* 4, 2 (Spring 1992):47-66.

________. "Postcoloniality and the Artifice of History: Who Speaks for 'Indian' Pasts?" *Representations*, no. 37 (Winter 1992):1-26.

________. "Marx after Marxism: A Subaltern Historian's Perspective." *EPW* 28, 22 (29 May 1933):1094-96.

________. "History as Cultural Performance: Some Reflections." *Australian Historical Association Bulletin*, forthcoming.

________. "Colonial Rule and the Domestic Order." In *Subaltern Studies*, Vol. 8. Edited by David Arnold and David Hardiman. Delhi: Oxford UP, forthcoming, 1994?

Chakravarti, Uma. "The development of the Sita myth: a case study of women in myth and literature." *Samya Shakti* 1, 1 (July 1983):68-75.

________. "Pativrata." *Seminar*, no. 318 (February 1986):17-20.

________. "Beyond the Altekarian Paradigm: Towards a New Understanding of Gender Relations in Early Indian History." *Social Scientist*, no. 183 (August 1988):44-52.

Chakravarti, Uma. "Women, men and beasts: The Jataka as Popular Tradition." *Studies in History* 9, 1 (Jan.-June 1993):43-70.

Chakravarty, Sumita S. "National Identity and Realist Aesthetic: Indian Cinema of the Fifties." *Quarterly Rv. of Film and Video* 11, 3 (1986).

________. *National Identity in Indian Popular Cinema 1947-1987*. Austin, Texas: University of Texas Press, 1993.

Chanda, P. Sita. "Birthing Terrible Beauties: Feminisms and 'Women's Magazines'". *EPW* 26, 43 (26 Oct. 1991) pp. WS-67 ff.

Chandan, Amarjit. *Indians in Britain*. New Delhi: Sterling, 1986.

________, ed. *Do Kinare*. British Punjabi Short Stories. Delhi: Navyug; London: Shakti, 1982.

________, ed. *Apne Aap Ton Dur*. British Punjabi Poetry. Amritsar: Balraj Sahni, 1985.

Chandhoke, Neera. "Teaching Marxism." *EPW* 27, 27 (4 July 1992):1391-94.

Chandra, Bipan. *Communalism in Modern India*. New Delhi: Vikas Publishing House, 1983.

________. "Nationalist Historians' Interpretations of the Indian National Movement." In *Situating Indian History—for Sarvepalli Gopal*. Edited by Sabyasachi Bhattacharya and Romila Thapar. Delhi: Oxford UP, 1986.

________. "Colonial India: British versus Indian Views of Development." *Review Fernand Braudel Center* 14, 1 (Winter 1991):81-167.

Chandra, Sudhir. "Communal Consciousness in Late Nineteenth Century Hindi Literature." In *Communal and Pan-Islamic Trends in Colonial India*, pp. 180-95. Edited by Mushirul Hasan. New Delhi: Manohar, 1981.

________. "Communal Elements in Late Nineteenth-Century Hindi Literature." *Jrl. of Arts and Ideas*, no. 6(Jan.-March 1984):5-18; also published as Occasional Papers on History and Society, no. 15. New Delhi: NMML, 1988.

________. "Literature and the Colonial Connection." Occasional Papers on History and Society, no. 5. New Delhi: NMML, 1986.

________. "Widow Remarriage and Later Nineteenth Century Indian Literature." Occasional Papers on History and Society, no. 24. New Delhi: NMML, 1986.

________. "Sati: The Dharmic Fallacy." *New Quest* (Mar.-Apr. 1988):111-14.

________. *The Oppressive Present: Literature and Consciousness in Colonial India*. Delhi: Oxford UP, 1992.

________. "Whose Laws? Notes on a Legitimising Myth of the Colonial Indian State?" Occasional Paper, no. 12. Surat: CSS, 1992.

Chatterjee, Gayatri. *Awara*. Pune: National Film Archive of India in association with Wiley Eastern, 1993.

Chatterjee, Indrani. "Refracted Reality: The 1935 Calcutta Police Survey of Prostitutes." *Manushi*, no. 57 (March-April 1990):26-36.

Chatterjee, Partha. "More on Modes of Power and the Peasantry." In *Subaltern Studies II*, pp. 311-349. Edited by Ranajit Guha. Delhi: Oxford UP, 1983.

________. *Bengal 1920-1947: Vol. I: The Land Question*. Calcutta: Published for the Centre for the Study of the Social Sciences by K. P. Bagchi, 1984.

________. "Gandhi and the Critique of Civil Society." In *Subaltern Studies III*, pp. 153-95. Edited by Ranajit Guha. Delhi: Oxford UP, 1984.

________. *Nationalist Thought and the Colonial World: A Derivative Discourse?* London: Zed Books, 1986; reprint paperback ed., Minneapolis: Univ. of Minnesota Press, 1992.

________. "Transferring a Political Theory: Early Nationalist Thought in India." *EPW* 221, 3 (1986).

________. "For an Indian History of Peasant Struggle." *Social Scientist*, no. 186 (November 1988):3-17.

________. *The Nationalist Resolution of the Women's Question*. Occasional Paper, no. 94. Calcutta: CSSS, 1988. Also published in *Recasting Women: Essays in Colonial History*, pp. 233-53. Edited by Kumkum Sangari and Sudesh Vaid. New Delhi: Kali for Women, 1989; New Brunswick, New Jersey: Rutgers UP, 1990; paperback ed., Delhi: Oxford UP, 1992.

________. "Caste and Subaltern Consciousness." In *Subaltern Studies VI*, pp. 169-209. Edited by Ranajit Guha. Delhi: Oxford UP, 1989; also published as Occasional Paper, no. 111. Calcutta: CSSS, 1989.

________. "Colonialism, Nationalism, and Colonized Women: The Contest in India." *American Ethnologist* 16, 4 (November 1989):622-33.

________. "A Response to Taylor's Invocation of Civil Society." *Working Papers and Proceedings,* no. 39. Chicago: Center for Psychosocial Studies, 1990. Also published as "A Response to Taylor's Modes of Civil Society." *Public Culture* 3, 1 (Fall 1990):119-32.

________. "History and the Nationalization of Hinduism." *Social Research* 59, 1 (Spring 1992):111-50.

________. "A Religion of Urban Domesticity: Sri Ramakrishna and the Calcutta Middle Class." In *Subaltern Studies 7: Writings on South Asian History and Society*, pp. 40-68. Edited by Gyanendra Pandey and Partha Chatterjee. Delhi: Oxford UP, 1992.

________. "Their Own Words? An Essay for Edward Said." In *Edward Said: A*

Critical Reader, pp. 194-220. Edited by Michael Sprinker. Oxford: Basil Blackwell, 1992.

Chatterjee, Partha. *The Nation and Its Fragments: Colonial and Post-Colonial Histories*. Princeton: Princeton UP, 1993.

Chatterjee, Partha and Pandey, Gyanendra, eds. *Subaltern Studies VII: Writings on South Asian History and Society*. New Delhi: Oxford UP, 1992.

Chatterjee, Roma. "Folklore and the Formation of Popular Consciousness in a Village in the Purulia District of West Bengal." Ph.D. thesis, University of Delhi, 1985.

Chatterjee, Sekhar. "The Colonial Theatre in India." *Theatre Research International* 8, 3 (Autumn 1983):233-34.

Chatterji, Lola, ed. *Woman/Image/Text: Feminist Readings of Literary Texts*. New Delhi: Trianka, 1986.

Chatterji, P. C. *Broadcasting in India*. 2nd ed. New Delhi: Sage Publications, 1991.

Chattopadhyay, Kamaladevi. *Inner Recesses, Outer Spaces*. New Delhi: Navrang, 1986.

Chattopadhyay, Ratnabali.* "The Alternative Vision, a Study of Indian Artistic Response to Orientalism." *Calcutta Historical Jrl.* (July 1986-June 1987).

________. "Nationalism and Form in Indian Painting: A Study of the Bengal School." *Jrl. of Arts and Ideas*, nos. 14-15 (July-Dec. 1987):5-46.

Chatwin, Bruce. "On the Road with Mrs Gandhi." *Granta* 26 (Spring 1989): 107-29.

Chaudhuri, K. N. *Trade and Civilisation in the Indian Ocean: An Economic History from the Rise of Islam to 1750*. Cambridge: Cambridge UP, 1985.

Chaudhuri, Nupur. "Memsahibs and motherhood in nineteenth-century colonial India." *Victorian Studies* 31, 4 (Summer 1988):517-535.

Chaudhuri, Sukanta, ed. *Calcutta, The Living City*. 2 vols. Calcutta: Oxford UP, 1990.

Chaudhury, Ajit K. "In Search of a Subaltern Lenin." In *Subaltern Studies V*, pp. 236-51. Edited by Ranajit Guha. Delhi: Oxford UP, 1987.

Chawla, Janet. "The Rig Vedic Slaying of Vrtra: Menstruation Taboos in Mythology." *Manushi*, no. 68 (Jan.-Feb. 1992):29-36.

Cheran, R. "Cultural Politics of Tamil Nationalism." *South Asia Bulletin* 12, 1 (1992):42-56.

Chhachhi, Amritha. "The State, Religious Fundamentalism and Women: Trends in South Asia." *EPW* (18 March 189):567-78.

________. "Forced Identities: the State, Communalism, Fundamentalism and

Women in India." In *Women, Islam and the State*, pp. 144-75. Edited by Deniz Kandiyoti. Philadelphia: Temple UP, 1991.

Chhachhi, Amritha. "In the Eye of the Storm: Women and Religious Fundamentalism in South Asia." *Sangarsh* [Bangalore], no. 3 (n.d.):8 ff.

Chowdhry, Kamla. "Poverty, Environment, Development." *Daedalus* (Winter 1989):141-58.

Chowdhry, Prem. "The Advantages of Backwardness: Colonial Policy and Agriculture in Haryana." *IESHR* 23, 3 (Oct.-Dec. 1986):236-88.

Clark, Alice W. *Gender and Political Economy: Explorations of South Asian Systems*. Delhi: Oxford UP, 1992.

Clarke, Colin *et al*, eds. *South Asians Overseas: Migration and Ethnicity*. Cambridge: Cambridge UP, 1990.

Clarke, M. *The Tempting Prospect: A Social History of English Watercolours*. London: British Museum Publications, 1981.

Clement, Catherine. "India: Of Crows and Democracy." *IICQ* 20, 1-2 (Spring-Summer 1993):51-60.

Cohn, Bernard S. "Representing Authority in Victorian India." In *The Invention of Tradition*, pp. 165-210. Edited by Eric Hobsbawm and Terence Ranger. Cambridge: Cambridge UP, 1983; paperback ed., 1984.

________. "The Census, Social Structure and Objectification in South Asia." *Folk* 26 (1984):25-49.

________. "The Command of Language and the Language of Command." In *Subaltern Studies IV*, pp. 276-329. Edited by Ranajit Guha. New Delhi: Oxford UP, 1985.

________. "The Transformation of Objects into Artifacts, Antiquities and Art in Nineteenth Century India." Paper delivered at National Endowment for the Humanities Conference, 'Patronage in Indian Culture', 1985.

________. *An Anthropologist among the Historians and Other Essays*. Delhi: Oxford UP, 1987.

________. "The Past in the Present: India as a Museum of Mankind." Paper delivered at Smithsonian Symposium, 'The Poetics and Politics of Representation', 1988.

________. "Cloth, Clothes, and Colonialism: India in the Nineteenth Century." In *Cloth and the Human Experience*, pp. 303-53. Edited by Annette B. Wiener and Jane Schneider. Washington, D.C.: Smithsonian Institution Press, 1989.

________. "Law and the Colonial State in India." In *History and Power: The Study of Law*, pp. 131-52. Edited by Jean Starr and Jane Collier. Ithaca, New York: Cornell UP, 1989.

Cohn, Bernard S. and Dirks, Nicholas B. "Beyond the Fringe: The Nation State, Colonialism and the Technologies of Power." *Jrl. of Historical Sociology* 1, 2 (June 1988):224-29.

Cohn-Sherbok, Dan, ed. *The Salman Rushdie Controversy in Interreligious Perspective.* Symposium Series Volume 27. Lewiston: The Edwin Mellen Press, 1990.

Contursi, Janet A. "Political Theology: Text and Practice in a Dalit Panther Community." *JAS* 52, 2 (May 1993):320-39.

Cook, Geoffrey. "Ananda K. Coomaraswamy and Medieval Sri Lankan Art." *Left Curve*, no. 15 (1991):75-81.

Cooper, Darius. "The Hindi Film Song and Guru Dutt." *East-West Film Journal* 2, 2 (June 1988):49-65.

________. "Colonialism in the Hindu Caste System: Satyajit Ray's *Sadgati* (*Deliverance*). *East-West Film Journal* 5, 2 (July 1991):66-76.

________. "Through a lens, uniquely: An essay on the narrative forms of *Kasba* and *Nazar*." *Cinema in India* (Sept. 1991):34-40.

Copley, Antony. "Indian secularism reconsidered: from Gandhi to Ayodhya." *Contemporary South Asia* 2, 1 (1993):47-66.

Corbridge, Stuart. "Industrialisation, Internal Colonialism and Ethnoregionalism: The Jharkhand, India, 1880-1980." *Jrl. of Historical Geography* 13, 3 (1987):249-66.

Correa, Charles. *The New Landscape: Urbanization in the Third World.* Bombay: The Book Society of India, 1985.

________. "The Public, the Private, and the Sacred." *Daedalus* (Fall 1989): 93-113.

Cosoto, Maria. "The Raj Films: A Study in Cultural Imperialism." *Splice*, no. 1 (Jan.-March 1992):5-13.

Cottle, Simon. "Reporting the Rushdie Affair: A Case Study in the Orchestration of Public Opinion." *Race and Class* 32, 4 (April-June 1991):45-64.

Crane, Ralph J. *Inventing India: A History of India in English-Language Fiction.* New York: St. Martin's Press, 1992.

Cruickshank, Dan. "Variations and Traditions." *Architectural Review*, no. 1086 (August 1987):51-61.

Cubitt, Sean. "Indian Cinema: Interview with Anand Patwardhan." *Framework* 30/31 (1986):60-67.

Curtis, William J. R. "Modernism and the search for an Indian identity." *Architectural Review* , no. 1086 (August 1987):33-38.

________. *Modern Architecture in an Indian Tradition: Balkrishna V. Doshi.* Ahmedabad: Mapin International, 1987.

Custers, Peter. *Women in the Tebhaga Uprising*. Delhi: Naya Prakash, 1987.

Dale, Stephen Frederic. "Religious Suicide in Islamic Asia: Anticolonial Terrorism in India, Indonesia, and the Philippines." *Jrl. of Conflict Resolution*.32, 1 (1988):37-59.

Dalmia, Manju. "Derozio: English Teacher." In *The Lie of the Land: English Literary Studies in India*, pp. 42-62. Edited by Rajeswari Sunder Rajan. New Delhi: Oxford UP, 1992.

Dalmia-Luderitz, Vasudha. "Friedrich Max Mueller: Appropriation of the Vedic Past." *Jrl. of Arts and Ideas*, nos. 20-21 (March 1991):43-58.

________. "'Sati' as a Religious Rite: *Parliamentary Papers on Widow Immolation, 1821-30*", *EPW* 27, 4 (25 January 1992):PE58-64.

________. "Encountering the Other, Accosting the Self." *Jrl. of Arts and Ideas*, no. 22 (April 1922):19-43.

________. "Reconsidering the Orientalist View." Special issue: "Perceiving India: Insight and Inquiry." *IICQ* 20, 1-2 (Spring-Summer 1993): 92-114.

Dangle, Arjun, ed. *Poisoned Bread: Translations from Modern Marathi Dalit Literature*. Hyderabad: Orient Longman, 1992.

Das, Arvind N. "Class in Itself, Caste for Itself: Social Articulation in Bihar." *EPW* (15 Sept. 1984):1616-19.

Das, Sanjukta. *Feminist Literary Criticism*. Occasional Paper, no. 99. Calcutta: CSSS, 1988.

Das, Veena. "The Mythological Film and Its Framework of Meaning: An Analysis of *Jai Santoshi Ma*." *IICQ* 8, 1 (March 1980):43-56.

________. "The Language of Sacrifice." *Man* (New Series) 18 (1983):445-62.

________. "Gender Studies, Cross-Cultural Comparison and the Colonial Organization of Knowledge." *Berkshire Review* 21 (1986):58-76.

________. "Femininity and the Orientation to the Body." In *Women, Socialization and Change*. Edited by Karuna Ahmed. Delhi: Orient Longmans, 1988.

________. "Science and Violence in Popular Fiction: Four Novels of Ira Levin." In *Science, Hegemony and Violence*, pp. 211-31. Edited by Ashis Nandy. Delhi: Oxford UP, 1992 [1988].

________. "Subaltern as Perspective." In *Subaltern Studies VI*, pp. 310-24. Edited by Ranajit Guha. Delhi: Oxford UP, 1989.

________. "Voices of Children." *Daedalus* (Fall 1989):263-94.

________."Composition of the Personal Voice: Violence and Migration." *Studies in History* (New Series) 7, 1 (Jan.-June 1991):65-77.

________. "Time, self, and community: Features of the Sikh militant discourse." *Contributions to Indian Sociology* (New Series) 26, 2 (July-Dec. 1992):245-59.

Das, Veena. "Force as a Residual Category in Max Weber." In *Marx and Weber: Modern Society on the Drawingboard*, ed. Surendra Munshi. Forthcoming.

Das, Veena, ed. *Mirrors of Violence: Communities, Riots and Survivors in South Asia*. Delhi: Oxford UP, 1990.

________. *The Word and the World: Fantasy, Symbol and Record*. New Delhi: Sage Publications, 1986.

Dasgupta, Chidananda. *Talking About Films*. New Delhi: Orient Longman, 1981.

________. "The Rural Base of an Urban Phenomenon." *East-West Film Journal* 3, 1 (Dec. 1988):88-96.

________. "Seeing and Believing, Science and Mythology: Notes on the 'Mythological' Genre." *Film Quarterly* 42, 4 (Summer 1989):121-28.

________. *The Painted Face: Studies in India's Popular Cinema*. Delhi: Roli Books, 1991.

Dasgupta, Probal. *Beyond Linguistic Limits: The Otherness of English, India's Auntie Tongue Syndrome*. New Delhi: Sage Publications, 1993.

Datta, Alokananda and Roy, Soma. "Adoor Gopalakrishnan in conversation." *Splice*, no. 2 (July 1986):23-30.

Datta, P. K. "Studies in Heterogeneity: A Reading of Two Recent Indo-Anglian Novels." *Social Scientist*, no. 202 (March 1990).

________. "War Over Music: The Riots of 1926 in Bengal." *Social Scientist*, nos. 205-6 (June-July 1990):38-48.

________. "Learning and Teaching: Keats' Odes." In *Ourstory: Indian Response to Nineteenth Century Literature*, pp. 25-40. Edited by Mohua Lahiri, Sanjay Kumar, and Anand Prakash. New Delhi: Academic Foundation, 1992.

________. "'Dying Hindus': Production of Hindu Communal Common Sense in Early 20th Century Bengal." *EPW* 28, 25 (19 June 1993):1305-19.

Datta, P.; Pati, B.; Sarkar, S.; Sarkar, T.; and Sen, S. "Understanding communal violence: Nizamuddin Riots." *EPW* 22, 45 (Nov. 1990):2487-95.

Datta, Santo. "Urbanisation of Indian Art." *Jrl. of Arts and Ideas*, no. 9 (Oct.-Dec. 1984):5-22.

Davis, Richard H. "Indian Art Objects as Loot." *JAS* 52, 1 (Feb. 1993):22-48.

De, Barun. *Problems of the Study of Indian History*. Occasional Paper, no. 116. Calcutta: CSSS, 1990.

de Alwis, Mala. "A Feminist Critique of [the] Gulf War." *EPW* 26, 36 (7 Sept. 1991):2086-88.

Debi, Rashsundari. *Amar Jiban (My Life)*. Edited with an introduction by Tanika Sarkar. New Delhi: Kali for Women, forthcoming 1993.

Dehejia, Vidya. "The Future of India's Past: Conservation of Cultural Heritage." In *India Briefing, 1990*, pp. 131-57. Edited by Marshall M. Bouton and Philip Oldenburg. Boulder: Westview Press, 1990.

Desai, A. R., ed. *Women's Liberation and Politics of Religious Personal Laws in India*. Bombay: C. G. Shah Memorial Trust Publications, 1986.

Desai, Chetan. "Martial Arts in Cinema." *Deep Focus* 2, 1 (Sept. 1989):32-41.

Desai, Gaurav. "The Invention of Invention." *Cultural Critique*, no. 24 (Spring 1993):119-42.

Desai, Meghnad. "Is Socialism Dead?" *Contention* 1, 2 (Winter 1992):143-58.

Deshingkar, G. D. "On the Banality of Reductionist Thinking." *Alternatives* 8, 1 (March 1982):127-30.

Deshpande, G. P. "Art in the Age of Mechanical and 'Utsav'ical' Reproduction." *EPW* 27, 8 (22 February 1992):401-4.

________. "Dialectics of Defeat: Some Reflections on Literature, Theatre and Music: Colonial India." *EPW* 22, 50 (12 Dec. 1982):2170-76.

Desmond, Ray. *History of the India Museum*. London, 1982.

________. "Photography in Victorian India." *Jrl. of the Royal Society of Arts* 134 (Dec. 1985):48-61.

Desnoes, Edmundo. "The Photographic Image of Underdevelopment." *Jump Cut*, no. 33 (1988).

Devalle, Susana B. C. *Discourses of Ethnicity: Culture and Protest in Jharkhand*. New Delhi: Sage, 1992.

Devji, Faisal F. "Gender and the Politics of Space: the Movement for Women's Reform in Muslim India, 1857-1900." *South Asia* (New Series) 14, 1 (1991):141-53.

________. "Hindu/Muslim/Indian." *Public Culture* 5, 1 (Fall 1992):1-18.

Devi, Ganesh N. "The Commonwealth Literature Period" and "Comparative Literature." In *Literature(s) in English: New Perspectives*, pp. 79-94. Edited by Wolfgang Zach. Frankfurt am Maim: Peter Lang, 1990.

Devi, Mahasweta. *Five Plays: Mother of 1084/Aajir/Bayen/Uvashi and Johnny/ Water*. Calcutta: Seagull Books, 1986.

Devy, G. N. *After Amnesia: Tradition and Change in Indian Literary Criticism*. Madras: Orient Longman, 1992.

Dhagamwar, Vasudha. *Law, Power and Justice: The Protection of Personal Rights in the Indian Penal Code*. New Delhi: Sage Publications, 1992.

Dhanagaare, D. N. "Subaltern Consciousness and Populism: Two Approaches in the Study of Social Movements." *Social Scientist*, no. 186 (Nov. 1988):18-35.

Dharampal. "A Note on the Disruption and Disorganisation of Indian Society in the Last Two Centuries." *PPST Bulletin* 3, 2 (Nov. 1983):18-47.

Dhareshwar, Vivek. "Self-Fashioning, Colonial Habitus and Double Exclusion: V. S. Naipual's 'The Mimic Men.'" *Criticism* 31, 1 (1989):73-102.

________. "Toward a Narrative Epistemology of the Postcolonial Predicament." *Inscriptions*, no. 5 (1989):135-57.

________. "The Predicament of Theory." In *Theory between the Disciplines: Authority/Vision/Politics*, pp. 231-50. Edited by Martin Kreiswirth and Mark Cheetham. Ann Arbor: University of Michigan Press, 1990.

Dhareshwar, V.; Niranjana, T.; Srivatsan, R; and Susie, S. "Blame it on the Victims." *Illustrated Weekly of India* (28 Oct.-3 Nov. 1990):42-45.

Dhondy, Faruukh. "Keeping Faith: Indian Film and Its World." *Deadalus* (Fall 1985):125-40.

Dhruvarajan, Vanaja. *Hindu Women and The Power of Ideology*. New Delhi: Sage Publications, 1989.

Dickason, Daniel G. "The Nineteenth-Century Indo-American Ice Trade: An Hyperborean Epic." *MAS* 25, 1 (1991):53-89.

Dickey, Sara Ann. "Going to the Pictures in Madurai." Unpublished Ph.D. Dissertation, University of California at San Diego, 1988.

________. "Accommodation and Resistance: Expression of Working-Class Values through Tamil Cinema." *Wide Angle* 11, 3 (July 1989): 26-32.

________. "The Politics of Adulation: Cinema and the Production of Politicians in South India." *JAS* 52, 2 (May 1993):340-72.

Dietrich, Gabriele. *Women's Movement in India: Conceptual and Religious Reflections*. Bangalore: Breakthrough Publications, 1988.

________. "Women, Ecology and Culture." *Lokayan Bulletin* 7, 1 (Jan.-Feb. 1989):7-26.

________. "The Development Debate and Gender Implications." *Lokayan Bulletin* 8, 1 (Jan.-Feb. 1990):39-56.

________. *Reflections on the Women's Movement in India: Religion, Ecology, Development*. New Delhi: Horizon India Books, 1992.

di Leonardo, Micaela, ed. *Gender at the Crossroads of Knowledge: Feminist Anthropology in the Postmodern Era*. Berkeley: Univ. of California Press, 1991.

Dimock, Edward C. *The Sound of Silent Guns and Other Essays*. New Delhi: Oxford UP, 1989. [Review by Vinay Lal, "Indian Poetics and Western Literary Criticism," *Indian Literature* 35, 1 (Jan.-Feb. 1992):101-7.]

Dirks, Nicholas B. "From Little King to Landlord: Property, Law, and the Gift Under the Madras Permanent Settlement." *CSSH* 28, 2 (1986):307-33; also published in revised form as "From Little King to Landlord: Colonial Discourse and Colonial Rule." In *Colonialism and Culture*, pp. 175-208. Edited by Nicholas Dirks. Ann Arbor, Michigan: Univ. of Michigan Press, 1992.

Dirks, Nicholas B. *The Hollow Crown: Ethnohistory of an Indian Kingdom*. Cambridge: Cambridge UP, 1987; 2nd edition, paperback, Ann Arbor: Univ. of Michigan Press, 1992.

________. "The Invention of Caste: Civil Society in Colonial India." *Social Analysis* 25 (1989):42-52.

________. "History as a Sign of the Modern." *Public Culture* 2, 2 (Spring 1990):25-33.

________. "Ritual and Resistance: Subversion as a Social Fact." In *Contesting Power: Resistance and Everday Social Relations in South Asia*, pp. 213-38. Edited by Douglas Haynes and Gyan Prakash. Delhi: Oxford UP, 1991.

________. "Castes of Mind." *Representations*, no. 37 (Winter 1992):56-78.

________. "Colonialism and Culture". Introduction to *Colonialism and Culture*, pp. 1-25. Edited by Nicholas Dirks. Ann Arbor, Michigan: Univ. of Michigan Press, 1992.

________. "Colonial Histories and Native Informants: Biography of an Archive." In *Orientalism and the Postcolonial Predicament*. Edited by Carol Breckenridge and Peter van der Veer. Philadelphia: Univ. of Pennsylvania Press, 1993.

________. "Is Vice Versa? Historical Anthropologies and Anthropological Histories." In *The Historic Turn in the Human Sciences*. Edited by Terence McDonald, forthcoming.

________, ed. *Colonialism and Culture*. Ann Arbor, Michigan: Univ. of Michigan Press, 1992.

Dirks, Nicholas B., Eley, Geoff; and Ortner, Sherry B., eds. *Culture/Power/History: A Reader in Contemporary Social Theory*. Princeton, New Jersey: Princeton UP, 1993.

Dirlik, Arif. "The Postcolonial Aura: Third World Criticism in the Age of Global Capitalism." *Critical Inquiry* 20, 2 (Winter 1994):328-56.

Dissanayake, Wimal. "Personality, Transpersonality and Impersonality." *Asian Culture* 10 (1982):2-35.

________. "Art, Vision, and Culture: Satyajit Ray's Apu Trilogy Revisited." *East-West Film Journal* 1, 1 (Dec. 1986):69-83.

________. "Film and Social Change: Notes Towards a Conceptual Analysis." *Splice*, no. 2 (1986):6-15.

________. "Self and Modernization in Malayalam Cinema." *East-West Film Journal* 1, 2 (June 1987):60-77.

Dissanayake, Wimal. "Questions of Female Subjectivity, Patriarchy, and Family: Perceptions of Three Indian Women Film Directors." *East-West Film Journal* 3, 2 (June 1989):74-90.

________. *Sholay: A Cultural Reading*. New Delhi: Wiley Eastern, 1992.

________, ed. *Cinema and Cultural Identity: Reflections on Films from Japan, India and China.* Lanham, Maryland: U. Press of America, 1988.

Dissanayake, Wimal and Alter, Stephen, eds. *The Penguin Book of Modern Indian Short Stories*. New Delhi: Penguin Books, 1989.

Dissanayake, Wimal and Sahai, Malti. *Raj Kapoor's Films: Harmony of Discourses*. New Delhi: Vikas Publishing House, 1988.

Divakaruni, Chitra Banerjee. *Black Candle: Poems about Women from India, Pakistan and Bangladesh.* Corvallis, Oregon: Calyx Books, 1991.

Dogra, Bharat. *Forests and People*. Delhi: Published by the author, 1984.

Doraiswamy, Rashmi. "Western interpretations of Bakhtin." *Journal of Arts and Ideas*, nos. 12-13 (Jan.-June 1987):93-122.

Dossal, Mariam. *Imperial Designs, Indian Realities: The Planning of Bombay City, 1845-1875*. Bombay: Oxford UP, 1991.

Duara, Prasenjit. "Rescuing History from the Nation-State." *Working Papers and Proceedings of the Center for Psychosocial Studies*, no. 48. Chicago: Center for Psychosocial Studies, 1992.

Durrans, Brian. "Competitive Pragmatism: Organising the 1982 Festival of India in Britain." *History and Anthropology* 6, 1 (1992):23-45.

Dutt, Ashok K., ed. *India: Cultural Patterns and Processes*. Boulder, Colorado: Westview, 1982.

Dutt, Srikant. *India and the Third World: Altruism or Hegemony?* London: Zed Books, 1984.

Dutta, Sangeeta. "Relinquishing the Halo: Portrayal of Mother in Indian Writing in English." *EPW* 25, 42-43 (25 Oct. 1990):WS84-94.

________. "Charlotte Bronte and the Woman Question." *EPW* 26, 40 (5 Oct. 1991):2311-16.

Edge, Sara and Morgan, Jill. *The Issue of Painting: Sutapa Biswas, Margaret Harrison, Glenys Johnson*. Rochdale, U.K.: Rochdale Art Gallery, 1986.

Edwards, Elizabeth. "The Image as Anthropological Document: Photographic 'Types': The Pursuit of Method." *Visual Anthropology* 3, 2-3 (1990): 235-58.

Engels, Dagmar. "The Age of Consent Act of 1891: Colonial Ideology in Bengal." *South Asia Research* 3, 2 (November 1983).

________. "The Limits of Gender Ideology: Bengali Women, the Colonial

State, and the Private Sphere, 1890-1930." *Women's Studies International Forum* 12, 4 (1989):425-37.

Engineer, Asghar Ali, ed. *The Shahbano Controversy*. Hyderabad: Orient Longman, 1987.

Ernst, Waltraud. *Mad Tales from the Raj: The European Insane in British India, 1800-1858*. Wellcome Institute Series in the History of Medicine. London: Routledge, 1991.

Escobar, Arturo. "Discourse and Power in Development: Michel Foucault and the Relevance of His Work to the Third World." *Alternatives* 10, 3 (September 1984):377-400.

Evans, Christopher. "'Power on Silt': Towards an Archaeology of the East India Company." *Antiquity* 84, no. 244 (Sept. 1990):643-61.

Evenson, Normal. *The Indian Metropolis: A View Toward the West*. New Haven: Yale UP, 1989.

Fahim, Hussein, ed. *Indigenous Anthropology in Non-Western Countries: Proceedings of a Burg Wartenstein Symposium*. Durham, North Carolina: Carolina Academic Press, 1982.

Falconer, J. "Ethnological Photogaphy in India, 1850-1900." *The Photographic Collector* 5, 1 (1984):16-46.

________. "Photography in Nineteenth-Century India." In *The Raj: India and the British 1600-1947*, pp. 264-77. Edited by C. A. Bayly. London: National Portrait Gallery Publications, 1990.

Farrell, Gerry. "Reflecting Surfaces: The Use of Elements from Indian Music in Popular Music in Jazz." *Popular Music* 7 (1988):189-205.

Fermor-Hesketh, Robert, ed. *Architecture of the British Empire*. London: Weidenfeld & Nicolson, 1986.

Fernandes, Walter and Menon, Geeta. *Tribal Women and Forest Economy: Deforestation, Exploitation, and Status Change*. Delhi: Indian Social Institute, 1987.

Fernando, Peter and Yasas, Frances M., ed. *Woman's Image Making and Shaping*. Pune: Ishvani Kendra, 1985.

Fischer, Michael M. J. and Abedi, Mehdi. *Debating Muslims: Cultural Dialogues in Postmodernity and Tradition*. [Chapter 7, "Postscriptual Parergon: Bombay Talkies, the Word and the World: Salman Rushdie's *Satanic Verses*", is relevant.] New Directions in Anthropological Writing. Madison, Wisconsin: The University of Wisconsin Press, 1990. [Review by Vinay Lal in *Middle East Report* 22, 4 (July-August 1992):46-47.]

Flora, Reis. "Miniature Paintings: Important Sources for Music History." *Asian Music* 18, 2 (Spring-Summer 1987):196-240.

Flueckiger, Joyce Burkhalter. "Bhoajli: Song, Goddess, Friend: A Chattisgarhi

Women's Oral Tradition." *Asian Folklore Studies* 42, 1 (1983):27-43.

Flueckiger, Joyce Burkhalter. "Land of Wealth, Land of Famine: The Sua nac (Parrot Dance) of Central India." *Jrl. of American Folklore* 100, no. 395 (Jan.-March 1987):39-57.

Forbes, Geraldine. "Caged Tigers: First-wave Feminists in India." *Women's Studies International Forum* 5, 6 (1982).

________. "In search of the 'pure heathen': missionary women in nineteenth century India." *EPW* 21, 17 (26 April 1986):WS2-8.

Fox, Richard G. "Gandhian Socialism and Hindu Nationalism: Cultural Domination in the World System." *Journal of Commonwealth and Comparative Politics* 25, 3 (1987):233-47.

________. *Gandhian Utopia: Experiments with Culture*. Boston: Beacon Press, 1989. [Review by Vinay Lal in *Gandhi Marg* 12, 2 (July-September, 1990):236-40.]

________, "East of Said." In *Edward Said: A Critical Reader*, pp. 144-56. Edited by Michael Sprinker. Oxford: Basil Blackwell, 1992.

Framework, no. 37. Special Issue on Sri Lanka Cinema. Guest Editors: Robert Crusz and Ashley Ratnavibhushana.

Franco, F. and Ramanathan, Suguna. "The recovery of religious meaning." *Textual Pratice* 5 (1991):183-93.

Frater, Judy. "In the Language of Folk." *El Palacio: Magazine of the Museum of New Mexico* 94, 3 (Spring 1989):44-53.

Freitag, Sandria. *Collective Action and Community*. Berkeley: Univ. of California Press, 1989.

________. *Culture and Power in Banaras: Community, Performance and Environment 1800-1980*. Delhi: Oxford UP, 1990.

________. "Crime in the Social Order of Colonial North India." *MAS* 25, 2 (1991):227-61.

________. "Enactments of Ram's Story and the Changing Nature of 'the Public' in British India." *South Asia* (New Series) 14, 1 (1991):65-90.

Frith, Edmund. "A Question of Order: a study of the Bhuleshwar temple complex and its tree shrine." Unpublished Ph.D. Dissertation, University of Cambridge, 1987.

Fryer, Peter. *Staying Power: The History of the Black People in Britain*. London: Pluto, 1984.

________. *Black People in the British Empire: An Introduction*. London: Pluto, 1989.

Frykenberg, "The Concept of 'Majority' as a Devilish Force in the Politics of Modern Indian History." *Jrl. of Commonwealth and Comparative Politics* 25, 3 (November 1987):267-74.

Gabriel, Teshome H. "Teaching Third World Cinema." *Screen* 24, 2 (March-April 1983): 60-64.

Gadgil, Madhav. "Towards an Ecological History of India." *EPW* (Special Number, November 1985):1909-38.

________. "Deforestation: Problems and Prospects." *Lokayan Bulletin* 7, 3 (May-June 1989):9-46.

Gandhi, Nandita. *When the Rolling Pins Hit the Streets: A Case Study of the Anti-Price Rise Movement in India.* New Delhi: Kali for Women, forthcoming 1993.

Gandhi, Nandita and Shah, Nandita. *The Issues at Stake: Theory and Practice in the Contemporary Women's Movement in India.* Delhi: Kali for Women, 1992.

Gandhi, Rajmohan. *Understanding the Muslim Mind.* New Delhi: Penguin, 1987.

Gandhi, Ramchandra. *Sita's Kitchen: A Testimony of Faith and Inquiry.* Albany: State Univ. of New York Press; New Delhi: Penguin Books, 1992.

Ganesh, Kamala. "Mother Who is Not a Mother: In Search of the Great Indian Goddess." *EPW* 25, 42-43 (20-27 Oct. 1990):WS58-64.

Ganguly, Keya. "Colonial Discourse and the History of Indian Art: A Revvisionist Reading." *Jrl. of Communication Inquiry* 12, 2 (1988):39-52.

________. "Migrant Identities: Personal Memory and the Construction of Selfhood." *Cultural Studies* 6, 1 (January 1992):27-50.

Ganguly, Suranjan. "One Single Blend: A Conversation with Satyajit Ray." *East-West Film Journal* 3, 2 (June 1989):91-95.

Gardezi, Fauzia. "Islam, Feminism, and the Women's Movement in Pakistan: 1981-1991." *South Asia Bulletin* 10, 2 (1990):18-24.

Garg, Mridula. "Bilingualism and the Creative Writer in India." *The Book Review* 14, 5 (Sept.-Oct. 1990):14-17.

________. "Metaphors of Womanhood in Indian Literature". *Alternatives* 16, 4 (Fall 1991):407-24.

Geetha, V. "Gender and Political Discourse." *EPW* 26, 7 (16 Feb. 1991):387-88.

George, Alex. "[Tipu] Sultan and the Saffron." *EPW* 25, 52 (29 Dec. 1990):2833-35.

George, K. M., et al. *Inner Spaces: New Writing by Women from Kerala.* New Delhi: Kali for Women, 1993.

Gessen, Elena and Brovchenko, Anatoli. "Shyam Benegal." *Soviet Literature*, no. 473 (1987):171-74.

Ghadially, Rehana. "Teaching the Psychology of Sex Roles to Engineers in India." *Women's Studies Quarterly* 16, 3-4 (Fall/Winter 1988):86-99.

Ghadially, Rehana. "Veiling the Unveiled: The Politics of Purdah in a Muslim Sect." *South Asia* (New Series) 12, 2 (1989):33-48.

________, ed. *Women in Indian Society: A Reader.* New Delhi: Sage Publications, 1988.

Ghai, Yash; Luckham, Robin; and Snyder, Francis, eds. *The Political Economy of Law: A Third World Reader.* Delhi: Oxford UP, 1987.

Ghosh, Amitav. "The Relations of Envy in an Egyptian Village." *Ethnology* (Trivandrum) 22, 3 (July 1983):211-23.

________. *The Circle of Reason.* London: Hamish Hamilton; New York: Viking, 1986.

________. "Tambiah on Ritual." *Contributions to Indian Sociology* (New Series) 21, 1 (Jan.-June 1987):217-24.

________. *The Shadow Lines.* New Delhi: Ravi Dayal Publisher; London: Bloomsbury, 1988.

________. "The Diaspora in Indian Culture." *Public Culture* 2, 1 (Fall 1989): 73-78.

________. "The Slave of Ms. H.6." Occasional Paper, no. 126. Calcutta: CSSS, 1990.

________. "The Slave of MS. H.6." In *Subaltern Studies 7: Wrtings on South Asian History and Society*, pp. 159-220. Edited by Partha Chatterjee and Gyanendra Pandey. Delhi: Oxford UP, 1992.

________. *In an Antique Land.* London: Granta; New Delhi: Ravi Dayal Publisher, 1992; New York: Knopf, 1993. [Review by Vinay Lal, "A Meditation on History", *Social Scientist*, nos. 242-42 (July-August 1993):89-98.]

________. "An obstacle course lunch." *Telegraph* (Calcutta), 11 Oct. 1993.

Ghosh, Anjan. *The Stricture of Structure, or, The Appropriation of an Anthropological Theory.* Occasional Papers, no. 107. Calcutta: CSSS, 1988. Also published in *Review Fernand Braudel Center* 14, 1 (Winter 1991):55-77.

Ghosh, Shohini and Chakravarti, Uma. "Hidden Agendas in the Alternative Media: Religion and Gender." *Samya Shakti* 6 (1991-92):81-97.

Ghosh, Sital Chandra and Roy, Arun Kumar, eds. *Twelve Indian Directors.* Calcutta: People's Book Publishing, 1981.

Gidwani, Vinay Krishin. "'Waste' and the Permanent Settlement in Bengal." *EPW* 27, 4 (25 January 1992):PE39-46.

Gillespie, Marie. "Technology and Tradition: Audio-Visual Culture Among South Asian Families in West London." *Cultural Studies* 3, 2 (1989).

Girdhar, Virendra K. "Towards an All-Inclusive Indian Architecture." *Indian Institute Magazine* (October-December 1986).

Gohain, Hiren. *The Idea of Popular Culture in the Early Nineteenth Century Bengal*. Calcutta: CSSS, 1991.

Gokhale, Shanta. "Mother in Sane Guruji's Shyamchi Ai." *EPW* 25, 42-43 (25 Oct. 1990):WS95-102.

Gonsalves, Paul. "Alternative Tourism: A Third World Perspective." *Lokayan Bulletin* 9, 2 (March-April 1991):23-28.

Goonatilake, Susantha. *Crippled Minds: Exploration into Colonial Culture*. New Delhi: Vikas Publishing, 1982.

________. *Colonial Culture and Endogenous Intellectual Creativity*. Tokyo: United Nations University, 1982.

________. *Aborted Discovery: Science and Creativity in the Third World*. London: Zed Books, 1984.

________. "Black Athena and Geopolitics of Knowledge." *EPW* 27, 42 (17 October 1992)P:2302-3 [review of Vol. II of Martin Bernal's *Black Athena*].

Gooneratne, Yasmine. *Diverse Inheritance: A Personal Perspective on Commonwealth Literature*. Adelaide: Center for Research in the New Literatures in English, 1980.

Gopal, Sarvepalli, et al. "The Political Abuse of History." *Social Scientist*, nos. 200-1 (Jan.-Feb. 1990):76-81.

________, ed. *Anatomy of a Confrontation: The Babri Masjid-Ram Janmabhumi Issue*. New Delhi: Viking, 1991; Penguin paperback ed., 1991.

Gopalan, Lalitha. "Putting Asunder: Fassbinder and The Marriage of Maria Braun." *Deep Focus* 1, 4 (Jan. 1989):50-57.

Gregory, R. G. *Quest for Equality: Asian Politics in East Africa (1900-1967)*. Hyderabad: Orient Longman, 1993.

Grewal, Inderpal. "The guidebook and the museum: imperialism, education and nationalism in the British Museum." *Bucknell Review* (1990):195-217.

Grewal, Shabnam, et al. *Charting the Journey: Writings by Black and Third World Women*. London: Sheba Feminist Publishers, 1988.

Gronow, Pekka. "Record Industry Comes to the Orient." *Ethnomusicology* 25, 2 (1981): 251-84.

Guha, Probir; Meduri, Avanthi; Neff, Deborah; and Zarrilli, Phillip. "The Aftermath: When Peter Brook Came to India" and "More Aftermath After Peter Brook", both in *The Drama Review* 30, 1 (1986):92-99 and 32 (Summer 1988):14-20.

Guha, Ramachandra. "Forestry in British and Post-British India: A Historical Analysis." *EPW* (29 Oct. 1983):1882-96.

Guha, Ramachandra. "Eco-Development Debate: A Critical Review." Occasional Paper, no. 73. Calcutta: CSSS, 1985.

________."Forestry and Social Protest in British Kumaon, c. 1893-1921." In *Subaltern Studies IV*. Edited by Ranajit Guha. Delhi: Oxford UP, 1985.

________. "Scientific Forestry and Social Change in Uttarakhand." *EPW* (Special Number, November 1985):1939-52.

________. *The Unquiet Woods: Ecological Change and Peasant Resistance in the Himalaya*. Delhi: Oxford UP; Berkeley: Univ. of California Press, 1989. [Reviewed by Amitava Kumar, "The Double Failure: Modernity in the Postcolonial Context", *Socialist Review* 22, 2 (April-June 1992):147-151; see also Rashmi Pant,"Man and Nature in the Himalayas", *Times of India Review of Books* 1, 1 (August-Sept. 1990): 30-31.]

________. "Ideological Tends in Indian Environmentalism." *EPW* (3 Dec. 1988):2578-81.

________. "Radical American Environmentalism and Wilderness Preservation: A Third World Critique." *Environmental Ethics* 11 (Spring 1989): 71-83.

________."Toward a Cross-Cultural Environmental Ethic." *Alternatives* 15, 4 (Fall 1990):431-47.

________. "Writing environmental history in India." *Studies in History* (New Series) 9, 1 (1993):119-29.

Guha, Ramachandra and Gadgil, Madhav. "State Forestry and Social Conflict in British India." *Past and Present*, no. 123 (1989):141-77.

________. *This Fissured Land: An Ecological History of India*. Delhi: Oxford UP, 1992.

Guha, Ranajit. "On Some Aspects of the Historiography of Colonial India." In *Subaltern Studies I*, pp. 1-8. Edited by Ranajit Guha. Delhi: Oxford UP, 1982.

________. *Elementary Aspects of Peasant Insurgency in Colonial India*. Delhi: Oxford UP, 1983.

________. "The Prose of Counter-Insurgency." In *Subaltern Studies II*, pp. 1-42. Edited by Ranajit Guha. Delhi: Oxford UP, 1983.

________. "Nationalism Reduced to 'Official Nationalism.'" *AAAS Review* 9, 1(July 1985):103-8. [Review of Benedict Anderson's *Imagined Communities*.]

________. "The Career of an Anti-God in Heaven and on Earth." In *The Truth Unites: Essays in Tribute to Samar Sen*. Edited by Asok Mitra. Calcutta: Subarnarekha, 1985.

Guha, Ranajit. "Chandra's Death." In *Subaltern Studies V*, pp. 166-202. Edited by Ranajit Guha. Delhi: Oxford UP, 1987.

________. *An Indian Historiography of India: A Nineteenth-Century Agenda and Its Implications*. Calcutta and New Delhi: K. P. Bagchi, for Centre for Studies in Social Sciences, 1988.

________. "Dominance Without Hegemony and Its Historiography." In *Subaltern Studies VI*, pp. 169-209. Edited by Ranajit Guha. Delhi: Oxford UP, 1989.

________. "Discipline and Mobilize." In *Subaltern Studies* VII, pp. 69-120. Edited by Partha Chatterjee and Gyanendra Pandey. Delhi: Oxford UP, 1992.

________, ed. *Subaltern Studies: Writings on South Asian History and Society*. 6 vols. Delhi: Oxford UP, 1982-89. [Volume I reviewed in *Social Scientist* 10, 8 (August 1982):55-63; *EPW* 19, 24-25 (16-23 June 1984): 942-45.]

Guha, Ranajit and Spivak, Gayatri Chakravorty, eds. *Selected Subaltern Studies*. With foreword by Edward W. Said. New York: Oxford UP, 1988.

Guhathakura. "Gender Violence in Bangladesh: The Role of the State." *Jrl. of Social Studies* 30 (1985):77-90.

Guillaume, Oliver. "Naive Anthropology in the Reconstruction of Indo-Greek History." *Indian Economic Social History Review* 27, 4 (Oct.-Dec. 1990):475-82.

________. *Analysis of Reasonings in Archaeology: The Case of Graeco-Bactrian and Indo-Greek Numismatics*. New Delhi: Oxford UP, 1991.

Gupta, Akhil. "The Song of the Nonaligned World: Transnational Identities and the Reinscription of Space in Late Capitalism." *Current Anthropology* 7, 1 (Feb. 1992):63-79.

________. "The Reincarnation of Souls and the Rebirth of Commodities: Representations of Time in 'East' and 'West.'" *Cultural Critique*, no. 22 (Fall 1992):187-211.

Gupta, Akhil and Ferguson, James. "Beyond 'Culture': Space, Identity, and the Politics of Difference." *Current Anthropology* 7, 1 (Feb. 1992):6-23.

Gupta, Anjuli. "English Writing in India: Fear of Experimentation, Fear of Appropriation — Death of Creativity?" In *Crisis and Creativity in the New Literatures in English: Cross/Cultures*, pp. 151-68. Edited by Geoffrey V. Davis and Hena Maes-Jelinek. Amsterdam: Rodopi, 1990.

Gupta, Bina, ed. *Sexual Archetypes, East and West*. A New Era Book. New York: Paragon House, 1987.

Gupta, Charu. "Politics of Gender: Women in Nazi Germany." *EPW* 26, 17 (27 April 1991):WS40-47.

________. "Portrayal of Women in Premchand's Stories: A Critique." *Social Scientist*, nos. 216-17 (May-June 1991):88-113.

Gupta, Dipankar. "From Varna to Jati: The Indian Caste System, from the Asiatic to the Feudal Mode of Production." *Jrl. of Contemporary Asia* 10, 3 (1980):249-71.

________. "Continuous Hierarchies and Discrete Castes." *EPW* 19, 46-48 (17-24 Nov. and 1 Dec. 1984):1955-58, 2003-5, 2049-53.

________. "Between general and particular 'others': Some observations on fundamentalism." *Contributions to Indian Sociology* (New Series) 27, 1 (Jan.-June 1993):119-37.

Gupta, Parthasarthi. "Music and Political Consciousness." Occasional Papers on History and Society, 2nd series, no. 15. New Delhi: NMML, 1989.

Gupta, Samita. "Sris Chandra Chatterjee: The quest for a national architecture." *IESHR* 28, 2 (1991):187-201.

Gupta, Sunetra. *Memories of Rain*. New York: Grove Press, 1991.

________. *The Glassblower's Breath*. New York: Grove Press, 1992.

Gupta, Sunil. "Northern Media, Southern Lives." In *Photography/Politics Two*, pp. 162-166. Edited by Patricia Holland, Jo Spence, and Simon Watney. London: Comedia, 1986.

________. "Fabled Territories: An Introduction". In *Fabled Territories: New Asian Photography in Britain.* Leeds: Leeds City Art Gallery, 1990.

________, ed. *An Economy of Signs: Contemporary Indian Photographs*. London and Boston: Rivers Oram Press, 1990.

Gupta, Sunil and Boffin, Tersa, eds. *Ecstatic Antibodies: Resisting the AIDS Mythology*. Winchester, Mass.: Oram Press; London: Unwin Hyman, 1990.

Gupta, Udayan. "New Visions in Indian Cinema: Interviews with Mrinal Sen, Girish Karnad, and Ketan Mehta." *Cineaste* 11, 4 (1982):18-24.

Guru, Gopal. "Hinduisation of Ambedkar in Maharashtra." *EPW* 26, 7 (16 Feb. 1991):339-341.

Gusterson, Hugh. "Orientalism and the Arms Race: An Analysis of the Neo-Colonial Discourse on Nuclear Non-Proliferation." *Working Papers and Proceedings of the Center for Psychosocial Studies*, no. 47. Chicago: Center for Psychosocial Studies, 1991.

Gutman, Judith Mara. *Through Indian Eyes*. With a foreword by Edward C. Dimock. New York: Oxford UP & International Center of Photography, 1982.

Gutman, Judith Mara. "Through Indian eyes: Indigenous photography in the subcontinent." *Impact of science on society*, no. 168 (1992):345-56.

Habib, Irfan. "Peasant and Artisan Resistance in Mughal India." *McGill Studies in International Development*, no. 34. Montreal: McGill University, Center for Developing Area Studies, 1984.

________. "Studying a Colonial Economy — Without Perceiving Colonialism." *Modern Asian Studies* 19, 4 (1985):355-81.

________. *Interpreting Indian History*. Shillong: North-Eastern Univ. Publications, 1987.

Habib, Irfan and Raina, Dhruva. "Copernicus, Columbus, Colonialism, and the Role of Science in Nineteenth-Century India." *Social Scientist*, nos. 190-91 (March 1989):51-66.

________. "The unfolding of an engagement: 'The Dawn' on science, technical education and industrialization: India, 1896-1912." *Studies in History* (New Series) 9, 1 (Jan.-June 1993):87-117.

Haggard, Sunil. "Mass Media and the Visual Arts in Twentieth-Century South Asia: Indian Film Posters 1947-Present." *South Asia Research* 8, 1 (May 1988):71-88.

Hanan, David. "Patriarchal Discourse in some early films of Satyajit Ray." *Deep Focus* 3, 1 (1990):30-57.

Hansen, Kathryn. "Hindi New Cinema: Basu Chatterji's *Sara Akash*." *South Asia* (New Series) 4, 1 (June 1981):15-21.

________. *Grounds for Play: The Nautanki Theatre of North India*. Berkeley: University of California Press, 1992.

Hanslot, Sehnaz and Spiro, Margherita. "Other Than This: 'An Economy of Signs' and 'Fabled Territories'." *Third Text*, no. 13 (Winter 1991): 49-56.

Haraksingh, Kusha. "Structure, Process and Indian Culture in Trinidad." *Immigrants and Minorities* 7,1 (1982):113-22.

Hardgrave, Robert. "Stars and Gods." In *Essays in the Political Sociology of South India*. New Delhi: Usha, 1979.

Hardiman, David. *Peasant Nationalists of Gujarat: Kheda District 1917-1934*. Delhi: Oxford UP, 1981.

________. "Adivasi Assertion in South Gujarat: The Devi Movement of 1922-3." In *Subaltern Studies III*, pp. 231-70. Edited by Ranajit Guha. Delhi: Oxford UP, 1984.

________. "From Custom to Crime: The Politics of Drinking in Colonial South Gujarat." In *Subaltern Studies IV*. Edited by Ranajit Guha. Delhi: Oxford UP, 1985.

Hardiman, David, ed. *Peasant Resistance in India, 1858-1914: Themes in Indian History*. Delhi: Oxford UP, 1992.

Harley, J. B. and Woodward, David, eds. *Cartography in the Traditional Islamic and South Asian Societies*. Volume Two, Book 1 of *The History of Cartography*. Chicago: Univ. of Chicago Press, 1992. [Review by Vinay Lal, "Mapping India", *The Book Review* 17, 9 (Sept. 1993):8-9.]

Harlow, Barbara. "Drawing the Line: Cultural Politics and the Legacy of Partition." *Polygraph*, no. 5 (1992):84-112.

Hasan, Zoya. "Minority Identity, Muslim Women Bill Campaign and the Political Process." *EPW* (7 Jan. 1989).

________, ed. *Identity Politics, Community and Gender: The Construction of Muslim Women in pre- and post-Independence India*. New Delhi: Kali for Women, forthcoming 1993.

Hasan, Zoya; Jha, S.N.; and Khan, Rasheeduddin, eds. *State, Political Processes and Identity*. London: Sage Publications, 1989.

Hashmi, Alamgir.* *Commonwealth Literature: An Essay towards the Redefinition of a Popular/Counter Culture*. Lahore, 1983.

________. "Pakistani Literature in English: Past, Present, and Future." *South Asia Bulletin* 10, 2 (Fall 1990):48-53.

________, ed. *The Worlds of Muslim Imagination*. Islamabad: Gulmohar, 1986.

Hashmi, Taj Ul-Islam. *Pakistan as a Peasant Utopia: The Communalization of Class Politics in East Bengal, 1920-1947*. Boulder, Colorado: Westview Press, 1992.

Hauff, Reinhard. *Ten Days in Calcutta: A Portrait of Mrinal Sen*. Calcutta: Seagull Books, 1989.

Haynes, Douglas. *Rhetoric and Ritual in Colonial India: The Shaping of a Public Culture in Surat City, 1852-1928*. Berkeley: Univ. of California Press, 1991. [Review by Vinay Lal, "Surat under the Raj", *EPW* 28, 18 (1 May 1993):863-65.]

Haynes, Douglas and Prakash, Gyan, eds. *Contesting Power: Resistance and Everyday Social Relations in South Asia*. Delhi: Oxford UP, 1991; Berkeley: University of California Press, 1992.

Hellmann-Rajanayagam, D. "The Concept of a 'Tamil Homeland' in Sri Lanka: Its Meaning and Development." *South Asia* 13, 2 (1988):79-110.

Helweg, Arthur W. "The Indian Diaspora: Influence on International Relations." In *Modern Diasporas in International Politics*, pp. 103-29. Edited by Gabriel Sheffer. New York: St. Martin's, 1986.

Heuze, Gerard. "Shiv Sena and 'National' Hindusim." In 2 parts. *EPW* 27, 40 (3 Oct. 1992):2189-95; Pt. II: 27, 41 (10 Oct. 1992):2253-63.

Hill, Christopher V. "Philosophy and Reality in Riparian South Asia: British Famine Policy and Migration in Colonial North India." *Modern Asian Studies* 25, 2 (May 1991):263-79.

Himid, Lubaina, exhibition selector. *The Thin Black Line*. London: Institute for Contemporary Arts, 1985. Catalogue includes Sutapa Biswas and Chila Burman.

Holmstrom, Lakshmi. *The Inner Courtyard: Stories by Indian Women*. London: Virago, 1990; reprint ed., Calcutta: Rupa, 1992.

Hore, Somnath. *Tebhaga: An Artist's Diary and Sketchbook*. Calcutta: Seagull Books, 1990.

Hovell, Laurie, trans. and introduction. "Dhasal, Namdeo: Poet and Author." *BCAS* 23, 2 (April-June 1991):77-83.

Hume, John Chandler Jr. "Colonialism and Sanitary Medicine: The Development of Preventive Health Policy in the Punjab, 1860 to 1900." *MAS* 20, 4 (1986):703-24.

Hussain, Nasser. "Hyphenated Identity: Nationalistic Discourse, History, and the Anxiety of Criticism in Salman Rushdie's *Shame*." *Qui Parle* 3, 2 (Fall 1989).

Hutt, Michael James, ed. and trans. *Himalayan Voices: An Introduction to Modern Nepali Literature*. Berkeley: Univ. of California Press, 1992.

Hyam, Ronald. "Empire and Sexual Opportunity." *Jrl. of Imperial and Commonwealth History* 14, 2 (Jan. 1986):34-89.

________. *Empire and Sexuality: The British Experience*. Studies in Imperialism. Manchester: Manchester UP, 1990.

Ifeka, C. "'Spiritual' and 'Statistical' Models of the Sexes in British India, 1871-1931." *South Asia* 5, 1 (1980):16-28.

Inden, Ronald. "Orientalist Constructions of India." *MAS* 20, 3 (1986):401-46.

________. *Imagining India*. Oxford: Basil Blackwell, 1990. [Reviewed by Declan Quigley, "The Power of Imagination", *MAS* 25, 2 (1991): 403-6.]

India, Government of. Directorate of Film Festivals. *The New Generation, 1960-1980: Film India: An Examination of India's New Cinema, Its Preoccupation with a Changing Society and the Status of Women*. New Delhi: Ministry of Information and Broadcasting, 1981.

Indra Deva. "Popular and Folk Culture in Contemporary India." *International Jrl. of Popular Culture* 2, 1 (1981):12-21.

Institute of Race Relations. *Southall: The Birth of a Black Community*. Campaign Against Racism and Fascism. London: Institute of Race Relations and Southall Rights, 1981.

Irving, Robert Grant. *Indian Summer: Lutyens, Baker and Imperial Delhi*. New Haven: Yale UP, 1981.

Ismail, Qadri. "Boys Will Be Boys: Gender and National Agency in Frantz Fanon and the Liberation Tigers of Tamil Eelam." *South Asia Bulletin* 11, 1-2 (1991):79-83.

Iyer, Pico. *Video Nights in Kathmandu*. New York: Alfred Knopf, 1988.

Iyer, V. R. Krishna. "India, Islam and the Fall of Postmodernism." *EPW* 27, 45 (7 Nov. 19920:2417-19 [review of Akbar S. Ahmed's *Postmodernism and Islam*].

Jahangir, B. K. *Problematics of Nationalism in Bangladesh*. Dhaka: Centre for Social Studies, 1986.

________. *Violence and Consent in a Peasant Society and Other Essays*. Calcutta: Centre for Social Studies, 1990.

Jain, Devaki. "Can Feminism be a Global Ideology?" *Quest* 4, 2 (Winter 1978):9-15.

________. *Woman's Quest for Power: Five Indian Case Studies*. Delhi: Vikas, 1980.

Jain, Jyotindra. "Ganga Devi: Tradition & Expression in Madhubani Painting." *Third Text* , no. 6 (1988).

Jain, Kulbhushan. "Realms of Transition: An Essay on the Physical and Cultural Attributes of In-between Architectural Spaces." *Architecture and Design* 3, 3 (March-April 1989):81-87.

Jain, Madhu. "The Curry Eastern Takeaway." *Public Culture* 2, 2 (1990).

Jain, Manju. *A Critical Reading of the "Selected Poems" of T. S. Eliot*. New Delhi: Oxford UP, 1991.

Jain, Sharada; Misra, Nirja; and Shrivastava, Kavita. "Deorala Episode: Women's Protest in Rajasthan." *EPW* (1987):1891-4.

Jain, Shobhita. "Women and People's Ecological Movement: A Case Study of Women's Rule in the Chipko Movement in Uttar Pradesh." *EPW* 19, 41 (13 Oct. 1984): 1788-94.

Jalal, Ayesha. "The Convenience of Subservience: Women and the State of Pakistan." In *Women, Islam and the State*, pp. 77-114. Edited by Deniz Kandiyoti. Philadelphia: Temple UP, 1991.

James, Adrian. "Walkeshwar, a Study in Urban Order." Unpublished Ph.D. Dissertation, University of Cambridge, 1987.

Jameson, Frederic. "Third-World Literature in the Era of Multinational Capitalism." *Social Text*, no. 15 (Fall 1986):65-88.

Janaky. "On the Trail of the Mahabharata: A Response." *EPW* 27, 37 (12 Sept. 1992):1997-99 [criticizes the search for ur-epics].

JanMohamed, Abdul R. "Humanism and Minority Literature: Toward a Definition of Counter-hegemonic Discourse." *boundary* 2 12, 3-13, 1 (Spring/Fall 1984):281-99.

Jayamanne, Laleen. "Speaking of 'Ceylon', a Clash of Cultures." In *Questions of Third Cinema*, pp. 150-69. Edited by Jim Pines and Paul Willemen. London: British Film Institute Publishing, 1989.

________. "Hunger for Images, Myths of Femininity in the Sri Lankan Cinema, 1947-1989." *South Asia Bulletin* 12, 1 (1992):57-75.

Jayamanne, Laleen; Thornton, Leslie; and Minh-ha, Trinh. "If Upon Leaving What We Have to Say We Speak: A Conversation Piece." In *Discourses: Conversations in Postmodern Art and Culture*, pp. 44-66. Edited by Russell Ferguson, William Olander, Marcia Tucker, and Karen Fiss. Cambridge, Mass.: MIT Press, 1990; paperback ed., 1992.

Jayawardena, Kumari. *Feminism and Nationalism in the Third World*. London: Zed Press, 1986.

________. "Some Comments on Feminism and the Left in South Asia." *South Asia Bulletin* 8, 1-2 (1988):88-91.

Jeffrey, Patricia. *Frogs in a Well: Indian Women in Purdah*. London: Zed Press, 1979.

Jeffrey, Patricia et al. *Labour Pains and Labour Power: Women and Childbearing in India*. London: Zed Books; Delhi: Manohar Publishers, 1989.

Jeffrey, Roger. *The Politics of Health in India*. Berkeley: Univ. of California Press, 1988.

Jha, J. C. *East Indians in the Caribbean: Colonialism and The Struggle for Identity*. London & New York, 1982.

Jhabvala, C. S. H. *Delhi: Stones and Streets*. Delhi: Ravi Dayal, 1991.

Jones, Kenneth W., ed. *Religious Controversy in British India: Dialogues in South Asian Languages*. Albany: State Univ. of New York Press, 1992.

Joseph, Ammu and Sharma, Kalpana. "Between the Lines: Women's Issues in English Language Newspapers." *EPW* 26, 43 (26 Oct. 1991):WS-75 ff.

Joseph, George Gheverghese. *The Crest of the Peacock: Non-Western Roots of Mathematics*. London: I. B. Tauris, 1991. [Reviewed in *EPW* 26, 24 (15 June 1991), p. 160.]

Joseph, Sarah. "Indigenous Social Science Project: Some Political Implications." *EPW* 26, 15 (13 April 1991):959-62.

________. "Culture and Political Analysis in India." *Social Scientist*, nos. 221-22 (Oct.-Nov. 1991):48-62.

________. "Changing Notions of Power: Some Implications for Women's Studies." *Samya Shakti* 6 (1991-92):17-27.

Josh, Bhagwan and Joshi, Shashi. *Struggle for Hegemony in India, 1920-47:*

The Colonial State, the Left and the National Movement. Vol. 1: 1920-34; Vol. 2: 1934-41; Vol. 3: 1941-47. New Delhi: Sage Publications, 1992-93.

Joshi, Barbara. *Untouchable: Voices of the Dalit Liberation Movement*. London: Zed Books, 1986.

Joshi, Pratima. "Problems in South Asian Architectural Historiography." *Architecture and Design* 5, 4 (May-June 1989):53-59.

Joshi, Svati. "'The Opposing Opposed': Marianne Moore and Possibilities of a Feminine Discourse." In *Woman/Image/Text: Feminist Readings of Literary Texts*, pp. 151-61. Edited by Lola Chatterji. Delhi: Trianka, 1986.

Joshi, Svati, ed. *Rethinking English: Essays in Literature, Language, History*. Delhi: Trianka, 1991.

Jussawalla, Feroza. *Family Quarrels: Towards a Criticism of Indian Writing in English*. Berne and New York: Peter Lang, 1985.

________. "Decolonizing the Decolonizers: Breaking the Colonial Habit of Mind." *North Dakota Quarterly* 55, 3 (1987):175-89.

________. "Rushdie's *Shame*: Problems in Communication." In *Studies in Indian Fiction in English*, pp. 1-13. Edited by Balarama Gupta. Gulbarga: JIWE Press, 1987.

________. "Resurrecting the Prophet: The Case of Salman, the Otherwise." *Public Culture* 2, 1 (Fall 1989):106-17.

Kabeer, Naila. "Subordination and Struggle: Women in Bangladesh." *New Left Review*, No. 168 (April/May 1988).

________. "The Quest for National Identity: Women, Islam and the State of Bangladesh." In *Women, Islam and the State*, pp.115-43. Edited by Deniz Kandiyoti. Philadelphia: Temple UP, 1991.

Kabir, Abulfazal M. Fazle. *The Libraries of Bengal, 1700-1947: The Story of [the] Bengal Renaissance*. New Delhi: Promilla & Co., 1990.

Kaiwar, Vasant. "Racism and the Writing of History, Part I." *South Asia Bulletin* 9, 2 (1989):32-56.

________. "On Provincialism and 'Popular Nationalism': Reflections on Samir Amin's Eurocentrism." *South Asia Bulletin* 11, 1-2 (1991):69-78.

Kakar, Sudhir. *The Inner World: A Psychoanalytic Study of Childhood and Society in India*. Delhi: Oxford UP, 1978.

________. "The Ties that Bind: Family Relationships in the Mythology of Hindi Cinema." *India International Centre Quarterly* 8 , 1 (1981):11-21.

________. "Reflections on Psychoanalysis, Indian Culture and Mysticism." *Journal of Indian Philosophy* 10 (1982):289-97.

Kakar, Sudhir. *Shamans, Mystics, and Doctors: A Psychological Inquiry into India and Its Healing Traditions*. Chicago: Univ. of Chicago Press, 1982.

________. *Intimate Relations: Exploring Indian Sexuality*. Chicago: Univ. of Chicago Press, 1989.

________. *The Analyst and the Mystic: Psychoanalytic Reflections on Religion and Mysticism*. Chicago: Univ. of Chicago Press; Delhi: Penguin Books, 1991.

Kala, Arvind. *Invisible Minority: The Unknown World of the Indian Homosexual*. New Delhi: Dynamic Books, [1992].

Kali for Women. *Truth Tales: Contemporary Writing by Indian Women*. Delhi: Kali for Women, 1986. Also published as *Truth Tales: Contemporary Stories by Women Writers of India*. With an introduction by Meena Alexander. New York: Feminist Press at City Univ. of New York, 1990.

Kannabiran, Vasanath and Kannabiran, Kalpana. "Caste and Gender: Understanding Dynamics of Power and Violence." *EPW* (14 Sept. 1991): 2130-33.

Kanwar, Asha S. "Raymond Williams and the English Novel." *Social Scientist*, no. 180 (May 1988):46-60.

Kanwar, Pamela. "The Changing Profile of the Summer Capital of British India: Simla 1864-1947." *Modern Asian Studies* 18, 2 (1984):215-36.

________. *Imperial Simla: The Political Culture of the Raj*. Delhi: Oxford UP, 1990.

Kapferer, Bruce. *A Celebration of Demons: Exorcism and the Aesthetics of Healing in Sri Lanka*. Bloomington: Indiana UP, 1983.

________. *Legends of People, Myths of State: Violence, Intolerance, and Political Culture in Sri Lanka and Australia*. Washington: Smithsonian Institution Press, 1988.

Kapur, Anuradha. "Actors, Pilgrims, Kings and Gods: The Ramlila at Ramnagar." *Contributions to Indian Sociology* (New Series) 19, 1 (1985).

________. *Actors, Pilgrims, Kings and Gods: The Ramlila at Ramnagar*. Calcutta: Seagull Books, 1990. [Reviewed by Avanthi Meduri, "Studies in Performance: Performance Studies", *Jrl. of Arts and Ideas*, no. 22 (April 1992):45-49.]

________. "Notions of the Authentic." *Jrl. of Arts and Ideas*, nos. 20-21 (March 1991):7-19.

________. "The Representation of Gods and Heroes: Parsi Mythological Drama of the Early Nineteenth Century." *Journal of Arts and Ideas*, nos. 23-24 (Jan. 1993):85-107.

Kapur, Geeta.* *Partisan Views on the Human Figure*. Place for People Exhibition Catalgoue. Bombay/New Delhi, 1981.

________. *K. G. Subramanyan*. New Delhi: Lalit Kala Akademi, 1987.

________. "Mythic Material in Indian Cinema." *Jrl. of Arts and Ideas*, nos. 14-15 (July-Dec. 1987):79-108; also published as Occasional Papers on History and Society. New Delhi: NMML, 1988.

________. "Ravi Varma: Representational Dilemmas of a Nineteenth Century Indian Painter." *Jrl. of Arts and Ideas*, nos. 17-18 (1988):59-80.

________."Articulating the Self into History: Ritwik Ghatak's *Jukti Takko aar Gappo*." In *Questions of Third Cinema*, pp. 179-94. Edited by Jim Pines and Paul Willemen. London: British Film Institute, 1989.

________. "Contemporary Cultural Practice: Some Polemical Categories." *Social Scientist*, no. 202 (March 1990):49-60.

________. "Contemporary Cultural Practice." Occasional Papers on History and Society, 2nd Series, no. 21. New Delhi: NMML, 1990.

________. "Ravi Varma." Occasional Papers on History and Society, 2nd Series, no. 22. New Delhi: NMML, 1990.

________."The Centre-Periphery Model or How are we Placed? Contemporary Cultural Practice in India." *Third Text*, nos. 16-17 (Autumn/Winter 1991):9-18.

________. "Further Narratives." *Jrl. of Arts and Ideas*, nos. 20-21 (March 1991):99-115.

________. "Cultural Creativity in the Third Decade: The Example of Satyajit Ray." *Jrl. of Arts and Ideas*, nos. 23-24 (Jan. 1993):17-49.

________."Revelation and Doubt: *Sant Tukaram* and *Devi*. In *Interrogating Modernity: Culture and Colonialism in India*. Edited by Tejaswini Niranjana, P. Sudhir, and Vivek Dhareshwar. Calcutta: Seagull Books, 1993.

________. "When Was Modernism in Indian/Third World Art?" *South Atlantic Quarterly* 92, 3 (Summer 1993):473-513.

Kapur, Jyotsna. "Putting Herself into the Picture: Women's Accounts of the Social Reform Campaign, Maharashtra." *Manushi*, no. 56 (Jan.-Feb. 1990):28-37.

Karan, Pradyuma P. "Landscape, Religion and Folk Art in Mithila: An Indian Cultural Region." *Journal of Cultural Geography* 5, 1 (Fall-Winter 1984):85-101.

Karlekar, Malavika. *Poverty and Women's Work: A Study of Sweeper Women in Delhi*. New Delhi: Vikas, 1982.

________."Constructions of Femininity in Nineteenth Century Bengal: Readings from *Janaika Grihabadhur Diary*." *Samya Shakti*, nos. 4- 5 (1989-90):11-29.

Karlekar, Malavika. *Voices from Within: Early Personal Narratives of Bengali Women*. Delhi: Oxford UP, 1991.

Karnad, Girish. "Theatre in India." *Architecture and Design* 7, 4 (July-August 1990):87-99.

Kasturi, Leela. "Rural Women in Struggle in Colonial India: Some Aporiae." *Samya Shakti* 6 (1991-92):65-80.

Katrak, Ketu. "Decolonizing Culture: Toward a Theory for Postcolonial Women's Texts." *Modern Fiction Studies* 35 (1989):157-79.

________. "Indian Nationalism, Gandhian 'Satyagraha', and Representation of Female Sexuality." In *Nationalisms and Sexualities*, pp. 395-406. Edited by Andrew Parker, Mary Russo, Doris Sommer, and Patricia Yaeger. New York: Routledge, 1992.

Katzenstein, May Fainsod. "Getting Women's Issues onto the Public Agenda: Body Politics in India." *Samya Shakti* 6 (1991-92):1-16.

Kaul, Suvir. "The Indian Academic and Resistance to Theory." In *The Lie of the Land: English Literary Studies in India*, pp. 207-28. Edited by Rajeswari Sunder Rajan. New Delhi: Oxford UP, 1992.

________. *Thomas Gray and Literary Authority: A Study in Ideology and Poetics*. Stanford: Stanford UP, 1992.

Kaviraj, Sudipta. "A Taste for Transgression: Liminality in the Novels of Bankim Chandra Chattopadhyay." Occasional Papers on History and Society, no. 48. New Delhi: NMML, 1987.

________. "The Myth of Praxis." Occasional Papers on History and Society, no. 53? New Delhi: NMML, 1988.

________. *Bankimchandra and the Making of Nationalist Consciousness*. Occasional Paper. Calcutta, 1989.

________. "Imaginary History." Occasional Papers on History and Society, 2nd series, no. 7. New Delhi: NMML, 1989.

________. *Perspectives on Capitalism: Marx, Keynes, Schumpeter, and Weber*. New Delhi and Newbury Park, California: Sage Publications, 1989.

________. "Signs of Madness: The Figure of Kamalakanta in the Work of Bankimchandra Chattopadhyay." *Jrl. of Arts and Ideas*, nos. 20-21 (March 1991):9-31.

________. "Some Observations on Marxism and Political Causality." Occasional Papers on History and Society. New Delhi: NMML, 1989.

________. "Capitalism and the Cultural Process." *Jrl. of Arts and Ideas*, no. 19 (May 1990):61-75.

Kaviraj, Sudipta. "Humor and the Prison of Reality." Occasional Papers on History and Society, 2nd series, no. 4. New Delhi: NMML, 1990.

________. "The Imaginary Institution of India." In *Subaltern Studies 7: Writings on South Asian History and Society*, pp. 1-39. Edited by Gyanendra Pandey and Dipesh Chakrabarty. Delhi: Oxford Univ. Press, 1992.

Kelkar, Govind. "The Woman Question on Bodh Gaya Movement, Bihar." Occasional Papers on History and Society, 2nd series, no. 12. New Delhi: NMML, 1989.

Kelkar, Govind and Nathan, Dev. *Gender and Tribe: Women, Land and Forests in Jharkand*. New Delhi: Kali for Women, 1992.

Kelly, John D. "From Holi to Diwali in Fiji: An Essay on Ritual and History." *Man* (New Series) 23 (1988):40-55.

________. *A Politics of Virtue: Hinduism, Sexuality, and Countercolonial Discourse in Fiji*. Chicago: Univ. of Chicago Press, 1991.

Kemper, Steven. *The Presence of the Past: Chronicles, Politics and Culture in Sinhala Life*. Ithaca, New York: Cornell UP, 1991.

Kennedy, Dane. "Guardians of Edenic Sanctuaries: Paharis, Lepchas, and Todas in the British Mind." *South Asia* (New Series) 14, 2 (Dec. 1991):57-78.

Kerr, David and Dhawan, R. K., eds. *Australian and Indian Literature: Studies in Mutual Response*. New Delhi: Indian Society for Commonwealth Studies, 1991.

Khan, Maqbool Hasan. "Without the 'Mind': Edward Dowden on Shakespeare's Art." In *Essays on Shakespeare in Honour of A. A. Ansari*, pp. 284-98. Edited by T. R. Sharma. Meerut, India: Shalabh Book House, 1986.

Khan, Rasheeduddin. "Minority Segments in Indian Polity: Muslim Situation and the Plight of Urdu." *EPW* (2 Sept. 1978).

Khanna, Satendra. *Indian Cinema and Indian Life*. Berkeley: Center for South and Southeast Asian Studies, 1980.

Khare, R. S. *The Untouchable as Himself: Ideology, Identity and Pragmatism among the Lucknow Chamars*. Cambridge: Cambridge UP, 1985.

Khondker, H. H. "Famine Policies in Pre-British India and the Question of Moral Economy." *South Asia* 9, 1 (1986):25-40.

Khopkar, Arun.* *Gurudatta: tin ankiya trasdi* [in Marathi]. Translated into Hindi by Nishkant Thakar. Madhya Pradesh Film Development Corporation.

Khosla, Romi. "Including Iconography and Images in Architecture." *Jrl. of Arts and Ideas* (April-June 1984):5-36.

________. "Those Wonderful Economic Arguments." *Architectural Review*, no. 1086 (August 1987):66-68.

Khubchandani, Lachman M., ed. *Language in a Plural World*. Delhi: Motilal Banarsidass; Simla: Indian Institute of Advanced Study, 1988.

King, Adele. "Shashi Deshpande: Portraits of an Indian Woman." In *The New Indian Novel in English: A Study of the 1980s*, pp. 159-68. Edited by Viney Kirpal. New Delhi: Allied Publishers, 1990.

King, Anthony D. "Colonial Architecture Re-visited: Some Issues for Further Debate." In *Changing South Asia: City and Culture*, pp. 99-106. Edited by Kenneth Ballhatchet and David Taylor. Hong Kong: Asian Research Service for Centre of South Asian Studies, SOAS, 1981.

Kipnis, Laura. "'The Phantom Twitchings of an Amputated Limb': Sexual Spectacle in the Post-Colonial Epic." *Wide Angle* 11, 4 (Oct. 1989): 42-51.

Kirpal, Viney. "What is the Third World Novel?" *Jrl. of Commonwealth Literature* 23, 1 (1988):144-56.

Kishwar, Madhu. "Arya Samaj and Women's Education: Kanya Mahavidyalaya, Jallandar." *EPW* 21, 17 (26 April 1986):9-24.

________. "Pro Women or Anti Muslim? The Shahbano Controversy." *Manushi*, no. 32 (1986):4-13.

________. *Gandhi and Women*. Delhi: Manushi Publications, 1987.

________. "Toiling without Rights: Ho Women of Singhbum." *EPW* 22, 3 (17 January 1987).

________. In *Man-Made Women: How New Reproductive Technologies Affect Women*. Edited by Gena Coea. London: Hutchinson, 1985; Bloomington: Indiana UP, 1987.

________. "Why I do not Call Myself a Feminist." *Manushi*, no. 61 (Nov.-Dec. 1990):2-8.

Kishwar, Madhu and Vanita, Ruth. "The Burning of Roop Kanwar." *Manushi*, nos. 42-43 (Sept.-Dec. 1987):15-25.

________, eds. *In Search of Answers: Indian Women's Voices from Manushi*. London: Zed Press, 1984.

Klass, Morton. *Singing with Sai Baba: The Politics of Revitalization in Trinidad*. Oxford: Westview Press, 1991.

________. "'When God Can Do Anything': Belief Systems in Collision." *Jrl. of the Society for the Anthropology of Consciousness* 2, 1-2 (1991).

Kleinhaus, Chuck and Pendakur, Manji. "Learning Together: Synthesizing Economic and Cultural Analysis in the Marxist Study of Third World Film and Video." *Jump Cut*, no. 33 (1987):82-91.

Kochhar, R. K. "Astronomy in British India: Science in the Service of the State." *Current Science* 60, 2 (25 Jan. 1991):124-29.

________. "French Astronomers in India During the 18th and 19th Centuries."

Journal of the British Astronomical Association 101, 2 (April 1991): 95-100.

Kochhar, R. K. "The Growth of Modern Astronomy in India, 1651-1960." *Vistas in Astronomy* 34, pts. 1-2 (1991):69-105.

________. "Science as a Tool in British India." *EPW* 26, 33 (17 August 1991):1927-33.

Kolff, Dirk H. A. *Naukar, Rajput and Sepoy: The Ethnohistory of the Military Labour Market in Hindustan, 1450-1850*. University of Cambridge Oriental Publications No. 43. Cambridge: Cambridge UP; Delhi: Manohar, 1990.

________. "A British Indian Circumambulation." *Itinerario* [Leiden] 16, 2 (1992):85-100.

Kopf, David. "A Look at Nehru's World History from the Dark Side of Modernity." *Journal of World History* 2, 1 (Spring 1991):47-63.

Kolenda, Pauline. "Woman as Tribute, Woman as Flower: Images of 'Woman' in Weddings in North and South India." *American Ethnologist* 11, 1 (Feb. 1984):98-117.

Korchagov, Yuri. 'Indian Films in the USSR." *Soviet Literature* Vol. 8 No. 473 (1987):190-192.

Korom, Frank J. "Inventing Traditions: Folklore and Nationalism as Historical Process in Bengal." In *Folklore and Historical Process,* pp. 57-83. Edited by D. Rihtman-Augustin and M. Povrzanovic. Zagreb: Institute of Folklore Research, 1989.

Kosambi, Meera. *Bombay in Transition: The Growth and Social Ecology of a Colonial City, 1880-1980*. Stockholm: Almqvist & Wiksell International, 1986.

________. "The Colonial City in Its Global Niche." *EPW* 25, 42-43 (20-27 Oct. 1990):2775-81.

________. "Images of Women and the Feminine in Maharashtra." *EPW* 26, 25 (22 June 1991):1519-24.

________. "Indian Response to Christianity, Church and Colonialism: Case of Pandita Ramabai." *EPW* 27, 43-44 (24 Oct. 1992):WS61-71.

Kosambi, Meera and Brush, John E. "Three Colonial Port Cities in India." *Geographical Review* 78, 1 (1988):32-47.

Kothari, Komal. "The Shrine: An Expression of Social Needs." In *Gods of the Byways*, pp. 5-31. Oxford: Museum of Modern Art, 1982.

Kothari, Manu L. and Mehta, Lopa. "Violence in Modern Medicine." In *Science, Hegemony and Violence: A Requiem for Modernity*, pp. 167-210. Edited by Ashis Nandy. Delhi: Oxford UP, 1992 [1988].

________. *The Tao of Death*. London: Marion Boyars, 1986.

Kothari, Rajni. "On Eco-Imperialism." *Alternatives* 7, 3 (Sept. 1981):385-394.

Kowlowski, Greg. "The Power of Language and the Language of Power: A Study of Mawlana Muhammad Ali's Political Rhetoric." *South Asia* 5, 1 (1982):29-41.

Krishen, Pradip. "Knocking at the Doors of Public Culture: India's Parallel Cinema." *Public Culture* 4, 1 (Fall 1991):25-42.

________, ed. "Indian Popular Cinema: Myth, Meaning and metaphor", special issue of *India International Centre Quarterly* 8, 1 (March 1981).

Krishna, Daya. *The Art of the Conceptual: Explorations in a Conceputal Maze Over Three Decades*. New Delhi: Munshiram Manoharlal and Indian Council for Philosophical Research, 1989.

________, ed. *India's Intellectual Traditions: Attempts at Conceptual Reconstructions*. New Delhi: Indian Council for Philosophical Research and Motilal Banarsidass, 1987.

Krishnan, Prabha. "In the Idiom of Loss: Ideology of Motherhood in Television Serials." *EPW* 25, 42-43 (25 Oct. 1990):WS103-16.

Krishnan, Prabha and Dighe, Anita. *Affirmation and Denial: Construction of Femininity on Indian Television*. New Delhi: Sage Publications, 1990.

Kumar, Amitava. "Towards Postmodern Marxist Theory: Ideology, State and the Politics of Critique." *Rethinking Marxism* 3, 3-4 (Fall-Winter 1990):149-55.

Kumar, Deepak. "Science, Resources and the Raj: A Case Study of Geological Works in Nineteenth-Century India." *Indian Historical Review* 10, 1-2 (July 1983-January 1984).

Kumar, Deepak, ed. *Science and Empire: Essays in Indian Context (1700-1947)*. Delhi: Anamika Prakashan, 1991.

Kumar, Kapil. "Peasants' Perception of Gandhi and his Programme, Oudh 1920-22." *Social Scientist* 11, 2 (February 1983).

________. *Peasants in Revolt: Tenants, Landlords, Congress and the Raj in Oudh 1886-1922*. Delhi: Manohar, 1984.

________. "Using the Ramcharitmanas as a Radical Text: Baba Ram Chandra in Oudh, 1920-50." In *Social Transformation and Creative Imagination*, pp. 311-34. Edited by Sudhir Chandra. Delhi: Allied, 1984. Also published as Occasional Papers on History and Society, no. 4. New Delhi: NMML, 1986.

________. "Rural Women in Oudh 1917-47: Baba Ramachandra and the Women's Question." In *Recasting Women*, pp. 337-69. Edited by Sudesh Vaid and Kumkum Sangari. New Delhi: Kali for Women, 1989.

________, ed. *Congress and Classes: Nationalism, Workers and Peasants*. Delhi: Manohar Publications, 1984.

Kumar, Krishan. *Utopianism*. Milton Keynes, England: Open UP, 1991.

Kumar, Krishna. "Origins of India's 'Textbook Culture.'" Occasional Papers on History and Society, no. 47. New Delhi: NMML, 1988.

________. "The Problem of Curriculum." Occasional Papers on History and Society. New Delhi: NMML, 1988.

________. *Social Character of Learning*. New Delhi: Sage Publications, 1989.

________. "Colonial Citizen as an Educational Ideal." Occasional Papers on History and Society, 2nd series, no. 13. New Delhi: NMML, 1990.

________. *Political Agenda of Education: A Study of Colonialist and Nationalist Ideas*. Newbury Park, Calif.: Sage Publications, 1991.

Kumar, Nita. *The Artisans of Banaras: Popular Culture and Identity*. Princeton, New Jersey: Princeton UP, 1988.

________. "Widows, Education and Social Change in Twentieth Century Banaras." *EPW* 26, 17 (27 April 1991):WS19-25.

________. "Class and Gender Politics in the Ramlila." *IESHR* 29, 1 (1992): 37-56.

________. *Friends, Keepers, and Informants: Memoirs of Fieldwork in Banaras*. Berkeley, California: Univ. of California Press, 1992.

Kumar, Radha. *The History of Doing: An Illustrated Account of the Women's Movement in India*. New Delhi: Kali for Women, 1993.

Kumar, Ravinder. *Essays in the Social History of Modern India*. Delhi: Oxford UP, 1983.

________. Introduction to *Myth and Reality: The Struggle for Freedom in India (1945-47)*. Edited by A. K. Gupta. New Delhi: Manohar Publications, 1987.

________. "The Role of Urban Society in Nationalist Politics." Occasional Papers on History and Society. New Delhi: NMML, 1988.

________. "The Past and the Present: An Indian Dialogue." *Daedalus* (Fall 1989):27-49.

________. "Chance and Determinism in History." Occasional Papers on History and Society, 2nd Series, no. 24. New Delhi: NMML, 1990.

________. *The Emergence of Modern India: Retrospect*. Delhi: Manohar, 1990.

________. "Exploring the Historical Conjuncture." *Social Scientist*, nos. 221-22 (Oct.-Nov. 1991):5-18.

________. "On Gender Theory, the Social Sciences and 'Relevant' Modernity." *Manushi*, no. 68 (Jan.-Feb. 1992):23-27.

________, ed. *A Centenary History of the Indian National Congress (1885-1985)*. Volume II, 1919-1935. New Delhi: All-India Congress Committee & Vikas, 1985.

Kumar, Sanjay. "Fiction or Historical Positioning?: A Reading of J. G. Farell's

The Siege of Krishnapur." In *Ourstory: Indian Response to Nineteenth Century Literature*, pp. 25-40. Edited by Mohua Lahiri, Sanjay Kumar, and Anand Prakash. New Delhi: Academic Foundation, 1992.

Kureishi, Hanif. *My Beautiful Laundrette and The Rainbow Sign*. Boston: Faber & Faber, 1986.

________. *Sammy and Rosie get laid*. New York: Penguin Books, 1988.

________. *The Buddha of Suburbia*. New York: Viking Books, 1990.

Kureishi, Hanif and Kermode, Frank. "Voice of the Almost English." Reprinted in *The Frontier Post: Kaleidoscope* (27 April 1990):9, 16.

Kurin, Richard. "Cultural Conservation through Representation: Festival of India Folklife Exhibitions at the Smithsonian Institution." In *Exhibiting Cultures: The Poetics and Politics of Museum Display*, pp. 315-43. Edited by Ivan Karp and Steven D. Lavine. Washington, D.C.: The Smithsonian Institution Press, 1991.

Kurtz, Stanley N. *All the Mothers Are One: Hindu India and the Cultural Reshaping of Psychoanalysis*. Foreword by S. J. Tambiah. New York: Columbia UP, 1992.

Lakshmi, C. S. "Feminism and the Cinema of Realism." *EPW* 21, 3 (18 Jan. 1986):113-15.

________. "Mother, Mother-Community and Mother-Politics in Tamil Nadu." *EPW* 25, 42-43 (25 Oct. 1990):WS72-83.

________. "Seeing in Gestalt?" *EPW* 26, 24 (15 June 1991):1487.

Lal, Brij V. "Veil of Dishonour: Sexual Jealousy and Suicide on Fiji Plantations." *Journal of Pacific History* (Australia) 20, 3-4 (1985):135-55.

Lal, Deepak. *Cultural Stability and Economic Stagnation: India, c1500 BC - AD 1980. The Hindu Equilibrium*, Vols. 1-2. Oxford: Clarendon, 1988-89.

Lal, Vinay. Review of Syed Amanuddin's *Creativity and Reception: Toward a Theory of Third World Criticism,* in *Indian Literature* 32, 3 (May-June, 1989):171-76.

________. "Indologists' India", review of Cleo McNelly Kearns, *T.S. Eliot and Indic Traditions*, *Indian Literature* 32, 5 (Sept.-Oct. 1989):167-72.

________. "Representing India," review-article on the special Daedalus issue, 'Another India', *New Quest*, no. 86 (March-April 1991):119-22.

________. "Literature from Below." *Indian Literature* 34, 3 (May-June 1991):111-18.

________. "The Politics of Representing AIDS", review of Richard and Rosalind Chirimuuta, *AIDS, Africa and Racism*, *EPW* 26, 47 (23 Nov. 1991): 2687-88.

________. Review of *Debating Muslims: Cultural Dialogues in Postmodernity and Tradition*, by Michael Fischer and Mehdi Abedi, *Middle Eastern*

Report 22, 4 (July-August 1992):46-47; slightly longer version also published as "De-Essentialising Islam" in *EPW* 27, 24-25 (13-20 June 1992):1257-58.

Lal, Vinay. "Committees of Inquiry and Discourses of 'Law and Order' in Twentieth-Century British India." 2 vols. Unpublished Ph.D. Dissertation, The University of Chicago, 1992.

________. "The Imperialism of Human Rights." *Focus on Law Studies* 8, 1 (Fall 1992), 5 ff.; reprinted in *Taking Sides: Clashing Views on Controversial Issues in Crime and Criminology*. Edited by Richard C. Monk. 3rd ed. Guilford, Connecticut: The Dushkin Publishing Group, Inc., 1993.

________. "Surat Under the Raj", review of Douglas Haynes, *Rhetoric and Ritual in Colonial India, EPW* 28, 18 (1 May 1993):863-65.

________. "The Incident of the Crawling Lane: Women in the Punjab Disturbances of 1919." *Genders* , no. 16 (Spring 1993):35-60.

Lalvani, Suren. "Photography, Epistemology and the Body." *Cultural Studies* 7, 3 (October 1993):442-65.

Lateef, Shahida. *Muslim Women in India: Political and Private Realities 1890s-1980s*. London: Zed Books; New Delhi: Kali for Women, 1990.

Lath, Mukund. *Half a Tale — A Study in the Interrelationship between Autobiography and History*. Translation and interpretation of *Ardhakathanaka*. Illustrated by Ganesh Pyne. Jaipur: Rajasthan Prakrit Bharati Sansthan, 1981.

________. "Aristotle and the roots of western rationality." *Journal of Indian Council of Philosophical Research* 9, 2 (January-April 1992):55-68.

Lariviere, Richard. "Adhikara — Right and Responsibility." In *Languages and Culture: Studies in Honor of Edgar C. Polome*. Edited by M. A. Jazayery et al. Berlin & N.Y.: De Gruyter, 1988.

Lazarus, Neil. "Postcolonialism and the Dilemma of Nationalism: Aijaz Ahmad's Critique of Third-Worldism." *Diaspora* 2, 3 (Winter 1993):373-400.

Lelyveld, David. *Aligarh's First Generation: Muslim Solidarity in British India*. Princeton, New Jersey: Princeton UP, 1978.

________. "Transmitters and Culture: The Colonial Roots of India Broadcasting." *South Asia Research* 10, 1 (Spring 1990).

________. "The Fate of Hindustani: Colonial Knowledge and the Project of a National Language." In *Orientalism and the Postcolonial Predicament*. Edited by Carol A. Breckenridge and Peter van der Veer. Philadelphia: Univ. of Pennsylvania Press, 1993.

Leonard, Karen Isaksen. "Punjabi Pioneers in California: Political Skills on a New Frontier." *South Asia* 12, 2 (1989):69-82.

Leonard, Karen Isaksen. *Making Ethnic Choices: California's Punjabi Mexican Americans*. Philadelphia: Temple UP, 1992.

Lesage, Julia. "Feminist Documentary in India: An Interview with Deepa Dhanraj." *Jump Cut*, no. 31 (March 1986):40-42.

Leslie, I. Julia. *The Perfect Wife: the Orthodox Hindu Woman according to the Stridharmapaddhati of Tryambakayajvan*. Delhi: Oxford UP, 1989.

Liddle, Joanna and Rama Joshi. "Gender and Colonialism: Women's Organisation under the Raj." *Women's Studies International Forum* 8, 5 (1985): 521-29.

________. *Daughters of Independence: Gender, Caste and Class in India*. London: Zed Books, 1986.

Loomba, Ania. "Disorderly Women in Jacobean Tragedy: Towards a Materialist Feminist Critique." Unpublished D. Phil. thesis, University of Sussex, 1987.

________. "Criticism and Pedagogy in the Indian Classroom." In *The Lie of the Land: English Literary Studies in India*, pp. 63-89. Edited by Rajeswari Sunder Rajan. New Delhi: Oxford UP, 1992.

________. *Gender, Race, Renaissance Drama*. Oxford India Paperback. Delhi: Oxford UP, 1992. [Reviewed by K. Vinod Chandran in *Social Scientist*, nos. 216-17 (May-June 1991):115-21.]

________. "Overworlding the Third World." *Oxford Literary Review* 13 (1991):164-91.

Lowis, Premila. *Social Action and the Labouring Poor: An Experience*. Vistaar, 1991.

Loy, David. "Indra's Postmodern Net." *Philosophy East and West* 43, 3 (July 1993):481-510.

Ludden, David. "Historians and Nation States." In *Perspectives, The American Historical Association Newsletter*. 24, 4 (1986):12-14.

________. "India's Development Regime." In *Colonialism and Culture*, pp. 247-87. Edited by Nicholas Dirks. Ann Arbor, Michigan: The Univ. of Michigan Press, 1992. A Comparative Studies in Society and History Book.

________. "Orientalist Empiricism: Transformations of Colonial Knowledge." Forthcoming in *Orientalism and Beyond: Perspectives from South Asia*. Edited by Carol Breckenridge and Peter Van der Veer.

Lutgendorf, Philip. "Ramayan: the Video." *The Drama Review* 34, 2 (Summer 1990).

________. *The Life of a Text: Tulsidas's Ramcaritmanas in Performance*. Berkeley: Univ. of California Press, 1991.

Lynch, Caitrin. "Nation, Woman, and the Indian Bourgeoisie: An Alternative Formulation." *Public Culture* 6, 2 (Winter 1994):425-37.

Lynch, Owen M., ed. *Divine Passions: The Social Construction of Emotion in India*. New Delhi: Oxford UP, 1990.

Maan, Bashir. *The New Scots: The Story of Asians in Scotland*. Edinburgh: Donald, 1992.

McDonaugh, Christian. "The Tharu House: Oppositions and Hierarchy." *Journal of the Anthropological Society of Oxford* 15, 1 (1984):1-14.

Mack, Phyllis. "Feminine Behavior and Radical Action: Franciscans, Quakers, and the Followers of Gandhi." *Signs* 11, 3 (1986):457-77.

McKean, Lise. "Militant Matriots: Devotion to Mother India in Hindu Nationalism." Unpublished paper, 1993.

McLean, M. D. "Are Ramakrishnaites Hindus? Some Implications of Recent Litigation on the Question." *South Asia* 14, 2 (Dec. 1991):99-117.

McLeod, W. H. *Popular Sikh Art*. Delhi: Oxford UP, 1991.

Mahajan, J. *Picturesque India*. Delhi: Lustre Press Pvt., Ltd., 1983.

________. *The Ganga Trail*. London: Books from India (UK) Ltd., 1984.

Maharaj, Sarat. "The Congo is Flooding the Acropolis: Art in Britain of the Immigrants." *Third Text* 15 (Summer 1991):77-90.

Majeed, Javed. *Ungoverned Imaginings: James Mill's 'The History of British India' and Orientalism*. Oxford English Monographs. Oxford: Oxford UP, 1992.

Makhijani, Arjun. *From Global Capitalism to Economic Justice: An Inquiry into the Elimination of Systemic Poverty, Violence and Environmental Destruction in the World Economy*. New York: Apex Press, 1992.

Mandal, D. *Ayodhya: Archaeology after Demolition; A Critique of the 'New' and 'Fresh' Discoveries*. Tracts for the Times, no. 5. Delhi: Orient Longman, 1993.

Mani, Lata. "Production of an Official Discourse on *Sati* in Early Nineteenth-Century Bengal." *EPW* 21, 17 (1986):WS32-40. Also published as "Contentious Traditions: The Debate on Sati in Colonial India." *Cultural Critique*, no. 7 (Fall 1987):119-56. For a different version, see "Cultural Theory, Colonial Texts: Reading Eyewitness Accounts of Widow Burning." In *Cultural Studies*, pp. 392-408. Edited by Lawrence Grossberg, Cary Nelson, and Paula Treichler. New York and London: Routledge, 1992; reprinted as "The Female Subject, the Colonial Gaze: Reading Eyewitness Accounts of Widow Burning." In *Interrogating Modernity: Culture and Colonialism in India*. Edited by Tejaswini

Niranjana, P. Sudhir, and Vivek Dhareshwar. Calcutta: Seagull Books, 1993.

Mani, Lata. Multiple Mediations: Feminist Scholarship in the Age of Multinational Reception." *Inscriptions*, no. 5 (1989), reprinted in *Feminist Review*, no. 35 (Summer 1990):24-41.

________. *Contentious Traditions: The Debate on Sati in Colonial India, 1780-1833*. Berkeley, California: University of California Press, forthcoming [1994].

Mani, Lata and Frankenberg, Ruth. "The Challenge of Orientalism." *Economy and Society* 14, 2 (1985):174-92.

________. "Crosscurrents, Crosstalk: Race, 'Postcoloniality' and the Politics of Location." *Cultural Studies* 7, 2 (May 1993):292-310.

Manogavan, Chelvadurai. *Ethnic Conflict and Reconciliation in Sri Lanka*. Honolulu: Univ. of Hawaii Press, 1987.

Manuel, Peter. "Formal Structure in Popular Music as Reflection of Socio-Economic Change." *International Review of the Aesthetics and Sociology of Music* 16, 2 (1985):163-80.

________. "Popular Music in India: 1901-1986." *Popular Music* 7 (1988): 157-76.

________. *Popular Music and Cassette Culture in North India*. Chicago: Univ. of Chicago Press, 1993.

Marglin, Frederique Apffel. *Wives of the God-King: The Rituals of the Devadasis of Puri*. Delhi: Oxford UP, 1985.

________. "Development and Repression: A Feminist Critique." *Lokayan Bulletin* 9, 1 (Jan.-Feb. 1991):9-26.

________."Smallpox in Two Systems of Knowledge." In *Dominating Knowledge: Development, Culture, and Resistance*, pp. 102-44. Edited by Frederique Apffel Marglin and Stephen A. Marglin. Oxford: Clarendon Press, 1990.

Marglin, Frederique Apffel and Marglin, Stephen A, eds. *Dominating Knowledge: Development, Culture and Resistance*. Oxford: Clarendon Press; New York: Oxford UP, 1990.

Marshall, P. J. "The Whites of British India, 1780-1830: A Failed Colonial Society?" *International History Review* 12, 1 (1990):26-44.

Marshall, P. J. and Williams, Glyndwr. *The Great Map of Mankind: British Perceptions of the World in the Age of Enlightenment*. London: J. M. Dent, 1982.

Martin, Carol. "Feminist Analysis across Cultures: Performing Gender in India." *Women and Performance* 3, 2 (1987-88):32-40.

Masani, P. "Humanization as De-Alienation: On the Theological Implications of Modern Science." *Alternatives* 7, 4 (Sept. 1981):265-90.

Massachusetts Review. Special issue entitled "Desh-Videsh: South Asian Expatriate Writing and Art." Volume 29, No. 4 (Winter 1988-89).

Masselos, Jim. "Spare Time and Recreation: Changing Behaviour Patterns in Bombay at the Turn of the Nineteenth Century." *South Asia* 7, 1 (1984):34-57.

________. "Audiences, Actors and Congress Dramas: Crowd Events in Bombay City in 1930." *South Asia* 8, 1-2 (1985):81-86.

________. "Appropriating Urban Space: Social Constructs of Bombay in the Time of the Raj." *South Asia* 14, 1 (1991):33-64.

________. "The Dis/Appearance of Subalterns: A Reading of a Decade of Subaltern Studies." *South Asia* (New Series) 15, 1 (June 1992):105-25.

Masson, Jeffrey M. *The Oceanic Feeling: The Origins of Religious Sentiment in Ancient India*. Dordrecht, Holland: D. Reidel Publishing Co., 1980.

Mathew, P. N. "Profile of a 'Non-Political' Struggle", *EPW* 19 34 (25 August 1984): 1458 ff.

Matilal, Bimal Krishna. *Scepticism and Mysticism in Indian Philosophy*. Occasional Paper, no. 81. Calcutta: CSSS, 1986.

________. *Confrontation of Cultures*. Calcutta: Published for CSSS by K. P. Bagchi, 1988.

Mazrui, Ali A. "*The Satanic Verses* or a Satanic Novel? Moral Dilemmas of the Rushdie Affair." *Alternatives* 15, 1 (Winter 1990):97-121.

Mazumdar, Pauline M. H. "Blood and Soil: The Serology of the Aryan Racial State." *Bulletin of the History of Medicine* 64 (1990):187-219.

Mazumdar, Ranjani. "Dialectic of Public and Private: Representation of Women in *Bhoomika* and *Mirch Masala*." *EPW* 26, 43 (26 Oct. 1991):WS-81 ff.

Mazumdar, Sucheta. "Racist Responses to Racism: The Aryan Myth and South Asians in the United States." *South Asia Bulletin* 9, 1 (1989):47-55.

Mazumdar, Vina. "Comment on Suttee." *Signs* 4, 2 (Winter 1978):269-73.

McBratney, John. "Images of Indian Women in Rudyard Kipling: A Case of Doubling Discourse." *Inscriptions* , nos. 3-4 (1988):47-57.

MacKenzie, John M. *Propaganda and Empire*. Manchester: Manchester UP, 1984.

McKenzie, Ray. "'The Laboratory of Mankind': John McCosh and the Beginnings of Photography in British India." *History of Photography* 11, 2 (April-June 1987):109-18.

Meade, Martin. "Europe in India." *Architectural Review* No. 1086 (August 1987):26-31.

Meduri, Avanthi. "*Bharatha Natyam* — What Are You?" *Asian Theatre Journal* 5, 1 (Spring 1988):1-23; briefly excerpted as "Dancing for gods — and men", in *Economic Times* (22 April 1992), p. 10.

________. "Western Feminist Theory, Asian Indian Performance, and a Notion of Agency." *Women and Performance* 5, 2 (Spring 1992):90-103.

________.* "History as an Image: Mimesis and Parody in Bharatnatyam." In *Proceedings of the Fifth Hongkong International Dance Performance*, Vol. 2, pp. 107-23. Hongkong: Hongkong Academy for the Performing Arts, 1990.

Mehta, J. L. *J. L. Mehta on Heidegger, Hermeneutics and Indian Tradition.* Foreword by William Halbfass. Introduction by Raimundo Pannikkar. Indian Thought, 2. Leiden: E. J. Brill, 1992.

Menon, A. G. Krishna. "Conservation in India." *Architecture and Design* (Nov.-Dec. 1989):22-27.

________. "Architectural Conundrums." *Jrl. of Arts and Ideas*, nos. 20-21 (March 1991):41-48.

Menon, Nivedita. "Orientalism and After." *EPW* 27, 39 (26 Sept. 1992):2133-36.

Menon, Parvathi. "Ayodhya and all that : Communalism and the discipline of history." *Frontline* (11-24 May 1991):47-48.

Mernissi, Fatima. *Women and Islam*: *An Historical and Theological Inquiry.* Delhi: Kali for Women, 1993.

Metcalfe, Thomas R. "Architecture and the Representation of Empire: India, 1860-1910." *Representations*, no. 6 (1984).

________. *An Imperial Vision: Indian Architecture and Britain's Raj.* Berkeley: Univ. of California Press, 1989.

Mies, Maria. "Capitalist Development and Subsistence Reproduction: Rural Women in India", *BCAS* 12, 4 (July 1985):57-88.

________. *Women: The Last Colony.* London: Zed Books, 1988.

Mies, Maria and Shiva, Vandana. *The World on the Brink: An Ecofeminist Perspective on Capital Accumulation, Ecological Destruction & People's Survival.* New Delhi: Kali for Women, forthcoming 1993.

Miller, Barbara Stoler, ed. *The Powers of Art*: *Patronage in Indian Culture.* Delhi: Oxford UP, 1992.

Miller, Barbara Stoler; Sen, Nabaneeta Dev; de Rayo, Agueda Pizarro. "Splitting the Mother Tongue: Bengali and Spanish Poems in English Translations." *Signs* 3, 3 (Spring 1978):608-21.

Miller, Dr. F. "'This Great Organisation of Ours': The Generations of Congress Discourse." *South Asia* 8, 1-2 (1985):141-53.

Minault, Gail. "Begamati Zuban: Women's Language and Culture in Nineteenth-Century Delhi." *IICQ* 11, 2 (June 1984):155-70.

Minhas, Balraj. *Dastavez*. Delhi: Shaoor Publications, 1982.

Mishra, Vijay. "Towards a Theoretical Critique of Bombay Cinema." *Screen* 26, 2-3 (1985):133-46.

________. "David Shulman and the Laughter of South Indian Kings and Clowns." *South Asia* (New series) 10, 1 (1987):83-88.

________. "Filmic Narrative: Text and Transformation in Bombay Cinema." *Continuum* [Australia] 2 (1988/89):9-43.

________. "The Centre Cannot Hold: Bailey, Indian Culture and the Sublime." *South Asia* (New series) 12, 1 (1989):119-37.

________. "The Texts of 'Mother India.'" *Kunapipi* 11, 1 (1989):119-37.

________. "Decentring History: Some Versions of Bombay Cinema." *East-West Film Journal* 6, 1 (Januay 1992):111-55.

Mishra, Vijay and Hodge, Bob. "What is post(-)colonialism?" *Textual Practice* 5, 3 (Winter 1991):399-414.

________. *The Dark Side of the Dream: Australian Literature and the Postcolonial Mind*. Sydney: Allen & Unwin, 1991.

Mishra, Vijay; Jeffrey, Peter; and Shoesmith, Brian. "The Actor as Parallel Text in Bombay." *Quarterly Review of Film and Video* 11 (1989): 49-67.

Mirtra, Ananda. "Desi BOND: The Cross-Cultural Transformation of James Bond into a Hero of Popular Indian Cinema." *Deep Focus* 2, 1 (Sept. 1989):42-47.

Mitra, Ashok. "Calcutta: A City of Processions." *Illustrated Weekly of India* 103, 44 (12 Dec. 1982).

Mitra, Indrani and Mitra, Madhu. "The Discourse of Liberal Feminism and Third World Women's Texts: Some Issues of Pedagogy." *College Literature* 18, 3 (October 1991).

Mitra, S. "Ecology as Science and Science Fiction." *EPW* 17 (1982):147-52.

Mitter, Partha. *Much Maligned Monsters*: *History of European Reactions to Indian Art*. Oxford: Clarendon Press, 1977; paperback ed., 1992.

________. "Indian Artists, Western Art and Tradition." In *Changing South Asia*: *City and Culture*, pp. 77-89. Edited by Kenneth Ballhatchet and David Taylor. Hong Kong: Asian Research Service for Centre of South Asian Studies, SOAS, 1981.

________. "The Early British Port Cities of India: Their Planning and Architecture circa 1640-1757." *Journal of the Society of Architectural Historians* 45, 2 (1986):95-114.

Mitter, Sara. *Dharma's Daughters: Contemporary Indian Women and Hindu Culture*. New Brunswick, N.J.: Rutgers Univ. Press, 1991.

Mitter, Swasti. *Common Fate, Common Bond: Women in the Global Economy*. London: Pluto Press, 1986.

Mohan, Peggy. "Two Faces of a Language Death" [on Trinidad Bhojpuri]." *IICQ* 11, 2 (June 1984):133-44.

Mohanty, Chandra. "Under Western Eyes: Feminist Scholarship and Colonial Discourses." *boundary* 2 12:3/13:1 (Spring/Fall 1984), reprinted in *Feminist Review*, no. 30 (1988), and (in a slightly revised form) in Mohanty, Russo and Torres, *Third World Women and the Politics of Feminism*, pp. 51-80.

________. "Feminist Encounters: Locating the Politics of Experience." *Copyright* 1 (1987):30-44; slight revised version in *Destabilizing Theory: Contemporary Feminist Debates*, pp. 74-92. Edited by Michele Barrett and Anne Phillips. Oxford: Polity Press, 1992. [For a discussion of this piece, see Kathleen M. Kirby, "Thinking through the Boundary: The Politics of Location, Subjects, and Space", *boundary* 2 20, 2 (Summer 1993):173-89.]

________. "On Race and Voice: Challenges for Liberal Education in the 1990s." *Cultural Critique* (Winter 1989-90):179-208.

________. "Cartographies of Struggle: Third World Women and the Politics of Feminism." Introduction to *Third World Women and the Politics of Women*, pp. 1-47. Bloomington, Indiana: Indiana UP, 1991.

Mohanty, Chandra and Martin, Biddy. "Feminist Politics: What's Home Got to Do with It?" In *Feminist Studies/Critical Studies*. Edited by Teresa de Lauretis. Bloomington: Indiana UP, 1986.

Mohanty, Chandra Talpade and Mohanty, Satya P. "Contradictions of Colonialism" [review of *Recasting Women*, eds. Kumkum Sangari and Sudesh Vaid (Delhi, 1989], *The Women's Review of Books* (March 1990): 19-21.

Mohanty, Chandra Talpade; Russo, Ann; and Torres, Lourdes, eds. *Third World Women and the Politics of Feminism*. Bloomington, Indiana: Indiana UP, 1991.

Mohanty, Satya P. "Us and Them: On the Philosophical Bases of Political Criticism." *Yale Journal of Criticism* 2 (Spring 1989):1-31; reprinted, with modifications, in *New Formations*, no. 8 (Summer 1989).

________. "Kipling's Children and the colour line." *Race and Class* 31, 1 (July-September 1989):21-39. Modified and lengthier version published as "Drawing the Color Line: Kipling and the Culture of Colonial Rule." In

The Bounds of Race: Perspectives on Hegemony and Resistance, pp. 311-44. Edited by Dominick LaCapra. Ithaca: Cornell Univ. Press, 1991.

Mohanty, Satya P. *Literary Theory and the Claims of History*. Oxford: Basil Blackwell, 1991.

________. "The Epistemic Status of Cultural Identity: On *Beloved* and the Postcolonial Condition." *Cultural Critique*, no. 24 (Spring 1993): 41-80.

Monar, Rooplall. *Backdam People*. Leeds: Peepal Tree Press, 1985.

Moore-Gilbert, B. J. *Kipling and 'Orientalism'*. London: Croom Helm; New York: St. Martin's Press, 1986.

Morris, J. and Winchester, S. *Stones of Empire*. Oxford: Oxford UP, 1983.

Mufti, Aamir. "Reading the Rushdie Affair: An Essay on Islam and Politics." *Social Text,* no. 29 (1991):95-116.

________. "The Satanic Verses and the Cultural Politics of 'Islam': A Response to Brennan." *Social Text*, nos. 31/32 (1992):277-82.

Mukherjee, Arun [Prabha]. "South Asian Poetry in Canada: In Search of a Place." *World Literature Written in English* 26, 1 (1986):84-98.

________. *The Gospel of Wealth in the Modern American Novel: A Study of Dreiser and Some of His Contemporaries*. London & Sydney: Croom Helm; Totowa, New Jersey: Barnes & Nobles Books, 1987.

________. *Towards an Aesthetic of Opposition: Essays on Literature Criticism and Cultural Imperialism*. Stratford, Ontario: Williams-Wallace, 1988.

________. "Whose Post-colonialism and Whose Postmodernism?" *World Literature Written in English* 30, 2 (1990):1-9.

________. "The Exclusions of Postcolonial Theory and Mulk Raj Anand's 'Untouchable': A Case Study." *Ariel, A Review of International English Literature* 22, 3 (July 1991):27-48.

Mukherjee, Bharati. "Mimicry and Reinvention." In *The Commonwealth in Canada*, pp. 147-57. Edited by Uma Parameswaran. Calcutta: Writers Workshop, 1983.

Mukherjee, Chandra. *From Graven Images: Patterns of Modern Materialism*. New York: Monthly Review Press, 1983.

Mukherjee, Meenakshi. "Macaulay's Imperishable Empire." *Literary Criterion* 17, 1 (1982), 38.

________. *Realism and Reality: The Novel and Society in India.* Delhi: Oxford UP, 1985. [Review by Alok Rai, "Plots on Reality", *Jrl. of Arts and Ideas*, no. 9 (Oct.-Dec. 1984):43-48.]

Mukherjee, Meenakshi. "Narrating a Nation." *Indian Literature* 35, 4 (July-August 1992): 138-49.

________. "Story, history and her story." *Studies in History* (New Series) 9, 1 (1993):71-85.

Mukherjee, Sujit. "Tigers in Fiction: An Aspect of the Colonial Encounter." *Kunapipi* 9, 1 (1987):1-13.

Mukherji, Chandra and Schudson, Michael. *Rethinking Popular Culture: Contemporary Perspectives in Cultural Studies*. Berkeley: Univ. of California Press, 1991.

Mumtaz, Khawar and Shaheed, Farida. *Women of Pakistan: Two Steps Forward, One Step Back*. London: Zed Press, 1987.

Murshid, Ghulam. *Reluctant Debutante: Response of Bengali Women to Modernisation, 1849-1905*. Rajshahi, Bangladesh: Sahitya Samsad, Rajshahi University, 1983.

Musselwhite, David. "The Trial of Warren Hastings." In *Literature, Politics and Theory: Papers from the Essex Conference 1976-84*, pp. 77-103. Edited by Francis Barker, Peter Hulme, Margaret Iversen, and Diana Loxley. London & New York: Methuen, 1986.

Nag, Dulali. "Fashion, Gender and the Bengali Middle Class." *Public Culture* 3, 2 (1991).

Naidoo, Thillayvel. *The Arya Samaj Movement in South Africa*. Delhi: Motilal Banarsidass, 1992.

Naim, C. M. "The Outrage of Bernard Lewis." *Social Text*, no. 30 (1992): 114-20.

Naipaul, V. S. *India: A Million Mutinies Now*. London: William Heinemann, 1990.

Nair, Janaki. "Uncovering the Zenana: Visions of Indian Womanhood in Englishmen's Writings, 1813-1940." *Journal of Women's History* 2, 1 (1990):8-34.

Nair, Kusum. *In Defense of the Irrational Peasant: Indian Agriculture after the Green Revolution*. Chicago: Univ. of Chicago Press, 1979.

Nair, Mira. "India Cabaret." In conversation with Ketali Sheth. *Splice*, no. 3 (1987):35-39, 41-44.

Nair, Mira and Sooni Taraporevala. "India Cabaret: Reflections and Reactions." *Discourse* 8 (Fall 1986-Winter 1987):58-71.

Nanda, B. R. *Gandhi and His Critics*. Delhi: Oxford UP, 1985.

Nanda, Meera. "Is Modern Science a Western, Patriarchal Myth? A Critique of the Populist Orthodoxy." *South Asia Bulletin* 11, 1-2 (1991): 32-61.

Nanda, Serena. "The Hijras of India: Cultural and Individual Dimensions of the Institutionalized Third Gender Role." *Journal of Homosexuality* 11, 3-4 (1986):35-54.

________. "The Third Gender: Hijra Community in India." *Manushi*, no. 72 (Sept.-Oct. 1992):9-16.

Nanda, Serena and Francher, J. Scott. "Culture and Homosexuality: A Comparison of Long-Term Male and Female Relationships." *Eastern Anthropologist* 33 (1980).

Nandy, Ashis. "Emancipating Science." In *Science and Technology and Future*. Edited by Buchholz and Wolfgang Gmelin. Munchen: K. G. Saur, 1979. Also in *Seminar*, no. 238 (June 1979).

________. "Herbert Marcuse: Metapsychologist — A Tribute." *Alternatives* 5, 3 (November 1979).

________. *Alternative Sciences: Creativity and Authenticity in Two Indian Scientists*. New Delhi: Allied Publishers, 1980; rev. ed. in paperback, New Delhi: Oxford Univ. Press, forthcoming [1994].

________. *At the Edge of Psychology: Essays in Politics and Culture.* Delhi: Oxford UP, 1980; paperback ed., 1990. [Reviewed by Veena Das, "Studies in Power and Authority", *Indian Express* (3 May 1981); Vol. 22, No. 3 of the *Journal of Commonwealth & Comparative Politics* (November 1984), with contributions by Franklin A. Presler, Lucian W. Pye, Arun Bose, Sanjukta Gupta, Richard Gombich and G. Morris Carstairs, and a 'response' by Ashis Nandy, "Cultures of Politics and Politics of Cultures", is devoted to a discussion of *At the Edge of Psychology*.]

________. "The Popular Hindi Film: Ideology and First Principles." *India International Centre Quarterly* 8, 1 (1980):89-96; reprinted as "The Supermarket of Dreams", *The Illustrated Weekly of India* (16 March 1986).

________. "A Post-colonial View of the East and the West." *Alternatives* 8, 1 (March 1982):25-48.

________. "Science for the Unafraid." *Deccan Herald* (30 May 1982); also in *Mainstream*, 26 June 1982; translated into Tamil by K. Manoharan, in *Vinayana Manobhava* (Madras: Lokayan, 1982).

________. *The Intimate Enemy: Loss and Recovery of Self Under Colonialism*. New Delhi: Oxford UP, 1983; paperback ed., 1988; translated into Gujarati as *Antarang Ari*, tr. Tridip S. Dave (Ahmedabad: Behavioural Sciences Centre, 1991), and into Hindi as *Antaranga Shatru*, tr. Pawan Agarwal, forthcoming.

Nandy, Ashis. "Towards an Alternative Politics of Psychology." *International Social Science Journal* 35, 2 (1983).

________. "Culture, State and the Rediscovery of Indian Politics." *EPW* 19, 49 (8 Dec. 1984):2078-83.

________. "Reconstructing Childhood: A Critique of the Ideology of Adulthood." *Alternatives* 10, 3 (Sept. 1984):359-75.

________. "An anti-secularist manifesto." *Seminar*, no. 314 (October 1985): 1-12.

________. "The Shadow State." *Illustrated Weekly of India* (24 Feb. 1985): 20-23.

________. "The Idea of Development: The Experience of Modern Psychology as a Cautionary Tale." In *Human Development in Its Social Context: A Collective Exploration*. Edited by Carlos Malmann and Oscar Nudler. London: Hodder and Stoughton, 1986. Earlier and shorter version first published in *Times of India*, July 5 and 6, 1983.

________. "Ranji, Cricket and Nationalism." *The Sunday Statesman Miscellany* (16 February 1986):1-4.

________. "An Intelligent Critic's Guide to Indian Cinema." *Deep Focus*, Pt. I, "The Cultural Matrix of the Popular Film", 1, 1 (Dec. 1987): 68-72; Pt. II, 1, 2 (June 1988):53-60; Pt. III, "The Double in Commercial Films", 1, 3 (Nov. 1988):58-61.

________. "Cultural Frames for Social Transformation: A Credo." *Alternatives* 12 (1987):113-23.

________. "Development and Authoritarianism: An Epitaph on Social Engineering." *Lokayan Bulletin* 5, 1 (1987):39-50; also published in *Journal fur Entwicklungspolitik* 1 (1987).

________. *Traditions, Tyranny and Utopias: Essays in the Politics of Awareness*. New Delhi: Oxford UP, 1987; paperback ed., 1992.

________. "Sati as Profit Versus Sati as Spectacle." *Illustrated Weekly of India* (17 January 1988).

________. "Science in Utopia: Equity, Plurality and Openness." In *Social Reality: Perspectives and Understanding*. Edited by Janak Pandey. New Delhi: Concept, 1988. Earlier version in *Indian International Centre Quarterly* 10, 1 (1983).

________. "After the Raj." *Seminar*, no. 361 (Sept. 1989):26-31.

________. "The Home and the World." *Illustrated Weekly of India* (30 July 1989).

________. "The Political Culture of the Indian State." *Daedalus* (Fall 1989): 1-26.

Nandy, Ashis. "Shamans, Savages and the Wilderness: On the Audibility of Dissent and the Future of Civilizations." *Alternatives* 14 (1989):263-77; portions published as "Liberation for Those who do not Speak the Language of Liberation." In *The Theory and Practice of Liberation at the End of the Twentieth Century*. Brussels: The Lelio Basso Foundation for the Rights and the Liberation of Peoples, 1988.

________. *The Tao of Cricket: On Games of Destiny and the Destiny of Games*. New Delhi: Viking and Penguin, 1989.

________. "The Discreet Charms of Indian Terrorism." *The Journal of Commonwealth and Comparative Politics* 12 (1990):25-43.

________. "The Politics of Secularism and the Recovery of Religious Tolerance." In *Mirrors of Violence: Communities, Riots and Survivors in South Asia*, pp. 69-93. Edited by Veena Das. Delhi: Oxford UP, 1990. Also reprinted in *The Book Review* 14, 6 (Nov.-Dec. 1990):23-29.

________. "Satyajit Ray's Secret Guide to Exquisite Murders: Creativity, Social Criticism, and the Partitioning of the Self." *East-West Film Journal* 4, 2 (1990):14-37.

________. "The Savage Freud: The First Non-Western Psychoanalyst and the Relegitimation of Depth Psychology in Colonial India." Mimeographed, 1990.

________. "Hinduism versus Hindutva: The Inevitability of a Confrontation." *Times of India* (18 Feb. 1991).

________. "The remembered city." *Seminar*, no. 379 (March 1991):43-47.

________. "Terrorism Indian Style." *Indian Express (Sunday) Magazine* (7 April 1991), pp. 1ff.

________. "Images of the Indian State." In *The State in Crisis: Dr. Mohan Sinha Mehta Memorial Lectures*. Edited by P. S. Sundaram. Bombay: Somaiya Publications, 1992.

________. "In the Name of God." *The Sunday Observor Colour Magazine* (6-12 Dec. 1992), 'Life' Section, p. 1.

________. "The Other Within: The Strange Case of Radhabinod Pal's Judgment on Culpability." *New Literary History* 23, 1 (Winter 1992):45-67.

________. "Secularism." *Seminar,* no. 394 (June 1992):29-30.

________. "State." In *The Development Dictionary: A Guide to Knowledge and Power*, pp. 264-74. Edited by Wolfgang Sachs. London: Zed Books, 1992.

________. "Terrorism—Indian Style." *Seminar*, no. 401 (January 1993):35-41.

________. *The Savage Freud and Other Essays in Possible and Retrievable Selves*. New Delhi: Oxford UP, forthcoming [1994].

Nandy, Ashis. *The Illegitimacy of Nationalism: Rabindranath Tagore and the Politics of Self*. New Delhi: Oxford UP, 1994.

________, ed. *Science, Hegemony and Violence: A Requiem for Modernity*. Tokyo: United Nations University; New Delhi: Oxford UP, 1988; paperback ed., 1990. [Review by T. G. Vaidyanathan in *Lokayan Bulletin* 7, 1 (Jan.-Feb. 1989):71-76.]

Nandy, Ashis and Das, Veena. "A New Kind of Rioting." *The Illustrated Weekly of India* (23 Dec. 1984).

________. "Violence, victimhood, and the language of silence." *CIS* 19, 1 (Jan.-June 1985):177-95. Reprinted in *The Word and the World: Fantasy, Symbol and Record*. Edited by Veena Das. New Delhi: Sage, 1986.

Nandy, Ashis; Das, Veena; Das, R. K.; and Mohanty, Manoranjan. "Only Widows and Orphans Left." *Indian Express* (16 Nov. 1984); also published in Hindi in *Jansatta* (19 Nov. 1984).

Nandy, Ashis and Kakar, Sudhir. "Culture and Personality in India." In *A Survey of Research in Psychology, 1971-1976*. Edited by Udai Pareekh. Bombay: Popular Prakashan, 1980.

Nandy, Ashis and Papastergiadis, Nikos. "Dialogue and the Diaspora." *Third Text* 11 (Summer 1990).

Nandy, Ashis; Trivedi, Shikha; and Mayaram, Sail. *The Emergence of Nationalities and the Creation of Minorities in India: The Ramjanmabhumi Movement and the Fear of Self*. Forthcoming, 1995.

Nandy, Ashis and Visvanathan, Shiv. "Modern Medicine and Its Non-Modern Critics: A Study in Discourse." In *Dominating Knowledge*, pp. 145-84. Edited by Frederique A. and Steve Marglin. Oxford: Clarendon Press, 1990.

Nandy, Ashis *et al*. *Comparative Electoral Systems: Report of a Non-Governmental Group on Bangladesh*. Colombo: International Centre for Ethnic Studies, 1990.

Nandy, Moti. "Football and Nationalism." Translated by Shampa Banerjee. In *The Calcutta Psyche*, pp. 241-54. Edited by Geeti Sen. New Delhi: Rupa & Co. and India International Center, 1990-91.

Narasimhan, Sakuntala. *Sati: Widow Burning in India*. New York and New Delhi: Viking, 1990.

Narayan, Kirin. *Storytellers, Saints, and Scoundrels: Folk Narrative in Hindu Religious Teaching*. Philadelphia: Univ. of Pennsylvania Press, 1989.

Narayan, Kirin; Lavie, Smadar; and Rosaldo, Renato, eds. *Creativity/Anthropology*. The Anthropology of Contemporary Issues. Ithaca, New York: Cornell UP, 1992.

Neelsen, John P, ed. *Gender, Caste and Power in South Asia: Social Status and*

Mobility in a Transitional Society. New Delhi: Manohar Publishers, 1992.

Nettl, Bruno and Bohlman, Philip, eds. *Comparative Musicology and the Anthropology of Music*. Chicago: Univ. of Chicago Press, 1991.

Neuman, Daniel M. "The Ecology of Indian Music in North America." *Bansuri* 1 (1984):9-15.

________. "Indian Music as a Cultural System." *Asian Music* 17, 1 (Fall/Winter 1985).

________. *The Life of Music in North India: The Organization of the Artistic Tradition*. Detroit: Wayne State Univ. Press, 1990.

Nevadomsky, Joseph. "Social Change and the East Indians in Rural Trinidad: a Critique of Methodologies." *Social and Economic Studies* 31 (1982):901-26.

Newman, R. S. "Orientalism for Kids: Postage Stamps and 'Creating' South Asia." *Jrl. of Developing Societies* 5, 1 (1989):70-82.

Nigam, Sanjay. "Disciplining and Policing the 'Criminals by Birth', Part I: The Making of a Colonial Stereotype — The Criminal Tribes and Castes of North India", *IESHR* 27, 2 (April-June 1990):131-64.

________. "Disciplining and Policing the 'Criminals by Birth', Part 2: The Development of a Disciplinary System, 1871-1900," *IESHR* 27, 3 (July-Sept. 1990):257-88.

Niranjana, Tejaswini, "Deconstructing Translation and History: Derrida on Benjamin." *Strategies* , no. 1 (Fall 1988):100-19.

________. "Representation, History and the Case of Translation." *Jrl. of Arts and Ideas*, nos. 17-18 (June 1989):109-16.

________. "Cinema, Femininity and Economy of Consumption." *EPW* 26,43 (26 Oct. 1991):WS-85 ff.

________. "Translation, Colonialism and the Rise of English." *EPW* 25, 15 (14 April 1990):773-79.

________. "'History, Really Beginning': Compulsions of Post-Colonial Pedagogy." *EPW* 25, 42-43 (20-27 October 1990):2379-84. Reprinted in *The Lie of the Land: English Literary Studies in India*, pp. 246-59. Edited by Rajeswari Sunder Rajan. New Delhi: Oxford UP, 1992.

________. *Siting Translation: History, poststructuralism and the colonial context.* Berkeley: Univ. of California Press, 1991.

________. "Colonialism and the Aesthetics of Translation." In *Interrogating Modernity: Culture and Colonialism in India*. Edited by Tejaswini Niranjana, P. Sudhir, and Vivek Dhareshwar. Calcutta: Seagull Books, 1993.

Niranjana, Tejaswini; Sudhir, P.; and Dhareshwar, Vivek, eds. *Interrogating*

Modernity: Culture and Colonialism in India. Calcutta: Seagull Books, 1993.

Nixon, Rob. *London Calling*: *V. S. Naipaul, Postcolonial Mandarin*. New York: Oxford UP, 1991.

Oberoi, Harjot Singh. "The 'New' Old Trope: The Application of Psychohistory in the Study of Socio-religious Movements in Colonial India." *Studies in History* (New Series) 2, 2 (July-Dec. 1986):255-73.

________. "The Worship of Pir Sakhi Sarvar: Illness, Healing and Popular Culture in the Punjab." *Studies in History* (New Series) 3, 1 (1987): 29-55.

Obeyesekere, Gananath. *Medusa's Hair*: *An Essay on Personal Symbols and Religious Experience*. Chicago: Univ. of Chicago Press, 1981; reprint ed., Princeton: Princeton UP, 1984.

________. *The Work of Culture*: *Symbolic Transformation in Psychoanalysis and Anthropology*. Chicago: Univ. of Chicago Press, 1990.

Obeyesekere, Ranjini. "The Problem of Language in the Sinhala Theater." In *Ediriweera Sarachchandra: Festschrift 1988*. Colombo, 1988.

________. "The Sinhala Literary Tradition: Polemics and Debate." *South Asia Bulletin* 12, 1 (Spring 1992):34-41.

Obeyesekere, Ranjini and Fernando, Chitra, eds. *An Anthology of Modern Writing from Sri Lanka*. Tuscon: University of Arizona Press, 1981.

Offredi, Mariola, ed. *Literature, Language and the Media in India*. New Delhi: Manohar Publishers, 1992.

Oldenburg, Veena Talwar. *The Making of Colonial Lucknow 1856-1877*. Princeton: Princeton UP, 1984; paperback ed., Delhi: Oxford UP, 1989.

________. "Lifestyle as Resistance: The Case of the Courtesans of Lucknow, India." *Feminist Studies* 16, 2 (Summer, 1990):259-87; slightly different version also published in *Contesting Power*: *Resistance and Everday Social Relations in South Asia*, pp. 23-61. Edited by Douglas Haynes and Gyan Prakash. Delhi: Oxford UP, 1991.

O'Hanlon, Rosalind. *Caste, Conflict and Ideology*: *Mahatma Jotirao Phule and Low-Caste Protest in Nineteenth-Century Western India*. New York: Cambridge University Press, 1985.

________. "Recovering the Subject: Subaltern Studies and Histories of Resistance in Colonial South Asia." *Modern Asian Studies* 22, 1 (1988):189-224.

________. "Cultures of Rule, Communities of Resistance: Gender, Discourse and Tradition in Recent South Asian Historiographies." *Social Analysis* 25 (1989).

________. "Issues of Widowhood: Gender and Resistance in Colonial Western

India." In *Contesting Power: Resistance and Everday Social Relations in South Asia*, pp. 62-108. Edited by Douglas Haynes and Gyan Prakash. Delhi: Oxford UP, 1991.

O'Hanlon, Rosalind and Washbrook, David. "After Orientalism: Culture, Criticism, and Politics in the Third World." *CSSH* 34, 1 (Jan. 1992): 141-67.

Omvedt, Gail. "The Downtrodden among the Downtrodden: An Interview with a Dalit Agricultural Laborer." *Signs* 4, 4 (1979):763-74.

________. "Adivasis, Culture and Modes of Production in India." *BCAS* 12 (January-March 1980): 15-22.

________. "'Once this land was ours': agricultural labourers and adivasis in India." *Race and Class* 21, 3 (Winter 1980):239-49.

________. *We Will Smash this Prison? Indian Women in Struggle*. London: Zed Press, 1980.

________. "Capitalist Agriculture and Rural Classes in India." *EPW* (26 Dec. 1981).

________. "Devdasi [sic] Custom and the Fight Against It." *Manushi* 19 (1983).

________.* "The 'New Peasant Movement' in India." *In the Wake of Marx* (Calcutta) 3 (1987):3-10.

________. "Violence, Exploitation, Sexuality: Theories of Women's Oppression and the Struggle for Liberation." *Lokayan Bulletin* 7, 2 (March-April 1993):35-51.

________. "Ambedkar and Dalit Labor Radicalism: Maharashtra, 1936-1942." *South Asia Bulletin* 10, 1(1990):12-22.

________. "The anti-caste movement and the discourse of power." *Race and Class* 33, 2 (Oct.-Dec. 1991):15-27.

________. "Red Green Movements in India." Forthcoming in *Capitalism Nature Socialism* (1993).

________, ed. *Land, Caste and Politics in Indian States*. Delhi: Authors Guild Publications, 1982.

Ostor, Akos. *Culture and Power: Legend, Ritual, Trade and Revolution in a Bengali Society*. Beverly Hill and New Delhi: Sage Publications, 1984.

________. "Cinema and Society in India and Senegal." *Splice*, no. 3 (1987): 6-30.

PPST Bulletin, Madras Group. "The Story of Scientific Forestry in India: Some Highlights." *PPST Bulletin* 3, 1 (May 1983):31-67.

________. "The Debate on the Building of New Delhi." *PPST Bulletin* 3, 2 (Nov. 1983):48-74.

Padikkal, Shivarama. "Inventing Modernity: The Emergence of the Novel in

India." In *Interrogating Modernity: Culture and Colonialism in India.* Edited by Tejaswini Niranjana, P. Sudhir, and Vivek Dhareshwar. Calcutta: Seagull Books, 1993.

Pal, Pratapaditya and Dehejia, Vidya. *From Merchants to Emperors: British Artists and India, 1757-1930.* Ithaca and London: Cornell UP, 1986.

Pande, Mrinal. *The Subject is Woman.* New Delhi: Sanchar Publishing House, 1991.

Pandey, Gyanendra. "A view of the observable: a positivist 'understanding' of agrarian society and political protest in colonial India." *Journal of Peasant Studies* 7, 3 (1980).

________. "Liberalism and the Study of Indian History: A Review of Writings on Communalism." *EPW* (15 Oct. 1983).

________. *The Congress and the Nation, c. 1917-1947.* Occasional Paper, no. 69. Calcutta: CSSS, 1985.

________. *The Construction of Communalism in Colonial North India.* Delhi: Oxford UP, 1990. [collects essays first published in *Subaltern Studies* and *EPW*].

________. "The Masjid and the Mandir: On the Horns of a Dilemma." *The India Magazine* (February 1990).

________. "Hindus and Others: The Militant Hindu Construction." *EPW* 26, 52 (28 Dec. 1991):2997-3005, 3008-9.

________. "In Defense of the Fragment: Writing About Hindu-Muslim Riots in India Today." *Representations,* no. 37 (Winter 1992):27-55; also in *EPW* (Annual Number) 26, 11-12 (March 1991):559-72.

Pandian, M. S. S. "Parasakhti: Life and Times of a DMK Film." *EPW* (Annual Number) 26, 11-12 (March 1991):759-70.

________. *The Image Trap: M. G. Ramachandran in Film and Politics.* Delhi: Sage, 1992.

________, Anandhi, S.; and Venkatachalpathy, A. R. "Of Maltova Mothers and Other Stories." *EPW* 26, 20 (20 April 1991):1059-64 [on C. S. Lakshmi].

Panikkar, R. "The Destiny of Technological Civilization: An Ancient Buddhist Legend *Romavisaya.*" *Alternatives* 10, 2 (June 1984):237-53.

________. "Alternatives to Modern Culture." *Interculture* 77 (1982):2-68.

________. "The Challenge of Modernity." *IICQ* 20, 1-2 (Spring-Summer 1993):182-92.

Pannikar, K. N. "The Intellectual History of Colonial India: Some Historiographical and Conceptual Questions." In *Situating Indian History—for Sarvepalli Gopal,* pp. 402-33. Edited by S. Bhattacharya and R. Thapar. Delhi: Oxford UP, 1986.

Pannikar, K. N. "Culture and Consciousness in Modern India: A Historical Perspective." *Social Scientist*, no. 203 (April 1990):3-32.

________, ed. *Communalism in India: History, Politics, and Culture*. Delhi: Manohar, 1991.

Papanek, Hanna and Minault, Gail, eds. *Separate Worlds: Studies of Purdah in South Asia*. Columbia, MO.: South Asia Books, 1982.

Parajuli, Pramod. "Power and Knowledge in Development Discourse: New Social Movements and the State in India." *International Social Science Journal* 20 (Feb. 1991):173-90.

Parameswaran, Uma. "Amid the Alien Corn: Biculturalism and the Challenge of Commonwealth Literary Criticism." *World Literature Written in English* 21, 1 (1982):240-53.

Paranjpe, Markarand. "The Invasion of 'Theory' — An Indian Response." *New Quest*, no. 81 (May-June 1990):151-62.

________. "Ideology as Form: Notes on the Third World Novel." *Social Scientist* 18, 8-9 (Aug.-Sept. 1990):71-84.

________. "A Critique of Indian Criticism: Options and Challenges." *New Quest*, no. 85 (Jan.-Feb. 1991):29-36.

________. "Caste of Indian English Novel." *EPW* 26, 40 (5 Oct. 1991): 2298-301.

________. *Decolonization and Development: Hind Swaraj Revisioned*. With a foreword by Ashis Nandy. New Delhi: Sage Publications, 1993.

Parasher, Aloka. "Attitudes towards the Mleccha in Early Northen India — up to ca. A.D. 600." *The Indian Historical Review* 9, 1-2 (1983): 1-30.

________. *Mlecchas in Early India*. Delhi: Munshiram Manoharlal, 1991.

Parekh, Bhikhu. "Gandhi's Concept of Ahimsa." *Alternatives* 13 (1988): 195-217.

________. *Colonialism, Tradition and Reform: An Analysis of Gandhi's Political Discourse*. New Delhi: Sage, 1989.

________. "The Rushdie Affair and the British Press." In *Social Studies Review* (November 1989), reprinted in *The Salman Rushdie Controversy in Interreligious Perspective*, pp. 71-96. Edited by Dan Cohn-Sherbok. Lewiston: Edwin Mellen Press, 1990.

Parker, Andrew; Russo, Mary; Sommer, Doris; and Yaeger, Patricia, eds., *Nationalisms and Sexualities*. New York: Routledge, 1992.

Parmar, Pratibha. "Gender, race and class: Asian Women in Resistance." In *The Empire Strikes Back*, pp. 236-75. A Publication of the Centre for Contemporary Cultural Studies. London: Hutchinson, 1980.

Parmar, Pratibha. "Hateful Contraries: Media Images of Asian Women." *Ten.8*, no. 16 (1984).

________. "Transitory Movements?" *Spectrum Women's Photography Festival Exhibition Catalogue* (1988).

________. "Other Kinds of Dreams." *Feminist Review* 31 (Spring 1989):55-66.

________. "Black Feminism: The Politics of Articulation." In *Identity, Community, Culture, Difference*, pp. 101-26. Edited by Jonathan Rutherford. London: Lawrence & Wishart, 1990.

Parrey, Eric. "Ritual of the City." *Architectural Review* No. 1086 (August 1987):14-24.

Parry, Benita. "Problems in Current Theories of Colonial Discourse." *Oxford Literary Review* 9, 1-2 (1987):27-58.

Parthasarthy, R. "Whoring after English Gods." In *Writers in East-West Encounter: New Cultural Bearings*. Edited by Guy Amirthanayagam. London: Macmillan, 1982.

Patankar, R. B. "Aesthetics: Some Important Problems." *Jrl. of Arts and Ideas*, no. 6 (Jan.-March 1984):43-66.

Patel, Amina. "Images of Asian Women in the (White) Media". *Artrage* no. 3/4 (Summer 1983).

Patel, Gieve. "Contemporary Indian Painting." *Daedalus* 118 (Fall 1989):171-203.

Patel, Sujata. "The Construction and Reconstruction of Woman in Gandhi." Occasional Papers on History and Society, no. 49. New Delhi: NMML, 1988; published in *EPW* (20 Feb. 1988):377-87.

Pathak, Bindeshwar. *Road to Freedom: A Sociological Study on the Abolition of Scavenging in India*. Delhi: Motilal Banarsidass, 1991.

Pathak, Zakhia. "Writing in Ourselves." In *Ourstory: Indian Response to Nineteenth Century Literature*, pp. 95-110. Edited by Mohua Lahiri, Sanjay Kumar, and Anand Prakash. New Delhi: Academic Foundation, 1992. Also published as "A Pedagogy for Postcolonial Feminists." In *Feminists Theorize the Political*, pp. 426-41. Edited by Judith Butler and Joan W. Scott. New York & London: Routledge, 1992.

Pathak, Zakhia; Sengupta, Saswati; and Purkayastha, Sharmila. "The Prisonhouse of Orientalism." *Textual Practice* 5, 2 (Summer 1991):195-218.

Patil, Anand B. "The Whirlgig of Literary Taste: Impact or Alienation." *Indian Literature* 36, 4 (July-August 1993):156-69.

Patnaik, Arun K. "Gramsci's Concept of Commonsense: Toward a Theory of Subaltern Consciousness in Hegemony Processes." Occasional Paper, no. 95. Calcutta: CSSS, 1987.

Patnaik, Arun K. "Reification of Intellect." *EPW* (27 Jan. 1990):PE12-19; also published as Occasional Paper, no. 118. Calcutta: CSSS, 1990.

Pattanayak, D. P. *Multilingualism and Mother-tongue Education*. Delhi: Oxford UP, 1981.

________. *Language and Social Issues*. Mysore: Prasaranga, Univ. of Mysore, 1982.

________. "Multilingualism and Language Politics in India." *IICQ* 11, 2 (June 1984):125-31.

________. "Diversity in Communication and Languages: A Predicament of a Multilingual National State: India, A Case Study." In *Language of Inequality*. Edited by Nessa Wolfson and Joan Manes. New York & Amsterdam: Mouton, 1985.

________. "Educational use of the Mother Tongue." In *Language and Education in Multilingual Settings*. Edited by Bernard Spolsky. San Diego: College-Hill Press, 1986.

________. "Literacy: Some Reflections." In *Aspects of Adult Literacy*. Munich: Goethe Institute, 1986.

________. *Multilingualism and multiculturalism: Britian and India*. Occasional Paper, No. 1. International Association of Intercultural Education, University of London. Institute of Education, 1987.

Paul, Ashit, ed. *Woodcut Prints of Nineteenth Century Calcutta*. Calcutta: Seagull Books, 1983.

Paxton, Nancy L. "Feminism Under the Raj: Complicity and Resistance in the Writings of Flora Annie Steel and Annie Besant." *Women's Studies International Forum* 13 (Spring 1990):333-46.

________. "Disembodied Subjects: English Women's Autobiography Under the Raj." In *De/Colonizing the Subject: The Politics of Gender in Women's Autobiography*, pp. 387-409. Edited by Sidone Smith and Julie Watson. Minneapolis: Univ. of Minnesota Press, 1992.

Peebles, Patrick. "Colonization and Ethnic Conflict in the Dry Zone of Sri Lanka." *Journal of Asian Studies* 49, 1 (1990):30-55.

Peers, Douglas. "'The Habitual Nobility of Being': British Officers and the Social Construction of the Bengal Army in the Early Nineteenth Century." *Modern Asian Studies* 25, 3 (July 1991):545-89.

Pendakur, Manjunath. "Film Policies in Canada: In Whose Interest?" *Media, Culture and Society* 3,2 (April 1981).

________. "U.S.-Canada Relations: Cultural Dependence and Conflict." In *Changing Patterns of Control in Communication*, Vol. 2. Edited by V. Mosco and J. Wasko. Philadelphia: Ablex, 1983.

Pendakur, Manjunath. "Dynamics in Cultural Policy Making: The U.S. Film Industry in India." *Journal of Communication* 35,4 (Autumn 1985): 52-72.

________. "New Cultural Technologies and the Fading Glitter of Indian Cinema." *Quarterly Rv. of Film and Video* 11, 3 (1986).

________. "The Indian Film Industry." In *Asian Film Industry*. Edited by J. A. Lent. Bromley: Christopher Helm, 1990.

Pereira, Winin and Seabrook, Jeremy. *Asking the Earth*. London: Earthscan Publications, 1990.

Persaud, Kamal. *Racism Against the Indians in the Eastern Caribbean*. Trinidad and Tobago: Battlefront Pointers, 1988.

Pines, Jim and Willemen, Paul. *Questions of Third Cinema*. London: British Film Institute Publishing, 1989.

Pinn, Fred. *The Road of Destiny: Darjeeling Letters 1839*. Oxford: Oxford UP, 1986; Oxford India Paperback, 1990.

Pinney, Christopher. "Classification and Fantasy in the Photographic Construction of Caste and Tribe." *Visual Anthropology* 3, 2-3 (1990).

________. "Representations of India: Normalisation and the Other." *Pacific Viewpoint* 29, 1 (May 1988):97-118.

Po'dar, Preym K. and Subba, Tanka B. "Demystifying Some Ethnographic Texts on the Himalayas." *Social Scientist*, nos. 219-220 (Aug.-Sept. 1991):78-84.

Pollock, Sheldon. "Raksasas and Others." *Indologica Taurinensia* 13 (1985-86): 263-81.

________. Introduction to *Ramayana of Valmiki, an Epic of Ancient India*, Volume II: *Ayodhyakanda*, translated by Sheldon Pollock. Princeton: Princeton UP, 1986.

________. "Mimamsa and the Problem of History in Traditional India." *JAOS* 109, 4 (1989):603-10.

________. "From Discourse of Ritual to Discourse of Power in Sanskrit Culture." *Journal of Ritual Studies* 4, 2 (Summer 1990):315-45.

________. "Ramayana and Political Imagination in India." *Jrl. of Asian Studies* 52, 2 (May 1993):261-97.

Powers, David S. "Orientalism, Colonialism, and Legal History: The Attack on Muslim Family Endowments in Algeria and India." *CSSH* 31, 3 (1989):535-71.

Powers, Harold S. "Classical music, cultural roots, and colonial rule: an Indic musicologist looks at the Muslim World." *Asian Music* 12, 1 (1980).

Prabhu, Shrikanth. "Singing in the Rain: An Analysis of Songs in Popular Cinema." *Deep Focus* 1, 4 (January 1989):42-48.

Pradhan, Kumar. *The Gorkha Conquests*. Delhi: Oxford UP, 1991.

Pradhan, S. V. "The Concept of Literary History: A Marxist Critique." *Jrl. of Arts and Ideas*, no. 6 (Jan.-March 1984):67-74.

Pradhan, Sudhir.* *Marxist Cultural Movement in India*. 2 vols. Calcutta, 1979.

Prakash, Gyan. *Bonded Histories: Genealogies of Labor Servitude in Colonial India*. Cambridge: Cambridge UP, 1990.

________. "Writing Post-Orientalist Histories of the Third World: Perspectives from Indian Historiography." *CSSH* 32, 2 (April 1990):383-408; also published in revised form as "Writing Post-Orientalist Histories of the Third World: Indian Historiography Is Good to Think", in *Colonialism and Culture*, pp. 353-88. Edited by Nicholas Dirks. Ann Arbor, Michigan: Univ. of Michigan Press, 1992.

________. "Can the 'Subaltern' Ride? A Reply to O'Hanlon and Washbrook." *CSSH* 34, 1 (Jan. 1992):168-85.

________. "Postcolonial Criticism and Indian Historiography." *Social Text*, nos. 31-32 (1992):8-19.

________. "Science 'Gone Native' in Colonial India." *Representations*, no. 40 (Fall 1992):153-78.

________, ed. *The World of the Rural Labourer in Colonial India*. New Delhi: Oxford UP, 1992.

Prakash, Vikramaditya. "Production of Identity in (Post) Colonial 'Indian' Architecture: Hegemony and Its Discontents in Nineteenth Century Jaipur." Unpublished Ph.D. Dissertation, Cornell University, 1994.

Prasad, Madhava. "Escape from Childhood: The Development of the Hero in Popular Cinema." *Deep Focus* 1, 1 (Dec. 1987):28-32.

________. "On the Question of a Theory of (Third World) Literature." *Social Text*, nos. 31-32 (1992):57-83.

________. "The 'Other' Worldliness of Postcolonial Discourse: a Critique." *Critical Quarterly* 34, 3 (Autumn 1992).

Prasad, Nageshwar, ed. *Hind Swaraj: A Fresh Look*. Delhi: Gandhi Peace Foundation, 1985.

Pritchett, Frances W. *Marvelous Encounters: Folk Romance in Urdu and Hindi*. New Delhi: Manohar, 1985.

Qureshi, Regula Burckhardt. *Sufi Music of India and Pakistan: Sound, Context and Meaning in Qawwali*. Cambridge: Cambridge UP, 1986; reprint ed., Calcutta: Seagull Books, 1990.

Race Today Collective. *The Struggle of Asian Workers in Britain*. London, 1983.

Radhakrishnan, R. "The Post-Modern Event and the End of Logocentrism." *boundary 2* 12, 1 (Fall 1983):33-62.

Radhakrishnan, R. "To Be: A Foucauldian Itinerary." *Works and Days* (Fall 1986):51-77.

________. "Reality, the Text, and Post-Modern Representation: A Question in Theory, or Theory in Question." In *Post-Modern Fiction: A Bio-Biblio-Graphic Guide*, pp. 229-42. Edited by Larry McCafferey. Westport, Conn.: Greenwood Press, 1986.

________. "Ethnic Identity and Post-Structuralist Differance." *Cultural Critique* (Spring 1987):199-220. Also published in *The Nature and Context of Minority Discourse*, pp. 50-71. Edited by Abdul JanMohamed and David Lloyd. New York: Oxford UP, 1990.

________. "Culture as Common Ground: Ethnicity and Beyond." *Melus* 14, 2 (Summer 1987):5-19.

________. "Negotiating Subject Positions in an Uneven World." In *Feminism and Institutions*, pp. 276-90. Edited by Linda Kauffman. Oxford: Basil Blackwell, 1989.

________. "Post-Structuralist Politics: Towards a Theory of Coalition." In *Jameson/Postmodernism/Critique*, pp. 301-32. Edited by Douglas Kellner. Washington, D.C.: Maisonneuve Press, 1989.

________. "The Changing Subject and the Politics of Theory." *Differences* 2, 2 (Summer 1990):126-52.

________. "Toward an Effective Intellectual: Foucault or Gramsci?" In *Intellectuals: Aesthetics, Politics, Academics*, pp. 57-99. Edited by Bruce Robbins. Minneapolis: University of Minnesota Press, 1990.

________. "Canonicity and Theory: Towards a Post-Structuralist Pedgagogy." In *Theory/Pedagogy/Politics*, pp. 112-35. Edited by Donald Morton and Mas'ud Zavarzadeh. Chicago: University of Illinois Press, 1991.

________. "Ethnicity in an Age of Diaspora." *Transition*, no. 54 (1991): 104-15.

________. "Nationalism, Gender and the Narrative of Identity." In *Nationalisms and Sexualities*, pp. 77-95. Edited by Andrew Parker, Mary Russo, Doris Sommer, and Patricia Yaeger. London: Routledge, 1992.

________. "Cultural Theory and the Politics of Location." In *Views Beyond the Border Country: Raymond Williams and Cultural Politics*, pp. 275-94. Edited by Dennis L. Dworkin and Leslie G. Roman. New York: Routledge, 1993.

________. "Postcoloniality and the Boundaries of Identity." *Callaloo* 16, 4 (Fall 1993):750-771.

Raheja, Gloria. "India: Caste, Kingship, and Dominance Reconsidered." *Annual Review of Anthropology* 17 (1988): 497-523.

Rahim, Amin-ur. "After the Last Journey: Some Reflections on Bangladeshi

Community Life in Ontario." *Polyphony: The Bulletin of the Multicultural Society of Ontario* 12 (1990):8-11.

Rahim, Amin-ur. "Multiculturalism or Ethnic Hegemony: A Critique of Multicultural Education in Toronto." *Jrl. of Ethnic Studies* 18, 3 (Fall 1990):29-46.

________. "The Political Economy of English Education in Muslim Bengal (1871-1912)." *Comparative Education Review* 36, 3 (August 1992): 309-21.

Rahnema, Majid. "A New Variety of AIDS and its Pathogens: Homo Economicus, Development and Aid." *Alternatives* 13, 1 (January 1988):117-36.

Rai, Alok. "Language and the Media: Seeing through the Newspapers." *IICQ* 11, 2 (June 1984):187-97.

________. "The Trauma of Independence: Some Aspects of Progressive Hindi Literature, 1945-47." *Jrl. of Arts and Ideas*, no. 6 (Jan.-March 1984): 19-34.

________. "Only Bigots Feel That Conversions Follow Invasions." *Times of India* (Lucknow ed.), 13 August 1990.

________. *Orwell and the Politics of Despair*. Cambridge: Cambridge UP, 1990.

________. "Black Skin, Black Masks." *EPW* 27, 39 (26 Sept. 1992):2099-103.

Raina, Badri. "Mikhail Bakhtin: The Politics of Language and Genre." *Jrl. of Arts and Ideas*, no. 9 (Oct.-Dec. 1984):65-78.

________. "The Politics of Development: A Statement and a Case. The Narmada River Project." *Jrl. of Arts and Ideas*, nos. 17-18 (June 1989):91-107.

Raina, M. L. "'I'm All Right Jack': Packaged Pleasures of the Middle Cinema." *Journal of Public Culture* 20, 2 (Fall 1986):131-41.

Rajadhyaksha, Ashish. *Ritwik Ghatak: A Return to the Epic*. Bombay: Screen Unit, 1982.

________. "Gandhiana and Gandhiology." *Framework*, nos. 22-3 (Autumn 1983).

________. "Art in Indian Cinema." In *70 Years of Indian Cinema* (1913-1983), pp. 224-236. Edited by T. M Ramachandran. Bombay: Cinema India International, 1985.

________. "Latin American Cinema: Political Cinema." *Jrl. of Arts and Ideas*, nos. 10-11 (Jan.-June 1985):87-98.

________. "Neo-traditionalism: Film as Popular Art in India." *Framework* 32/33 (1986):20-67.

________. "The Phalke Era: Conflict of Traditional Form and Modern Technology." *Jrl. of Arts and Ideas*, nos. 14-15 (July-Dec. 1987):47-78. Also reprinted in *Interrogating Modernity: Culture and Colonialism in*

India. Edited by Tejaswini Niranjana, P. Sudhir, and Vivek Dhareshwar. Calcutta: Seagull Books, 1993.

Rajadhyaksha, Ashish. "Debating the Third Cinema." In *Questions of Third Cinema*, pp. 170-78. Edited by Jim Pines and Paul Willmen. London: British Film Institute, 1989.

________. "Beaming Messages to the Nation." *Jrl. of Arts and Ideas*, no. 19 (May 1990):33-52.

________. "Satyajit Ray, Ray's Films, and Ray-Movie." *Jrl. of Arts and Ideas*, nos. 23-24 (Jan. 1993):7-16. Short version, entitled "Beyond Orientalism", in *Sight and Sound* (1992).

Rajadhyaksha, Ashish and Shahani, Kumar. "Dossier: Shahani." [Kumar Shahani's essays on film.] *Framework*, nos. 30/31 (1986):68-100.

Rajadhyaksha, Ashish and Gangar, Amrit, eds. *Ritwik Ghatak: Arguments/ Stories*. Bombay: Screen Unit/Research Centre for Cinema Studies, 1987.

Rajadhyaksha, Ashish and Muller, Marco, eds. *Le Avventurose storie del cinema indiano*. 2 vols. Venice: Mostra Internazionale del Nuovo Ninema, Pesaro Marsilio Editori, 1985.

Rajagopal, Arvind. "Uses of the Past: The Television Broadcast of an Ancient Epic and its Reception in Indian Society." Unpublished Ph.D. Dissertation, University of California, Berkeley, 1992.

________. "Postcolonial Improvisations on Orientalism: A Hindu Epic Goes Prime Time." Unpublished ms., 1993.

________. "The Rise of National Programming: The Case of Indian Television." *Media, Culture and Society* 15, 1 (January 1993):91-111.

Rajakrishnan, V. "Narrative Structure in Malayalam Cinema." *Deep Focus* 3, 2 (1990):35-39.

Rajam, V. S. "*Ananku*: A Notion Semantically Reduced to Signify Female Sacred Power." *JAOS* 106 (1986):257-72.

Rajan, Gita. "Subversive-Subaltern Identity: Indira Gandhi as the Speaking Subject." In *De/Colonizing the Subject: The Politics of Gender in Women's Autobiography*, pp. 196-222. Edited by Sidone Smith and Julie Watson. Minneapolis: U. of Minnesota Press, 1992.

Rajan, Rajeswari Sunder. "After 'Orientalism': Colonialism and English Literary Studies in India." *Social Scientist*, no. 158 (July 1986):23-35.

________. "Katherine Mansfield and the Question of Women's Writing." In *Woman/Image/Text: Feminist Readings of Literary Texts*, pp. 133-50. Edited by Lola Chatterji. Delhi: Trianka, 1986.

________. "The Subject of Sati: Pain and Death in the Contemporary Discourse on Sati." *Yale Journal of Criticism* 3, 2 (Spring 1990):1-28. Also published in *Interrogating Modernity: Culture and Colonialism in India.* Edited by Tejaswini Niranjana, P. Sudhir, and Vivek Dhareshwar. Calcutta: Seagull Books, 1993.

________. "An Exhilarating Anthology." *The Book Review* 16, 3 (May-June 1992):16-17 [review of Susie Tharu & K. Lalita, eds., *Women Writing in India*, Vol. I].

________. "Brokering English Studies: The British Council in India." In *The Lie of the Land: English Literary Studies in India*, pp. 130-55. Edited by Rajeswari Sunder Rajan. New Delhi: Oxford UP, 1992.

________. "Fixing English: Nation,Language, Subject." In *Lie of the Land: English Literary Studies in India*, pp. 7-28. Edited by Rajeswari Sunder Rajan. Delhi: Oxford UP, 1992.

________. *Real and Imagined Women: Gender, Culture, and Post-colonialism.* London: Routledge, 1994.

________, ed. *Lie of the Land: English Literary Studies in India.* Delhi: Oxford UP, 1992.

Rajan, Rajeswari Sunder and Pathak, Zakia. "'Shahbano.'" *Signs* 14, 3 (Spring 1989):558-82; also published in *Feminists Theorize the Political*, pp. 257-79. Edited by Judith Butler and Joan W. Scott. New York & London: Routledge, 1992.

Rajan, Roby. "The Discourse of Exploitation and the Exploitation of Discourse." *Alternatives* 15 (1990):29-52.

________. "Pathological Rationality/Rational Pathologies." *Alternatives* 17 (1992):339-70.

Rajan, Tillotma. "Displacing Post-Structuralism: Romantic Studies after Paul de Man." *Studies in Romanticism* 24, 4 (Winter 1985):451-74.

Ram, Kalpana. *Mukkuvar Women: Gender, Hegemony and Capitalist Transformation in a South Indian Fishing Community.* London: Zed Books, 1991.

Ram, Susan. "Ram's Englishman." *EPW* 27, 40 (3 Oct. 1992):2172-74. [Review of Mark Tully's *No Full Stops in India* (1991)].

Ramakrishnan, E. V. "'Unachieved Absolute Expression' and the Modernity of Muktibodh." *New Quest*, no. 87 (May-June 1991):149-56.

Raman, N. Kalyan. "Individualism and the Pseudo-Epic Sensibility." *Deep Focus* 3, 2 (1990):72-81.

Ramanathan, Suguna and Franco, F. "The recovery of religious meaning." *Textual Practice* 5, 2 (Summer 1991):183-94.

Ramanujan, A. K. "Hanchi: A Kannada Cinderella." In *Cinderella: A Folklore Casebook*, pp. 259-275. New York: Garland Publishing, 1982.

________."The Indian Oedipus." In *Oedipus: A Folklore Casebook*, pp. 234-61.

Edited by Alan Dundes and Lowell Edmunds. New York: Garland Press, 1983.

Ramanujan, A. K. "Two Realms of Kannada Folklore." In *Another Harmony: New Essays on the Folklore of India*, pp. 41-75. Edited by Stuart Blackburn and A. K. Ramanujan. Berkeley: U. of California Press, 1986.

________. "The Relevance of South Asian Folklore." In *Indian Folklore II*, pp. 79-156. Edited by Peter Claus, J. Handoo, and D. P. Pattanayak. Mysore: Central Institute of Indian Languages, 1987.

________. "Where Mirrors are Windows: Toward an Anthology of Reflections." *History of Religions* 28, 3 (February 1989):187-216.

________. "Telling Tales." *Daedalus* (Fall 1989):239-61.

________. "Is There an Indian Way of Thinking?" *The Book Review* (Jan.-Feb. 1990); also published in *Contributions to Indian Sociology* (1990).

________. *Who Needs Folklore? The Relevance of Oral Traditions to South Asian Studies*. South Asian Occasional Paper Series, No. 1. Honolulu: Center for South Asian Studies, University of Hawaii, 1990. Also reprinted in *Manushi*, no. 69 (March-April 1992):2-16.

________, trans. *Hymns for the Drowning*: *Poems for Visnu by Nammalvar*. Princeton, New Jersey: Princeton UP, 1981. See especially the "Afterword."

________, trans. *Poems of Love and War*. New York: Columbia UP, 1985.

Ranade, Sudhanshu. "A Communist Persepctive on Development Strategy for Rural India." *Jrl. of Peasant Studies* 16 (1988-89):542-74.

Ranga, Haripriya. "Romancing the Environment: Popular Environmental Action in the Garhwal Himalayas." In *In Defense of Livelihood: Comparative Studies on Environmental Action*, pp. 155-81. Edited by John Friedman and Haripriya Ranga. West Hartford, Conn.: Kumarian Press, Inc., 1993.

Rao, Amiya and Rao, B. G. *The Blue Devil*: *Indigo and Colonial Bengal*. New Delhi: Oxford UP, 1992.

Rao, D. Venkat. "Self-Formations: Speculations on the Question of Postcoloniality." *Wasafiri* , no. 13 (Spring 1991).

________. "The Strutting Lebensraum: Sudhir Kakar and the Subject of Postcoloniality." *Jrl. of Contemporary Thought* 1, 1 (1991):111-24.

Rao, Leela. "Woman in Indian films — a paradigm of continuity and change." *Media, Culture and Society* 11, 4 (Oct. 1989):443-58.

Rao, Mohan. "Of Cholera and the Post-Modern World." *EPW* 27, 34 (22 August 1992):1792-95.

Rao, S. Balu. *Last Mile Together: An Anthology of South African Poems*. The Afro-Asian Writers' Association, 1991.

Rashid, Ian Iqbal. *Black Markets, White BoyFriends and Other Acts of Elusion*. Toronto: Toronto South Asian Review, 1991.

Rathore, Nasha. "On Colonies and Classes: The Myth of Aryan Invasion." *New Quest*, no. 87 (May-June 1991):141-48.

Ravindran, K. T. "Indigenous India." *Architectural Review* No. 1086 (August 1987):63-65.

Ray, Bharati. "Bengali Women and Politics of Joint Family." *EPW* 26, 52 (28 Dec. 1991):3015-21.

Ray, Rabindra. "And why an Indian sociology?" *Contributions to Indian Sociology* (New Series) 24, 2 (July-Dec. 1990):265-75.

Raychaudhuri, Tapan. "Indian Nationalism as Animal Politics." *Historical Journal* 22 (1979):747-63.

Reddi, Usha. "Media and culture in Indian society: conflict or co-operation?" *Media, Culture and Society* 11, 4 (Oct. 1989):395-413.

"Reworking Myths: Sutapa Biswas", interview with Yasmin Kureishi, in *Visibly Female: Feminism and Art: An Anthology,* pp. 37-42. Edited by Hilary Robinson. London: Camden Press, 1987; New York: Universe Books, 1988.

Risseeuw, Carla. *Gender Transformation, Power and Resistance among Women in Sri Lanka: The Fish Don't Talk about the Water*. Leiden: Brill, 1988; Delhi: Manohar, 1991.

________. "Gender, Kinship and State Formation: Case of Sri Lanka Under Colonial Rule." *EPW* 27, 43-44 (24-31 Oct. 1992):WS46-54.

Robb, Peter. "New Directions in South Asian History." *South Asia Research* 7, 2 (1979):123-42.

Roberge, Gaston. *Mediation: The Action of the Media in Our Society*. New Delhi: Manohar, 1980.

________. *Another Cinema for Another Society*. Calcutta: Seagull Books, 1985.

________. *The Ways of Film Studies: Film Theory and the Interpretation of Film*. With an essay on Freud by Somnath Zutshi. New Delhi: Ajanta, 1992.

Roberts, Michael. "From Southern India to Lanka: The Traffic in Commodities, Bodies and Myths from the Thirteenth Century Onwards." *South Asia* 3, 1 (1980):36-47.

________. "'Our Duty to Act': Brown Sahibs in Universal Suits: A Review Article on the Abortive 1962 Coup in Sri Lanka." *South Asia* 6, 2 (1983):62-77.

Roberts, Michael. "Ethnicity in Riposte at a Cricket Match: The Past for the Present." *CSSH* 27 (1985):401-29.

Robinson, Andrew. *Satyajit Ray: The Inner Eye*. Berkeley: U. of California Press, 1990.

Rogers, John D. *Crime, Justice and Society in Colonial Sri Lanka*. London: Curzon; Maryland: Riverdale Press, 1987.

________. "Cultural Nationalism and Social Reform: The 1904 Temperance Movement in Sri Lanka." *IESHR* 26 (1989):319-41.

________. "Culture and Social Resistance: Gambling in Colonial Sri Lanka." In *Contesting Power: Resistance and Everyday Social Relations in South Asia*, pp. 175-212. Edited by Douglas Haynes & Gyan Prakash. Oxford: Oxford UP, 1991; Berkeley: University of California Press, 1992.

Rorty, Richard. "A Pragmatist View of Rationality and Cultural Difference." *Philosophy East and West* 42, 4 (Oct. 1992):581-96 [comments on Ashis Nandy].

Routledge, Paul. "Modernity as a vision of conquest: development and culture in India." *Cultural Survival Qtly.* 11, 3 (1987):63-66.

________. "Putting politics in its place: Baliapal, India as a terrain of resistance." *Political Geography* 11, 6 (Nov. 1992):588-611.

Roy, Arundahti. "Over the (Electric) Moon." *Sunday* (12-18 April 1992):76-84.

Roy, Debal K. Singha. *Women in Peasant Movements: Tebhaga, Naxalite and After*. Delhi: Manohar Publishers, 1992.

Roy, Kumkum. "The King's Household: Structure/Space in the Sastric Tradition." *EPW* 27, 43-44 (24-31 October 1992):WS55-60.

Roy, Ramashray; Walker, R. B. J.; and Ashley, Richard K. "Dialogue: Towards a Critical Social Theory of International Politics." *Alternatives* 13, 1 (January 1988):77-102.

Rubin, Arnold. "Tattoo Trends in Gujarat." In *Marks of Civilization: Artistic Transformations of the Human Body*, pp. 140-53. Edited by Arnold Rubin. Los Angeles: Museum of Cultural History, University of California, 1988.

Rudolph, Lloyd. "The Media and Cultural Politics." *EPW* 27, 28 (11 July 1992):1489-96.

Rushdie, Salman. *Midnight's Children*. New York: Alfred Knopf, 1980; various other editions.

________. *Shame*. London: Cape; New York: Alfred Knopf, 1983.

________. *Satanic Verses*. New York and London: Viking, 1988.

________. *Imaginary Homelands: Essays and Criticism 1981-1991*. London: Granta/Penguin, 1991.

Ruthven, Malise. *Salman Rushdie and the Rage of Islam*. London: Chatto & Windus, 1990.

Saberwal, Satish. *India: The Roots of Crisis*. New Delhi: Oxford UP, 1986.

________. "On the Rise of Institutions, or, the Church and Kingship in Medieval Europe." *Studies in History* 7 (1991):107-34.

________. "Segmentation and Literacy." *EPW* 26 (Annual No. 1991):723-738.

________. "On the Making of Europe: Reflections from Delhi." *History Workshop Journal*, no. 33 (1992):145-51.

Sabin, Margery. "The Suttee Romance." *Raritan* 11, 2 (Fall 1991):1-24.

Sahai, Malti. "Raj Kapoor and the Indianization of Charlie Chaplin." *East-West Film Journal* 2, 1 (Dec. 1987):62-76.

Sahni, Kalpana. "Oriental Phantoms." *Social Scientist* 16, 7 (July 1986):36-45.

Sakata, Hiromi Lorraine. "Musicians Who Do Not Perform; Performers who are not Musicians." *Asian Music* 17,1 (Fall/Winter 1985).

Samaraweera, Vijaya. "The 'Village Community' and Reform in Colonial Sri Lanka." *Ceylon J. of Historical and Social Studies* (New Series) 8 (1980):68-75.

Sandahl, Stella. "To Psychoanalyse a Civilization." *Journal of Indian Philosophy* 10 (1982): 299-303.

Sangari, Kumkum. "The Changing Text." *Journal of Arts and Ideas*, no. 8 (July-Sept. 1984):61-76.

________."Marquez and the Politics of the Possible." *Journal of Arts and Ideas*, no. 10 (Dec. 1985):37-48, 53-58; also published in *Cultural Critique*, no. 7 (Fall 1987):157-79.

________. "Of Ladies, Gentlemen, and the Short Cut: *The Portrait of a Lady*." In *Woman/Image/Text*. Edited by Lola Chatterjee. Delhi: Trianka, 1986.

________. "Perpetuating the Myth." *Seminar* [special issue on Sati], no. 342 (Feb. 1988):24-30; reprinted in *Sati,* ed. Mulk Raj Anand (1990).

________. "Mirabai and the Spritual Economy of Bhakti." *EPW* 15, 27-28 (7, 14 July 1990); also published as Occasional Papers, 2nd series, no. 29, New Delhi: NMML, 1990.

________. "Figures for the Unconscious." *Journal of Arts and Ideas*, nos. 20-21 (1991):67-84.

________. "Relating Histories: Literature, Literacy and Gender in Early Nineteenth Century Calcutta and England." In *Rethinking English*, pp. 32-123. Edited by Swati Joshi. Delhi: Trianka, 1991; also published as Occasional Paper, NMML.

________. "Consent, Agency and Rhetorics of Incitement." *EPW* 28, 18 (1 May 1993):867-882.

Sangari, Kumkum and Vaid, Sudesh. "Sati in Modern India." *EPW* 16, 31 (August 1981).

________. "Institutions, Ideologies, Beliefs: Widow Immolation in Contemporary Rajasthan." *EPW* (7 and 14 July 1990).

________, eds. *Women and Culture*. Bombay: S.N.D.T. University Monographs, 1985.

________, eds. *Recasting Women*. Delhi: Kali for Women, 1989; New Brunswick: Rutgers UP, 1990.

Sangwan, Satpal. *Science, Technology and Colonisation: An Indian Experience 1757-1857*. Delhi: Anamika Prakashan, 1991.

Sanyal, Hitesranjan. "Trends of Change in the Bhakti Movement in Bengal." Occasional Paper, no. 76. Calcutta: CSSS, 1985.

Sardar, Ziauddin. *Information and the Muslim World: A Strategy for the Twenty-First Century*. London: Mansell, 1988.

________. "Science and Health: Medicine and Metaphysics." In *The Revenge of Athena*, pp. 106-119. Edited by Z. Sardar. London & New York: Mansell Publishing, 1988.

________. "Surviving the Terminator: The Postmodern Mental Condition." *Futures* 22, 2 (March 1990):203-10.

________. "Total Recall: Aliens, 'Others', and Amnesia in Postmodernist Thought." *Futures* 23, 2 (March 1991):189-203.

________. "Paper, printing and compact disks: the making and unmaking of Islamic culture." *Media, Culture and Society* 15, 1 (January 1993): 43-59.

________, ed. *The Revenge of Athena: Science, Exploitation & the Third World*. London & New York: Mansell Publishing, 1988.

Sardar, Ziauddin and Davies, Merryl Wyn. *Distorted Imagination: Lessons from the Rushdie Affair*. London: Gray Seal Books, 1990.

Sarkar, Saral. "Marxism and Productive Forces: A Critique." *Alternatives* 9, 1 (March 1983):145-76.

Sarkar, Sumit. *Modern India, 1885-1947*. Delhi: Macmillan, 1983.

________. *'Popular Movements' and 'Middle Class' Leadership in Late Colonial India: Problems and Perspectives of a 'History from Below.'* Calcutta: K. P. Bagchi, for CSSS, 1983.

________. "The Conditions and Nature of Subaltern Militancy: Bengal from Swadeshi to Non-Co-operation, c. 1905-22." In *Subaltern Studies III*, pp. 271-320. Edited by Ranajit Guha. Delhi: Oxford UP, 1984.

________. *A Critique of Colonial India*. Calcutta: Papyrus, 1985.

________. "Social History: Predicament and Possibilities." In *Fresh Perspec-*

tives on India and Pakistan: Essays on Economics, Politics, and Culture, pp. 256-74. Edited by Iqbal Khan. Oxford, 1985.

Sarkar, Sumit. "The *Kathamrita* as a Text." Occasional Papers on History and Society, no. 22. New Delhi: NMML, 1986.

________. "The Kalki-Avatar of Bikrampur: A Village Scandal in Early Twentieth Century Bengal." In *Subaltern Studies VI*, pp. 1-53. Edited by Ranajit Guha. Delhi: Oxford UP, 1989.

________. "Ramakrishna and the Calcutta of His Times." In *The Calcutta Psyche*, pp. 99-121. Edited by Geeti Sen. New Delhi: Rupa & Co. and India International Centre, 1990-91.

________. *Marxian Approaches to the History of Indian Nationalism*. Presidency College Historical Pamphlets, no. 1. New Delhi & Calcutta: K. P. Bagchi, 1990. Reprinted in *The Book Review* 15, 4 (July-Aug. 1991):17-20.

Sarkar, Tanika. *Bengal, 1928-1934: The Politics of Protest*. Delhi: Oxford UP, 1987.

________. "The Woman as Communal Subject: Rashtrasevika Samiti and Ram Janmabhoomi Movement." *EPW* (31 August 1991):2057-2062.

Sarkar, Tanika and Butalia, Urvashi, eds. *Women of the Hindu Right: A Collection of Essays*. New Delhi: Kali for Women, forthcoming [1995].

Sastrowardoyo, Robi Sularto. "Identity in Diversity." *Jrl. of Arts and Ideas*, no. 7 (April-June 1984):53-64.

Saunders, Rebecca Ann. "Gender, Colonialism, and Exile: Flora Annie Steel and Sara Jeannette Duncan in India." In *Women's Writing in Exile*, pp. 303-24. Edited by Mary Lynn Broe and Angela Ingram. Chapel Hill: Univ. of North Carolina Press, 1989.

________. "The Politics of Exile: Links between Feminism and Imperialism: British and North American Women Writers in India — Sara Jeanette Duncan, Flora Annie Steel, Maud Diver, Margaret Wilson." Ph. D. Dissertation, abstracted in *Dissertation Abstracts International* 51, 6 (Dec. 1990):2029A.

Sax, William S. *Mountain Goddess: Gender and Politics in a Himalayan Pilgrimage*. New York: Oxford UP, 1991.

Sayer, Derek. "British Reaction to the Amritsar Massacre, 1919-1920." In *Crossing Cultures: Essays in the Displacement of Western Civilization*, pp. 142-81. Edited by Daniel Segal. Tuscon and London: Univ. of Arizona Press, 1992. A slightly different version published in *Past and Present* 131 (1991).

Schechner, Richard. "The Ramlila of Ramnagar"; "Perfomer Training

Interculturally"; and "Performers and Spectators Transported and Transformed", all in *Between Theater and Anthropology*. Philadelphia: Univ. of Pennsylvania Press, 1985.

Schechner, Richard. "Magnitudes of Performance." In *Performance Theory*. London & New York: Routledge, 1988.

________. *Performative Circumstances from the Avant Garde to Ramlila*. Calcutta: Seagull Books, 1990.

________. "Wayang Kulit in the Colonial Margin", and "Striding Through the Cosmos", in *The Future of Ritual: Writings on Culture and Performance*. London & New York: Routledge, 1993.

Schomer, Karine. *Mahadevi Varma and the Chhayavad Age of Modern Hindi Poetry*. Berkeley: Univ. of California Press, 1983.

Schwarz, Henry. "Provocations Toward a Theory of Third World Literature." *Mississippi Review* 49/50 (1989):177-201.

Scott, David. "The Demonology of Nationalism: On the Anthropology of Ethnicity and Violence in Sri Lanka." *Economy and Society* 19, 4 (1990):491-510.

________. "The Cultural Poetics of Eyesight in Sri Lanka: Composure, Vulnerability, and the Sinhala Concept of *Distiya*." *Dialetical Anthropology* 16, 1 (1991):85-102.

Scott, David. "Conversion and Demonism: Colonial Christian Discourse and Religion in Sri Lanka." *CSSH* 34, 2 (April 1992):331-65.

________. *Formations of Ritual: Colonial and Anthropological Discourses on the Sinhala Yaktovil*. Minneapolis: Univ. of Minnesota Press, 1994.

Scrase, Timothy J. *Image, Ideology and Inequality: Cultural Domination, Hegemony and Schooling in India*. New Delhi: Sage Publications, 1993.

Seabrook, Jeremy. *Life and Labour in a Bombay Slum*. London & New York: Quartet, 1987.

Seed, David. "Disorientation and Commitment in the Fiction of Empire: Kipling and Orwell." *Dutch Quarterly Review of Anglo-American Letters* 14, 4 (1984):269-80.

Seigel, Lee. *Laughing Matters: Comic Tradition in India*. Chicago: Univ. of Chicago Press, 1987; Delhi: Motilal Banarsidass, 1980.

________. *Net of Magic: Wonders and Deceptions in India*. Chicago: Univ. of Chicago Press, 1991.

Seminar. Issue on "The Sexist Media: A Symposium on How Patriarchy Exploits the Woman." No. 300. August, 1984.

________. Issue on "Purdah Culture." No. 318. February, 1986.

Sen, Amartya. "Gender and Cooperative-Conflict." In *Persistent Inqequalities*. Edited by Irene Tinker. New York: Oxford UP, 1990.

Sen, Anup Kumar. "A Discourse on Nineteenth Century Bengal." *EPW* 26, 1-2 (5-12 Jan. 1991):66-68 [on Sumanta Banerjee's *The Parlour and The Street]*.

Sen, Asok. "'Subaltern Studies': Tinti ba Du-ti prashna ja ami karte pari" [in Bengali]. *Anustup* (Autumn 1985).

________. "Subaltern Studies: Capital, Class and Community." In *Subaltern Studies* V, pp. 203-35. Edited by Ranajit Guha. Delhi: Oxford UP, 1987.

________. *The Limits of 'Economic Man'*. Occasional Paper, no. 112. Calcutta: CSSS, 1989.

Sen, Geeti. *The Mind's Eye*: *Meera Mukherjee, Jogen Chowdhury, Ganesh Pyne, Arpita Singh, and Manjit Bawa*. Calcutta: Seagull Books, 1990.

________, ed. *The Calcutta Psyche*. Delhi: India International Centre and Rupa & Co., 1990-91.

Sen, Gita and Caren Grown. *Development Crises and Alternative Visions*: *Third World Women's Perspectives*. New York: Monthly Review Press, 1987.

Sen Gupta, Suddhabrata. "Sexual Politics of Television Mythology." *EPW* 26, 45 (9 Nov. 1991):2558-60. [See Janaky, "On the Trail of the Mahabharata: A Response", *EPW* 27, 37 (12 Sept. 1992):1997-99.]

Sen, Ilina, ed. *A Space within the Struggle — Women's Participation in People's Movements*. New Delhi: Kali for Women, 1990.

Sen, Indrani. "Jean Genet and Colonialism." *Jrl. of Arts and Ideas*, no. 9 (Oct.-Dec. 1984):85-92.

Sen, Surojit. "A Passage to India: The Book and the Film." *Splice*, no. 1 (Jan.-March 1986):14-18.

Sena, Vinod and Verma, Rajiva. *New Essays on T. S. Eliot*. New Delhi: Oxford UP,1992.

Sequiera, Isaac. "The Study of Popular Culture in India: a Frontier Situation." *International Jrl. of Popular Culture* 2, 1 (1981):6-11.

________. "India." *Journal of Popular Culture* 20, 2 (Fall 1986):123-92.

Sethi, Harsh. "Culture as Politics or Politics as Culture." *EPW* 22, 12 (21 March 1987).

________. "Towards an Anthropology of Power." *EPW* 26, 19 (11 May 1991):1216-18 [review of Raj Thapar's *All These Years* (1990)].

________. "The Politics of Health in India." *National Medical Journal of India* 5, 2 (March-April 1992).

Sethia, Tara. "Railways, Raj, and the Indian States: Policy of Collaboration and Coercion in Hyderabad." In *Railway Imperialism*, pp. 103-120. Contributions in Comparative Colonial Studies, No. 26. Edited by

Clarence B. Davis & Kenneth E. Wilburn, Jr. Westport, Conn.: Greenwood Press, 1991.

Shahani, Kumar. "Film as a Contemporary Art." *Social Scientist*, no. 202 (March 1990):33-59.

________. "Notes Towards an Aesthetic of Cinema Sound." *Jrl. of Arts and Ideas*, no. 5, reprinted in *Framework*, nos. 30/31 (1986).

________. "Interrogating Internationalism." *Jrl. of Arts and Ideas*, no. 19 (May 1990):5-19.

Shaheed, Farida. "Legal Systems, Islam and Women in Pakistan." *Ethnic Studies Report* 3, 1 (1985).

Shaikh, Farzana. "The language of representation: towards a Muslim political order in nineteenth-century India." In *Language, History and Class*, pp. 204-26. Edited by Penelope J. Corfield. Oxford: Basil Blackwell, 1991.

Shankaranarayanam, Vasanthi. "The goddess-chattel syndrome: Representation of Women in Malayalam Cinema." *Deep Focus* 3, 1 (1990):66-74.

Shanmugaratnam, N. "Development and Environment: a View from the South." *Race and Class* 29, 3 (Jan.-March 1989), Special Issue, 'Un-Greening the Third World'.

Sharma, Dhirendra. "Anti-nuclear Movement in India." *Science as Critique*, no. 12 (1991).

Sharma, Kumud. "Women in Struggle: A Case Study of the Chipko Movement." *Samya Shakti*: *A Journal of Women's Studies* 1, 2 (1984):58 ff.

Sharma, Ram. *Architecture in India.* Paris: Electa Moniteur, 1985.

Sharma, Suresh. "Cultural Survival in the Age of Progress." *Alternatives* 13, 4 (October 1988):485-513.

Sharma, T. R. S. "Chinua Achebe and V. S. Naipaul: One Version and Two Postures on Post-Colonial Societies." In *The Colonial and the Neo-Colonial Encounters in Commonwealth Literature*, pp. 83-93. Mysore: Prasaragana Univ., 1983.

Sharpe, Jennifer. "Scenes of an Encounter: A Double Discourse of Colonialism and Nationalism." Ph. D. Dissertation, 1988. Abstracted in *Dissertation Abstracts Intl.* 48, 10 (April 1988):2623A.

Sharpe, Jenny. "Figures of Colonial Resistance." *Modern Fiction Studies* 35, 1 (Spring 1989):137-55.

________. "The Unspeakable Limits of Rape: Colonial Violence and Counter-Insurgency." *Genders*, no. 10 (Spring 1991):24-46.

________. *Allegories of Empire: The Figure of Woman in the Colonial Text.* Minneapolis: U. of Minnesota Press, 1993.

Sharpe, Jenny. "The Violence of Light in the Land of Desire; or, How William Jones Discovered India." *boundary* 2 20, 2 (Summer 1993):26-46.

Sharrad, Paul. "The Books behind the Film: Paul Scott's Raj Quartet." *East-West Film Journal* 1, 2 (June 1987):60-77.

Sheikh, Ghulam Mohammed. "Viewer's View: Looking at Pictures." In *Interrogating Modernity: Culture and Colonialism in India*. Edited by Tejaswini Niranjana, P. Sudhir, and Vivek Dhareshwar. Calcutta: Seagull Books, 1993.

Sheth, D. L. "Grass-roots Stirrings and the Future of Politics." *Alternatives* 9, 1 (March 1983):1-24.

________. "Movements, Intellectuals and the State: Social Policy in Nation-Building." *EPW* 27, 8 (22 February 1992):425-29.

Shiva, Vandana. "Ecology Movements in India." *Alternatives* 11, 2 (April 1986):255-73.

________. "The Violence of Reductionist Science." *Alternatives* 12, 2 (April 1987):243-61. Reprinted as "Reductionist Science as Epistemological Violence" in *Science, Hegemony and Violence*, pp. 232-56. Edited by Ashis Nandy. Delhi: Oxford UP, 1992 [1988].

________. *Staying Alive: Women, Ecology and Survival in India*. London: Zed Books, 1988; Delhi: Kali for Women, 1988.

________. *Violence of the Green Revolution: Ecological Degradation and Political Conflict in Punjab*. Dehra Dun: Research Foundation for Science and Ecology, 1989.

________. *Ecology and the Politics of Survival: Conflicts over Natural Resources in India*. New Delhi: United Nations University Press, 1991.

________. "Let us Survive: Women, Ecology and Development." *Sangarsh*, no. 3 [Bangalore], n.d.

________, ed. *Minding Our Lives: Women from the South and North Reconnect Ecology and Health*. New Delhi: Kali for Women, 1993.

Shiva, Vandana and Bandyopadhyay, Jayanta. "The History, Structure and Impact of the Chipko Movement." *Mountain Research & Development* 6, 2 (1986):113-41.

________. "Chipko." *Seminar*, no. 330 (February 1987).

________. "The Large and Fragile Community of Scientists in India." *New Quest*, no. 79 (Jan.-Feb. 1990):5-22.

Shrivastava, Aseem. "Overpopulation: The Great Red Herring?" *EPW* 27, 38 (19 Sept. 1992):2032-38.

Shukla, Sonal. "Cultivating Minds: 19th Century Gujarati Women's Journals." *EPW* 26, 43 (26 Oct. 1991):WS-63 ff.

Shulman, David. "Battle as Metaphor in Tamil Folk and Classical Traditions." In *Another Harmony*, pp. 105-30. Edited by Stuart Blackburn and A. K. Ramanujan. Berkeley: Univ. of California Press, 1986.

________. *The King and the Clown in South Indian Myth and Poetry*. Princeton, New Jersey: Princeton UP, 1985.

Siddiqi, Majid Hayat. "History and Society in a Popular Rebellion: Mewat, 1920-1933." *CSSH* (1986):442-67.

________. "Bluff, Doubt and Fear: The Kheiri Brothers and the Colonial State, 1904-45." *IESHR* 24, 3 (July-Sept. 1987):233-63.

Simeon, Dilip. "Communalism in Modern India: A Theoretical Examination." *Social Science Probings* 4, 1 (March 1987).

Singer, Milton, *et al.* "Boundaries of Power, Boundaries of Communication." *Working Papers and Proceedings of the Center for Psychosocial Studies*, nos. 42-46. Chicago: Center for Psychosocial Studies, 1991.

Singh, K. S. *Tribal Society in India: An Anthropo-historical Perspective*. New Delhi, 1985.

________. *History of the Anthropological Survey of India*. Calcutta: Seagull Books, 1992.

________. *Visual Anthropology and India*. Calcutta: Seagull Books, 1992.

Singh, Madan Gopal. "Through the Realist Defile." *Jrl. of Arts and Ideas*, nos. 20-21 (March 1991):85-97.

Singh, Namvar. "Decolonising the Indian Mind", trans. Harish Trivedi. *Indian Literature* 35, 5 (Sept.-Oct. 1992):145-56.

Singh, Randhir. "Theorising Communalism — A Fragmentary Note in the Marxist Mode." *EPW* (23 July 1888):1541-48.

Singha, Radhika. "A 'despotism of law': British criminal justice and public authority in North India, 1872-1837." Unpublished Ph.D. Dissertation, Cambridge University, 1990.

________. "'Providential' Circumstances: The Thuggee Campaign of the 1830's and Legal Innovation." *Modern Asian Studies* 27, 1 (Feb. 1993):83-146.

Sinha, Mrinalini. "Gender and Imperialism: Colonial Policy and the Ideology of Moral Imperialism in Late Nineteenth-Century Bengal." In *Changing Men: New Directions in Research of Men and Masculinity*. Edited by Michael S. Kimmel. London: Sage, 1987.

Sircar, Ajanta. "Imagining Metropolitan Subjectivity: Salman Rushdie's *Midnight's Children* and Amitav Ghosh's *The Shadow Lines*." Unpublished M.Phil. Dissertation, Department of English, University of Hyderabad, 1991.

Sircar, Ajanta. "Individualising History: The 'Real' Self in *The Shadow Lines*." *Social Scientist*, no. 223 (Dec. 1991):33-46.

________. "Production of Authenticity: The Indo-Anglian Critical Tradition." *EPW* 27, 36 (5 Sept. 1992):1921-26.

Sivanandan, A. *A Different Hunger: Writings on Black Resistance*. London: Pluto, 1982.

________. "Sri Lanka: Racism and the Politics of Underdevelopment." *Race and Class* 25, 1 (Summer 1984):1-38.

________. *Communities of Resistance: Writings on Black Struggles for Socialism*. London: Verso, 1990.

Sivaramakrishnan, Arvind. "The Slave with Two Hearts: The Asymmetry of Cultural Assimilation." *Third Text*, no. 7 (Summer 1989):3-10.

________. "Percipere aut Percipi: Reading of Readings." *IICQ* 20, 1-2 (Spring-Summer 1993):251-63.

Sivathamby, Karthigesu. *The Tamil Film as a Medium of Political Communication*. Madras: New Century, 1981.

Skillman, Teri. "The Bombay Hindi Film Song Genre: A Historical Survey." *Yearbook for Traditional Music* 18 (1986):133-44.

Smith, Richard Saumarez. "Rule-by-Records and Rule-by-Reports: Complementary Aspects of the British Imperial Rule of Law." *CIS* 19, 1 (1985):153-76.

Southhall Black Sisters. *Against the Grain: A Celebration of Survival and Struggle*. London, 1990.

Souza, Francis N. "Nirvana of a Maggot . . ." *Third Text*, no. 19 (Summer 1992):41-48.

Spitz, Pierre. "Food Systems and Society in India: The Origins of An Interdisciplinary Approach." *International Social Science Journal* 37, 3 (1985):371-88.

Spivak, Gayatri Chakravorty. "Can the Subaltern Speak? Speculations on Widow Sacrifice." *Wedge*, nos. 7/8 (Winter/Spring 1985):120-30. Also in *Marxism and the Interpretation of Culture*, pp. 271-313. Edited by Gary Nelson and Lawrence Gorssberg. Urbana: Univ. of Illinois Press, 1988.

________. "The Rani of Sirmur." In *Europe and Its Others*. Edited by Francis Barker et al. Colchester: Univ. of Essex, 1985.

________. "Imperialism and Sexual Difference." *Oxford Literary Review* 8, 1-2 (1986):225-40.

________. *In Other Worlds: Essays in Cultural Politics*. New York: Routledge, 1987; reprint ed., Calcutta: Seagull Books, 1990.

Spivak, Gayatri Chakravorty. "Feminism and Deconstruction, Again." In *Between Feminism and Psychoanalysis*. Edited by Teresa Brennan. London and New York: Routledge, 1989.

________. "In a Word." Interview with Ellen Rooney. *Differences* 1, 2 (Summer 1989):124-56.

________. "The Political Economy of Women." In *Coming to Terms: Feminism, Theory, Politics*. Edited by Elizabeth Weed. New York: Routledge, 1989.

________. "Reading *The Satanic Verses*." *Public Culture* 2, 1 (Fall 1989): 79-99.

________. "Who Claims Alterity?" *In Remaking History*, pp. 269-92. Edited by Barbara Kruger and Phil Mariani. Dia Art Foundation, Discussions in Contemporary Culture, Number 4. Seattle: Bay Press, 1989.

________. "Constitutions and Culture Studies." *Yale Jrl. of Law and the Humanities* 2, 1 (1990):133-47.

________. "Inscriptions of Truth to Size." In *Inscription* (exhibition catalogue, Dunlop Art Gallery, Regina, Saskatchewan, 15 Sept.-21 Oct. 1990), pp. 9-11, 14-15.

________. "The Making of Americans, the Teaching of English, and the Future of Cultural Studies." *New Literary History* 21, 4 (1990):781-98.

________. *The Post-Colonial Critic: Interviews, Strategies, Dialogues*. Ed. Sarah Harasym. New York: Routledge, 1990.

________. "Poststructuralism, Postcoloniality, Marginality, and Value." In *Literary Theory Today*, pp. 219-44. Edited by Peter Collier and Helga Geyer-Ryan. Cambridge: Polity, 1990.

________. "Versions of the Margin: Coetzee's *Foe* reading Defoe's *Crusoe/ Roxana*." In *Theory and Its Consequences*. Edited by Jonathan Arac and Barbara Johnson. Baltimore: Johns Hopkins UP, 1990.

________. "Feminism in Colonization." *Differences* 3, 3 (1991):139-70.

________. "Identity and Alterity." An interview with Nikos Papastergiadis. *Arena*, no. 97 (1991):65-76.

________. "Neocolonialism and the Secret Agent of Knowledge." *Oxford Literary Review* 13 (1991):220-51.

________. "Time and Timing: Law and History." In *Chronotypes: the Construction of Time*, pp. 99-117. Edited by John Bender and David Wellbery. Stanford: Stanford UP, 1991.

________. "Acting Bits/Identity Talk." *Critical Inquiry* 18, 4 (Summer 1992): 770-803.

________. "Asked to Talk About Myself . . ." *Third Text*, no. 19 (Summer 1992):9-18.

Spivak, Gayatri Chakravorty. "The Burden of English Studies." In *The Lie of the Land: English Literary Studies in India*, pp. 275-99. Edited by Rajeswari Sunder Rajan. New Delhi: Oxford UP, 1992.

________. "Echo." Unpublished ms. Columbia University, Seminar on 'Women and Society', 1992.

________. "French Feminism Revisisted: Ethics and Politics." In *Feminists Theorize the Political*, pp. 54-85. Edited by Judith Butler and Joan W. Scott. New York & London: Routledge, 1992.

________. "More on Power/Knowledge." In *Rethinking Power*, pp. 149-73. Edited by Thomas E. Warternberg. Albany, New York: State Univ. of New York Press, 1992.

________. "The Politics of Translation." In *Destabilzing Theory: Contemporary Feminist Debates*. Edited by Michele Barrett and Anne Phillips. Stanford: Stanford UP, 1992.

________. *Thinking Academic Freedom in Gendered Post-coloniality*. Cape Town: Univ. of Cape Town, 1992.

________. "Woman in Difference: Mahasweta Devi's 'Douloti the Beautiful.' In *Nationalisms and Sexualities*, pp. 96-117. Edited by Andrew Parker, Mary Russo, Doris Sommer, and Patricia Yaeger. New York: Routledge, 1992.

________. Interview with Sara Danius and Stefan Jonsson. *boundary 2* 20, 2 (Summer 1993):24-50.

________. *Outside in the Teaching Machine*. London: Routledge, 1993.

________. "Remembering the Limits: Difference, Identity, and Place." In *Socialism and the Limits of Liberalism*. Edited by Peter Osborne. London: Verso, forthcoming.

Srinath, C. N. *The Literary Landscape: Essays on Indian Fiction and Poetry in English*. Delhi: Mittal, 1986.

Srinivas, K. Ravi. "Popular Culture and Pop Sociology." *EPW* 27, 33 (15 August 1992):1763-64.

Srinivas, M. D. "Logical and Methodological Foundations of Indian Science." In *The Revenge of Athena: Science, Exploitation & the Third World*, pp. 261-89. Edited by Ziauddin Sardar. London & New York: Mansell Publishing, 1988.

Srinivasan, Amrita. "The Hindu Temple Dancer: Prostitute or Nun." *Cambridge Anthropology* 8, 1 (1983):73-99.

________. "Reform and Revival: The Devadasi and Her Dance." *EPW* 20, 44 (1985):1869-76.

________. "Reform or Conformity? Temple 'Prostitution' and the Community in the Madras Presidency." In *State, Community and Household in*

Modernizing Asia. Edited by Bina Agarwal. Delhi: Kali for Women, 1988.

Srinivasan, Cheenu Raman. "Goods and Gods: Cultures of Technology of India, 1900-1990." Unpublished Ph.D. Dissertation, University of Pennsylvania, 1993.

________. "No Free Launch: Designing the Indian National Satellite." Unpublished manuscript, Dept. of History and Sociology of Science, Univ. of Pennsylvania, 1993.

Srivastava, Aruna. "The Empire Writes Back: Language and History.in *Shame* and *Midnight's Children.*" In *Past the Last Post: Theorizing Post-Colonialism and Post-Modernism*, pp. 65-78. Edited by Ian Adam and Helen Tiffin. Calgary: Univ. of Calgary Press, 1990.

Srivastava, Mukesh. "Mosaic of Narrative Manipulations: Power and Production of Subjectivity in (Post) Colonial India." *EPW* 27, 4 (25 January 1992):PE47-57.

Srivastava, Vinay Kumar. The Ethnographer and the People: Reflections on Field Work." *EPW* 26, 22-23 (1-8 June 1991):1408-1414; Pt. II in 26, 24 (15 June 1991):1475-81.

Srivatsan, R. "Looking at Film Hoardings: Labour, Gender, Subjectivity and Everyday Life in India." *Public Culture* 4, 1 (Fall 1991):1-24.

________. "Photography and Society: Icon Building in Action." *EPW* (Annual Number) 26, 11-12 (March 1991):771-88.

________. "Welcoming 'Popular' Critique." *EPW* 27, 49-50 (5-12 Dec. 1992):2667-68.

________. "Imaging Truth and Desire: Photography and the Visual Field in India." In *Interrogating Modernity: Culture and Colonialism in India.* Edited by Tejaswini Niranjana, P. Sudhir, and Vivek Dhareshwar. Calcutta: Seagull Books, 1993.

Stam, Robert. "College Course File: Third World Cinema." *Journal of Film and Video* 36, 4 (Fall 1984):50-61.

Steedman, Carolyn. *The Radical Soldier's Tale*. London: Routledge, 1988.

Stein, Burton. "Notes on 'Peasant Insurgency' in Colonial Mysore: Events and Process." *South Asia Research* 5, 1 (1985):11-27.

________. "State Formation and Economy Reconsidered: Part One." *Modern Asian Studies* 19, 3 (1985):387-413.

________. "A decade of historical efflorescence." *South Asia Research* 10, 2 (Nov. 1990):125-38.

________, ed. *The Making of Agrarian Policy in British India, 1770-1900.* Delhi: Oxford UP, 1992.

Stein, Dorothy K. "Women to Burn: Suttee as a Normative Institution." *Signs* 4, 2 (Winter 1978):253-68.

Stephens, Julie. "Feminist Fictions: A Critique of the Category 'Non-Western Woman' in Feminist Writings on India." In *Subaltern Studies VI*, pp. 92-125. Edited by Ranajit Guha. Delhi: Oxford UP, 1989. And see response by Susie Tharu, pp. 126-31 in same volume.

Stieg, Margaret F. "Indian Romances: Tracts for the Times." *Journal of Popular Culture* 18, 4 (Spring 1985):2-15.

Stirrat, R. L. *Power and Religiosity in a Post-Colonial Setting: Sinhala Catholics in Contemporary Sri Lanka*. Cambridge: Cambridge UP, 1992.

Storey, William K. "Big Cats and Imperialism: Lion and Tiger Hunting in Kenya and Northern India, 1898-1930." *Journal of World History* 2, 2 (Fall 1991):135-73.

Stree Shakti Sangathana. *We Were Making History: Women and the Telengana Uprising*. London: Zed Press; Delhi: Kali for Women, 1990.

Studdert-Kennedy, Gerald. *British Christians, Indian Nationalists and the Raj*. Delhi: Oxford UP, 1992.

Subramaniam, K. N. with Tripathy, Ratnakar. *Flashback — Cinema in the 'Times of India'*. Bombay: Times of India, 1990.

Subramaniam, V. "Karmayoga and the Rise of the Indian Middle Class." *Jrl. of Arts and Ideas*, nos. 14-15 (July-Dec. 1987).

Subramanyam, K. G. *Moving Focus: Essays on Indian Art*. New Delhi: Lalit Kala Akademi, 1978.

________. *Our Friends, the Ogres*. Calcutta: Seagull Books, 1985.

________. *When God first made the animals, he made them all alike*. Calcutta: Seagull Books, 1985.

________. *The Living Tradition: Perspectives on Modern Indian Art*. Calcutta: Seagull Books, 1987.

Subramanyam, Sanjay. "The Tail wags the Dog: Or Some Aspects of the external relations of the *Estado da India*, 1570-1600." *Studies in History* (New Series) 9, 1 (1993):131-46.

________. "The 'Kaffirs of Europe': A comment on Portugal and the historiography of European expansion in Asia." *Studies in History* (New Series) 9, 1 (1993):131-46.

Subramanyam, Sanjay and Thomaz, Luis Filipe. "Evolution of Empire: The Portugese in the Indian Ocean during the 16th century." In *The Political Economy of Merchant Empires*. Edited by James D. Tracy. Cambridge & New York: Cambridge UP, 1991.

Sudhir, P. "Colonialism and the Vocabularies of Dominance." In *Interrogating*

Modernity: Culture and Colonialism in India. Edited by Tejaswini Niranjana, P. Sudhir, and Vivek Dhareshwar. Calcutta: Seagull Books, 1993.

Suleri, Sara. "Amorphous India: Questions of Geography." *Southwest Review* 71, 3 (Summer 1986):389-400.

________. "Naipaul's Arrival." *The Yale Journal of Criticism* 2, 1 (Fall 1988):25-50.

________. "Contraband Histories: Salman Rushdie and the Embodiment of Blasphemy." *The Yale Review* 78, 4 (Summer 1989).

________. *Meatless Days*. Chicago: Univ. of Chicago Press, 1989; paperback ed., 1991.

________. "Whither Rushdie." *Transition*, no. 51 (1991):198-212.

________. "Karachi, 1990." *Raritan* 11, 4 (Spring 1992):50-71.

________. *The Rhetoric of English India*. Chicago: Univ. of Chicago Press, 1992.

________. "Woman Skin Deep: Feminism and the Postcolonial Condition." *Critical Inquiry* 18, 4 (Summer 1992):756-69.

Sullivan, Nancy. "Sangam: Signs of India." *Public Culture* 6, 1 (Fall 1993): 195-99.

Sullivan, Zohreh T. *Narratives of Empire*: *The Fictions of Rudyard Kipling*. New York: Cambridge UP, 1993.

Sundara Rajan, R. *Innovative Competence and Social Change*. Pune: Indian Philosophical Quarterly Publications, 1986. No. 10.

________. *Towards a Critique of Cultural Reason*. ICPR Series in Philosophy of Natural and Social Sciences. Delhi: Oxford UP, 1987.

________. *The Primacy of the Political*. New Delhi: Indian Council for Philosophical Research & Oxford UP, 1991.

________. *Studies in Phenomenology, Hermeneutics, and Deconstruction*. New Delhi: Indian Council for Philosophical Research, 1991.

Sundaram, Ravi. "Modernity and Its Victims." *EPW* 27, 9 (29 February 1992):459-64.

Sutherland, Sally J. M., ed. *Bridging Worlds*: *Studies on Women in South Asia*. Delhi: Oxford UP, 1992.

Tambiah, Stanley J. "Bridewealth and Dowry Revisited: The Position of Women in Sub-Saharan Africa and North India." *Current Anthropology* 30, 4 (Aug.-Oct. 1989):413-35.

Thakurta, Tapati Guha. "Westernization and Tradition in South Indian Painting in the Nineteenth Century: The Case of Raja Ravi Varma (1848-1906)." *Studies in History* 2, 2 (July-Dec. 1986):165-98.

________. "Artists, Artisans and Mass Picture Production in Late Nineteenth-

and Early Twentieth-Century Calcutta: The Changing Iconography of Popular Prints." *South Asia Research* 8, 1 (1988):3-45.

Thakurta, Tapati Guha. "Women as 'Calendar Art' Icons: Emergence of Pictorial Stereotype in Colonial India." *EPW* 26, 43 (26 Oct. 1991): WS-91 ff.

________. *The Making of a New 'Indian' Art: Artists, Aesthetics and Nationalism in Bengal, c. 1850-1920*. Cambridge: Cambridge UP, 1992.

Thapan, Meenakshi. "Sociology in India: A View from Within." *EPW* 26, 19 (11 May 1991):1229-34.

Thapar, Romila. "Epic and History: Tradition, Dissent and Politics in India." *Past and Present*, no. 125 (1989):3-26.

________. "Imagined Religious Communities? Ancient History and the Modern Search for a Hindu Identity." *Modern Asian Studies* 23, 2 (May 1989):209-31.

________. "Communalism and the Historical Legacy: Some Facts." *Social Scientist*, nos. 205-6 (June-July 1990):4-20.

________. *Interpreting Early India*. Delhi: Oxford UP, 1992; Oxford India Paperback, 1993.

________. "Interpretations of Indian History." In converation with Kunal Chakrabarti and Geeti Sen. *IICQ* 20, 1-2 (Spring-Summer 1993): 115-35.

Tharu, Susie. "Decoding [Mulk Raj] Anand's Humanism." *Kunapipi* 4, 2 (1982):30-41.

________. "Constructing the Orient." *New Quest* 43 (Jan.-Feb. 1984):53-58.

________. "Third World Women's Cinema: Notes on Narrative, Reflections on Opacity." *EPW* 21, 20 (17 May 1986):864-66.

________. "Thinking the Nation Out: Some Reflections on Nationalism and Theory." *Jrl. of Arts and Ideas*, nos. 17-18 (June 1989):81-89.

________. "Tracing Savitri's Pedigree: Victorian Racism and the Image of Women in Indo-Anglian Literature." In *Recasting Women*, pp. 254-68. Edited by Kumkum Sangari and Sudesh Vaid. New Delhi: Kali for Women, 1989.

________. "Introducing Anveshi." *Lokayan Bulletin* 8, 3 (May-June 1990): 59-63.

________. "Women Writing in India." *Jrl. of Arts and Ideas*, nos. 20-21 (March 1991):49-66.

Tharu, Susie and Lalita, K. "Empire, Nation, and the Literary Text." In *Interrogating Modernity: Culture and Colonialism in India*. Edited by Tejaswini Niranjana, P. Sudhir, and Vivek Dhareshwar. Calcutta: Seagull Books, 1993.

Tharu, Susie and Lalita, K, eds. *Women Writing in India*. 2 vols. New York: Feminist Press: Volume 1, 1991; Volume 2, 1993. Volume 1 reprinted as Oxford India paperback, 1992. [Review of Vol. 1 by Meenakshi Mukherjee, "Recovering 'Lost' Texts", *Jrl. of Arts and Ideas*, no. 22 (April 1992):7-18.

Third Text, special issue entitled "The Other Story: AfroAsian Artists in Britain", Nos.8/9 (1989), with contributions from Geeta Kapur (writing on Francis Newton Souza) and Shelagh Hourahane (writing on Avtarjeet Dhanjal).

Third Text, special issue entitled "Beyond the Rushdie Affair", No. 11 (Summer 1990), with contributions from, among others, Ali A. Mazrui, Gayatri Spivak, Tariq Madood, Rustom Bharucha, and Ashis Nandy.

Thomas, Rosie. "Indian Cinema: Pleasures and Popularity." *Screen* 26 (1985):116-31.

________. "Sanctity and Scandal: The Mythologization of Mother India." *Quarterly Rv. of Film and Video* 11, 3 (1986).

Tillotson, G. H. R. *The Tradition of Indian Architecture: Continuity, Controversy, and Change since 1850*. New Haven: Yale UP, 1989.

Tirumalesh, K. V. "Writing-English versus Writing-in-English: New Notes on an Old Theme." *EPW* 26, 47 (23 Nov. 1991):2670-72.

Tiwari, Laxmi G. *The Splendor of Worship: Women's Fasts, Rituals, Stories and Art*. Delhi: Manohar, 1991.

Tulika, Amrita. "Science and History." *EPW* 27, 48 (28 Nov. 1992):2600-02 [review of *Bharat ki Chaap* by Chayanika Shah, Suhas Paranjpe, and Swatija Manorama].

Tull, Barbara Mitchell, ed. *Affectionately, Rachel: Letters from India, 1860-1884*. Athens, Ohio: Ohio State University Press, 1992.

Tyagi, Amita and Uberoi, Ptricia. "Adjustment is the Key: Postmarital Romance in Popular Indian Fiction." *Manushi*, no. 61 (Nov.-Dec. 1990):15-21.

Uberoi, J. P. Singh. *Science and Culture*. Delhi: Oxford UP, 1978.

________. *The Other Mind of Europe: Goethe as a Scientist*. Delhi: Oxford UP, 1984.

________. "Right, Left, and Centre in the Science of Nature." In *Hind Swaraj: A Fresh Look*, pp. 106-111. Edited by Nageshwar Prasad. New Delhi: Gandhi Peace Foundation, 1985.

________. "The Other European Science of Nature?" *Journal of Indian Council of Philosophical Research* 5, 1 (Sept.-Dec. 1987).

Uberoi, Patricia. "Feminine Identity and National Ethos in Indian Calendar Art." *EPW* (28 April 1990).

Uberoi, Patricia. "Some Reflections on Teaching the Sociology of Gender." *Samya Shakti* Vols. 4-5 (1989-90):279-89.

Upreti, H. C. and Upreti, Nandini. *The Myth of Sati: Some Dimensions of Widow Burning*. Delhi: Motilal Banarsidass, 1991.

Vaid, Baldev Krishna. "The Burden of Ambivalence and Dialogue with the West." *Bahuvachan: An Occasional of the Arts and Ideas* (1988): 87-94.

Vaid, Sudesh. "Ideologies on Women in Nineteenth Century Britain, 1850s-70s." *EPW* 20, 43 (26 Oct. 1985):WS63-67.

Vaid, Sudesh and Sangari, Kumkum. "Institutions, Beliefs, Ideologies: Widow Immolation in Contemporary Rajasthan." *EPW* 26, 17 (27 April 1991):WS2-18.

Vaidyanathan, T. G. "Authority and Identity in India." *Daedalus* (Fall 1989): 147-69.

Valicha, Kishore. "Femininity and the Indian Film." *Cinema India International* 5, 1 (1988).

________. *Moving Image: A Study of Indian Cinema*. London: Sangam Books, 1988.

________. "Sex and the Indian Film." *New Quest*, no. 75 (May-June 1989): 167-69.

________. Indian Cinema: Mahesh Bhatt's *Arth* — A textual analysis." *New Quest*, no. 80 (March-April 1990):107-14.

________. "Repetitiveness as a Structuring Principle in Indian Cinema: Some Considerations." *New Quest*, no. 83 (Sept.-Oct. 1990):299-301.

________. "The Image of Ashok Kumar." *New Quest*, no. 87 (May-June 1991):171-75.

van der Veer, Peter. "God must be liberated! A Hindu liberation movement in Ayodhya." *Modern Asian Studies* 21 (1987).

________. *Gods on Earth: The Management of Religious Experience and Identity in a North Indian Pilgrimage Centre*. London: Athlone Press, 1988. LSE Monographs on Social Anthropology, 59.

________. "Satanic or Angelic? The Politics of Religious and Literary Inspiration." *Public Culture* 2, 1 (Fall 1989):100-5.

________. "Hindu 'Nationalism' and the discourse of 'modernity': The Vishva Hindu Parishad." In *The Dynamics of Fundamentalist Movements* Edited by Martin Marty and S. Appleby. Chicago: Univ. of Chicago Press, 1991.

________. "Ayodhya and Somnath: Eternal Shrines, Contested Histories." *Social Research* 59, 1 (Spring 1992):85-110.

van Erven, Eugene. "The Theatre of Liberation of India, Indonesia, and the Philippines." *Australasian Drama Studies* 10 (April 1987):5-18.

Vanaik, Achin. "The Indian Left." *New Left Review*, no. 159 (Sept./Oct. 1986):49-80.

________. *The Painful Transition: Bourgeois Democracy in India*. London: Verso, 1990.

Varma, Pavan K. "Do Indians Have a Sense of History?" *Times of India Review of Books* 1, 1 (August-Sept. 1990):42-43 [review of Nirmal Verma's *Word and Memory*].

Varma, Vijaya Shankar. "Bhopal: The Unfolding of a Tragedy." *Alternatives* 11, 1 (Jan. 1986):133-45.

Vasavada, Ravindra, compiler. *Reflections*: a volume of essays issued to commemorate the National Convention of the Indian Institute of Architects held in Ahmedabad in February 1987. Ahmedabad: Indian Institute of Architects, 1987.

Vassanji, M. G. *Gunny Sack*. Oxford and Portsmouth, N.H.: Heinemann, 1989. African Writers Series.

________. *No New Land*. Toronto: McClelland & Stewart, 1991.

________, ed. *A Meeting of Streams: South Asian Canadian Literature*. Toronto: T[oronto] S[outh] A[sian] R[eview] Publications, 1985.

Vasudev, Aruna and Lenglet, Phillipe, eds. *Indian Cinema Superbazaar*. Delhi: Vikas Publishing House, 1983. [Review by Sanjeev Prakash, "Genres in Indian Cinema", *Jrl. of Arts and Ideas*, no. 9 (Oct.-Dec. 1984):23ff.]

Vasudeva, Sunita and Chakravarty, Pradip. "The epistemology of Indian mass communication research." *Media, Culture and Society* 11, 4 (Oct. 1989):415-33.

Vasudevan, Ravi. "The Melodramatic Mode and the Commercial Hindi Cinema." *Screen* 30 (1989):29-50.

________. "Indian Commerical Cinema." *Screen* 31, 4 (Winter 1990):446-53.

________. "The cultural space of a film narrative: Interpreting *Kismet* (Bombay Talkies, 1943)." *IESHR* 28, 2 (1991):183 ff.

________. "Shifting Codes, Dissolving Identities: The Hindi Social Film of the 1950s as Popular Culture." *Jrl. of Arts and Ideas*, nos. 23-24 (Jan. 1993):51-84.

Vatsyayan, Kapila. "Ecology and Indian Myth." *IICQ* 19, 2 (Spring-Summer 1992):157-80.

Venkatesth, Sudhir Alladi. "Learnin' the Trade: Conversation with a Gangsta.'" *Public Culture* 6, 2 (Winter 1994):319-42.

Verma, Nirmal. *Word and Memory*. Bikaner: Vagdevi Prakashan, 1988.

Verma, Nirmal. "India and Europe: The Self and the Other." *IICQ* 20, 1-2 (Spring-Summer 1993):137-63.

Vertovec, Steven. "Religion and Ethnic Ideology: The Hindu Youth Movement in Trinidad." *Ethnic and Racial Studies* 13, 2 (1990):225-49.

________. *Hindu Trinidad: Religion, Ethnicity and Socio-Economic Change.* London: Macmillan Caribbean, 1992.

Vicziany, Marika. "Imperialism, Botany, and Statistics in Early Nineteenth-Century India: The Surveys of Francis Buchanan (1762-1829)." *Modern Asian Studies* 20 (1986):625-50.

Vidyarthi, Govind. *Cultural Neocolonialism*. New Delhi: Allied Publishers, 1988.

Vilanilam, John. "Television advertising and the Indian poor." *Media, Culture and Society* 11, 4 (Oct. 1989):485-97.

Vingadassamy-Engel, Lotus. "The Hindu Diaspora in the French West Indies." *India International Centre Quarterly* 19, 3 (Monsoon 1992):6-26.

Virdi, Jyotika. "(Mis)representing child labor: SALAAM BOMBAY!" *Jump Cut*, no. 37 (July 1992):29-36.

Visram, Rozima. *Ayahs, Lascars and Princes: Indians in Britain 1700-1947.* London: Pluto Press, 1986.

Viswanathan, Gauri. "Some Other Time: Johannes Fabian's *Time and the Other.*" *New Ideas in Psychology* 4, 3 (1986):395-400.

________. "The Beginnings of English Literary Study in British India." *Oxford Literary Review* 9, 1-2 (1987):2-26.

________. "Currying Favor: The Beginnings of English Literary Study in British India." *Social Text*, nos. 19/20 (Fall 1988):85-104.

________. "The Empire Within: How the Canon Divides and Conquers." *Voice Literary Supplement* (December 1988).

________. *Masks of Conquest: Literary Study and British Rule in India.* New York: Columbia UP, 1989; London: Faber & Faber, 1990. [Reviewed by Henry Schwarz in *Polygraph*, no. 5 (1992):263-69.]

________. "Raymond Williams and British Colonialism." *Yale Jrl. of Criticism* 4, 2 (1991):47-66.

________. "English in a Literate Society." In *The Lie of the Land: English Literary Studies in India.* Edited by R. S. Rajan. Delhi: Oxford UP, 1992.

________. "Ronald Inden's *Imagining India.*" *Nineteenth-Century Prose* 19, 2 (1992).

________. "Raymond Williams and British Colonialism: The Limits of Metropolitan Cultural Theory." In *Views Beyond the Border Country:*

Raymond Williams and Cultural Politics, pp. 217-30. Edited by Dennis Dworkin and Leslie Roman. New York & London: Routledge, 1993.

Viswanathan, Gauri. "Coping with (Civil) Death: The Christian Convert's Rights of Passage." Forthcoming in *After Colonialism: Imperialism and the Colonial Aftermath*. Edited by Natalie Z. Davis and Gyan Prakash. Princeton: Princeton UP, 1993.

________. "Elihu Yale, British Imperialism, and American Higher Education: The Naming of Yale College." Forthcoming in *Cultures of American Imperialism*. Edited by Donald Pease and Amy Kaplan. Durham, N.C.: Duke UP, 1993.

Visvanathan, Shiv. "Atomic Physics: The Career of an Imagination." *Alternatives* 10, 2 (June 1984):193-236; reprinted in *Science, Hegemony and Violence*, pp. 257-88. Edited by Ashis Nandy. New Delhi: Oxford UP, 1992 [1988].

________. *Organizing for Science: The Making of an Industrial Research Laboratory*. New Delhi: Oxford UP, 1985.

________. "Bhopal: The Imagination of a Disaster." *Alternatives* 11, 1 (Jan. 1986):147-65.

________. "On Ancestors and Epigones." *Seminar*, no. 330 (Feb. 1987):14-24.

________. "On the Annals of the Laboratory State." Reprinted in *Science, Hegemony and Violence*, pp. 257-88. Edited by Ashis Nandy. New Delhi: Oxford UP, 1988.

________. "Reflections on the Technology of Transfer: Notes on the New Panopticon." *Lokayan Bulletin* 6, 1-2 (Jan.-April 1988):147-60.

________. "The Glasnot Spy." *Alternatives* 15, 1 (Winter 1988):83-96.

________. "Mrs. Brundtland's Non-Magical Cosmos." *Lokayan Bulletin* 9, 1 (Jan-Feb. 1991):47-54; also published in *Alternatives* 16, 3 (Summer 1991).

________. "The House of Bamboo." *IUMDA Newsletter*, no. 4 (1991):39-48; reprinted in *Lokayan Bulletin* 9, 5 (Sept.-Oct. 1991):47-55.

________. "Reinventing Gandhi." *IUMDA Newsletter*, no. 5 (1992).

Visvanathan, Shiv and Sethi, Harsh. "Bhopal: A Report from the Future." *Lokayan Bulletin* 7, 3 (May-June 1989):47-67.

Visweswaran, Kamala. "Defining Feminist Ethnography." *Inscriptions* Nos.3/4 (1988): 27-46.

________. "Family Subjects: An Ethnography of the 'Women's Question' in Indian Nationalism." Unpublished Ph.D. Dissertation, Stanford University, 1990.

Visweswaran, Kamala. *Fictions of Feminist Ethnography*. Minneapolis: Univ. of Minnesota Press, 1994.

Wade, Bonnie C. and Pescatello, Ann M. "The Status of Women in the Performing Arts of India and Iberia: Cross-Cultural Perspectives from Historical Accounts and Field." In *The Performing Arts: Music and Dance*, pp. 119-37. Edited by John Blacking and Joann W. Kealiinohomoku. The Hague: Mouton, 1979.

Wang, Georgette and Dissanayake, Wimal. *Continuity and Change in Communication Systems: An Asian Perspective*. Norwood, New Jersey: Ablex Publishing Corporation, 1986.

Ware, Vron. *Beyond the Pale: White Women, Racism and History*. London and New York: Verso, 1992. Pt. III, "Britannia's Other Daughters."

Washbrook, D. A. "Ethnicity and Racialism in Colonial Indian Society." In *Racism and Colonialism: Essays on Ideology and Social Structure*. Edited by R. Ross. The Hague: Nijhoff, 1982.

________. "Law, State and Agrarian Society in Colonial India." *Modern Asian Studies* 15, 3 (1981).

________. "Progress and Problems: South Asian Economic and Social History c. 1720-1860." *Modern Asian Studies* 22, 1 (1988): 57-96.

________. "'To Each a Language of His Own': Language, Culture and Society in Colonial India." In *Language, History and Class*, pp. 179-203. Edited by Penelope J. Corfield. Oxford: Basil Blackwell, 1991.

Weber, Jacques. "Chanemongam, 'King of French India': Social and Political Foundations of an Absolute Power under the Third Republic." *EPW* 26, 6 (9 Feb. 1991):291-302.

Weingarden, Lauren S. "A Transcendentalist Discourse in the Poetics of Technology: Louis Sullivan's Transportation Building and Walt Whitman's 'Passage to India.'" *Word and Image* 3, 2 (April-June 1987):202-21.

Weiss, Anita M. "South Asian Muslims in Hong Kong: Creation of a 'Local Boy' Identity." *MAS* 25, 3 (1991):417-53.

West, Michael. "Indian Politics in South Africa: 1860 to the Present." *South Asia Bulletin* 7 (1987):97-111.

White, Sarah C. *Arguing with the Crocodile: Gender and Class in Bangladesh*. London: Zed Books, 1992.

Whitehead, Judy. "The State and Oppositional Discourse in Central Uttar Pradesh." *Social Scientist*, nos. 219-20 (Aug.-Sept. 1991):3-27.

Wickremeratne, Ananda. *The Genesis of an Orientalist: Thomas Williams Rhys Davids and Buddhism in Sri Lanka*. Delhi: Motilal Banarsidass, 1984.

Willemen, Paul. "Negotiating the Transition to Capitalism: The Case of Andaz." *East-West Film Journal* 5, 1 (Jan. 1991):56-66.

Williams, Sylvia. "Marguerite Duras' India Song — Texte Threate Film." *Australian Journal of French Studies* 23, 3 (Sept.-Dec. 1986):277-89.

Willis, Janice D., ed. *Feminine Ground: Essays on Women and Tibet*. Ithaca, New York: Snow Lion Publications, 1989.

Wilson, Kalpana. "Globalisation and 'Muslim Belt': Reshaping of British Racism." *EPW* 28, 25 (19 June 1993):1288-90.

Wolf, Gita. "Construction of Gender Identity: Women in Popular Tamil Magazines." *EPW* 26, 43 (26 Oct. 1991):WS-71 ff.

Worboys, Michael. "Science and British Colonial Imperialism: 1895-1940." Unpublished D. Phil. thesis, University of Sussex, 1980.

Wurgaft, Lewis D. *The Imperial Imagination: Magic and Myth in Kipling's India*. Middletown, Conn.: Wesleyan UP, 1983.

Yang, Anand. "Disciplining 'Natives': Prisons and Prisoners in Early Nineteenth Century India." *South Asia* 10, 2 (1987):29-46.

________. "Whose Sati? Widow Burning in English Nineteenth Century India." *Journal of Women's History* 1, 2 (1989):8-33.

________. *The Limited Raj: Agrarian Relations in Colonial India, Saran District, 1793-1920*. Berkeley: Univ. of California Press, 1989.

________, ed. *Crime and Criminality in British India*. Tuscon, Arizona: Published for the Association for Asian Studies by the Univ. of Arizona Press, 1985.

Young, Robert M. *White Mythologies: Writing History and the West*. London & New York: Routledge, 1990.

Zene, Cosimo. "The Authority of the Face: Missionary Representations in South-West Bangladesh." *History and Anthropology* 6, 2-3 (1993):125-55.

Zutshi, Somnath. "White Nightmares/Dark Dreams: Racist Images in Hollywood Cinema." *Deep Focus* 2, 1 (Sept. 1989):20-30.

________. "Women, Nation and the Outsider in Contemporary Hindi Cinema." In *Interrogating Modernity: Culture and Colonialism in India*. Edited by Tejaswini Niranjana, P. Sudhir, and Vivek Dhareshwar. Calcutta: Seagull Books, 1993.

BIBLIOGRAPHY OF CONTEMPORARY SOUTH ASIAN CULTURAL STUDIES, ARRANGED THEMATICALLY

I. Art and Architecture

Araeen, Rasheed. *The Other Story: Afro-Asian Artists in Post-War Britain*. London: South Bank Centre, 1989.

Architectural Review. Special issue on "Indian Identity." Vol. 182, No. 1086 (August 1987).

Bell, L. "Artists and Empire: Victorian Representations of Subject People." *Art History* (March 1982):73-86.

Bhatt, Vikram and Scriver, Peter. *After the Masters: Contemporary Indian Architecture*. Ahmedabad: Mapin Publishing, 1991.

Burman, Chila, interviewed by Errol Lloyd. *Artrage*, no. 11 (1986).

Burman, Chila. "Ask How I Feel/ Automatic Rap/ My New Work." *Third Text*, no. 19 (Summer 1992):79-86.

Burman, Chila. "There Have Always Been Great Blackwomen Artists." In *Visibly Female, Feminism and Art: An Anthology*, pp. 195-99. Edited by Hilary Robinson. London: Camden Press, 1987.

Chattopadhyay, Ratnabali.* "The Alternative Vision, a Study of Indian Artistic Response to Orientalism." *Calcutta Historical Jrl.* (July 1986-June 1987).

Chattopadhyay, Ratnabali. "Nationalism and Form in Indian Painting: A Study of the Bengal School." *Jrl. of Arts and Ideas*, nos. 14-15 (July-Dec. 1987):5-46.

Clarke, M. *The Tempting Prospect: A Social History of English Watercolours*. London: British Museum Publications, 1981.

Cohn, Bernard S. "The Transformation of Objects into Artifacts, Antiquities and Art in Nineteenth Century India." Paper delivered at National Endowment for the Humanities Conference, 'Patronage in Indian Culture', 1985.

Cook, Geoffrey. "Ananda K. Coomaraswamy and Medieval Sri Lankan Art." *Left Curve*, no. 15 (1991):75-81.

Correa, Charles. *The New Landscape: Urbanization in the Third World*. Bombay: The Book Society of India, 1985.

Correa, Charles. "The Public, the Private, and the Sacred." *Daedalus* (Fall 1989):93-113.

Cruickshank, Dan. "Variations and Traditions." *Architectural Review*, no. 1086 (August 1987):51-61.

Curtis, William J. R. *Modern Architecture in an Indian Tradition: Balkrishna V. Doshi.* Ahmedabad: Mapin International, 1987.

Curtis, William J. R. "Modernism and the search for an Indian identity." *Architectural Review* , no. 1086 (August 1987):33-38.

Datta, Santo. "Urbanisation of Indian Art." *Jrl. of Arts and Ideas*, no. 9 (Oct.-Dec. 1984):5-22.

Davis, Richard H. "Indian Art Objects as Loot." *JAS* 52, 1 (Feb. 1993):22-48.

Dehejia, Vidya. "The Future of India's Past: Conservation of Cultural Heritage." In *India Briefing, 1990*, pp. 131-157. Edited by Marshall M. Bouton and Philip Oldenburg. Boulder: Westview Press, 1990.

Desmond, Ray. *History of the India Museum*. London, 1982.

Dossal, Mariam. *Imperial Designs, Indian Realities: The Planning of Bombay City, 1845-1875*. Bombay: Oxford UP, 1991.

Edge, Sara and Morgan, Jill. *The Issue of Painting: Sutapa Biswas, Margaret Harrison, Glenys Johnson*. Rochdale, U.K.: Rochdale Art Gallery, 1986.

Evenson, Normal. *The Indian Metropolis: A View Toward the West*. New Haven: Yale UP, 1989.

Fermor-Hesketh, Robert, ed. *Architecture of the British Empire*. London: Weidenfeld & Nicolson, 1986.

Ganguly, Keya. "Colonial Discourse and the History of Indian Art: A Revvisionist Reading." *Jrl. of Communication Inquiry* 12, 2 (1988):39-52.

Girdhar, Virendra K. "Towards an All-Inclusive Indian Architecture." *Indian Institute Magazine* (October-December 1986).

Grewal, Inderpal. "The guidebook and the museum: imperialism, education and nationalism in the British Museum." *Bucknell Review* (1990): 195-217.

Gupta, Samita. "Sris Chandra Chatterjee: The quest for a national architecture." *IESHR* 28, 2 (1991):187-201.

Himid, Lubaina, exhibition selector. *The Thin Black Line*. London: Institute for Contemporary Arts, 1985. Catalogue includes Sutapa Biswas and Chila Burman.

Irving, Robert Grant. *Indian Summer: Lutyens, Baker and Imperial Delhi*. New Haven: Yale UP, 1981.

Jain, Jyotindra. "Ganga Devi: Tradition & Expression in Madhubani Painting." *Third Text* , no. 6 (1988).

Jain, Kulbhushan. "Realms of Transition: An Essay on the Physical and Cultural

Attributes of In-between Architectural Spaces." *Architecture and Design* 3, 3 (March-April 1989):81-87.

Jhabvala, C. S. H. *Delhi: Stones and Streets*. Delhi: Ravi Dayal, 1991.

Joshi, Pratima. "Problems in South Asian Architectural Historiography." *Architecture and Design* 5, 4 (May-June 1989):53-59.

Kapur, Anuradha. *K. G. Subramanyan*. New Delhi: Lalit Kala Akademi, 1987.

Kapur, Geeta.* *Partisan Views on the Human Figure*. Place for People Exhibition Catalgoue. Bombay/New Delhi, 1981.

Kapur, Geeta. "Ravi Varma." Occasional Papers on History and Society, 2nd Series, no. 22. New Delhi: NMML, 1990.

Kapur, Geeta. "Ravi Varma: Representational Dilemmas of a Nineteenth Century Indian Painter." *Jrl. of Arts and Ideas*, nos. 17-18 (1988): 59-80.

Kapur, Geeta. "When Was Modernism in Indian/Third World Art?" *South Atlantic Quarterly* 92, 3 (Summer 1993):473-513.

Karan, Pradyuma P. "Landscape, Religion and Folk Art in Mithila: An Indian Cultural Region." *Journal of Cultural Geography* 5, 1 (Fall-Winter 1984):85-101.

Khosla, Romi. "Including Iconography and Images in Architecture." *Jrl. of Arts and Ideas* (April-June 1984):5-36.

Khosla, Romi. "Those Wonderful Economic Arguments." *Architectural Review*, no. 1086 (August 1987):66-68.

King, Anthony D. "Colonial Architecture Re-visited: Some Issues for Further Debate." In *Changing South Asia: City and Culture*, pp. 99-106. Edited by Kenneth Ballhatchet and David Taylor. Hong Kong: Asian Research Service for Centre of South Asian Studies, SOAS, 1981.

Kosambi, Meera and Brush, John E. "Three Colonial Port Cities in India." *Geographical Review* 78, 1 (1988):32-47.

Kosambi, Meera. *Bombay in Transition: The Growth and Social Ecology of a Colonial City, 1880-1980*. Stockholm: Almqvist & Wiksell International, 1986.

Kosambi, Meera. "The Colonial City in Its Global Niche." *EPW* 25, 42-43 (20-27 Oct. 1990):2775-81.

Kothari, Komal. "The Shrine: An Expression of Social Needs." In *Gods of the Byways*, pp. 5-31. Oxford: Museum of Modern Art, 1982.

Maharaj, Sarat. "The Congo is Flooding the Acropolis: Art in Britain of the Immigrants." *Third Text* 15 (Summer 1991):77-90.

McDonaugh, Christian. "The Tharu House: Oppositions and Hierarchy." *Journal of the Anthropological Society of Oxford* 15, 1 (1984):1-14.

Meade, Martin. "Europe in India." *Architectural Review* No. 1086 (August 1987):26-31.

Menon, A. G. Krishna. "Architectural Conundrums." *Jrl. of Arts and Ideas*, nos. 20-21(March 1991):41-48.

Menon, A. G. Krishna. "Conservation in India." *Architecture and Design* (Nov.-Dec. 1989):22-27.

Metcalfe, Thomas R. *An Imperial Vision: Indian Architecture and Britain's Raj*. Berkeley: Univ. of California Press, 1989.

Metcalfe, Thomas R. "Architecture and the Representation of Empire: India, 1860-1910." *Representations*, no. 6 (1984).

Miller, Barbara Stoler, ed. *The Powers of Art: Patronage in Indian Culture*. Delhi: Oxford UP, 1992.

Mitter, Partha. "Indian Artists, Western Art and Tradition." In *Changing South Asia City and Culture*. Edited by Kenneth Ballhatchet and David Taylor. Hong Kong: Published for SOAS by Asian Research Service, 1984.

Mitter, Partha. "Indian Artists, Western Art and Tradition." In *Changing South Asia: City and Culture*, pp. 77-89. Edited by Kenneth Ballhatchet and David Taylor. Hong Kong: Asian Research Service for Centre of South Asian Studies, SOAS, 1981.

Mitter, Partha. *Much Maligned Monsters: History of European Reactions to Indian Art*. Oxford: Clarendon Press, 1977; paperback ed., 1992.

Mitter, Partha. "The Early British Port Cities of India: Their Planning and Architecture circa 1640-1757." *Journal of the Society of Architectural Historians* 45, 2 (1986):95-114.

Morris, J. and Winchester, S. *Stones of Empire*. Oxford: Oxford UP, 1983.

Pal, Pratapaditya and Dehejia, Vidya. *From Merchants to Emperors: British Artists and India, 1757-1930*. Ithaca and London: Cornell UP, 1986.

Parrey, Eric. "Ritual of the City." *Architectural Review* No. 1086 (August 1987):14-24.

Patankar, R. B. "Aesthetics: Some Important Problems." *Jrl. of Arts and Ideas*, no. 6 (Jan.-March 1984):43-66.

Patel, Gieve. "Contemporary Indian Painting." *Daedalus* 118 (Fall 1989):171-203.

PPST Bulletin, Madras Group. "The Debate on the Building of New Delhi." *PPST Bulletin* 3, 2 (Nov. 1983):48-74.

Prakash, Vikramaditya. "Production of Identity in (Post) Colonial 'Indian' Architecture: Hegemony and Its Discontents in Nineteenth Century

Jaipur." Unpublished Ph.D. Dissertation, Cornell University, 1994.

Ravindran, K. T. "Indigenous India." *Architectural Review* No. 1086 (August 1987):63-65.

"Reworking Myths: Sutapa Biswas", interview with Yasmin Kureishi, in *Visibly Female: Feminism and Art: An Anthology,* pp. 37-42. Edited by Hilary Robinson. London: Camden Press, 1987; New York: Universe Books, 1988.

Sen, Geeti. *The Mind's Eye: Meera Mukherjee, Jogen Chowdhury, Ganesh Pyne, Arpita Singh, and Manjit Bawa.* Calcutta: Seagull Books, 1990.

Sharma, Ram. *Architecture in India.* Paris: Electa Moniteur, 1985.

Sheikh, Ghulam Mohammed. "Viewer's View: Looking at Pictures." In *Interrogating Modernity: Culture and Colonialism in India.* Edited by Tejaswini Niranjana, P. Sudhir, and Vivek Dhareshwar. Calcutta: Seagull Books, 1993.

Subramanyam, K. G. *Moving Focus: Essays on Indian Art.* New Delhi: Lalit Kala Akademi, 1978.

Subramanyam, K. G. *The Living Tradition: Perspectives on Modern Indian Art.* Calcutta: Seagull Books, 1987.

Thakurta, Tapati Guha. "Artists, Artisans and Mass Picture Production in Late Nineteenth- and Early Twentieth-Century Calcutta: The Changing Iconography of Popular Prints." *South Asia Research* 8, 1 (1988):3-45.

Thakurta, Tapati Guha. *The Making of a New 'Indian' Art: Artists, Aesthetics and Nationalism in Bengal, c. 1850-1920.* Cambridge: Cambridge UP, 1992.

Thakurta, Tapati Guha. "Westernization and Tradition in South Indian Painting in the Nineteenth Century: The Case of Raja Ravi Varma (1848-1906)." *Studies in History* 2, 2 (July-Dec. 1986):165-98.

Thakurta, Tapati Guha. "Women as 'Calendar Art' Icons: Emergence of Pictorial Stereotype in Colonial India." *EPW* 26, 43 (26 Oct. 1991): WS-91 ff.

Third Text, special issue entitled "The Other Story: AfroAsian Artists in Britain", Nos.8/9 (1989), with contributions from Geeta Kapur (writing on Francis Newton Souza) and Shelagh Hourahane (writing on Avtarjeet Dhanjal).

Tillotson, G. H. R. *The Tradition of Indian Architecture: Continuity, Controversy, and Change since 1850.* New Haven: Yale UP, 1989.

Uberoi, Patricia. "Feminine Identity and National Ethos in Indian Calendar Art." *EPW* (28 April 1990).

Vasavada, Ravindra, compiler.* *Reflections*: a volume of essays issued to commemorate the National Convention of the Indian Institute of Architects held in Ahmedabad in February 1987. Ahmedabad: Indian Institute of Architects, 1987.

II. Cinema and Media

Agrawal, Binod C. "Indianness of the Indian Cinema." In *Continuity and Change in Communication Systems: An Asian Perspective*, pp. 181-91. Edited by Georgette Wang, Wimal Dissanayake, and Emile G. McAnany. Norwood, New Jersey: Ablex, 1984.

Armes, Roy. *Third World Film Making and the West.* Berkeley: Univ. of California Press, 1987.

Arnold, Alison. "Popular Film Song in India: A Case of Mass-Market Musical Eclecticism." *Popular Music* 7, 2 (May 1988):177-88.

Arora, V. N. "Popular Songs in Hindi Films." *Journal of Popular Culture* 20, 2 (Fall 1986):143-66.

Balagopal, K. "Perception and Presentation: A Telugu Film on Naxalites." *EPW* 26, 29 (20 July 1991):1727-31.

Baskaran, S. Theodore. "Music for the Masses: Film Songs of Tamil Nadu." *EPW* (Annual Number) 26, 11-12 (March 1991):755-58.

Bhalla, Alok. "A Historical Map for a World of Fables: Notes, hypotheses, reflections on a cinematic phenomenon." *J. of Arts and Ideas*, nos. 10-11 (Jan.-June 1985):99-131.

Bhattacharya, Rinki.* "Feminism and the Cinema of Racism." *Women, Take One* 1 (1986).

Binford, Mira Reym, ed. *Quarterly Review of Film and Video:* [Special issue on] *Indian Cinema.* 11, 3 (1989):1-108.

Binford, Mira Reym. "The New Cinema of India." *Quarterly Review of Film Studies* 8, 4 (Fall 1983):47-67.

Burra, Rani, ed. *Indian Cinema 1980-85*. New Delhi: Directorate of Film Festivals, 1986.

Center for Psychosocial Studies, Chicago. "Center Forum Group: Televising the Discovery of India: A Discussion with Film-Maker Shyam Benegal." *Working Papers and Proceedings of the Center for Psychosocial Studies* No. 38 (1990).

Chakravarty, Sumita S. "National Identity and Realist Aesthetic: Indian Cinema of the Fifties." *Quarterly Rv. of Film and Video* 11, 3 (1986).

Chakravarty, Sumita S. *National Identity in Indian Popular Cinema 1947-1987*. Austin, Texas: University of Texas Press, 1993.

Chatterjee, Gayatri. *Awara*. Pune: National Film Archive of India in association with Wiley Eastern, 1993.

Cooper, Darius. "Colonialism in the Hindu Caste System: Satyajit Ray's *Sadgati* (*Deliverance*). *East-West Film Journal* 5, 2 (July 1991): 66-76.

Cooper, Darius. "The Hindi Film Song and Guru Dutt." *East-West Film Journal* 2, 2 (June 1988):49-65.

Cooper, Darius. "Through a lens, uniquely: An essay on the narrative forms of *Kasba* and *Nazar*." *Cinema in India* (Sept. 1991):34-40.

Cosoto, Maria. "The Raj Films: A Study in Cultural Imperialism." *Splice*, no. 1 (Jan.-March 1992):5-13.

Cubitt, Sean. "Indian Cinema: Interview with Anand Patwardhan." *Framework* 30/31 (1986):60-67.

Das, Veena. "The Mythological Film and Its Framework of Meaning: An Analysis of *Jai Santoshi Ma*." *IICQ* 8, 1 (March 1980):43-56.

Dasgupta, Chidananda. "Seeing and Believing, Science and Mythology: Notes on the 'Mythological' Genre." *Film Quarterly* 42, 4 (Summer 1989): 121-28.

Dasgupta, Chidananda. *Talking About Films*. New Delhi: Orient Longman, 1981.

Dasgupta, Chidananda. *The Painted Face: Studies in India's Popular Cinema*. Delhi: Roli Books, 1991.

Dasgupta, Chidananda. "The Rural Base of an Urban Phenomenon." *East-West Film Journal* 3, 1 (Dec. 1988):88-96.

Datta, Alokananda and Roy, Soma. "Adoor Gopalakrishnan in conversation." *Splice*, no. 2 (July 1986):23-30.

Desai, Chetan. "Martial Arts in Cinema." *Deep Focus* 2, 1 (Sept. 1989):32-41.

Dhondy, Faruukh. "Keeping Faith: Indian Film and Its World." *Deadalus* (Fall 1985):125-40.

Dickey, Sara Ann. "Accommodation and Resistance: Expression of Working-Class Values through Tamil Cinema." *Wide Angle* 11, 3 (July 1989): 26-32.

Dickey, Sara Ann. "Going to the Pictures in Madurai." Unpublished Ph.D. Dissertation, University of California at San Diego, 1988.

Dickey, Sara Ann. "The Politics of Adulation: Cinema and the Production of Politicians in South India." *JAS* 52, 2 (May 1993):340-72.

Dissanayake, Wimal. "Art, Vision, and Culture: Satyajit Ray's Apu Trilogy Revisited." *East-West Film Journal* 1, 1 (Dec. 1986):69-83.

Dissanayake, Wimal. "Film and Social Change: Notes Towards a Conceptual Analysis." *Splice*, no. 2 (1986):6-15.

Dissanayake, Wimal. "Questions of Female Subjectivity, Patriarchy, and Family: Perceptions of Three Indian Women Film Directors." *East-West Film Journal* 3, 2 (June 1989):74-90.

Dissanayake, Wimal. "Self and Modernization in Malayalam Cinema." *East-West Film Journal* 1, 2 (June 1987):60-77.

Dissanayake, Wimal. *Sholay: A Cultural Reading*. New Delhi: Wiley Eastern, 1992.

Dissanayake, Wimal, ed. *Cinema and Cultural Identity: Reflections on Films from Japan, India and China*. Lanham, Maryland: U. Press of America, 1988.

Dissanayake, Wimal and Sahai, Malti. *Raj Kapoor's Films: Harmony of Discourses*. New Delhi: Vikas Publishing House, 1988.

Framework, no. 37. Special Issue on Sri Lanka Cinema. Guest Editors: Robert Crusz and Ashley Ratnavibhushana.

Gabriel, Teshome H. "Teaching Third World Cinema." *Screen* 24, 2 (March-April 1983): 60-64.

Ganguly, Suranjan. "One Single Blend: A Conversation with Satyajit Ray." *East-West Film Journal* 3, 2 (June 1989):91-95.

George, Alex. "[Tipu] Sultan and the Saffron." *EPW* 25, 52 (29 Dec. 1990):2833-35.

Gessen, Elena and Anatoli Brovchenko. "Shyam Benegal." *Soviet Literature*, no. 473 (1987):171-74.

Ghosh, Sital Chandra and Roy, Arun Kumar, eds. *Twelve Indian Directors*. Calcutta: People's Book Publishing, 1981.

Gillespie, Marie. "Technology and Tradition: Audio-Visual Culture Among South Asian Families in West London." *Cultural Studies* 3, 2 (1989).

Gopalan, Lalitha. "Putting Asunder: Fassbinder and The Marriage of Maria Braun." *Deep Focus* 1, 4 (Jan. 1989):50-57.

Gupta, Udayan. "New Visions in Indian Cinema: Interviews with Mrinal Sen, Girish Karnad, and Ketan Mehta." *Cineaste* 11, 4 (1982):18-24.

Haggard, Sunil. "Mass Media and the Visual Arts in Twentieth-Century South Asia: Indian Film Posters 1947-Present." *South Asia Research* 8, 1 (May 1988):71-88.

Hanan, David. "Patriarchal Discourse in some early films of Satyajit Ray." *Deep Focus* 3, 1 (1990):30-57.

Hansen, Kathryn. "Hindi New Cinema: Basu Chatterji's *Sara Akash*." *South Asia* (New Series) 4, 1 (June 1981):15-21.

Hardgrave, Robert. "Stars and Gods." In *Essays in the Political Sociology of South India*. New Delhi: Usha, 1979.

Hauff, Reinhard. *Ten Days in Calcutta: A Portrait of Mrinal Sen*. Calcutta: Seagull Books, 1989.

India, Government of. Directorate of Film Festivals. *The New Generation, 1960-1980: Film India: An Examination of India's New Cinema, Its Preoccupation with a Changing Society and the Status of Women*. New Delhi: Ministry of Information and Broadcasting, 1981.

Janaky. "On the Trail of the Mahabharata: A Response." *EPW* 27, 37 (12 Sept. 1992):1997-99 [criticizes the search for ur-epics].

Jayamanne, Laleen. "Hunger for Images, Myths of Femininity in the Sri Lankan Cinema, 1947-1989." *South Asia Bulletin* 12, 1 (1992):57-75.

Kakar, Sudhir. "The Ties that Bind: Family Relationships in the Mythology of Hindi Cinema." *India International Centre Quarterly* 8, 1 (1981): 11-21.

Kapur, Geeta. "Articulating the Self into History: Ritwik Ghatak's *Jukti Takko aar Gappo*." In *Questions of Third Cinema*, pp. 179-94. Edited by Jim Pines and Paul Willemen. London: British Film Institute, 1989.

Kapur, Geeta. "Cultural Creativity in the Third Decade: The Example of Satyajit Ray." *Jrl. of Arts and Ideas*, nos. 23-24 (Jan. 1993):17-49.

Kapur, Geeta. "Mythic Material in Indian Cinema." *Jrl. of Arts and Ideas*, nos. 14-15 (July-Dec. 1987):79-108; also published as Occasional Papers on History and Society. New Delhi: NMML, 1988.

Kapur, Geeta. "Revelation and Doubt: *Sant Tukaram* and *Devi*. In *Interrogating Modernity: Culture and Colonialism in India*. Edited by Tejaswini Niranjana, P. Sudhir, and Vivek Dhareshwar. Calcutta: Seagull Books, 1993.

Khanna, Satendra. *Indian Cinema and Indian Life*. Berkeley: Center for South and Southeast Asian Studies, 1980.

Khopkar, Arun.* *Gurudatta: tin ankiya trasdi*. Translated into Hindi by Nishkant Thakar. Madhya Pradesh Film Development Corporation.

Kipnis, Laura. "'The Phantom Twitchings of an Amputated Limb': Sexual Spectacle in the Post-Colonial Epic." *Wide Angle* 11, 4 (Oct. 1989): 42-51.

Kleinhaus, Chuck and Pendakur, Manji. "Learning Together: Synthesizing Economic and Cultural Analysis in the Marxist Study of Third World Film and Video." *Jump Cut*, no. 33 (1987):82-91.

Korchagov, Yuri. 'Indian Films in the USSR." *Soviet Literature* Vol. 8 No. 473 (1987):190-92.

Krishen, Pradip, ed. "Indian Popular Cinema: Myth, Meaning and metaphor", special issue of *India International Centre Quarterly* 8, 1 (March 1981).

Krishen, Pradip. "Knocking at the Doors of Public Culture: India's Parallel Cinema." *Public Culture* 4 , 1 (Fall 1991):25-42.

Lesage, Julia. "Feminist Documentary in India: An Interview with Deepa Dhanraj." *Jump Cut*, no. 31 (March 1986):40-42.

Mirtra, Ananda. "Desi BOND: The Cross-Cultural Transformation of James Bond into a Hero of Popular Indian Cinema." *Deep Focus* 2, 1 (Sept. 1989):42-47.

Mishra, Vijay. "Decentring History: Some Versions of Bombay Cinema." *East-West Film Journal* 6, 1 (Januay 1992):111-55.

Mishra, Vijay. "Filmic Narrative: Text and Transformation in Bombay Cinema." *Continuum* [Australia] 2 (1988/89):9-43.

Mishra, Vijay. "The Texts of 'Mother India.'" *Kunapipi* 11, 1 (1989):119-37.

Mishra, Vijay. "Towards a Theoretical Critique of Bombay Cinema." *Screen* 26, 2-3 (1985):133-46.

Mishra, Vijay; Jeffrey, Peter; and Shoesmith, Brian. "The Actor as Parallel Text in Bombay." *Quarterly Review of Film and Video* 11 (1989):49-67.

Nair, Mira and Sooni Taraporevala. "India Cabaret: Reflections and Reactions." *Discourse* 8 (Fall 1986-Winter 1987):58-71.

Nair, Mira. "India Cabaret." In conversation with Ketali Sheth. *Splice*, no. 3 (1987):35-39, 41-44.

Nandy, Ashis. "An Intelligent Critic's Guide to Indian Cinema." *Deep Focus*, Pt. I, "The Cultural Matrix of the Popular Film", 1, 1 (Dec. 1987):68-72; Pt. II, 1, 2 (June 1988):53-60; Pt. III, "The Double in Commercial Films", 1, 3 (Nov. 1988):58-61.

Nandy, Ashis. "Satyajit Ray's Secret Guide to Exquistite Murders: Creativity, Social Criticism, and the Partitioning of the Self." *East-West Film Journal* 4, 2 (1990):14-37.

Nandy, Ashis. "The Popular Hindi Film: Ideology and First Principles." *India International Centre Quarterly* 8, 1 (1980):89-96; reprinted as "The Supermarket of Dreams", *The Illustrated Weekly of India* (16 March 1986).

Niranjana, Tejaswani. "Cinema, Femininity and Economy of Consumption." *EPW* 26,43 (26 Oct. 1991):WS-85 ff.

Ostor, Akos. "Cinema and Society in India and Senegal." *Splice*, no. 3 (1987): 6-30.

Pandian, M. S. S. "Parasakhti: Life and Times of a DMK Film." *EPW* (Annual Number) 26, 11-12 (March 1991):759-70.

Pandian, M. S. S. *The Image Trap: M. G. Ramachandran in Film and Politics*. Delhi: Sage, 1992.

Pendakur, Manjunath. "Dynamics in Cultural Policy Making: The U.S. Film Industry in India." *Journal of Communication* 35,4 (Autumn 1985): 52-72.

Pendakur, Manjunath. "New Cultural Technologies and the Fading Glitter of Indian Cinema." *Quarterly Rv. of Film and Video* 11, 3 (1986).

Pendakur, Manjunath. "The Indian Film Industry." In *Asian Film Industry*. Edited by J. A. Lent. Bromley: Christopher Helm, 1990.

Pines, Jim and Willemen, Paul. *Questions of Third Cinema*. London: British Film Institute Publishing, 1989.

Prabhu, Shrikanth. "Singing in the Rain: An Analysis of Songs in Popular Cinema." *Deep Focus* 1, 4 (January 1989):42-48.

Prasad, Madhava. "Escape from Childhood: The Development of the Hero in Popular Cinema." *Deep Focus* 1, 1 (Dec. 1987):28-32.

Raina, M. L. "'I'm All Right Jack': Packaged Pleasures of the Middle Cinema." *Journal of Public Culture* 20, 2 (Fall 1986):131-41.

Rajadhyaksha, Ashish. "Art in Indian Cinema." In *70 Years of Indian Cinema* (1913-1983), pp. 224-36. Edited by T. M. Ramachandran. Bombay: Cinema India International, 1985.

Rajadhyaksha, Ashish. "Debating the Third Cinema." In *Questions of Third Cinema*, pp. 170-78. Edited by Jim Pines and Paul Willmen. London: British Film Institute, 1989.

Rajadhyaksha, Ashish. "Latin American Cinema: Political Cinema." *Jrl. of Arts and Ideas*, nos. 10-11 (Jan.-June 1985):87-98.

Rajadhyaksha, Ashish. "Neo-traditionalism: Film as Popular Art in India." *Framework* 32/33 (1986):20-67.

Rajadhyaksha, Ashish. *Ritwik Ghatak: A Return to the Epic*. Bombay: Screen Unit, 1982.

Rajadhyaksha, Ashish. "Satyajit Ray, Ray's Films, and Ray-Movie." *Jrl. of Arts and Ideas*, nos. 23-24 (Jan. 1993):7-16. Short version, entitled "Beyond Orientalism", in *Sight and Sound* (1992).

Rajadhyaksha, Ashish. "The Phalke Era: Conflict of Traditional Form and Modern Technology." *Jrl. of Arts and Ideas*, nos. 14-15 (July-Dec. 1987):47-78. Also reprinted in *Interrogating Modernity: Culture and Colonialism in India*. Edited by Tejaswini Niranjana, P. Sudhir, and Vivek Dhareshwar. Calcutta: Seagull Books, 1993.

Rajadhyaksha, Ashish and Gangar, Amrit, eds. *Ritwik Ghatak: Arguments/ Stories*. Bombay: Screen Unit/Research Centre for Cinema Studies, 1987.

Rajadhyaksha, Ashish and Muller, Marco, eds. *Le Avventurose storie del cinema indiano*. 2 vols. Venice: Mostra Internazionale del Nuovo Ninema, Pesaro Marsilio Editori, 1985.

Rajadhyaksha, Ashish and Shahani, Kumar. "Dossier: Shahani." [Kumar Shahani's essays on film.] *Framework*, nos. 30/31 (1986):68-100.

Rajagopal, Arvind. "Postcolonial Improvisations on Orientalism: A Hindu Epic Goes Prime Time." Unpublished ms., 1993.

Rajagopal, Arvind. "Uses of the Past: The Television Broadcast of an Ancient Epic and its Reception in Indian Society." Unpublished Ph.D. Dissertation, University of California, Berkeley, 1992.

Rajakrishnan, V. "Narrative Structure in Malayalam Cinema." *Deep Focus* 3, 2 (1990):35-39.

Rao, Leela. "Woman in Indian films — a paradigm of continuity and change." *Media, Culture and Society* 11, 4 (Oct. 1989):443-58.

Roberge, Gaston. *Another Cinema for Another Society.* Calcutta: Seagull Books, 1985.

Roberge, Gaston. *Mediation: The Action of the Media in Our Society*. New Delhi: Manohar, 1980.

Roberge, Gaston. *The Ways of Film Studies: Film Theory and the Interpretation of Film*. With an essay on Freud by Somnath Zutshi. New Delhi: Ajanta, 1992.

Robinson, Andrew. *Satyajit Ray: The Inner Eye*. Berkeley: Univ. of California Press, 1990.

Roy, Arundahti. "Over the (Electric) Moon." *Sunday* (12-18 April 1992):76-84.

Sahai, Malti. "Raj Kapoor and the Indianization of Charlie Chaplin." *East-West Film Journal* 2, 1 (Dec. 1987):62-76.

Sen, Surojit. "A Passage to India: The Book and the Film." *Splice*, no. 1 (Jan.-March 1986):14-18.

Shahani, Kumar. "Film as a Contemporary Art." *Social Scientist*, no. 202 (March 1990):33-59.

Shahani, Kumar. "Notes Towards an Aesthetic of Cinema Sound." *Jrl. of Arts and Ideas*, no. 5, reprinted in *Framework*, nos. 30/31 (1986).

Shankaranarayanam, Vasanthi. "The goddess-chattel syndrome: Representation of Women in Malayalam Cinema." *Deep Focus* 3, 1 (1990):66-74.

Sharrad, Paul. "The Books behind the Film: Paul Scott's Raj Quartet." *East-West Film Journal* 1, 2 (June 1987):60-77.

Sivathamby, Karthigesu. *The Tamil Film as a Medium of Political Communication*. Madras: New Century, 1981.

Skillman, Teri. "The Bombay Hindi Film Song Genre: A Historical Survey." *Yearbook for Traditional Music* 18 (1986):133-44.

Srivatsan, R. "Looking at Film Hoardings: Labour, Gender, Subjectivity and Everyday Life in India." *Public Culture* 4, 1 (Fall 1991):1-24.

Stam, Robert. "College Course File: Third World Cinema." *Journal of Film and Video* 36, 4 (Fall 1984):50-61.

Subramaniam, K. N. with Tripathy, Ratnakar. *Flashback — Cinema in the "Times of India"*. Bombay: Times of India, 1990.

Tharu, Susie. "Third World Women's Cinema: Notes on Narrative, Reflections on Opacity." *EPW* 21, 20 (17 May 1986):864-66.

Thomas, Rosie. "Indian Cinema: Pleasures and Popularity." *Screen* 26 (1985):116-31.

Thomas, Rosie. "Sanctity and Scandal: The Mythologization of Mother India." *Quarterly Rv. of Film and Video* 11, 3 (1986).

Valicha, Kishore. "Femininity and the Indian Film." *Cinema India International* 5, 1 (1988).

Valicha, Kishore. Indian Cinema: Mahesh Bhatt's *Arth* — A textual analysis." *New Quest*, no. 80 (March-April 1990):107-14.

Valicha, Kishore. *Moving Image: A Study of Indian Cinema*. London: Sangam Books, 1988.

Valicha, Kishore. "Repetitiveness as a Structuring Principle in Indian Cinema: Some Considerations." *New Quest*, no. 83 (Sept.-Oct. 1990):299-301.

Valicha, Kishore. "Sex and the Indian Film." *New Quest*, no. 75 (May-June 1989):167-69.

Valicha, Kishore. "The Image of Ashok Kumar." *New Quest*, no. 87 (May-June 1991):171-75.

Vasudev, Aruna and Lenglet, Phillipe, eds. *Indian Cinema Superbazaar*. Delhi: Vikas Publishing House, 1983. [Review by Sanjeev Prakash, "Genres in Indian Cinema", *Jrl. of Arts and Ideas*, no. 9 (Oct.-Dec. 1984):23ff.]

Vasudevan, Ravi. "Indian Commerical Cinema." *Screen* 31, 4 (Winter 1990): 446-53.

Vasudevan, Ravi. "Shifting Codes, Dissolving Identities: The Hindi Social Film of the 1950s as Popular Culture." *Jrl. of Arts and Ideas*, nos. 23-24 (Jan. 1993):51-84.

Vasudevan, Ravi. "The cultural space of a film narrative: Interpreting *Kismet* (Bombay Talkies, 1943)." *IESHR* 28, 2 (1991):183 ff.

Vasudevan, Ravi. "The Melodramatic Mode and the Commercial Hindi Cinema." *Screen* 30 (1989):29-50.

Virdi, Jyotika. "(Mis)representing child labor: SALAAM BOMBAY!" *Jump Cut*, no. 37 (July 1992):29-36.

Willemen, Paul. "Negotiating the Transition to Capitalism: The Case of Andaz." *East-West Film Journal* 5, 1 (Jan. 1991):56-66.

Zutshi, Somnath. "White Nightmares/Dark Dreams: Racist Images in Hollywood Cinema." *Deep Focus* 2, 1 (Sept. 1989):20-30.

Zutshi, Somnath. "Women, Nation and the Outsider in Contemporary Hindi Cinema." In *Interrogating Modernity: Culture and Colonialism in India*. Edited by Tejaswini Niranjana, P. Sudhir, and Vivek Dhareshwar. Calcutta: Seagull Books, 1993.

III. Criticism, Critical Theory, Literary Theory

Ahmad, Aijaz. "'Third World Literature' and the Nationalist Ideology." *Journal of Arts and Ideas*, nos. 17-18 (June, 1987):117-35.

Ahmad, Aijaz. "Between Orientalism and Historicism: Anthropological Knowledge of India." *Studies in History* (New Series) 7, 1 (Jan.-June 1991):135-63.

Ahmad, Aijaz. *In Theory: Nations, Classes, Literatures*. London: Verso, 1992. [Reviewed by Benita Parry, "A Critique Mishandled", *Social Text*, no. 35 (1993):121-33. Almost an entire issue of *Public Culture* (6, 1 [Fall 1993]), with contributions by Michael Sprinker, Talal Asad, Vivek Dhareshwar, Partha Chatterjee, Nivedita Menon, Peter van der Veer, Marjorie Howes, Marjorie Levinson, and Andrew Parker, and a response by Aijaz Ahmad, is devoted to the discussion of *In Theory*.]

Ahmad, Aijaz. "Jameson's Rhetoric of Otherness and the 'National Allegory.'" *Social Text* , no. 17 (1985):3-25.

Ahmad, Aijaz. "Orientalism and After: Ambivalence and Cosmopolitan Location in the Work of Edward Said." *EPW* 27, 30 (25 July 1992):PE98-116.

Appadurai, Arjun. "Center and Periphery in Anthropological Theory." *CSSH* 28, 2 (1986):356-61.

Appadurai, Arjun. "Commodities and the Politics of Value." In *The Social Life of Things*, pp. 3-63. Edited by A. Appadurai. New York: Cambridge UP, 1986.

Appadurai, Arjun. "Disjuncture and Difference in the Global Cultural Economy." *Public Culture* 2, 2 (1990):1-24.

Appadurai, Arjun. Is Homo Hieraarchicus — A Review Essay." *American Ethnologist* 13, 4 (1986):745-61.

Appadurai, Arjun. "Patriotism and Its Futures." *Public Culture* 5 (Spring 1993):1-19; portions published as "The Heart of Whiteness", *Callaloo* 16, 4 (Fall 1993):796-807.

Appadurai, Arjun, ed. *The Social Life of Things: Commodities in Cultural Perspective*. Cambridge: Cambridge UP, 1986.

Ashcroft, Bill and Tiffin, Helen. *The Empire Writes Back: Theory and Practice in Post-Colonial Literature*. London: Routledge, 1989.

Banuri, Tariq. "Development and the Politics of Knowledge: A Critical Interpretation of the Social Role of Modernization." In *Dominating Knowledge: Development, Culture, and Resistance*, pp. 29-72. Edited by Frederique Apffel Marglin and Stephen A. Marglin. Oxford: Clarendon Press, 1990.

Banuri, Tariq. "Modernization and Its Discontents: A Cultural Perspective on Theories of Development." In *Dominating Knowledge: Development, Culture, and Resistance*, pp. 73-101. Edited by Frederique Apffel Marglin and Stephen A. Marglin. Oxford: Clarendon Press, 1990.

Baucon, Ian. "Narrating the Nation." *Transition*, no. 55 (1992):144-53.

Bhabha, Homi. "Location, Intervention, Incommensurability: A Conversation with Homi Bhabha", *Emergences* 1 (Fall 1989):63-88.

Bhabha, Homi. "Of Mimicry and Man: The Ambivalence of Colonial Discourse." *October* 28 (Spring 1984):125-33.

Bhabha, Homi. "Race and the Humanities: The 'Ends' of Modernity?" *Public Culture* 4, 2 (Spring 1992):81-85.

Bhabha, Homi. "Remembering Fanon." Introduction to Frantz Fanon, *Black Skins White Masks*. London: Pluto Press/Zwan, 1986. Reprinted in *Remaking History*, pp. 131-48. Dia Art Foundation, Discussions in Contemporary Culture, no. 4. Edited by Barbara Kruger and Phil Mariani. Seattle: Bay Press, 1989.

Bhabha, Homi. "The Commitment to Theory." *New Formations* No. 5 (Summer 1988): 5-23; also in *Questions of Third Cinema*, ed. Jim Pines and Paul Willemen (London: BFI Publishing, 1989), pp. 111-32.

Bhabha, Homi. *The Location of Culture*. London: Routledge, 1993.

Bhabha, Homi. "The Other Question — The Stereotype and Colonial Discourse." *Screen* 24, 6 (1983):18-36.

Bhabha, Homi. "The Other question: difference, discrimination and the discourse of colonialism." In *Literature, Politics and Theory: Papers from the Essex Conference 1976-84*. Edited by Francis Barker et al. London: Methuen, 1986.

Bhargava, Rajeev. "The Right to Culture." *Social Scientist*, no. 209 (Oct. 1990):50-57.

Bhatnagar, Rashmi. "Uses and limits of Foucault: a study of the theme of origins in Edward Said's *Orientalism*." *Social Scientist*, no. 158 (July 1986).

Breckenridge, Carol A. and van der Veer, Peter, eds. *Orientalism and the Postcolonial Predicament*. Philadelphia: Univ. of Pennsylvania Press, 1993.

Brennan, Timothy. "India, Nationalism, and Other Failures." *South Atlantic Quarterly* 87, 1 (Winter 1988).

Chakrabarty, Dipesh. "The Death of History? Historical Consciousness and the Culture of Late Capitalism." *Public Culture* 4, 2 (Spring 1992): 47-66.

Chandra, Sudhir. *The Oppressive Present: Literature and Consciousness in Colonial India*. Delhi: Oxford UP, 1992.

Dalmia-Luderitz, Vasudha. "Reconsidering the Orientalist View." Special issue: "Perceiving India: Insight and Inquiry." *IICQ* 20, 1-2 (Spring-Summer 1993):92-114.

Desai, Gaurav. "The Invention of Invention." *Cultural Critique*, no. 24 (Spring 1993):119-42.

Dhareshwar, Vivek. "The Predicament of Theory." In *Theory between the Disciplines: Authority/Vision/Politics*, pp. 231-50. Edited by Martin Kreiswirth and Mark Cheetham. Ann Arbor: University of Michigan Press, 1990.

Dirks, Nicholas; Eley, Geoff; and Ortner, Sherry B., eds. *Culture/Power/History: A Reader in Contemporary Social Theory*. Princeton, New Jersey: Princeton UP, 1993.

Doraiswamy, Rashmi. "Western interpretations of Bakhtin." *Journal of Arts and Ideas*, nos. 12-13 (Jan.-June 1987):93-122.

Escobar, Arturo. "Discourse and Power in Development: Michel Foucault and the Relevance of His Work to the Third World." *Alternatives* 10, 3 (September 1984):377-400.

Gupta, Akhil. and Ferguson, James. "Beyond 'Culture': Space, Identity, and the Politics of Difference." *Current Anthropology* 7, 1 (Feb. 1992):6-23.

Gupta, Akhil. "The Reincarnation of Souls and the Rebirth of Commodities: Representations of Time in 'East' and 'West.'" *Cultural Critique*, no. 22 (Fall 1992):187-211.

Gupta, Akhil. "The Song of the Nonaligned World: Transnational Identities and the Reinscription of Space in Late Capitalism." *Current Anthropology* 7, 1 (Feb. 1992):63-79.

Inden, Ronald. *Imagining India*. Oxford: Basil Blackwell, 1990. [Reviewed by Declan Quigley, "The Power of Imagination", *MAS* 25, 2 (1991): 403-6.]

Inden, Ronald. "Orientalist Constructions of India." *MAS* 20, 3 (1986):401-46.

Jameson, Frederic. "Third-World Literature in the Era of Multinational Capitalism." *Social Text*, no. 15 (Fall 1986):65-88.

JanMohamed, Abdul R. "Humanism and Minority Literature: Toward a Definition of Counter-hegemonic Discourse." *boundary 2* 12, 3-13, 1 (Spring/Fall 1984):281-99.

Jayamanne, Laleen; Thornton, Leslie; and Minh-ha, Trinh. "If Upon Leaving What We Have to Say We Speak: A Conversation Piece." In *Discourses: Conversations in Postmodern Art and Culture*, pp. 44-66. Edited by Russell Ferguson, William Olander, Marcia Tucker, and Karen Fiss. Cambridge, Mass.: MIT Press, 1990; paperback ed., 1992.

Joshi, Svati, ed. *Rethinking English: Essays in Literature, Language, History*. Delhi: Trianka, 1991.

Kaiwar, Vasant. "Racism and the Writing of History, Part I." *South Asia Bulletin* 9, 2 (1989):32-56.

Kapur, Geeta. "Contemporary Cultural Practice." Occasional Papers on History and Society, 2nd Series, no. 21. New Delhi: NMML, 1990.

Kapur, Geeta. "Contemporary Cultural Practice: Some Polemical Categories." *Social Scientist*, no. 202 (March 1990):49-60.

Kapur, Geeta. "Further Narratives." *Jrl. of Arts and Ideas*, nos. 20-21 (March 1991):99-115.

Kapur, Geeta. "The Centre-Periphery Model or How are we Placed? Contemporary Cultural Practice in India." *Third Text*, nos. 16-17 (Autumn/Winter 1991):9-18.

Kaviraj, Sudipta. "Capitalism and the Cultural Process." *Jrl. of Arts and Ideas*, no. 19 (May 1990):61-75.

Kaviraj, Sudipta. "The Imaginary Institution of India." In *Subaltern Studies 7: Wrtings on South Asian History and Society*, pp. 1-39. Edited by Gyanendra Pandey and Dipesh Chakrabarty. Delhi: Oxford Univ. Press, 1992.

Kirpal, Viney. "What is the Third World Novel?" *Jrl. of Commonwealth Literature* 23, 1 (1988):144-56.

Kumar, Amitava. "Towards Postmodern Marxist Theory: Ideology, State and the Politics of Critique." *Rethinking Marxism* 3, 3-4 (Fall-Winter 1990):149-55.

Lal, Vinay. Review of *Debating Muslims: Cultural Dialogues in Postmodernity and Tradition,* by Michael Fischer and Mehdi Abedi, *Middle Eastern Report* 22, 4 (July-August 1992):46-47; slightly longer version also published as "De-Essentialising Islam" in *EPW* 27, 24-25 (13-20 June 1992):1257-58.

Lal, Vinay. "The Imperialism of Human Rights." *Focus on Law Studies* 8, 1 (Fall 1992), 5 ff.; reprinted in *Taking Sides: Clashing Views on Controversial Issues in Crime and Criminology*. Edited by Richard C. Monk. 3rd ed. Guilford, Connecticut: The Dushkin Publishing Group, Inc., 1993.

Ludden, David. "Orientalist Empiricism: Transformations of Colonial Knowledge." Forthcoming in *Orientalism and Beyond: Perspectives from South Asia*. Edited by Carol Breckenridge and Peter Van der Veer.

Mani, Lata and Frankenberg, Ruth. "The Challenge of Orientalism." *Economy and Society* 14, 2 (1985):174-92.

Marglin, Frederique Apffel and Marglin, Stephen A, eds. *Dominating Knowledge: Development, Culture and Resistance*. Oxford: Clarendon Press; New York: Oxford UP, 1990.

Mohanty, Chandra. "Feminist Encounters: Locating the Politics of Experience." *Copyright* 1 (1987):30-44; slight revised version in *Destabilizing Theory: Contemporary Feminist Debates*, pp. 74-92. Edited by Michele Barrett and Anne Phillips. Oxford: Polity Press, 1992. [For a discussion of this piece, see Kathleen M. Kirby, "Thinking through the Boundary: The Politics of Location, Subjects, and Space", *boundary 2* 20, 2 (Summer 1993):173-89.]

Mohanty, Chandra. "On Race and Voice: Challenges for Liberal Education in the 1990s." *Cultural Critique* (Winter 1989-90):179-208.

Mohanty, Satya P. *Literary Theory and the Claims of History*. Oxford: Basil Blackwell, 1991.

Mohanty, Satya P. "Us and Them: On the Philosophical Bases of Political Criticism." *Yale Journal of Criticism* 2 (Spring 1989):1-31; reprinted, with modifications, in *New Formations*, no. 8 (Summer 1989).

Nandy, Ashis. *At the Edge of Psychology: Essays in Politics and Culture*. Delhi: Oxford UP, 1980; paperback ed., 1990. [Reviewed by Veena Das, "Studies in Power and Authority", *Indian Express* (3 May 1981); Vol. 22, No. 3 of the *Journal of Commonwealth & Comparative Politics* (November 1984), with contributions by Franklin A. Presler, Lucian W. Pye, Arun Bose, Sanjukta Gupta and Richard Gombich, G. Morris Carstairs, and a 'response' by Ashis Nandy, "Cultures of Politics and Politics of Cultures", is devoted to a discussion of *At the Edge of Psychology*.]

Nandy, Ashis. "Cultural Frames for Social Transformation: A Credo." *Alternatives* 12 (1987):113-23.

Nandy, Ashis. "Shamans, Savages and the Wilderness: On the Audibility of Dissent and the Future of Civilizations." *Alternatives* 14 (1989):263-77;

portions published as "Liberation for Those who do not Speak the Language of Liberation." In *The Theory and Practice of Liberation at the End of the Twentieth Century*. Brussels: The Lelio Basso Foundation for the Rights and the Liberation of Peoples, 1988.

Nandy, Ashis. "The Discreet Charms of Indian Terrorism." *The Journal of Commonwealth and Comparative Politics* 12 (1990):25-43.

Nandy, Ashis. *The Intimate Enemy: Loss and Recovery of Self Under Colonialism*. New Delhi: Oxford UP, 1983; paperback ed., 1988; translated into Gujarati as *Antarang Ari*, tr. Tridip S. Dave (Ahmedabad: Behavioural Sciences Centre, 1991), and into Hindi as *Antaranga Shatru*, tr. Pawan Agarwal, forthcoming.

Nandy, Ashis. "The Politics of Secularism and the Recovery of Religious Tolerance." In *Mirrors of Violence: Communities, Riots and Survivors in South Asia*, pp. 69-93. Edited by Veena Das. Delhi: Oxford UP, 1990. Also reprinted in *The Book Review* 14, 6 (Nov.-Dec. 1990): 23-29.

Nandy, Ashis. *The Savage Freud and Other Essays in Possible and Retrievable Selves*. New Delhi: Oxford UP, forthcoming [1994].

Nandy, Ashis. *The Tao of Cricket: On Games of Destiny and the Destiny of Games*. New Delhi: Viking and Penguin, 1989.

Nandy, Ashis. *Traditions, Tyranny and Utopias: Essays in the Politics of Awareness*. New Delhi: Oxford UP, 1987; paperback ed., 1992.

Niranjana, Tejaswini, Sudhir, P., and Dhareshwar, Vivek, eds. *Interrogating Modernity: Culture and Colonialism in India.* Calcutta: Seagull Books, 1993.

Niranjana, Tejaswini. "Colonialism and the Aesthetics of Translation." In *Interrogating Modernity: Culture and Colonialism in India.* Edited by Tejaswini Niranjana, P. Sudhir, and Vivek Dhareshwar. Calcutta: Seagull Books, 1993.

Niranjana, Tejaswini. "Deconstructing Translation and History: Derrida on Benjamin." *Strategies* , no. 1 (Fall 1988):100-19.

Niranjana, Tejaswini. "Representation, History and the Case of Translation." *Jrl. of Arts and Ideas*, nos. 17-18 (June 1989):109-116.

Niranjana, Tejaswini. *Siting Translation: History, poststructuralism and the colonial context.* Berkeley: Univ. of California Press, 1991.

Padikkal, Shivarama. "Inventing Modernity: The Emergence of the Novel in India." In *Interrogating Modernity: Culture and Colonialism in India.* Edited by Tejaswini Niranjana, P. Sudhir, and Vivek Dhareshwar. Calcutta: Seagull Books, 1993.

Parker, Andrew; Russo, Mary; Sommer, Doris; Yaeger, Patricia, eds., *Nationalisms and Sexualities*. New York: Routledge, 1992.

Parry, Benita. "Problems in Current Theories of Colonial Discourse." *Oxford Literary Review* 9, 1-2 (1987):27-58.

Pathak, Zakhia; Śengupta, Saswati; and Purkayastha, Sharmila. "The Prisonhouse of Orientalism." *Textual Practice* 5, 2 (Summer 1991):195-218.

Radhakrishnan, R. "Canonicity and Theory: Towards a Post-Structuralist Pedgagogy." In *Theory/Pedagogy/Politics*, pp. 112-135. Edited by Donald Morton and Mas'ud Zavarzadeh. Chicago: University of Illinois Press, 1991.

Radhakrishnan, R. "Cultural Theory and the Politics of Location." In *Views Beyond the Border Country: Raymond Williams and Cultural Politics*, pp. 275-94. Edited by Dennis L. Dworkin and Leslie G. Roman. New York: Routledge, 1993.

Radhakrishnan, R. "Culture as Common Ground: Ethnicity and Beyond." *Melus* 14, 2 (Summer 1987):5-19.

Radhakrishnan, R. "Ethnic Identity and Post-Structuralist Differance." *Cultural Critique* (Spring 1987):199-220. Also published in *The Nature and Context of Minority Discourse*, pp. 50-71. Edited by AbdulJan Mohamed and David Lloyd. New York: Oxford UP, 1990.

Radhakrishnan, R. "Nationalism, Gender and the Narrative of Identity." In *Nationalisms and Sexualities*, pp. 77-95. Edited by Andrew Parker, Mary Russo, Doris Sommer, and Patricia Yaeger. London: Routledge, 1992.

Radhakrishnan, R. "Negotiating Subject Positions in an Uneven World." In *Feminism and Institutions*, pp. 276-90. Edited by Linda Kauffman. Oxford: Basil Blackwell, 1989.

Radhakrishnan, R. "Post-Structuralist Politics: Towards a Theory of Coalition." In *Jameson/Postmodernism/Critique*, pp. 301-32. Edited by Douglas Kellner. Washington, D.C.: Maisonneuve Press, 1989.

Radhakrishnan, R. "Reality, the Text, and Post-Modern Representation: A Question in Theory, or Theory in Question." In *Post-Modern Fiction: A Bio-Biblio-Graphic Guide*, pp. 229-42. Edited by Larry McCafferey. Westport, Conn.: Greenwood Press, 1986.

Radhakrishnan, R. "The Changing Subject and the Politics of Theory." *Differences* 2, 2 (Summer 1990):126-52.

Radhakrishnan, R. "The Post-Modern Event and the End of Logocentrism." *boundary 2* 12, 1 (Fall 1983):33-62.

Radhakrishnan, R. "To Be: A Foucauldian Itinerary." *Works and Days* (Fall 1986):51-77.

Radhakrishnan, R. "Toward an Effective Intellectual: Foucault or Gramsci?" In *Intellectuals: Aesthetics, Politics, Academics*, pp. 57-99. Edited by Bruce Robbins. Minneapolis: University of Minnesota Press, 1990.

Raina, Badri. "Mikhail Bakhtin: The Politics of Language and Genre." *Jrl. of Arts and Ideas*, no. 9 (Oct.-Dec. 1984):65-78.

Rajan, Tillotma. "Displacing Post-Structuralism: Romantic Studies after Paul de Man." *Studies in Romanticism* 24, 4 (Winter 1985):451-74.

Rorty, Richard. "A Pragmatist View of Rationality and Cultural Difference." *Philosophy East and West* 42, 4 (Oct. 1992):581-596 [comments on Ashis Nandy].

Rushdie, Salman. *Imaginary Homelands: Essays and Criticism 1981-1991*. London: Granta/Penguin, 1991.

Sardar, Ziauddin. "Surviving the Terminator: The Postmodern Mental Condition." *Futures* 22, 2 (March 1990):203-210.

Sardar, Ziauddin. "Total Recall: Aliens, 'Others', and Amnesia in Postmodernist Thought." *Futures* 23, 2 (March 1991):189-203.

Schwarz, Henry. "Provocations Toward a Theory of Third World Literature." *Mississippi Review* 49/50 (1989):177-201.

Shahani, Kumar. "Interrogating Internationalism." *Jrl. of Arts and Ideas*, no. 19 (May 1990):5-19.

Sivaramakrishnan, Arvind. "The Slave with Two Hearts: The Asymmetry of Cultural Assimilation." *Third Text* , no. 7 (Summer 1989):3-10.

Spivak, Gayatri Chakravorty. "Asked to Talk About Myself . . ." *Third Text*, no. 19 (Summer 1992):9-18.

Spivak, Gayatri Chakravorty. "Constitutions and Culture Studies." *Yale Jrl. of Law and the Humanities* 2, 1 (1990):133-47.

Spivak, Gayatri Chakravorty. "Feminism in Colonization." *Differences* 3, 3 (1991):139-70.

Spivak, Gayatri Chakravorty. "Identity and Alterity." An interview with Nikos Papastergiadis. *Arena*, no. 97 (1991):65-76.

Spivak, Gayatri Chakravorty. *In Other Worlds: Essays in Cultural Politics*. New York: Routledge, 1987; reprint ed., Calcutta: Seagull Books, 1990.

Spivak, Gayatri Chakravorty. "More on Power/Knowledge." In *Rethinking Power*, pp. 149-73. Edited by Thomas E. Warternberg. Albany, New York: State Univ. of New York Press, 1992.

Spivak, Gayatri Chakravorty. "Neocolonialism and the Secret Agent of Knowledge." *Oxford Literary Review* 13 (1991):220-51.

Spivak, Gayatri Chakravorty. *Outside in the Teaching Machine*. London: Routledge, 1993.

Spivak, Gayatri Chakravorty. "Poststructuralism, Postcoloniality, Marginality, and Value." In *Literary Theory Today*, pp. 219-44. Edited by Peter Collier and Helga Geyer-Ryan. Cambridge: Polity, 1990.

Spivak, Gayatri Chakravorty. "The Burden of English Studies." In *The Lie of the Land: English Literary Studies in India*, pp. 275-99. Edited by Rajeswari Sunder Rajan. New Delhi: Oxford UP, 1992.

Spivak, Gayatri Chakravorty. "The Making of Americans, the Teaching of English, and the Future of Cultural Studies." *New Literary History* 21, 4 (1990):781-98.

Spivak, Gayatri Chakravorty. "The Politics of Translation." In *Destabilzing Theory: Contemporary Feminist Debates*. Edited by Michele Barrett and Anne Phillips. Stanford: Stanford UP, 1992.

Spivak, Gayatri Chakravorty. "Time and Timing: Law and History." In *Chronotypes: the Construction of Time*, pp. 99-117. Edited by John Bender and David Wellbery. Stanford: Stanford UP, 1991.

Spivak, Gayatri Chakravorty. "Who Claims Alterity?" *In Remaking History*, pp. 269-92. Edited by Barbara Kruger and Phil Mariani. Dia Art Foundation, Discussions in Contemporary Culture, Number 4. Seattle: Bay Press, 1989.

Spivak, Gayatri Chakravorty. "Woman in Difference: Mahasweta Devi's 'Douloti the Beautiful.' In *Nationalisms and Sexualities*, pp. 96-117. Edited by Andrew Parker, Mary Russo, Doris Sommer, and Patricia Yaeger. New York: Routledge, 1992.

Srivastava, Mukesh. "Mosaic of Narrative Manipulations: Power and Production of Subjectivity in (Post) Colonial India." *EPW* 27, 4 (25 January 1992):PE47-57.

Sudhir, P. "Colonialism and the Vocabularies of Dominance." In *Interrogating Modernity: Culture and Colonialism in India*. Edited by Tejaswini Niranjana, P. Sudhir, and Vivek Dhareshwar. Calcutta: Seagull Books, 1993.

Suleri, Sara. *The Rhetoric of English India*. Chicago: Univ. of Chicago Press, 1992.

Tharu, Susie and Lalita, K. "Empire, Nation, and the Literary Text." In *Interrogating Modernity: Culture and Colonialism in India*. Edited by Tejaswini Niranjana, P. Sudhir, and Vivek Dhareshwar. Calcutta: Seagull Books, 1993.

Tharu, Susie. "Thinking the Nation Out: Some Reflections on Nationalism and Theory." *Jrl. of Arts and Ideas*, nos. 17-18 (June 1989):81-89.

Tharu, Susie. "Women Writing in India." *Jrl. of Arts and Ideas*, nos. 20-21 (March 1991):49-66.

Uberoi, J. P. Singh. *Science and Culture*. Delhi: Oxford UP, 1978.

Uberoi, J. P. Singh. *The Other Mind of Europe: Goethe as a Scientist*. Delhi: Oxford UP, 1984.

Vidyarthi, Govind. *Cultural Neocolonialism*. New Delhi: Allied Publishers, 1988.

Viswanathan, Gauri. "Elihu Yale, British Imperialism, and American Higher Education: The Naming of Yale College." Forthcoming in *Cultures of American Imperialism*. Edited by Donald Pease and Amy Kaplan. Durham, N.C.: Duke UP, 1993.

Viswanathan, Gauri. "Raymond Williams and British Colonialism." *Yale Jrl. of Criticism* 4, 2 (1991):47-66; also published as "Raymond Williams and British Colonialism: The Limits of Metropolitan Cultural Theory." In *Views Beyond the Border Country: Raymond Williams and Cultural Politics*, pp. 217-30. Edited by Dennis Dworkin and Leslie Roman. New York & London: Routledge, 1993.

Young, Robert M. *White Mythologies: Writing History and the West*. London & New York: Routledge, 1990.

IV. The Diaspora — Indians Abroad

Barz, R. K. "The Cultural Significance of Hindi in Mauritius." *South Asia* 3, 1 (1973):1-13.

Barz, Richard K. and Seigel, Jeff, eds. *Language Transplanted: The Development of Overseas Hindi*. Wiesbaden: Harrassowitz, 1988.

Bhachu, Parminder. *Twice Migrants: East African Sikh Settlers in Britain*. London & New York: Tavistock Publications, 1985.

Bhachu, Parminder and Light, Ivan, eds. *Immigration and Entrepreneurship: Culture, Capital, and Ethnic Networks*. New Brunswick, N.J.: Transaction Books, 1993.

Bhachu, Parminder and Westwood, Sallie, eds. *Enterprising Women: Home, Work, and Minority Cultures in Britain*. London & New York: Routledge, 1988.

Bhattacharjee, Anannya. "The Habit of Ex-Nomination: Nation, Woman, and the Indian Immigrant Bourgeoisie." *Public Culture* 5, 1 (Fall 1992): 19-44.

Birbalsingh, Frank, ed. *Indenture and Exile: The Indo-Caribbean Experience*. Toronto: The South Asian Review, 1989.

Birbalsingh, Frank. "Indo-Caribbean Test Cricketers." *The Toronto South Asian Review* 5, 1 (1986):105-17.

Birbalsingh, Frank. *Passion and Exile: Essays on Caribbean Literature*. London: Hausib, 1988.

Chandan, Amarjit, ed. *Apne Aap Ton Dur*. British Punjabi Poetry. Amritsar: Balraj Sahni, 1985.

Chandan, Amarjit, ed. *Do Kinare*. British Punjabi Short Stories. Delhi: Navyug; London: Shakti, 1982.

Chandan, Amarjit. *Indians in Britain*. New Delhi: Sterling, 1986.

Clarke, Colin et al, eds. *South Asians Overseas: Migration and Ethnicity*. Cambridge: Cambridge UP, 1990.

Fryer, Peter. *Black People in the British Empire: An Introduction*. London: Pluto, 1989.

Fryer, Peter. *Staying Power: The History of the Black People in Britain*. London: Pluto, 1984.

Ganguly, Keya. "Migrant Identities: Personal Memory and the Construction of Selfhood." *Cultural Studies* 6, 1 (January 1992):27-50.

Ghosh, Amitav. "An obstacle course lunch." *Telegraph* (Calcutta), 11 Oct. 1993.

Ghosh, Amitav. "The Diaspora in Indian Culture." *Public Culture* 2, 1 (Fall 1989):73-78.

Gregory, R. G. *Quest for Equality: Asian Politics in East Africa (1900-1967)*. Hyderabad: Orient Longman, 1993.

Grewal, Inderpal. "Reading and Writing the South Asian Diaspora: Feminism and Nationalism in North America." In *Our Feet Walk the Sky: Women of the South Asian Diaspora*, pp. 226-36. Edited by The Women of the South Asian Descent Collective. San Francisco: Aunt Lute Books, 1993.

Haraksingh, Kusha. "Structure, Process and Indian Culture in Trinidad." *Immigrants and Minorities* 7,1 (1982):113-22.

Helweg, Arthur W. "The Indian Diaspora: Influence on International Relations." In *Modern Diasporas in International Politics*, pp. 103-29. Edited by Gabriel Sheffer. New York: St. Martin's, 1986.

Institute of Race Relations. *Southall: The Birth of a Black Community*. Campaign Against Racism and Fascism. London: Institute of Race Relations and Southall Rights, 1981.

Jha, J. C. *East Indians in the Caribbean: Colonialism and The Struggle for Identity*. London & New York, 1982.

Kelly, John D. *A Politics of Virtue: Hinduism, Sexuality, and Countercolonial Discourse in Fiji*. Chicago: Univ. of Chicago Press, 1991.

Kelly, John D. "From Holi to Diwali in Fiji: An Essay on Ritual and History." *Man* (New Series) 23 (1988):40-55.

Klass, Morton. *Singing with Sai Baba: The Politics of Revitalization in Trinidad*. Oxford: Westview Press, 1991.

Lal, Brij V. "Veil of Dishonour: Sexual Jealousy and Suicide on Fiji Plantations." *Journal of Pacific History* (Australia) 20, 3-4 (1985): 135-55.

Leonard, Karen Isaksen. *Making Ethnic Choices: California's Punjabi Mexican Americans*. Philadelphia: Temple UP, 1992.

Leonard, Karen Isaksen. "Punjabi Pioneers in California: Political Skills on a New Frontier." *South Asia* 12, 2 (1989):69-82.

Lynch, Caitrin. "Nation, Woman, and the Indian Bourgeoisie: An Alternative Formulation." *Public Culture* 6, 2 (Winter 1994):425-37.

Maan, Bashir. *The New Scots: The Story of Asians in Scotland*. Edinburgh: Donald, 1992.

Maharaj, Sarat. "The Congo is Flooding the Acropolis: Art in Britain of the Immigrants." *Third Text* 15 (Summer 1991):77-90.

Mazumdar, Sucheta. "Racist Responses to Racism: The Aryan Myth and South Asians in the United States." *South Asia Bulletin* 9, 1 (1989): 47-55.

Mohan, Peggy. "Two Faces of a Language Death" [on Trinidad Bhojpuri]." *IICQ* 11, 2 (June 1984):133-44.

Mukherjee, Arun [Prabha]. "South Asian Poetry in Canada: In Search of a Place." *World Literature Written in English* 26, 1 (1986):84-98.

Naidoo, Thillayvel. *The Arya Samaj Movement in South Africa*. Delhi: Motilal Banarsidass, 1992.

Nandy, Ashis and Papastergiadis, Nikos. "Dialogue and the Diaspora." *Third Text* 11 (Summer 1990).

Nevadomsky, Joseph. "Social Change and the East Indians in Rural Trinidad: a Critique of Methodologies." *Social and Economic Studies* 31 (1982): 901-26.

Persaud, Kamal. *Racism Against the Indians in the Eastern Caribbean*. Trinidad and Tobago: Battlefront Pointers, 1988.

Race Today Collective. *The Struggle of Asian Workers in Britain*. London, 1983.

Radhakrishnan, R. "Ethnicity in an Age of Diaspora." *Transition*, no. 54 (1991):104-15.

Rahim, Amin-ur. "Multiculturalism or Ethnic Hegemony: A Critique of Multicultural Education in Toronto." *Jrl. of Ethnic Studies* 18, 3 (Fall 1990):29-46.

Rao, S. Balu. *Last Mile Together: An Anthology of South African Poems*. The Afro-Asian Writers' Association, 1991.

Sivanandan, A. *A Different Hunger: Writings on Black Resistance*. London: Pluto, 1982.

Sivanandan, A. *Communities of Resistance: Writings on Black Struggles for Socialism*. London: Verso, 1990.

Southhall Black Sisters. *Against the Grain: A Celebration of Survival and Struggle*. London, 1990.

Vassanji, M. G., ed. *A Meeting of Streams: South Asian Canadian Literature*. Toronto: T[oronto] S[outh] A[sian] R[eview] Publications, 1985.

Vertovec, Steven. *Hindu Trinidad: Religion, Ethnicity and Socio-Economic Change*. London: Macmillan Caribbean, 1992.

Vertovec, Steven. "Religion and Ethnic Ideology: The Hindu Youth Movement in Trinidad." *Ethnic and Racial Studies* 13, 2 (1990):225-49.

Vingadassamy-Engel, Lotus. "The Hindu Diaspora in the French West Indies." *India International Centre Quarterly* 19, 3 (Monsson 1992): 6-26.

Visram, Rozima. *Ayahs, Lascars and Princes: Indians in Britain 1700-1947*. London: Pluto Press, 1986.

Weiss, Anita M. "South Asian Muslims in Hong Kong: Creation of a 'Local Boy' Identity." *MAS* 25, 3 (1991):417-53.

West, Michael. "Indian Politics in South Africa: 1860 to the Present." *South Asia Bulletin* 7 (1987):97-111.

V. Ecology and Environment

Agarwal, Anil and Narain, Sunita. *Towards a Green World: Should Global Environmental Management Be Built on Legal Conventions or Human Rights?* New Delhi: Centre for Science and Environment, 1992.

Agarwal, Anil. "Human-Nature Interactions in a Third World Country." *The Environmentalist* 6, 2 (1986).

Agarwal, Bina. *Cold Hearths and Barren Slopes: The Woodfuel Crisis in the Third World*. London: Zed Books, 1986.

Agarwal, Bina. "Engendering the Environment Debate: Lessons from the Indian Subcontinent." CASID Distinguished Speaker Series, Discussion Paper No. 8. Michigan State University Press, 1991.

Agarwal, Bina. "The Gender and Environment Debate: Lessons from India." *Feminist Studies* 18, 1 (Spring 1992):119-159.

Agarwal, Bina. "Under the Cooking Pot: The Political Economy of the Domestic Fuel Crisis in Rural South Asia." *IDS Bulletin* 18, 1 (1987): 11-22.

Agarwal, Bina. "Who Sows? Who Reaps? Women and Land Rights in India." *Jrl. of Peasant Studies* 15, 4 (1988):531-581. Reprinted as booklet by the Institute of Economic Growth, University Enclave, Delhi.

Bajaj, Jatinder K. "Green Revolution: A Historical Perspective." *PPST Bulletin* 2 (1982):87-112.

Bajaj, Jatinder K. "The Bhopal Tragedy: The Responsibility of the Scientific Community." *PPST Bulletin* 5 (1985):6-14.

Baxi, Upendra. *Inconvenient Forum and Convenient Catastrophe: the Bhopal Case*. Bombay: N. M. Tripathi, 1986.

Chowdhry, Kamla. "Poverty, Environment, Development." *Daedalus* (Winter 1989):141-158.

Dietrich, Gabriele. "Women, Ecology and Culture." *Lokayan Bulletin* 7, 1 (Jan.-Feb. 1989):7-26.

Dogra, Bharat. *Forests and People*. Delhi: Published by the author, 1984.

Fernandes, Walter and Menon, Geeta. *Tribal Women and Forest Economy: Deforestation, Exploitation, and Status Change*. Delhi: Indian Social Institute, 1987.

Gadgil, Madhav. "Deforestation: Problems and Prospects." *Lokayan Bulletin* 7, 3 (May-June 1989):9-46.

Gadgil, Madhav. "Towards an Ecological History of India." *EPW* (Special Number, November 1985):1909-38.

Guha, Ramachandra. "Eco-Development Debate: A Critical Review." Occasional Paper, no. 73. Calcutta: CSSS, 1985.

Guha, Ramachandra. "Forestry in British and Post-British India: A Historical Analysis." *EPW* (29 Oct. 1983):1882-96.

Guha, Ramachandra. "Ideological Tends in Indian Environmentalism." *EPW* (3 Dec. 1988):2578-81.

Guha, Ramachandra. "Radical American Environmentalism and Wilderness Preservation: A Third World Critique." *Environmental Ethics* 11 (Spring 1989):71-83.

Guha, Ramachandra. "Toward a Cross-Cultural Environmental Ethic." *Alternatives* 15, 4 (Fall 1990):431-47.

Guha, Ramachandra. "Writing environmental history in India." *Studies in History* (New Series) 9, 1 (1993):119-29.

Guha, Ramachandra and Gadgil, Madhav. *This Fissured Land: An Ecological History of India*. Delhi: Oxford UP, 1992.

Jain, Shobhita. "Women and People's Ecological Movement: A Case Study of Women's Rule in the Chipko Movement in Uttar Pradesh." *EPW* 19, 41 (13 Oct. 1984): 1788-94.

Kelkar, Govind and Nathan, Dev. *Gender and Tribe: Women, Land and Forests in Jharkand*. New Delhi: Kali for Women, 1992.

Kothari, Rajni. "On Eco-Imperialism." *Alternatives* 7, 3 (Sept. 1981):385-94.

Mies, Maria and Shiva, Vandana. *The World on the Brink: An Ecofeminist*

Perspective on Capital Accumulation, Ecological Destruction & People's Survival. New Delhi: Kali for Women, 1993.

Mitra, S. "Ecology as Science and Science Fiction." *EPW* 17 (1982):147-52.

Nanda, Meera. "Is Modern Science a Western, Patriarchal Myth? A Critique of the Populist Orthodoxy." *South Asia Bulletin* 11, 1-2 (1991):32-61.

Parajuli, Pramod. "Power and Knowledge in Development Discourse: New Social Movements and the State in India." *International Social Science Journal* 20 (Feb. 1991):173-90.

Pereira, Winin and Seabrook, Jeremy. *Asking the Earth*. London: Earthscan Publications, 1990.

PPST Bulletin, Madras Group. "The Story of Scientific Forestry in India: Some Highlights." *PPST Bulletin* 3, 1 (May 1983):31-67.

Ranga, Haripriya. "Romancing the Environment: Popular Environmental Action in the Garhwal Himalayas." In *In Defense of Livelihood: Comparative Studies on Environmental Action*, pp. 155-81. Edited by John Friedman and Haripriya Ranga. West Hartford, Conn.: Kumarian Press, Inc., 1993.

Routledge, Paul. "Putting politics in its place: Baliapal, India as a terrain of resistance." *Political Geography* 11, 6 (Nov. 1992):588-611.

Shanmugaratnam, N. "Development and Environment: a View from the South." *Race and Class* 29, 3 (Jan.-March 1989), Special Issue, 'Un-Greening the Third World'.

Sharma, Kumud. "Women in Struggle: A Case Study of the Chipko Movement." *Samya Shakti: A Journal of Women's Studies* 1, 2 (1984):58 ff.

Shiva, Vandana. *Ecology and the Politics of Survival: Conflicts over Natural Resources in India*. New Delhi: United Nations University Press, 1991.

Shiva, Vandana. "Ecology Movements in India." *Alternatives* 11, 2 (April 1986):255-73.

Shiva, Vandana. "Let us Survive: Women, Ecology and Development." *Sangarsh*, no. 3 [Bangalore], n.d.

Shiva, Vandana. *Staying Alive: Women, Ecology and Survival in India*. London: Zed Books, 1988; Delhi: Kali for Women, 1988.

Shiva, Vandana. "The Violence of Reductionist Science." *Alternatives* 12, 2 (April 1987):243-61. Reprinted as "Reductionist Science as Epistemological Violence" in *Science, Hegemony and Violence*, pp. 232-56. Edited by Ashis Nandy. Delhi: Oxford UP, 1992 [1988].

Shiva, Vandana. *Violence of the Green Revolution: Ecological Degradation and Political Conflict in Punjab*. Dehra Dun: Research Foundation for Science and Ecology, 1989.

Shiva, Vandana and Bandyopadhyay, Jayanta. "Chipko." *Seminar*, no. 330 (February 1987).

Shiva, Vandana and Bandyopadhyay, Jayanta. "The History, Structure and Impact of the Chipko Movement." *Mountain Research & Development* 6, 2 (1986):113-41.

Vatsyayan, Kapila. "Ecology and Indian Myth." *IICQ* 19, 2 (Spring-Summer 1992):157-80.

VI. English Studies

Amur, G. S. and Desai, S. K., eds. *Colonial Consciousness in Commonwealth Literature*. Bombay, Madras and New Delhi: Somanja Publications, 1984.

Anagol, Padma J. "Literature as Ideology: Rudyard Kipling's Creative World." *Studies in History* 3, 1 (1987):75-96.

Anniah Gowda, H. H., ed. *The Colonial and the Neo-Colonial Encounters in Commonwealth Literature*. Mysore: Prasaragana University, 1983.

Bailey, G. M. "On the De-construction of Culture in Indian Literature: A Tentative Response to Vijay Mishra's Article." *South Asia* (New Series) 12, 1 (1989):85-102.

Bhalla, Alok. *Politics of Atrocity and Lust: The Vampire Tale as a Nightmare History of England in the Nineteenth Century*. New Delhi: Sterling, 1988.

Bhatnagar, Rashmi. "A Reading of Pope's *The Rape of the Lock*." In *Woman/Image/Text*, pp. 40-53. Edited by Lola Chatterjee. New Delhi: Trianka, 1986.

Bhatnagar, Rashmi. "Genre and gender: a reading of Tagore's *The Broken Nest* and R. K. Narayan's *The Dark Room*." In *Woman/Image/Text: Feminist Readings of Literary Texts*, pp. 172-87. Edited by Lola Chatterjee. New Delhi: Trianka, 1986.

Bhattacharya, Nandini. "Ethnopolitical Dynamics and the Language of Gendering in Dryden's *Aureng-Zebe*." *boundary 2* 20, 2 (Summer 1993):153-76.

Bhattacharyya, Gargi. "Cultural Education in Britain." *Oxford Literary Review*, no. 13 (1991):4-19.

Brennan, Timothy. *Salman Rushdie and the Third World: Myths of the Nation*. London: Macmillan, 1989.

Chatterji, Lola, ed. *Woman/Image/Text: Feminist Readings of Literary Texts*. New Delhi: Trianka, 1986.

Crane, Ralph J. *Inventing India: A History of India in English-Language Fiction*. New York: St. Martin's Press, 1992.

Dalmia, Manju. "Derozio: English Teacher." In *The Lie of the Land: English Literary Studies in India*, pp. 42-62. Edited by Rajeswari Sunder Rajan. New Delhi: Oxford UP, 1992.

Das, Sanjukta. *Feminist Literary Criticism*. Occasional Paper, no. 99. Calcutta: CSSS, 1988.

Das, Veena. "Science and Violence in Popular Fiction: Four Novels of Ira Levin." In *Science, Hegemony and Violence*, pp. 211-31. Edited by Ashis Nandy. Delhi: Oxford UP, 1992 [1988].

Dasgupta, Probal. *Beyond Linguistic Limits: The Otherness of English, India's Auntie Tongue Syndrome*. New Delhi: Sage Publications, 1993.

Datta, P. K. "Learning and Teaching: Keats' Odes." In *Ourstory: Indian Response to Nineteenth Century Literature*, pp. 25-40. Edited by Mohua Lahiri, Sanjay Kumar, and Anand Prakash. New Delhi: Academic Foundation, 1992.

Datta, P. K. "Studies in Heterogeneity: A Reading of Two Recent Indo-Anglian Novels." *Social Scientist*, no. 202 (March 1990).

Devi, Ganesh N. "The Commonwealth Literature Period" and "Comparative Literature." In *Literature(s) in English: New Perspectives*, pp. 79-94. Edited by Wolfgang Zach. Frankfurt am Maim: Peter Lang, 1990.

Devy, G. N. *After Amnesia: Tradition and Change in Indian Literary Criticism*. Madras: Orient Longman, 1992.

Dhareshwar, Vivek. "Self-Fashioning, Colonial Habitus and Double Exclusion: V. S. Naipual's 'The Mimic Men.'" *Criticism* 31, 1 (1989):73-102.

Dutta, Sangeeta. "Charlotte Bronte and the Woman Question." *EPW* 26, 40 (5 Oct. 1991):2311-16.

Gooneratne, Yasmine. *Diverse Inheritance: A Personal Perspective on Commonwealth Literature*. Adelaide: Center for Research in the New Literatures in English, 1980.

Gupta, Anjuli. "English Writing in India: Fear of Experimentation, Fear of Appropriation — Death of Creativity?" In *Crisis and Creativity in the New Literatures in English: Cross/Cultures*, pp. 151-68. Edited by Geoffrey V. Davis and Hena Maes-Jelinek. Amsterdam: Rodopi, 1990.

Hashmi, Alamgir.* *Commonwealth Literature: An Essay towards the Redefinition of a Popular/Counter Culture*. Lahore, 1983.

Hashmi, Alamgir. "Pakistani Literature in English: Past, Present, and Future." *South Asia Bulletin* 10, 2 (Fall 1990):48-53.

Jain, Manju. *A Critical Reading of the "Selected Poems" of T. S. Eliot*. New Delhi: Oxford UP, 1991.

Johsi, Svati. "'The Opposing Opposed': Marianne Moore and Possibilities of a Feminine Discourse." In *Woman/Image/Text: Feminist Readings of Literary Texts*, pp. 151-61. Edited by Lola Chatterji. Delhi: Trianka, 1986.

Joshi, Svati, ed. *Rethinking English: Essays in Literature, Language, History*. Delhi: Trianka, 1991.

Jussawalla, Feroza. "Decolonizing the Decolonizers: Breaking the Colonial Habit of Mind." *North Dakota Quarterly* 55, 3 (1987):175-89.

Jussawalla, Feroza. *Family Quarrels: Towards a Criticism of Indian Writing in English*. Berne and New York: Peter Lang, 1985.

Jussawalla, Feroza. "Rushdie's *Shame*: Problems in Communication." In *Studies in Indian Fiction in English*, pp. 1-13. Edited by Balarama Gupta. Gulbarga: JIWE Press, 1987.

Kanwar, Asha S. "Raymond Williams and the English Novel." *Social Scientist*, no. 180 (May 1988):46-60.

Kaul, Suvir. "The Indian Academic and Resistance to Theory." In *The Lie of the Land: English Literary Studies in India*, pp. 207-28. Edited by Rajeswari Sunder Rajan. New Delhi: Oxford UP, 1992.

Kaul, Suvir. *Thomas Gray and Literary Authority: A Study in Ideology and Poetics*. Stanford: Stanford UP, 1992.

Khan, Maqbool Hasan. "Without the 'Mind': Edward Dowden on Shakespeare's Art." In *Essays on Shakespeare in Honour of A. A. Ansari*, pp. 284-98. Edited by T. R. Sharma. Meerut, India: Shalabh Book House, 1986.

King, Adele. "Shashi Deshpande: Portraits of an Indian Woman." In *The New Indian Novel in English: A Study of the 1980s*, pp. 159-68. Edited by Viney Kirpal. New Delhi: Allied Publishers, 1990.

Kumar, Sanjay. "Fiction or Historical Positioning?: A Reading of J. G. Farell's The Siege of Krishnapur." In *Ourstory: Indian Response to Nineteenth Century Literature*, pp. 25-40. Edited by Mohua Lahiri, Sanjay Kumar, and Anand Prakash. New Delhi: Academic Foundation, 1992.

Kureishi, Hanif and Kermode, Frank. "Voice of the Almost English." Reprinted in *The Frontier Post: Kaleidoscope* (27 April 1990):9, 16.

Lal, Vinay. Review of Syed Amanuddin's *Creativity and Reception: Toward a Theory of Third World Criticism*, in *Indian Literature* 32, 3 (May-June, 1989):171-76.

Loomba, Ania. "Criticism and Pedagogy in the Indian Classroom." In *The Lie of the Land: English Literary Studies in India*, pp. 63-89. Edited by Rajeswari Sunder Rajan. New Delhi: Oxford UP, 1992.

Loomba, Ania. "Disorderly Women in Jacobean Tragedy: Towards a Materialist

Feminist Critique." Unpublished D. Phil. thesis, University of Sussex, 1987.

Loomba, Ania. *Gender, Race, Renaissance Drama*. Oxford India Paperback. Delhi: Oxford UP, 1992. [Reviewed by K. Vinod Chandran in *Social Scientist*, nos. 216-17 (May-June 1991):115-21.]

McBratney, John. "Images of Indian Women in Rudyard Kipling: A Case of Doubling Discourse." *Inscriptions* , nos. 3-4 (1988):47-57.

Mitra, Indrani and Mitra, Madhu. "The Discourse of Liberal Feminism and Third World Women's Texts: Some Issues of Pedagogy." *College Literature* 18, 3 (October 1991).

Mohanty, Satya P. "Kipling's Children and the colour line." *Race and Class* 31, 1 (July-September 1989):21-39. Modified and lengthier version published as "Drawing the Color Line: Kipling and the Culture of Colonial Rule." In *The Bounds of Race: Perspectives on Hegemony and Resistance*, pp. 311-44. Edited by Dominick LaCapra. Ithaca: Cornell Univ. Press, 1991.

Mohanty, Satya P. "The Epistemic Status of Cultural Identity: On *Beloved* and the Postcolonial Condition." *Cultural Critique*, no. 24 (Spring 1993): 41-80.

Moore-Gilbert, B. J. *Kipling and 'Orientalism'*. London: Croom Helm; New York: St. Martin's Press, 1986.

Mukherjee, Arun [Prabha]. *The Gospel of Wealth in the Modern American Novel: A Study of Dreiser and Some of His Contemporaries*. London & Sydney: Croom Helm; Totowa, New Jersey: Barnes & Nobles Books, 1987.

Mukherjee, Arun [Prabha]. *Towards an Aesthetic of Opposition: Essays on Literature Criticism and Cultural Imperialism*. Stratford, Ontario: Williams-Wallace, 1988.

Mukherjee, Meenakshi. "Macaulay's Imperishable Empire." *Literary Criterion* 17, 1 (1982), 38.

Mukherjee, Meenakshi. "Narrating a Nation." *Indian Literature* 35, 4 (July-August 1992):138-49.

Mukherjee, Meenakshi. *Realism and Reality: The Novel and Society in India.* Delhi: Oxford UP, 1985. [Review by Alok Rai, "Plots on Reality", *Jrl. of Arts and Ideas*, no. 9 (Oct.-Dec. 1984):43-48.]

Mukherjee, Meenakshi. "Story, history and her story." *Studies in History* (New Series) 9, 1 (1993):71-85.

Mukherjee, Sujit. "Tigers in Fiction: An Aspect of the Colonial Encounter." *Kunapipi* 9, 1 (1987):1-13.

Niranjana, Tejaswini. "Translation, Colonialism and the Rise of English." *EPW* 25, 15 (14 April 1990):773-79.

Parthasarthy, R. "Whoring after English Gods." In *Writers in East-West Encounter: New Cultural Bearings*. Edited by Guy Amirthanayagam. London: Macmillan, 1982.

Pathak, Zakhia. "Writing in Ourselves." In *Ourstory: Indian Response to Nineteenth Century Literature*, pp. 95-110. Edited by Mohua Lahiri, Sanjay Kumar, and Anand Prakash. New Delhi: Academic Foundation, 1992. Also published as "A Pedagogy for Postcolonial Feminists." In *Feminists Theorize the Political*, pp. 426-41. Edited by Judith Butler and Joan W. Scott. New York & London: Routledge, 1992.

Patil, Anand B. "The Whirlgig of Literary Taste: Impact or Alienation." *Indian Literature* 36, 4 (July-August 1993):156-69.

Rai, Alok. *Orwell and the Politics of Despair*. Cambridge: Cambridge UP, 1990.

Rajan, Rajeswari Sunder. "After 'Orientalism': Colonialism and English Literary Studies in India." *Social Scientist*, no. 158 (July 1986):23-35.

Rajan, Rajeswari Sunder. "Brokering English Studies: The British Council in India." In *The Lie of the Land: English Literary Studies in India*, pp. 130-55. Edited by Rajeswari Sunder Rajan. New Delhi: Oxford UP, 1992.

Rajan, Rajeswari Sunder. "Fixing English: Nation, Language, Subject." In *Lie of the Land: English Literary Studies in India*, pp. 7-28. Edited by Rajeswari Sunder Rajan. Delhi: Oxford UP, 1992.

Rajan, Rajeswari Sunder. "Katherine Mansfield and the Question of Women's Writing." In *Woman/Image/Text: Feminist Readings of Literary Texts*, pp. 133-50. Edited by Lola Chatterji. Delhi: Trianka, 1986.

Rajan, Rajeswari Sunder, ed. *Lie of the Land: English Literary Studies in India*. Delhi: Oxford UP, 1992.

Sangari, Kumkum. "Of Ladies, Gentlemen, and the Short Cut: *The Portrait of a Lady*." In *Woman/Image/Text*. Edited by Lola Chatterjee. Delhi: Trianka, 1986.

Sangari, Kumkum. "Relating Histories: Literature, Literacy and Gender in Early Nineteenth Century Calcutta and England." In *Rethinking English*, pp. 32-123. Edited by Swati Joshi. Delhi: Trianka, 1991; also published as Occasional Paper, NMML.

Sangari, Kumkum. "The Changing Text." *Journal of Arts and Ideas*, no. 8 (July-Sept. 1984):61-76.

Seed, David. "Disorientation and Commitment in the Fiction of Empire: Kipling and Orwell." *Dutch Quarterly Review of Anglo-American Letters* 14, 4 (1984):269-80.

Sena, Vinod and Verma, Rajiva. *New Essays on T. S. Eliot.* New Delhi: Oxford UP,1992.

Sharma, T. R. S. "Chinua Achebe and V. S. Naipaul: One Version and Two Postures on Post-Colonial Societies." In *The Colonial and the Neo-Colonial Encounters in Commonwealth Literature*, pp. 83-93. Mysore: Prasaragana Univ., 1983.

Sircar, Ajanta. "Imagining Metropolitan Subjectivity: Salman Rushdie's *Midnight's Children* and Amitav Ghosh's *The Shadow Lines*." Unpublished M.Phil. Dissertation, Department of English, University of Hyderabad, 1991.

Sircar, Ajanta. "Individualising History: The 'Real' Self in *The Shadow Lines*." *Social Scientist*, no. 223 (Dec. 1991):33-46.

Sircar, Ajanta. "Production of Authenticity: The Indo-Anglian Critical Tradition." *EPW* 27, 36 (5 Sept. 1992):1921-26.

Spivak, Gayatri Chakravorty. "The Burden of English Studies." In *The Lie of the Land: English Literary Studies in India*, pp. 275-99. Edited by Rajeswari Sunder Rajan. New Delhi: Oxford UP, 1992.

Spivak, Gayatri Chakravorty. "The Making of Americans, the Teaching of English, and the Future of Cultural Studies." *New Literary History* 21, 4 (1990):781-98.

Spivak, Gayatri Chakravorty. "Versions of the Margin: Coetzee's *Foe* reading Defoe's *Crusoe/Roxana*." In *Theory and Its Consequences*. Edited by Jonathan Arac and Barbara Johnson. Baltimore: Johns Hopkins U. Press, 1990.

Srinath, C. N. *The Literary Landscape: Essays on Indian Fiction and Poetry in English*. Delhi: Mittal, 1986.

Srivastava, Aruna. "The Empire Writes Back: Language and History in *Shame* and *Midnight's Children*." In *Past the Last Post: Theorizing Post-Colonialism and Post-Modernism*, pp. 65-78. Edited by Ian Adam and Helen Tiffin. Calgary: Univ. of Calgary Press, 1990.

Suleri, Sara. "Naipaul's Arrival." *The Yale Journal of Criticism* 2, 1 (Fall 1988):25-50.

Suleri, Sara. *The Rhetoric of English India*. Chicago: Univ. of Chicago Press, 1992.

Sullivan, Zohreh T. *Narratives of Empire: The Fictions of Rudyard Kipling*. New York: Cambridge UP, 1993.

Tharu, Susie. "Decoding [Mulk Raj] Anand's Humanism." *Kunapipi* 4, 2 (1982):30-41.

Tharu, Susie. "Tracing Savitri's Pedigree: Victorian Racism and the Image of Women in Indo-Anglian Literature." In *Recasting Women*, pp. 254-68. Edited by Kumkum Sangari and Sudesh Vaid. New Delhi: Kali for Women, 1989.

Viswanathan, Gauri. "Currying Favor: The Beginnings of English Literary Study in British India." *Social Text*, nos. 19/20 (Fall 1988):85-104.

Viswanathan, Gauri. "English in a Literate Society." In *The Lie of the Land: English Literary Studies in India*. Edited by R. S. Rajan. Delhi: Oxford UP, 1992.

Viswanathan, Gauri. *Masks of Conquest: Literary Study and British Rule in India*. New York: Columbia UP, 1989; London: Faber & Faber, 1990. [Reviewed by Henry Schwarz in *Polygraph*, no. 5 (1992):263-69.]

Viswanathan, Gauri. "The Beginnings of English Literary Study in British India." *Oxford Literary Review* 9, 1-2 (1987):2-26.

VII. Gender and Women's Studies

Aden, Michael and Mukherjee, S. N., eds. *Women in India and Nepal*. ANU Monographs on South Asia, No. 8. Canberra: Australian National University, 1982.

Agarwal, Bina and Afshar, Haleh, eds. *Women, Poverty, and Ideology: Contradictory Pressures, Uneasy Solutions*. London: Macmillan, 1989.

Agarwal, Bina, ed. *State, Community and Household in Modernizing Asia*. Delhi: Kali for Women, 1988.

Agarwal, Bina. "The Gender and Environment Debate: Lessons from India." *Feminist Studies* 18, 1 (Spring 1992):119-59.

Agarwal, Bina. "Who Sows? Who Reaps? Women and Land Rights in India." *Jrl. of Peasant Studies* 15, 4 (1988):531-81. Reprinted as booklet by the Institute of Economic Growth, University Enclave, Delhi.

Agarwal, Bina. "Women, Poverty, and Agricultural Growth in India." *Jrl. of Peasant Studies* 13 (July 1986):165-220.

Ahmad, Karuna. "Gandhi, Women's Roles, and the Freedom Movement." Occasional Papers on History and Society, no. 19. New Delhi: NMML, 1988.

Ahmed, Rehnuma. "Women's Movement in Bangladesh and the Left's Understanding of the Women Question." *Jrl. of Social Studies*, no. 30 (1985):27-56.

Amos, Valerie and Parmar, Pratibha. "Challenging Imperial Feminism." *Feminist Review* 17 (1984):3-19.

Amos, Valerie and Parmar, Pratibha. "Resistance and Responses: The Experiences of Black Girls in Britain." In *Feminism for Girls: An Adventure Story*. Edited by Angela McRobbie et al. Boston and London: Routledge & Kegan Paul, 1981.

Anandhi, S. "Representing Devadasis: 'Dasigal Mosavalai' as a Radical Text." *EPW* (Annual Number) 26, 11-12 (March 1991):739-46.

Anandhi, S. "Women's Question in the Dravidian Movement c. 1925-1948." *Social Scientist*, nos. 216-217 (May-June 1991):24-41.

Aranha, Celine; Fernando, Peter; and Mahale, Prabha. *Beyond the Fire Line: Perceptions of Eight Tribal Women*. New Delhi: Indian Social Institute, 1991.

Babb, Lawrence A. Indigenous Feminism in a Modern Hindu Sect." *Signs* 9, 3 (1984):399-416.

Bagchi, Jasodhara. "Representing Nationalism: Ideology of Motherhood in Colonial Bengal." *EPW* 25, 42-43 (25 Oct. 1990):WS65-71.

Balasubrahmanyan, Vimal. *Mirror Image: The Media and the Women's Question*. Bombay: Centre for Education and Documentation, 1988.

Bald, Suresht Renjen. "From 'Satyartha Prakash' to 'Manushi': An Overview of the Women's Movement in India." *Univ. of Michigan Working Paper*, no. 23 (April 1983).

Bandopadhyay, Sibaj; Chatterjee, Ratnabali; and Bagchi, Joasodhara. *Femininity Redefined: Politics of Home and the World in Colonial Bengal*. New Delhi: Kali for Women, forthcoming 1993.

Banerji, Himani. "Fashioning a Self: Educational Proposals for and by Women in Popular Magazines in Colonial Bengal." *EPW* 26, 43 (26 Oct. 1991):WS 50 ff.

Bardhan, Kalpana. "Being a Woman in South Asia." *Jrl. of Women's History* 2, 1 (Spring 1990):200-19.

Bardhan, Kalpana. "Women, Work, Welfare and Status: Forces of Tradition and Change in India". *South Asia Bulletin* 6, 1(Spring 1986):3-16.

Basu, Amrtia. "The Challenge of Difference in the Women's Movement in India." *Feminist Studies* 16 (1990).

Beneria, Lourdes and Sen, Gita. "Accumulation, Reproduction and Women's Role in Economic Development: Boserup Revisited", *Signs* 7, 2 (1982): 279-98.

Bhagwat, Vidyut. "Man-Woman Relations in the Writings of the Saint Poetesses." *New Quest*, no. 82 (July-August 1990):223-32.

Bhasin, Kamla and Khan, Nighat Said. *Some Questions on Feminism and Its Relevance in South Asia*. New Delhi: Kali for Women, 1986.

Bhasin, Kamla. *What is Patriarchy?* New Delhi: Kali for Women, forthcoming.

Bhattacharjee, Anannya. "The Habit of Ex-Nomination: Nation, Woman, and the Indian Immigrant Bourgeoisie." *Public Culture* 5, 1 (Fall 1992): 19-44.

Bhattacharji, Sukumari. "Motherhood in Ancient India." *EPW* 25, 2-43 (20-27 Oct. 1990):WS50-57.

Bhattacharji, Sukumari. "Sita in the TV Uttararamayana." *Social Scientist*, nos. 200-1 (Jan.Feb. 1990):66-71.

Bhattacharya, Nandini."Ethnopolitical Dynamics and the Language of Gendering in Dryden's *Aureng-Zebe*." *boundary* 2 20, 2 (Summer 1993):153-76.

Bhave, Sumitra. *Pan on Fire: Eight Dalit Women Tell Their Story*. Translated by Gauri Deshpande. Delhi: Indian Social Institute, 1988.

Bhavni, Kum Kum and Coulson, Margaret. "Transforming socialist-feminism: the challenge of racism." *Feminist Review*, no. 23 (Summer 1986).

Bhushan, Madhu. "Vimochana: Women's Struggles, Nonviolent Militancy and Direct Action in the Indian Context." *Women's Studies International Forum* 12, 1 (1989):25-33.

Borthwick, Meredith. *The Changing Role of Women in Bengal, 1849-1905*. Princeton, New Jersey: Princeton UP, 1984.

Burton, Antoinette M. "The White Woman's Burden: British Feminists and the Indian Woman, 1865-1915." *Women's Studies International Forum* 13, 4 (Winter 1990).

Chaki-Sircar, Manjusri. *Feminism in a Traditional Society: Women of the Manipur Valley*. New Delhi: Shakti Books, 1984.

Chakravarti, Uma. "Beyond the Altekarian Paradigm: Towards a New Understanding of Gender Relations in Early Indian History." *Social Scientist*, no. 183 (August 1988):44-52.

Chakravarti, Uma. "Pativrata." *Seminar*, no. 318 (February 1986):17-20.

Chakravarti, Uma. "The development of the Sita myth: a case study of women in myth and literature." *Samya Shakti* 1, 1 (July 1983):68-75.

Chanda, P. Sita. "Birthing Terrible Beauties: Feminisms and 'Women's Magazines'". *EPW* 26, 43 (26 Oct. 1991) pp. WS-67 ff.

Chatterjee, Partha. "Colonialism, Nationalism, and Colonized Women: The Contest in India." *American Ethnologist* 16, 4 (November 1989): 622-33.

Chatterji, Lola, ed. *Woman/Image/Text: Feminist Readings of Literary Texts*. New Delhi: Trianka, 1986.

Chaudhuri, Nupur. "Memsahibs and motherhood in nineteenth-century colonial India." *Victorian Studies* 31, 4 (Summer 1988):517-35.

Chawla, Janet. "The Rig Vedic Slaying of Vrtra: Menstruation Taboos in Mythology." *Manushi*, no. 68 (Jan.-Feb. 1992):29-36.

Chhachhi, Amritha. "Forced Identities: the State, Communalism, Fundamentalism and Women in India." In *Women, Islam and the State*, pp. 144-75. Edited by Deniz Kandiyoti. Philadelphia: Temple UP, 1991.

Chhachhi, Amritha. "In the Eye of the Storm: Women and Religious Fundamentalism in South Asia." *Sangarsh* [Bangalore], no. 3 (n.d.):8 ff.

Chhachhi, Amritha. "The State, Religious Fundamentalism and Women: Trends in South Asia." *EPW* (18 March 189):567-78.

Clark, Alice W. *Gender and Political Economy: Explorations of South Asian Systems*. Delhi: Oxford UP, 1992.

Custers, Peter. *Women in the Tebhaga Uprising*. Delhi: Naya Prakash, 1987.

Dalmia-Luderitz, Vasudha. "'Sati' as a Religious Rite: *Parliamentary Papers on Widow Immolation, 1821-30"*, *EPW* 27, 4 (25 January 1992):PE 58-64.

Das, Veena. "Femininity and the Orientation to the Body." In *Women, Socialization and Change.* Edited by Karuna Ahmed. Delhi: Orient Longmans, 1988.

Das, Veena. "Gender Studies, Cross-Cultural Comparison and the Colonial Organization of Knowledge." *Berkshire Review* 21 (1986):58-76.

Debi, Rashsundari. *Amar Jiban (My Life)*. Edited with an introduction by Tanika Sarkar. New Delhi: Kali for Women, forthcoming 1994.

Desai, A. R., ed. *Women's Liberation and Politics of Religious Personal Laws in India*. Bombay: C. G. Shah Memorial Trust Publications, 1986.

Dhruvarajan, Vanaja. *Hindu Women and The Power of Ideology*. New Delhi: Sage Publications, 1989.

Dietrich, Gabriele. *Reflections on the Women's Movement in India: Religion, Ecology, Development*. New Delhi: Horizon India Books, 1992.

Dietrich, Gabriele. "The Development Debate and Gender Implications." *Lokayan Bulletin* 8, 1 (Jan.-Feb. 1990):39-56.

Dietrich, Gabriele. *Women's Movement in India: Conceptual and Religious Reflections*. Bangalore: Breakthrough Publications, 1988.

Dietrich, Gabriele. "Women, Ecology and Culture." *Lokayan Bulletin* 7, 1 (Jan.-Feb. 1989):7-26.

Dutta,,Sangeeta. "Relinquishing the Halo: Portrayal of Mother in Indian Writing in English." *EPW* 25, 42-43 (25 Oct. 1990):WS84-94.

Engineer, Asghar Ali, ed. *The Shahbano Controversy*. Hyderabad: Orient Longman, 1987.

Fernandes, Walter and Menon, Geeta. *Tribal Women and Forest Economy:*

Deforestation, Exploitation, and Status Change. Delhi: Indian Social Institute, 1987.

Fernando, Peter and Yasas, Frances M., ed. *Woman's Image Making and Shaping*. Pune: Ishvani Kendra, 1985.

Forbes, Geraldine. "Caged Tigers: First-wave Feminists in India." *Women's Studies International Forum* 5, 6 (1982).

Forbes, Geraldine. "In search of the 'pure heathen': missionary women in nineteenth century India." *EPW* 21, 17 (26 April 1986):WS2-8.

Gandhi, Nandita. *When the Rolling Pins Hit the Streets: A Case Study of the Anti-Price Rise Movement in India.* New Delhi: Kali for Women, forthcoming 1994.

Gandhi, Nandita and Shah, Nandita. *The Issues at Stake: Theory and Practice in the Contemporary Women's Movement in India*. Delhi: Kali for Women, 1992.

Ganesh, Kamala. "Mother Who is Not a Mother: In Search of the Great Indian Goddess." *EPW* 25, 42-43 (20-27 Oct. 1990):WS58-64.

Gardezi, Fauzia. "Islam, Feminism, and the Women's Movement in Pakistan: 1981-1991." *South Asia Bulletin* 10, 2 (1990):18-24.

Garg, Mridula. "Metaphors of Womanhood in Indian Literature". *Alternatives* 16, 4 (Fall 1991):407-24.

Geetha, V. "Gender and Political Discourse." *EPW* 26, 7 (16 Feb. 1991):387-88.

Ghadially, Rehana, ed. *Women in Indian Society: A Reader*. New Delhi: Sage Publications, 1988.

Ghadially, Rehana. "Teaching the Psychology of Sex Roles to Engineers in India." *Women's Studies Quarterly* 16, 3-4 (Fall/Winter 1988):86-99.

Ghadially, Rehana. "Veiling the Unveiled: The Politics of Purdah in a Muslim Sect." *South Asia* (New Series) 12, 2 (1989):33-48.

Ghosh, Shohini and Chakravarti, Uma. "Hidden Agendas in the Alternative Media: Religion and Gender." *Samya Shakti* 6 (1991-92):81-97.

Gokhale, Shanta. "Mother in Sane Guruji's 'Shyamchi Ai.'" *EPW* 25, 42-43 (25 Oct. 1990):WS95-102.

Gupta, Bina, ed. *Sexual Archetypes, East and West*. A New Era Book. New York: Paragon House, 1987.

Gupta, Charu. "Politics of Gender: Women in Nazi Germany." *EPW* 26, 17 (27 April 1991):WS40-47.

Gupta, Charu. "Portrayal of Women in Premchand's Stories: A Critique." *Social Scientist*, nos. 216-17 (May-June 1991):88-113.

Hasan, Zoya. "Minority Identity, Muslim Women Bill Campaign and the Political Process." *EPW* (7 Jan. 1989).

Hasan, Zoya, ed. *Identity Politics, Community and Gender: The Construction of Muslim Women in pre- and post-Independence India*. New Delhi: Kali for Women, forthcoming 1994.

Hyam, Ronald. "Empire and Sexual Opportunity." *Jrl. of Imperial and Commonwealth History* 14, 2 (Jan. 1986):34-89.

Hyam, Ronald. *Empire and Sexuality: The British Experience*. Studies in Imperialism. Manchester: Manchester UP, 1990.

Ifeka, C. "'Spiritual' and 'Statistical' Models of the Sexes in British India, 1871-1931." *South Asia* 5, 1 (1980):16-28.

Ismail, Qadri. "Boys Will Be Boys: Gender and National Agency in Frantz Fanon and the Liberation Tigers of Tamil Eelam." *South Asia Bulletin* 11, 1-2 (1991):79-83..

Jain, Devaki. "Can Feminism be a Global Ideology?" *Quest* 4, 2 (Winter 1978):9-15.

Jain, Devaki. *Woman's Quest for Power: Five Indian Case Studies*. Delhi: Vikas, 1980.

Jain, Sharada; Misra, Nirja; and Kavita Shrivastava. "Deorala Episode: Women's Protest in Rajasthan." *EPW* (1987):1891-94.

Jain, Shobhita. "Women and People's Ecological Movement: A Case Study of Women's Rule in the Chipko Movement in Uttar Pradesh." *EPW* 19, 41 (13 Oct. 1984): 1788-94.

Jayawardena, Kumari. *Feminism and Nationalism in the Third World*. London: Zed Press, 1986.

Jayawardena, Kumari. "Some Comments on Feminism and the Left in South Asia." *South Asia Bulletin* 8, 1-2 (1988):88-91.

Jeffrey, Patricia. *Frogs in a Well: Indian Women in Purdah*. London: Zed Press, 1979.

Jeffrey, Patricia *et al*. *Labour Pains and Labour Power: Women and Childbearing in India*. London: Zed Books; Delhi: Manohar Publishers, 1989.

Joseph, Ammu and Sharma, Kalpana. "Between the Lines: Women's Issues in English Language Newspapers." *EPW* 26, 43 (26 Oct. 1991):WS-75 ff.

Joseph, Sarah. "Changing Notions of Power: Some Implications for Women's Studies." *Samya Shakti* 6 (1991-92):17-27.

Kannabiran, Vasanath and Kannabiran, Kalpana. "Caste and Gender: Understanding Dynamics of Power and Violence." *EPW* (14 Sept. 1991): 2130-33.

Kapur, Jyotsna. "Putting Herself into the Picture: Women's Accounts of the Social Reform Campaign, Maharashtra." *Manushi*, no. 56 (Jan.-Feb. 1990):28-37.

Karlekar, Malavika. "Constructions of Femininity in Nineteenth Century Bengal:

Readings from *Janaika Grihabadhur Diary*." *Samya Shakti*, nos. 4-5 (1989-90):11-29.

Karlekar, Malavika. *Poverty and Women's Work: A Study of Sweeper Women in Delhi*. New Delhi: Vikas, 1982.

Karlekar, Malavika. *Voices from Within: Early Personal Narratives of Bengali Women*. Delhi: Oxford UP, 1991.

Kasturi, Leela. "Rural Women in Struggle in Colonial India: Some Aporiae." *Samya Shakti* 6 (1991-92):65-80.

Katrak, Ketu. "Decolonizing Culture: Toward a Theory for Postcolonial Women's Texts." *Modern Fiction Studies* 35 (1989):157-79.

Katrak, Ketu. "Indian Nationalism, Gandhian 'Satyagraha', and Representation of Female Sexuality." In *Nationalisms and Sexualities*, pp. 395-406. Edited by Andrew Parker, Mary Russo, Doris Sommer, and Patricia Yaeger. New York: Routledge, 1992.

Katzenstein, May Fainsod. "Getting Women's Issues onto the Public Agenda: Body Politics in India." *Samya Shakti* 6 (1991-92):1-16.

Kelkar, Govind. "The Woman Question on Bodh Gaya Movement, Bihar." Occasional Papers on History and Society, 2nd series, no. 12. New Delhi: NMML, 1989.

Kelkar, Govind and Nathan, Dev. *Gender and Tribe: Women, Land and Forests in Jharkand*. New Delhi: Kali for Women, 1992.

Kishwar, Madhu. "Arya Samaj and Women's Education: Kanya Mahavidyalaya, Jallandar." *EPW* 21, 17 (26 April 1986):9-24.

Kishwar, Madhu. *Gandhi and Women*. Delhi: Manushi Publications, 1987.

Kishwar, Madhu. In *Man-Made Women: How New Reproductive Technologies Affect Women*. Edited by Gena Coea. London: Hutchinson, 1985; Bloomington: Indiana UP, 1987.

Kishwar, Madhu. "Pro Women or Anti Muslim? The Shahbano Controversy." *Manushi*, no. 32 (1986):4-13.

Kishwar, Madhu. "Toiling without Rights: Ho Women of Singhbum." *EPW* 22, 3 (17 January 1987).

Kishwar, Madhu. "Why I do not Call Myself a Feminist." *Manushi*, no. 61 (Nov.-Dec. 1990):2-8.

Kishwar, Madhu and Vanita, Ruth. "The Burning of Roop Kanwar." *Manushi*, nos. 42-43 (Sept.-Dec. 1987):15-25.

Kishwar, Madhu and Vanita, Ruth, eds. *In Search of Answers: Indian Women's Voices from Manushi*. London: Zed Press, 1984.

Kolenda, Pauline. "Woman as Tribute, Woman as Flower: Images of 'Woman' in Weddings in North and South India." *American Ethnologist* 11, 1 (Feb. 1984):98-117.

Kosambi, Meera. "Images of Women and the Feminine in Maharashtra." *EPW* 26, 25 (22 June 1991):1519-24.

Kosambi, Meera. "Indian Response to Christianity, Church and Colonialism: Case of Pandita Ramabai." *EPW* 27, 43-44 (24 Oct. 1992):WS61-71.

Krishnan, Prabha and Dighe, Anita. *Affirmation and Denial: Construction of Femininity on Indian Television*. New Delhi: Sage Publications, 1990.

Krishnan, Prabha. "In the Idiom of Loss: Ideology of Motherhood in Television Serials." *EPW* 25, 42-43 (25 Oct. 1990):WS103-16.

Kumar, Nita. "Class and Gender Politics in the Ramlila." *IESHR* 29, 1 (1992): 37-56.

Kumar, Nita. "Widows, Education and Social Change in Twentieth Century Banaras." *EPW* 26, 17 (27 April 1991):WS19-25.

Kumar, Radha. *The History of Doing: An Illustrated Account of the Women's Movement in India*. New Delhi: Kali for Women, 1993.

Kumar, Ravinder. "On Gender Theory, the Social Sciences and 'Relevant' Modernity." *Manushi*, no. 68 (Jan.-Feb. 1992):23-27.

Lakshmi, C. S. "Feminism and the Cinema of Realism." *EPW* 21, 3 (18 Jan. 1986):113-15.

Lakshmi, C. S. "Mother, Mother-Community and Mother-Politics in Tamil Nadu." *EPW* 25, 42-43 (25 Oct. 1990):WS72-83.

Lateef, Shahida. *Muslim Women in India: Political and Private Realities 1890s-1980s*. London: Zed Books; New Delhi: Kali for Women, 1990.

Leslie, I. Julia. *The Perfect Wife: the Orthodox Hindu Woman according to the 'Stridharmapaddhati' of Tryambakayajvan*. Delhi: Oxford UP, 1989.

Liddle, Joanna and Rama Joshi. *Daughters of Independence: Gender, Caste and Class in India*. London: Zed Books, 1986.

Liddle, Joanna and Rama Joshi. "Gender and Colonialism: Women's Organisation under the Raj." *Women's Studies International Forum* 8, 5 (1985): 521-29.

Loomba, Ania. *Gender, Race, Renaissance Drama*. Oxford India Paperback. Delhi: Oxford UP, 1992. [Reviewed by K. Vinod Chandran in *Social Scientist*, nos. 216-17 (May-June 1991):115-21.]

Lynch, Caitrin. "Nation, Woman, and the Indian Bourgeoisie: An Alternative Formulation." *Public Culture* 6, 2 (Winter 1994):425-37.

Mack, Phyllis. "Feminine Behavior and Radical Action: Franciscans, Quakers, and the Followers of Gandhi." *Signs* 11, 3 (1986):457-77.

Mani, Lata. *Contentious Traditions: The Debate on Sati in Colonial India, 1780-1833*. Berkeley, California: University of California Press, forthcoming [1994].

Mani, Lata. Multiple Mediations: Feminist Scholarship in the Age of Multinational Reception." *Inscriptions*, no. 5 (1989), reprinted in *Feminist Review*, no. 35 (Summer 1990):24-41.

Mani, Lata. "Production of an Official Discourse on *Sati* in Early Nineteenth-Century Bengal." *EPW* 21, 17 (1986):WS32-40. Also published as "Contentious Traditions: The Debate on Sati in Colonial India." *Cultural Critique*, no. 7 (Fall 1987):119-56. For a different version, see "Cultural Theory, Colonial Texts: Reading Eyewitness Accounts of Widow Burning." In *Cultural Studies*, pp. 392-408. Edited by Lawrence Grossberg, Cary Nelson, and Paula Treichler. New York and London: Routledge, 1992; reprinted also as "The Female Subject, the Colonial Gaze: Reading Eyewitness Accounts of Widow Burning." In *Interrogating Modernity: Culture and Colonialism in India*. Edited by Tejaswini Niranjana, P. Sudhir, and Vivek Dhareshwar. Calcutta: Seagull Books, 1993.

Marglin, Frederique Apffel. "Development and Repression: A Feminist Critique." *Lokayan Bulletin* 9, 1 (Jan.-Feb. 1991):9-26.

Marglin, Frederique Apffel. *Wives of the God-King: The Rituals of the Devadasis of Puri*. Delhi: Oxford UP, 1985.

Martin, Carol. "Feminist Analysis across Cultures: Performing Gender in India." *Women and Performance* 3, 2 (1987-88):32-40.

Mazumdar, Ranjani. "Dialectic of Public and Private: Representation of Women in *Bhoomika* and *Mirch Masala*." *EPW* 26, 43 (26 Oct. 1991):WS-81 ff.

Mazumdar, Vina. "Comment on Suttee." *Signs* 4, 2 (Winter 1978):269-73.

McBratney, John. "Images of Indian Women in Rudyard Kipling: A Case of Doubling Discourse." *Inscriptions* , nos. 3-4 (1988):47-57.

McKean, Lise. "Militant Matriots: Devotion to Mother India in Hindu Nationalism." Unpublished paper, 1993.

Meduri, Avanthi. "Western Feminist Theory, Asian Indian Performance, and a Notion of Agency." *Women and Performance* 5, 2 (Spring 1992): 90-103.

Mernissi, Fatima. *Women and Islam: An Historical and Theological Inquiry*. Delhi: Kali for Women, 1993.

Mies, Maria and Shiva, Vandana. *The World on the Brink: An Ecofeminist Perspective on Capital Accumulation, Ecological Destruction & People's Survival*. New Delhi: Kali for Women, 1993.

Mies, Maria. "Capitalist Development and Subsistence Reproduction: Rural Women in India", *BCAS* 12, 4 (July 1985):57-88.

Mies, Maria. *Women: The Last Colony*. London: Zed Books, 1988.

Minault, Gail. "Begamati Zuban: Women's Language and Culture in Nineteenth-Century Delhi." *IICQ* 11, 2 (June 1984):155-70.

Mitra, Indrani and Mitra, Madhu. "The Discourse of Liberal Feminism and Third World Women's Texts: Some Issues of Pedagogy." *College Literature* 18, 3 (October 1991).

Mitter, Sara. *Dharma's Daughters: Contemporary Indian Women and Hindu Culture*. New Brunswick, N.J.: Rutgers UP, 1991.

Mitter, Swasti. *Common Fate, Common Bond: Women in the Global Economy*. London: Pluto Press, 1986.

Mohanty, Chandra. "Cartographies of Struggle: Third World Women and the Politics of Feminism." Introduction to *Third World Women and the Politics of Women*, pp. 1-47. Bloomington, Indiana: Indiana Univ. Press, 1991.

Mohanty, Chandra. "Under Western Eyes: Feminist Scholarship and Colonial Discourses." *boundary 2* 12:3/13:1 (Spring/Fall 1984), reprinted in *Feminist Review*, no. 30 (1988), and (in a slightly revised form) in Mohanty, Russo and Torres, *Third World Women and the Politics of Feminism*, pp. 51-80.

Mohanty, Chandra and Martin, Biddy. "Feminist Politics: What's Home Got to Do with It?" In *Feminist Studies/Critical Studies*. Edited by Teresa de Lauretis. Bloomington: Indiana Univ. Press, 1986.

Mohanty, Chandra Talpade and Mohanty, Satya P. "Contradictions of Colonialism" [review of *Recasting Women*, eds. Kumkum Sangari and Sudesh Vaid (Delhi, 1989], *The Women's Review of Books* (March 1990): 19-21.

Mohanty, Chandra Talpade; Russo, Ann; and Torres, Lourdes, eds. *Third World Women and the Politics of Feminism*. Bloomington, Indiana: Indiana Univ. Press, 1991.

Mumtaz, Khawar and Shaheed, Farida. *Women of Pakistan: Two Steps Forward, One Step Back*. London: Zed Press, 1987.

Nag, Dulali. "Fashion, Gender and the Bengali Middle Class." *Public Culture* 3, 2 (1991).

Nair, Janaki. "Uncovering the Zenana: Visions of Indian Womanhood in Englishmen's Writings, 1813-1940." *Journal of Women's History* 2, 1 (1990):8-34.

Nanda, Meera. "Is Modern Science a Western, Patriarchal Myth? A Critique of the Populist Orthodoxy." *South Asia Bulletin* 11, 1-2 (1991):32-61.

Nanda, Serena. "The Hijras of India: Cultural and Individual Dimensions of the Institutionalized Third Gender Role." *Journal of Homosexuality* 11, 3-4 (1986):35-54.

Nanda, Serena. "The Third Gender: Hijra Community in India." *Manushi*, no. 72 (Sept.-Oct. 1992):9-16.

Nandy, Ashis. "Sati as Profit Versus Sati as Spectacle." *Illustrated Weekly of India* (17 January 1988).

Neelsen, John P, ed. *Gender, Caste and Power in South Asia: Social Status and Mobility in a Transitional Society.* New Delhi: Manohar Publishers, 1992.

Oldenburg, Veena. "Lifestyle as Resistance: The Case of the Courtesans of Lucknow, India." *Feminist Studies* 16, 2 (Summer, 1990):259-87; slightly different version also published in *Contesting Power: Resistance and Everday Social Relations in South Asia*, pp. 23-61. Edited by Douglas Haynes and Gyan Prakash. Delhi: Oxford UP, 1991.

Omvedt, Gail."Devdasi [sic] Custom and the Fight Against It." *Manushi* 19 (1983).

Omvedt, Gail. "Violence, Exploitation, Sexuality: Theories of Women's Oppression and the Struggle for Liberation." *Lokayan Bulletin* 7, 2 (March-April 1993):35-51.

Omvedt, Gail. *We Will Smash this Prison? Indian Women in Struggle.* London: Zed Press, 1980.

Pande, Mrinal. *The Subject is Woman.* New Delhi: Sanchar Publishing House, 1991.

Papanek, Hanna and Minault, Gail, eds. *Separate Worlds: Studies of Purdah in South Asia.* Columbia, MO.: South Asia Books, 1982.

Parker, Andrew; Russo, Mary; Sommer, Doris; and Yaeger, Patricia, eds., *Nationalisms and Sexualities.* New York: Routledge, 1992.

Parmar, Pratibha. "Black Feminism: The Politics of Articulation." In *Identity, Community, Culture, Difference*, pp. 101-26. Edited by Jonathan Rutherford. London: Lawrence & Wishart, 1990.

Parmar, Pratibha. "Gender, race and class: Asian Women in Resistance." In *The Empire Strikes Back*, pp. 236-75. A Publication of the Centre for Contemporary Cultural Studies. London: Hutchinson, 1980.

Parmar, Pratibha. "Hateful Contraries: Media Images of Asian Women." *Ten.8*, no. 16 (1984).

Parmar, Pratibha. "Other Kinds of Dreams." *Feminist Review* 31 (Spring 1989):55-66.

Parmar, Pratibha. "Transitory Movements?" *Spectrum Women's Photography Festival Exhibition Catalogue* (1988).

Patel, Amina. "Images of Asian Women in the (White) Media". *Artrage* no. 3/4 (Summer 1983).

Patel, Sujata. "The Construction and Reconstruction of Woman in Gandhi." Occasional Papers on History and Society, no. 49. New Delhi: NMML, 1988; published in *EPW* (20 Feb. 1988):377-87.

Paxton, Nancy L. "Disembodied Subjects: English Women's Autobiography Under the Raj." In *De/Colonizing the Subject: The Politics of Gender in Women's Autobiography*, pp. 387-409. Edited by Sidone Smith and Julie Watson. Minneapolis: Univ. of Minnesota Press, 1992.

Paxton, Nancy L. "Feminism Under the Raj: Complicity and Resistance in the Writings of Flora Annie Steel and Annie Besant." *Women's Studies International Forum* 13 (Spring 1990):333-46.

Rajan, Gita. "Subversive-Subaltern Identity: Indira Gandhi as the Speaking Subject." In *De/Colonizing the Subject: The Politics of Gender in Women's Autobiography*, pp. 196-222. Edited by Sidone Smith and Julie Watson. Minneapolis: Univ. of Minnesota Press, 1992.

Rajan, Rajeswari Sunder and Pathak, Zakia. "'Shahbano.'" *Signs* 14, 3 (Spring 1989):558-582; also published in *Feminists Theorize the Political*, pp. 257-79. Edited by Judith Butler and Joan W. Scott. New York & London: Routledge, 1992.

Rajan, Rajeswari Sunder. "An Exhilarating Anthology." *The Book Review* 16, 3 (May-June 1992):16-17 [review of Susie Tharu & K. Lalita, eds., *Women Writing in India*, Vol. I].

Rajan, Rajeswari Sunder. *Real and Imagined Women: Gender, Culture, and Post-colonialism*. London: Routledge, 1994.

Rajan, Rajeswari Sunder. "The Subject of Sati: Pain and Death in the Contemporary Discourse on Sati." *Yale Journal of Criticism* 3, 2 (Spring 1990):1-28. Also published in *Interrogating Modernity: Culture and Colonialism in India*. Edited by Tejaswini Niranjana, P. Sudhir, and Vivek Dhareshwar. Calcutta: Seagull Books, 1993.

Ram, Kalpana. *Mukkuvar Women: Gender, Hegemony and Capitalist Transformation in a South Indian Fishing Community*. London: Zed Books, 1991.

Ray, Bharati. "Bengali Women and Politics of Joint Family." *EPW* 26, 52 (28 Dec. 1991):3015-21.

Risseeuw, Carla. *Gender Transformation, Power and Resistance among Women in Sri Lanka: The Fish Don't Talk about the Water*. Leiden: Brill, 1988; Delhi: Manohar, 1991.

Risseeuw, Carla. "Gender, Kinship and State Formation: Case of Sri Lanka Under Colonial Rule." *EPW* 27, 43-44 (24-31 Oct. 1992):WS46-54.

Roy, Debal K. Singha. *Women in Peasant Movements: Tebhaga, Naxalite and After*. Delhi: Manohar Publishers, 1992.

Sangari, Kumkum. "Mirabai and the Spritual Economy of Bhakti." *EPW* 15, 27-28 (7, 14 July 1990); also published as Occasional Papers, 2nd series, no. 29, New Delhi: NMML, 1990.

Sangari, Kumkum. "Perpetuating the Myth." *Seminar* [special issue on Sati], no. 342 (Feb. 1988):24-30; reprinted in *Sati,* ed. Mulk Raj Anand (1990).

Sangari, Kumkum and Vaid, Sudesh. "Institutions, Ideologies, Beliefs: Widow Immolation in Contemporary Rajasthan." *EPW* (7 and 14 July 1990).

Sangari, Kumkum and Vaid, Sudesh. "Sati in Modern India." *EPW* 16, 31 (August 1981).

Sangari, Kumkum and Vaid, Sudesh, eds. *Recasting Women* Delhi: Kali for Women, 1989; New Brunswick: Rutgers UP, 1990.

Sangari, Kumkum and Vaid, Sudesh, eds. *Women and Culture.* Bombay: S.N.D.T. University Monographs, 1985.

Sarkar, Tanika. "The Woman as Communal Subject: Rashtrasevika Samiti and Ram Janmabhoomi Movement." *EPW* (31 August 1991):2057-2062.

Sarkar, Tanika and Butalia, Urvashi, eds. *Women of the Hindu Right: A Collection of Essays.* New Delhi: Kali for Women, forthcoming [1995].

Saunders, Rebecca Ann. "Gender, Colonialism, and Exile: Flora Annie Steel and Sara Jeannette Duncan in India." In *Women's Writing in Exile,* pp. 303-24. Edited by Mary Lynn Broe and Angela Ingram. Chapel Hill: Univ. of North Carolina Press, 1989.

Saunders, Rebecca Ann. "The Politics of Exile: Links between Feminism and Imperialism: British and North American Women Writers in India — Sara Jeanette Duncan, Flora Annie Steel, Maud Diver, Margaret Wilson." Ph. D. Dissertation, abstracted in *Dissertation Abstracts International* 51, 6 (Dec. 1990):2029A.

Sax, William S. *Mountain Goddess: Gender and Politics in a Himalayan Pilgrimage.* New York: Oxford UP, 1991.

Seminar. Issue on "Purdah Culture." No. 318. February, 1986.

Seminar. Issue on "The Sexist Media: A Symposium on How Patriarchy Exploits the Woman." No. 300. August, 1984.

Sen, Amartya. "Gender and Cooperative-Conflict." In *Persistent Inqeualities.* Edited by Irene Tinker. New York: Oxford UP, 1990.

Sen, Ilina, ed. *A Space within the Struggle — Women's Participation in People's Movements.* New Delhi: Kali for Women, 1990.

Shankaranarayanam, Vasanthi. "The goddess-chattel syndrome: Representation of Women in Malayalam Cinema." *Deep Focus* 3, 1 (1990):66-74.

Sharpe, Jenny. *Allegories of Empire: The Figure of Woman in the Colonial Text.* Minneapolis: Univ. of Minnesota Press, 1993.

Sharpe, Jenny. "The Unspeakable Limits of Rape: Colonial Violence and Counter-Insurgency." *Genders,* no. 10 (Spring 1991):24-46.

Shiva, Vandana. *Staying Alive: Women, Ecology and Survival in India.* London: Zed Books, 1988; Delhi: Kali for Women, 1988.

Shiva, Vandana, ed. *Minding Our Lives: Women from the South and North Reconnect Ecology and Health*. New Delhi: Kali for Women, 1993.

Shukla, Sonal. "Cultivating Minds: 19th Century Gujarati Women's Journals." *EPW* 26, 43 (26 Oct. 1991):WS-63 ff.

Sinha, Mrinalini. "Gender and Imperialism: Colonial Policy and the Ideology of Moral Imperialism in Late Nineteenth-Century Bengal." In *Changing Men: New Directions in Research of Men and Masculinity*. Edited by Michael S. Kimmel. London: Sage, 1987.

Southhall Black Sisters. *Against the Grain: A Celebration of Survival and Struggle*. London, 1990.

Spivak, Gayatri Chakravorty. "Can the Subaltern Speak? Speculations on Widow Sacrifice." *Wedge*, nos. 7/8 (Winter/Spring 1985):120-30. Also in *Marxism and the Interpretation of Culture*, pp. 271-313. Edited by Gary Nelson and Lawrence Gorssberg. Urbana: U. of Illinois Press, 1988.

Spivak, Gayatri Chakravorty. "Feminism and Deconstruction, Again." In *Between Feminism and Psychoanalysis*. Edited by Teresa Brennan. London and New York: Routledge, 1989.

Spivak, Gayatri Chakravorty. "Feminism in Colonization." *Differences* 3, 3 (1991):139-70.

Spivak, Gayatri Chakravorty. "French Feminism Revisisted: Ethics and Politics." In *Feminists Theorize the Political*, pp. 54-85. Edited by Judith Butler and Joan W. Scott. New York & London: Routledge, 1992.

Spivak, Gayatri Chakravorty. "Imperialism and Sexual Difference." *Oxford Literary Review* 8, 1-2 (1986):225-40.

Spivak, Gayatri Chakravorty. "The Political Economy of Women." In *Coming to Terms: Feminism, Theory, Politics*. Edited by Elizabeth Weed. New York: Routledge, 1989.

Spivak, Gayatri Chakravorty. "The Rani of Sirmur." In *Europe and Its Others*. Edited by Francis Barker et al. Colchester: Univ. of Essex, 1985.

Spivak, Gayatri Chakravorty. *Thinking Academic Freedom in Gendered Post-coloniality*. Cape Town: Univ. of Cape Town, 1992.

Spivak, Gayatri Chakravorty. "Woman in Difference: Mahasweta Devi's 'Douloti the Beautiful.' In *Nationalisms and Sexualities*, pp. 96-117. Edited by Andrew Parker, Mary Russo, Doris Sommer, and Patricia Yaeger. New York: Routledge, 1992.

Srinivasan, Amrita. "Reform and Revival: The Devadasi and Her Dance." *EPW* 20, 44 (1985):1869-76.

Srinivasan, Amrita. "Reform or Conformity? Temple 'Prostitution' and the Community in the Madras Presidency." In *State, Community and Household in Modernizing Asia*. Edited by Bina Agarwal. Delhi: Kali for Women, 1988.

Srinivasan, Amrita. "The Hindu Temple Dancer: Prostitute or Nun." *Cambridge Anthropology* 8, 1 (1983):73-99.

Stephens, Julie. "Feminist Fictions: A Critique of the Category 'Non-Western Woman' in Feminist Writings on India." In *Subaltern Studies VI*, pp. 92-125. Edited by Ranajit Guha. Delhi: Oxford UP, 1989. And see response by Susie Tharu, pp. 126-31, in same volume.

Stree Shakti Sangathana. *We Were Making History: Women and the Telengana Uprising*. London: Zed Press; Delhi: Kali for Women, 1990.

Suleri, Sara. "Woman Skin Deep: Feminism and the Postcolonial Condition." *Critical Inquiry* 18, 4 (Summer 1992):756-69.

Sutherland, Sally J. M., ed. *Bridging Worlds: Studies on Women in South Asia*. Delhi: Oxford UP, 1992.

Tambiah, Stanley J. "Bridewealth and Dowry Revisited: The Position of Women in Sub-Saharan Africa and North India." *Current Anthropology* 30, 4 (Aug.-Oct. 1989):413-35.

Tharu, Susie. "Introducing Anveshi." *Lokayan Bulletin* 8, 3 (May-June 1990): 59-63.

Tharu, Susie. "Tracing Savitri's Pedigree: Victorian Racism and the Image of Women in Indo-Anglian Literature." In *Recasting Women*, pp. 254-68. Edited by Kumkum Sangari and Sudesh Vaid. New Delhi: Kali for Women, 1989.

Tharu, Susie. "Women Writing in India." *Jrl. of Arts and Ideas*, nos. 20-21 (March 1991):49-66.

Tharu, Susie and Lalita, K., eds. *Women Writing in India*. 2 vols. New York: Feminist Press: Volume 1, 1991; Volume 2, 1993. Volume 1 reprinted as Oxford India paperback, 1992. [Review of Vol. 1 by Meenakshi Mukherjee, "Recovering 'Lost' Texts", *Jrl. of Arts and Ideas*, no. 22 (April 1992):7-18.

Tiwari, Laxmi G. *The Splendor of Worship: Women's Fasts, Rituals, Stories and Art*. Delhi: Manohar, 1991.

Uberoi, Patricia. "Feminine Identity and National Ethos in Indian Calendar Art." *EPW* (28 April 1990).

Uberoi, Patricia. "Some Reflections on Teaching the Sociology of Gender." *Samya Shakti* Vols. 4-5 (1989-90):279-89.

Upreti, H. C. and Upreti, Nandini. *The Myth of Sati: Some Dimensions of Widow Burning*. Delhi: Motilal Banarsidass, 1991.

Vaid, Sudesh and Sangari, Kumkum. "Institutions, Beliefs, Ideologies: Widow Immolation in Contemporary Rajasthan." *EPW* 26, 17 (27 April 1991): WS2-18.

Vaid, Sudesh. "Ideologies on Women in Nineteenth Century Britain, 1850s-70s." *EPW* 20, 43 (26 Oct. 1985):WS63-67.

Visweswaran, Kamala. "Defining Feminist Ethnography." *Inscriptions* Nos.3/4 (1988):27-46.

Visweswaran, Kamala. "Family Subjects: An Ethnography of the 'Women's Question' in Indian Nationalism." Unpublished Ph.D. Dissertation, Stanford University, 1990.

Visweswaran, Kamala. *Fictions of Feminist Ethnography*. Minneapolis: Univ. of Minnesota Press, 1994.

Ware, Vron. *Beyond the Pale: White Women, Racism and History*. London and New York: Verso, 1992. Pt. III, "Britannia's Other Daughters."

Willis, Janice D., ed. *Feminine Ground: Essays on Women and Tibet*. Ithaca, New York: Snow Lion Publications, 1989.

Wolf, Gita. "Construction of Gender Identity: Women in Popular Tamil Magazines." *EPW* 26, 43 (26 Oct. 1991):WS-71 ff.

VIII. Identity and Ethnicity

Ahmed, Akbar S. *Postmodernism and Islam*. London: Routledge, 1992. [Reviews in *Indian Express*, 5 July 1992, p. 6; *Guardian* (London), 25 June 1992, p. 29.]

Alexander, Meena. *Fault Lines: A Memoir*. The Cross-Cultural Memoir Series. New York: The Feminist Press at the City Univ. of New York, 1993.

Alexander, Meena. "The Poem's Second Life: Writing and Self Identity." *Toronto South Asian Review* (Fall-Winter 1987-88):77-85.

Appaurai, Arjun. "Patriotism and Its Futures." *Public Culture* 5 (Spring 1993):1-19; portions published as "The Heart of Whiteness", *Callaloo* 16, 4 (Fall 1993):796-807.

Araeen, Rasheed. *Making Myself Visible*. London: Kala Press, 1985.

Araeen, Rasheed. *The Other Story: Afro-Asian Artists in Post-War Britain*. London: South Bank Centre, 1989.

Bilgrami, Akeel. "What Is a Muslim? Fundmental Commitment and Cultural Identity." *Critical Inquiry* 18, 4 (Summer 1992):821-42; also published in *EPW* 27, 20-21 (16-23 May 1992):1071-78.

Contursi, Janet A. "Political Theology: Text and Practice in a Dalit Panther Community." *JAS* 52, 2 (May 1993):320-39.

Dangle, Arjun, ed. *Poisoned Bread: Translations from Modern Marathi Dalit Literature*. Hyderabad: Orient Longman, 1992.

Das, Veena. "Composition of the Personal Voice: Violence and Migration." *Studies in History* (New Series) 7, 1 (Jan.-June 1991):65-77.

Das, Veena. "Time, self, and community: Features of the Sikh militant discourse." *Contributions to Indian Sociology* (New Series) 26, 2 (July-Dec. 1992):245-59.

Joshi, Barbara. *Untouchable: Voices of the Dalit Liberation Movement*. London: Zed Books, 1986.

Khare, R. S. *The Untouchable as Himself: Ideology, Identity and Pragmatism among the Lucknow Chamars*. Cambridge: Cambridge UP, 1985.

Nandy, Ashis and Papastergiadis, Nikos. "Dialogue and the Diaspora." *Third Text* 11 (Summer 1990).

Radhakrishnan, R. "Ethnicity in an Age of Diaspora." *Transition*, no. 54 (1991):104-15.

IX. Literature

Ahmad, Rukhsana, ed. *Right of Way: Prose and Poetry*. Asian Women Writers' Workshop. London: Women's Press, 1988.

Ahmad, Rukhsana, trans. *Beyond Belief: Contemporary Feminist Urdu Poetry*. Lahore: ASR Publications, 1990.

Alexander, Meena. *Fault Lines: A Memoir*. The Cross-Cultural Memoir Series. New York: The Feminist Press at the City Univ. of New York, 1993.

Butalia, Urvashi and Menon, Ritu, eds. *In Other Worlds: New Writing by Indian Women*. New Delhi: Kali for Women, 1992.

Chandan, Amarjit, ed. *Apne Aap Ton Dur*. British Punjabi Poetry. Amritsar: Balraj Sahni, 1985.

Chandan, Amarjit, ed. *Do Kinare*. British Punjabi Short Stories. Delhi: Navyug; London: Shakti, 1982.

Debi, Rashsundari. *Amar Jiban (My Life)*. Edited with an introduction by Tanika Sarkar. New Delhi: Kali for Women, forthcoming 1994.

Devi, Mahasweta. *Five Plays: Mother of 1084/Aajir/Bayen/Uvashi and Johnny/Water*. Calcutta: Seagull Books, 1986.

Divakaruni, Chitra Banerjee. *Black Candle: Poems about Women from India, Pakistan and Bangladesh*. Corvallis, Oregon: Calyx Books, 1991.

George, K. M., et al. *Inner Spaces: New Writing by Women from Kerala.* New Delhi: Kali for Women, 1993.

Ghosh, Amitav. *In an Antique Land.* London: Granta; New Delhi: Ravi Dayal Publisher, 1992; New York: Knopf, 1993.

Ghosh, Amitav. *The Circle of Reason.* London: Hamish Hamilton; New York: Viking, 1986.

Ghosh, Amitav. *The Shadow Lines.* New Delhi: Ravi Dayal Publisher; London: Bloomsbury, 1988.

Grewal, Shabnam, et al. *Charting the Journey: Writings by Black and Third World Women.* London: Sheba Feminist Publishers, 1988.

Gupta, Sunetra. *Memories of Rain.* New York: Grove Press, 1991.

Gupta, Sunetra. *The Glassblower's Breath.* New York: Grove Press, 1992.

Holmstrom, Lakshmi. *The Inner Courtyard: Stories by Indian Women.* London: Virago, 1990; reprint ed., Calcutta: Rupa, 1992.

Hovell, Laurie, trans. and introduction. "Dhasal, Namdeo: Poet and Author." *BCAS* 23, 2 (April-June 1991):77-83.

Iyer, Pico. *Video Nights in Kathmandu.* New York: Alfred Knopf, 1988.

Kali for Women. *Truth Tales: Contemporary Writing by Indian Women.* Delhi: Kali for Women, 1986. Also published as *Truth Tales: Contemporary Stories by Women Writers of India.* With an introduction by Meena Alexander. New York: Feminist Press at City Univ. of New York, 1990.

Kureishi, Hanif. *My Beautiful Laundrette and The Rainbow Sign.* Boston: Faber & Faber, 1986.

Kureishi, Hanif. *Sammy and Rosie get laid.* New York: Penguin Books, 1988.

Kureishi, Hanif. *The Buddha of Suburbia.* New York: Viking Books, 1990.

Massachusetts Review. Special issue entitled "Desh-Videsh: South Asian Expatriate Writing and Art." Volume 29, No. 4 (Winter 1988-89).

Miller, Barbara Stoler; Sen, Nabaneeta Dev; and de Rayo, Agueda Pizarro. "Splitting the Mother Tongue: Bengali and Spanish Poems in English Translations." *Signs* 3, 3 (Spring 1978):608-21.

Monar, Rooplall. *Backdam People.* Leeds: Peepal Tree Press, 1985.

Obeyesekere, Ranjini and Fernando, Chitra, eds. *An Anthology of Modern Writing from Sri Lanka.* Tuscon: University of Arizona Press, 1981.

Ramanujan, A. K., trans. *Hymns for the Drowning: Poems for Visnu by Nammalvar.* Princeton, New Jersey: Princeton UP, 1981. See especially the "Afterword."

Ramanujan, A. K., trans. *Poems of Love and War.* New York: Columbia UP, 1985.

Rao, S. Balu. *Last Mile Together: An Anthology of South African Poems.* The Afro-Asian Writers' Association, 1991.

Rashid, Ian Iqbal. *Black Markets, White BoyFriends and Other Acts of Elusion*. Toronto: Toronto South Asian Review, 1991.

Rushdie, Salman. *Midnight's Children*. New York: Alfred Knopf, 1980; various other editions.

Rushdie, Salman. *Satanic Verses*. New York and London: Viking, 1988.

Rushdie, Salman. *Shame*. London: Cape; New York: Alfred Knopf, 1983.

Suleri, Sara. *Meatless Days*. Chicago: Univ. of Chicago Press, 1989; paperback ed., 1991.

Tharu, Susie and Lalita, K., eds. *Women Writing in India*. 2 vols. New York: Feminist Press: Volume 1, 1991; Volume 2, 1993. Volume 1 reprinted as Oxford India paperback, 1992. [Review of Vol. 1 by Meenakshi Mukherjee, "Recovering 'Lost' Texts", *Jrl. of Arts and Ideas*, no. 22 (April 1992):7-18.

Vassanji, M. G. *Gunny Sack*. Oxford and Portsmouth, N.H.: Heinemann, 1989. African Writers Series.

Vassanji, M. G. *No New Land*. Toronto: McClelland & Stewart, 1991.

X. Music

Blum, Stephen; Bohlman, Philip V.; and Neuman, Danield M., eds. *Ethnomuscicology and Modern Music History*. Chicago: Univ. of Illinois Press, 1991.

Bohlman, Philip. *The Study of Folk Music in the Modern World*. Bloomington, Indiana: Indiana UP, 1988.

Capwell, Charles. "Musical Life in Nineteenth-Century Calcutta." *Asian Music* 18, 1 (Fall/Winter 1986).

Deshpande, G. P. "Dialectics of Defeat: Some Reflections on Liteature, Theatre and Music: Colonial India." *EPW* 22, 50 (12 Dec. 1982):2170-76.

Farrell, Gerry. "Reflecting Surfaces: The Use of Elements from Indian Music in Popular Music in Jazz." *Popular Music* 7 (1988):189-205.

Flora, Reis. "Miniature Paintings: Important Sources for Music History." *Asian Music* 18, 2 (Spring-Summer 1987):196-240.

Gronow, Pekka. "Record Industry Comes to the Orient." *Ethnomusicology* 25, 2 (1981): 251-84.

Gupta, Parthasarthi. "Music and Political Consciousness." Occasional Papers on History and Society, 2nd series, no. 15. New Delhi: NMML, 1989.

Manuel, Peter. "Formal Structure in Popular Music as Reflection of Socio-Economic Change." *International Review of the Aesthetics and Sociology of Music* 16, 2 (1985):163-80.

Manuel, Peter. *Popular Music and Cassette Culture in North India*. Chicago: Univ. of Chicago Press, 1993.

Manuel, Peter. "Popular Music in India: 1901-1986." *Popular Music* 7 (1988): 157-76.

Nettl, Bruno and Bohlman, Philip, eds. *Comparative Musicology and the Anthropology of Music*. Chicago: Univ. of Chicago Press, 1991.

Neuman, Daniel M. "Indian Music as a Cultural System." *Asian Music* 17, 1 (Fall/Winter 1985).

Neuman, Daniel M. "The Ecology of Indian Music in North America." *Bansuri* 1 (1984):9-15.

Neuman, Daniel M. *The Life of Music in North India: The Organization of the Artistic Tradition*. Detroit: Wayne State Univ. Press, 1990.

Powers, Harold S. "Classical music, cultural roots, and colonial rule: an Indic musicologist looks at the Muslim World." *Asian Music* 12, 1 (1980).

Qureshi, Regula Burckhardt. *Sufi Music of India and Pakistan: Sound, Context and Meaning in Qawwali*. Cambridge: Cambridge UP, 1986; reprint ed., Calcutta: Seagull Books, 1990.

Sakata, Hiromi Lorraine. "Musicians Who Do Not Perform; Performers who are not Musicians." *Asian Music* 17,1 (Fall/Winter 1985).

XI. Photography

Desmond, Ray. "Photography in Victorian India." *Jrl. of the Royal Society of Arts* 134 (Dec. 1985):48-61.

Desnoes, Edmundo. "The Photographic Image of Underdevelopment." *Jump Cut*, no. 33 (1988).

Edwards, Elizabeth. "The Image as Anthropological Document: Photographic 'Types': The Pursuit of Method." *Visual Anthropology* 3, 2-3 (1990): 235-58.

Falconer, J. "Ethnological Photogaphy in India, 1850-1900." *The Photographic Collector* 5, 1 (1984):16-46.

Falconer, J. "Photography in Nineteenth-Century India." In *The Raj: India and the British 1600-1947*, pp. 264-77. Edited by C. A. Bayly. London: National Portrait Gallery Publications, 1990.

Gupta, Sunil. "Fabled Territories: An Introduction". In *Fabled Territories: New Asian Photography in Britain.* Leeds: Leeds City Art Gallery, 1990.

Gupta, Sunil. "Northern Media, Southern Lives." In *Photography/Politics Two*, pp. 162-66. Edited by Patricia Holland, Jo Spence, and Simon Watney. London: Comedia, 1986.

Gupta, Sunil, ed. *An Economy of Signs: Contemporary Indian Photographs*. London and Boston: Rivers Oram Press, 1990.

Gutman, Judith Mara. *Through Indian Eyes*. With a foreword by Edward C. Dimock. New York: Oxford UP & International Center of Photography, 1982.

Gutman, Judith Mara. "Through Indian eyes: Indigenous photography in the subcontinent." *Impact of science on society*, no. 168 (1992):345-56.

Hanslot, Sehnaz and Spiro, Margherita. "Other Than This: 'An Economy of Signs' and 'Fabled Territories'." *Third Text*, no. 13 (Winter 1991): 49-56.

Lalvani, Suren. "Photography, Epistemology and the Body." *Cultural Studies* 7, 3 (October 1993):442-65.

McKenzie, Ray. "'The Laboratory of Mankind': John McCosh and the Beginnings of Photography in British India." *History of Photography* 11, 2 (April-June 1987):109-18.

Pinney, Christopher. "Classification and Fantasy in the Photographic Construction of Caste and Tribe." *Visual Anthropology* 3, 2-3 (1990).

Pinney, Christopher. "Representations of India: Normalisation and the Other." *Pacific Viewpoint* 29, 1 (May 1988):97-118.

Srivatsan, R. "Imaging Truth and Desire: Photography and the Visual Field in India." In *Interrogating Modernity: Culture and Colonialism in India*. Edited by Tejaswini Niranjana, P. Sudhir, and Vivek Dhareshwar. Calcutta: Seagull Books, 1993.

Srivatsan, R. "Photography and Society: Icon Building in Action." *EPW* (Annual Number) 26, 11-12 (March 1991):771-88.

XII. Post-coloniality, Post-orientalism

Ahmad, Aijaz. *In Theory: Nations, Classes, Literatures*. London: Verso, 1992. [Reviewed by Benita Parry, "A Critique Mishandled", *Social Text*, no. 35 (1993):121-33. Almost an entire issue of *Public Culture* (6, 1 [Fall 1993]), with contributions by Michael Sprinker, Talal Asad, Vivek Dhareshwar, Partha Chatterjee, Nivedita Menon, Peter van der Veer, Marjorie Howes, Marjorie Levinson, and Andrew Parker, and a response by Aijaz Ahmad, is devoted to the discussion of *In Theory*.]

Bhabha, Homi. "'Race', Time, and the Revision of Modernity." *Oxford Literary Review* 13 (1991):193-219.

Bhabha, Homi. "Interrogating Identity." *Identity Documents* [Institute for Contemporary Arts, London] 6 (1991):5-11. Also published as "Interrogating Identity: The Postcolonial Prereogative." In *Anatomy of Racism*, pp. 183-209. Edited by David Theo Goldberg. Minneapolis: U. of Minnesota Press, 1990.

Bhabha, Homi. "Postcolonial Authority and Postmodern Guilt." In *Cultural Studies*, pp. 56-68. Edited by Lawrence Grossberg, Cary Nelson, and Paula Treichler. New York & London: Routledge, 1992.

Bhabha, Homi. "Postcolonial Criticism." In *Redrawing the Boundaries: The Transformation of English and American Literary Studies*. Edited by Stephen Greenblatt and Giles Gunn. New York: Modern Language Association, 1992.

Bhabha, Homi. "The Commitment to Theory." *New Formations,* no. 5 (Summer 1988): 5-23; also in *Questions of Third Cinema*, ed. Jim Pines and Paul Willemen (London: BFI Publishing, 1989), pp. 111-132.

Bhabha, Homi. *The Location of Culture*. London: Routledge, 1993.

Bhabha, Homi. "The Postcolonial Critic: Homi Bhabha Interviewed by David Bennett and Terry Collits." *Arena* 96 (Spring 1991):47-63.

Chakrabarty, Dipesh. "Postcoloniality and the Artifice of History: Who Speaks for 'Indian' Pasts?" *Representations*, no. 37 (Winter 1992): 1-26.

Dhareshwar, Vivek. "Toward a Narrative Epistemology of the Postcolonial Predicament." *Inscriptions*, no. 5 (1989):135-57.

Dirlik, Arif. "The Postcolonial Aura: Third World Criticism in the Age of Global Capitalism." *Critical Inquiry* 20, 2 (Winter 1994):328-56.

Katrak, Ketu. "Decolonizing Culture: Toward a Theory for Postcolonial Women's Texts." *Modern Fiction Studies* 35 (1989):157-79.

Lazarus, Neil. "Postcolonialism and the Dilemma of Nationalism: Aijaz Ahmad's Critique of Third-Worldism." *Diaspora* 2, 3 (Winter 1993):373-400.

Loomba, Ania. "Overworlding the Third World." *Oxford Literary Review* 13 (1991):164-91.

Mani, Lata and Frankenberg, Ruth. "Crosscurrents, Crosstalk: Race, 'Postcoloniality' and the Politics of Location." *Cultural Studies* 7, 2 (May 1993):292-310.

Menon, Nivedita. "Orientalism and After." *EPW* 27, 39 (26 Sept. 1992): 2133-36.

Mishra, Vijay and Hodge, Bob. *The Dark Side of the Dream: Australian Literature and the Postcolonial Mind*. Sydney: Allen & Unwin, 1991.

Mishra, Vijay and Hodge, Bob. "What is post(-)colonialism?" *Textual Practice* 5, 3 (Winter 1991):399-414.

Mukerjhi, Chandra and Schudson, Michael. *Rethinking Popular Culture: Contemporary Perspectives in Cultural Studies*. Berkeley: Univ. of California Press, 1991.

Mukherjee, Arun [Prabha]. "The Exclusions of Postcolonial Theory and Mulk

Raj Anand's 'Untouchable': A Case Study." *Ariel, A Review of International English Literature* 22, 3 (July 1991):27-48.

Mukherjee, Arun [Prabha]. "Whose Post-colonialism and Whose Postmodernism?" *World Literature Written in English* 30, 2 (1990): 1-9.

Niranjana, Tejaswini. "'History, Really Beginning': Compulsions of Post-Colonial Pedagogy." *EPW* 25, 42-43 (20-27 October 1990):2379-84. Reprinted in *The Lie of the Land: English Literary Studies in India*, pp. 246-59. Edited by Rajeswari Sunder Rajan. New Delhi: Oxford UP, 1992.

Nixon, Rob. London Calling: *V. S. Naipaul, Postcolonial Mandarin*. New York: Oxford UP, 1991.

Prakash, Gyan. "Postcolonial Criticism and Indian Historiography." *Social Text,* nos. 31-32 (1992):8-19.

Prakash, Gyan. "Writing Post-Orientalist Histories of the Third World: Perspectives from Indian Historiography." *CSSH* 32, 2 (April 1990): 383-408; also published in revised form as "Writing Post-Orientalist Histories of the Third World: Indian Historiography Is Good to Think", in *Colonialism and Culture*, pp. 353-88. Edited by Nicholas Dirks. Ann Arbor, Michigan: Univ. of Michigan Press, 1992.

Prasad, Madhav. "On the Question of a Theory of (Third World) Literature." *Social Text*, nos. 31-32 (1992):57-83.

Prasad, Madhav. "The 'Other' Worldliness of Postcolonial Discourse: a Critique." *Critical Quarterly* 34, 3 (Autumn 1992).

Radhakrishnan, R. "Postcoloniality and the Boundaries of Identity." *Callaloo* 16, 4 (Fall 1993):750-71.

Rajan, Rajeswari Sunder. *Real and Imagined Women: Gender, Culture, and Post-colonialism*. London: Routledge, 1994.

Rao, D. Venkat. "Self-Formations: Speculations on the Question of Postcoloniality." *Wasafiri*, no. 13 (Spring 1991).

Rao, D. Venkat. "The Strutting Lebensraum: Sudhir Kakar and the Subject of Post-coloniality." *Jrl. of Contemporary Thought* 1, 1 (1991):111-24.

Spivak, Gayatri Chakravorty. *Outside in the Teaching Machine*. London: Routledge, 1993.

Spivak, Gayatri Chakravorty. *The Post-Colonial Critic: Interviews, Strategies, Dialogues*. Ed. Sarah Harasym. New York: Routledge, 1990.

Spivak, Gayatri Chakravorty. *Thinking Academic Freedom in Gendered Post-coloniality*. Cape Town: Univ. of Cape Town, 1992.

Suleri, Sara. "Woman Skin Deep: Feminism and the Postcolonial Condition." *Critical Inquiry* 18, 4 (Summer 1992):756-69.

XIII. Public and Popular Culture

Appadurai, Arjun. "Street Culture." *The India Magazine* 8, 1 (December 1987):3-23.

Appadurai, Arjun and Breckernridge, Carol. "Public Culture in Late Twentieth Century India." *Items, Newsletter of the Social Science Research Council* 44, 4 (Dec. 1990).

Appadurai, Arjun and Breckernridge, Carol. "Why Public Culture?" *Public Culture* 1 (Fall 1988):5-11.

Chatterjee, Roma. "Folklore and the Formation of Popular Consciousness in a Village in the Purulia District of West Bengal." Ph.D. thesis, University of Delhi, 1985.

Gohain, Hiren. *The Idea of Popular Culture in the Early Nineteenth Century Bengal*. Calcutta: CSSS, 1991.

Indra Deva. "Popular and Folk Culture in Contemporary India." *International Jrl. of Popular Culture* 2, 1 (1981):12-21.

Kothari, Komal. "The Shrine: An Expression of Social Needs." In *Gods of the Byways*, pp. 5-31. Oxford: Museum of Modern Art, 1982.

Kumar, Nita. *The Artisans of Banaras: Popular Culture and Identity*. Princeton, New Jersey: Princeton UP, 1988.

Kurin, Richard. "Cultural Conservation through Representation: Festival of India Folklife Exhibitions at the Smithsonian Institution." In *Exhibiting Cultures: The Poetics and Politics of Museum Display*, pp. 315-343. Edited by Ivan Karp and Steven D. Lavine. Washington, D.C.: The Smithsonian Institution Press, 1991.

Nag, Dulali. "Fashion, Gender and the Bengali Middle Class." *Public Culture* 3, 2 (1991).

Oberoi, Harjot Singh. "The Worship of Pir Sakhi Sarvar: Illness, Healing and Popular Culture in the Punjab." *Studies in History* (New Series) 3, 1 (1987):29-55.

Rajadhyaksha, Ashish. "Neo-traditionalism: Film as Popular Art in India." *Framework* 32/33 (1986):20-67.

Ramanujan, A. K. "The Relevance of South Asian Folklore." In *Indian Folklore II*, pp. 79-156. Edited by Peter Claus, J. Handoo, and D. P. Pattanayak. Mysore: Central Institute of Indian Languages, 1987.

Ramanujan, A. K. *Who Needs Folklore? The Relevance of Oral Traditions to South Asian Studies*. South Asian Occasional Paper Series, No. 1. Honolulu: Center for South Asian Studies, University of Hawaii, 1990. Also reprinted in *Manushi*, no. 69 (March-April 1992):2-16.

Sequiera, Isaac. "India." *Journal of Popular Culture* 20, 2 (Fall 1986):123-92.

Sequiera, Isaac. "The Study of Popular Culture in India: a Frontier Situation." *International Jrl. of Popular Culture* 2, 1 (1981):6-11.

Srivatsan, R. "Looking at Film Hoardings: Labour, Gender, Subjectivity and Everyday Life in India." *Public Culture* 4, 1 (Fall 1991):1-24.

Srivatsan, R. "Photography and Society: Icon Building in Action." *EPW* (Annual Number) 26, 11-12 (March 1991):771-88.

Stieg, Margaret F. "Indian Romances: Tracts for the Times." *Journal of Popular Culture* 18, 4 (Spring 1985):2-15.

Sullivan, Nancy. "Sangam: Signs of India." *Public Culture* 6, 1 (Fall 1993): 195-99.

Tyagi, Amita and Uberoi, Patricia. "Adjustment is the Key: Postmarital Romance in Popular Indian Fiction." *Manushi*, no. 61 (Nov.-Dec. 1990): 15-21.

XIV. The Rushdie Affair

Afshari, Reza. "Ali-Mazrui or Salman Rushdie: The Satanic Verses and Islamist Practices." *Alternatives* 16, 1 (Winter 1991):107-14.

Ahmad, Aijaz. "Rushdie's Shame: Postmodernism, Migrancy and the Representation of Women." *EPW* 26, 24 (15 June 1991):1461-71.

Al-Azm, Sadik J. "The Importance of Being Earnest About Salman Rushdie." *South Asia Bulletin* 11, 1-2 (1991):1-20.

Appignanesi, Lisa and Maitland, Sara. *The Rushdie File*. Syracuse, New York: Syracuse UP, 1990.

Aravamudan, Srinivas. "'Being God's Postman Is No Fun, Yaar': Salman Rushdie's *The Satanic Verses.*" *Diacritics* 19, 2 (1989): 3-20.

Asad, Talal. "Ethnography, Literature, and Politics: Some Readings and Uses of Salman Rushdie's *The Satanic Verses.*" *Cultural Anthropology* 5, 3 (1990):239-90.

Asad, Talal. "Multiculturalism and British Identity in the Wake of the Rushdie Affair." *Politics and Society* 18, 4 (December 1990):455-80.

Bilgrami, Akeel. "Rushdie and the Reform of Islam." *Grand Street* 8 (Summer 1989):170-84.

Bilgrami, Akeel. "Rushdie, Islam and Postcolonial Defensiveness." *Yale Jrl. of Criticism* 4 (Fall 1990):301-11.

Bilimoria, Purusottama. "The Jaina Spirit in Salman Rushdie." *South Asia Bulletin* 9, 2 (1989):57-64.

Brennan, Timothy. "Rushdie, Islam, and Postcolonial Criticism." *Social Text*, nos. 31/32 (1992):271-76.

Cohn-Sherbok, Dan, ed. *The Salman Rushdie Controversy in Interreligious*

Perspective. Symposium Series Volume 27. Lewiston: The Edwin Mellen Press, 1990.

Cottle, Simon. "Reporting the Rushdie Affair: A Case Study in the Orchestration of Public Opinion." *Race and Class* 32, 4 (April-June 1991):45-64.

Fischer, Michael M. J. and Abedi, Mehdi. *Debating Muslims: Cultural Dialogues in Postmodernity and Tradition.* [Chapter 7, "Postscriptual Parergon: Bombay Talkies, the Word and the World: Salman Rushdie's *Satanic Verses*", is relevant.] New Directions in Anthropological Writing. Madison, Wisconsin: The University of Wisconsin Press, 1990. [Review by Vinay Lal in *Middle East Report* 22, 4 (July-August 1992):46-47.]

Hussain, Nasser. "Hyphenated Identity: Nationalistic Discourse, History, and the Anxiety of Criticism in Salman Rushdie's *Shame*." *Qui Parle* 3, 2 (Fall 1989).

Jussawalla, Feroza. "Resurrecting the Prophet: The Case of Salman, the Otherwise." *Public Culture* 2, 1 (Fall 1989):106-17.

Mazrui, Ali A. "*The Satanic Verses* or a Satanic Novel? Moral Dilemmas of the Rushdie Affair." *Alternatives* 15, 1 (Winter 1990):97-121.

Mufti, Aamir. "Reading the Rushdie Affair: An Essay on Islam and Politics." *Social Text,* no. 29 (1991):95-116.

Mufti, Aamir. "The Satanic Verses and the Cultural Politics of 'Islam': A Response to Brennan." *Social Text*, nos. 31/32 (1992):277-82.

Parekh, Bhikhu. "The Rushdie Affair and the British Press." In *Social Studies Review* (November 1989), reprinted in *The Salman Rushdie Controversy in Interreligious Perspective*, pp. 71-96. Edited by Dan Cohn-Sherbok. Lewiston: Edwin Mellen Press, 1990.

Ruthven, Malise. *Salman Rushdie and the Rage of Islam*. London: Chatto & Windus, 1990.

Sardar, Ziauddin and Davies, Merryl Wyn. *Distorted Imagination: Lessons from the Rushdie Affair*. London: Gray Seal Books, 1990.

Spivak, Gayatri Chakravorty. "Reading *The Satanic Verses*." *Public Culture* 2, 1 (Fall 1989):79-99.

Suleri, Sara. "Contraband Histories: Salman Rushdie and the Embodiment of Blasphemy." *The Yale Review* 78, 4 (Summer 1989).

Suleri, Sara. "Whither Rushdie." *Transition*, no. 51 (1991):198-212.

Third Text, special issue entitled "Beyond the Rushdie Affair", No. 11 (Summer 1990), with contributions from, among others, Ali A. Mazrui, Gayatri Spivak, Tariq Madood, Rustom Bharucha, and Ashis Nandy.

van der Veer, Peter. "Satanic or Angelic? The Politics of Religious and Literary Inspiration." *Public Culture* 2, 1 (Fall 1989):100-5.

XV. Science, Medicine, and Technology

Alvares, Claude. *Homo Faber: Technology and Culture in India, China and the West: 1500 to the Present Day*. New Delhi: Allied Publishers, 1979; Hague: Martinus Nijhoff, 1980. *Reprinted as Decolonizing History: Technology and Culture in India, China and the West: 1492 to the Present Day*. New York: Apex Press and Mapusa, Goa: The Other India Press, 1991.

Alvares, Claude. "Science, Colonialism and Violence: A Luddite View." In *Science, Hegemony and Violence: A Requiem for Modernity*, pp. 68-112. Edited by Ashis Nandy. Tokyo: United Nations Univ., 1988; Delhi: Oxford UP, 1990.

Bajaj, Jatinder K. "Francis Bacon, the First Philosopher of Modern Science: A Non-Western View." In *Science, Hegemony and Violence: A Requiem for Modernity*. Edited by Ashis Nandy. Delhi: Oxford UP, 1992 [1988].

Bala, Poonam. *Imperialism and Medicine in Bengal: A Socio-Historical Perspective*. Delhi: Sage Publications, 1991.

Goonatilake, Susantha. *Aborted Discovery: Science and Creativity in the Third World*. London: Zed Books, 1984.

Goonatilake, Susantha. "Black Athena and Geopolitics of Knowledge." *EPW* 27, 42 (17 October 1992)P:2302-3 [review of Vol. II of Martin Bernal's *Black Athena*].

Gupta, Sunil and Boffin, Tersa, eds. *Ecstatic Antibodies: Resisting the AIDS Mythology*. Winchester, Mass.: Oram Press; London: Unwin Hyman, 1990.

Habib, Irfan and Raina, Dhruva. "Copernicus, Columbus, Colonialism, and the Role of Science in Nineteenth-Century India." *Social Scientist*, nos. 190-91 (March 1989):51-66.

Habib, Irfan and Raina, Dhruva. "The unfolding of an engagement: 'The Dawn' on science, technical education and industrialization: India, 1896-1912." *Studies in History* (New Series) 9, 1 (Jan.-June 1993): 87-117.

Jeffrey, Roger. *The Politics of Health in India*. Berkeley: Univ. of California Press, 1988.

Joseph, George Gheverghese. *The Crest of the Peacock: Non-Western Roots of Mathematics*. London: I. B. Tauris, 1991. [Reviewed in EPW 26, 24 (15 June 1991), p. 160.]

Kochhar, R. K. "Astronomy in British India: Science in the Service of the State". *Current Science* 60, 2 (25 Jan. 1991):124-29.

Kochhar, R. K. "French Astronomers in India During the 18th and 19th Centuries." *Journal of the British Astronomical Association* 101, 2 (April 1991):95-100.

Kochhar, R. K. "Science as a Tool in British India." *EPW* 26, 33 (17 August 1991):1927-33.

Kochhar, R. K. "The Growth of Modern Astronomy in India, 1651-1960." *Vistas in Astronomy* 34, pts. 1-2 (1991):69-105.

Kothari, Manu L. and Mehta, Lopa. *The Tao of Death*. London: Marion Boyars, 1986.

Kothari, Manu L. and Mehta, Lopa. "Violence in Modern Medicine." In *Science, Hegemony and Violence: A Requiem for Modernity*, pp. 167-210. Edited by Ashis Nandy. Delhi: Oxford UP, 1992 [1988].

Kumar, Deepak, ed. *Science and Empire: Essays in Indian Context (1700-1947)*. Delhi: Anamika Prakashan, 1991.

Kumar, Deepak. "Science, Resources and the Raj: A Case Study of Geological Works in Nineteenth-Century India." *Indian Historical Review* 10, 1-2 (July 1983-January 1984).

Lal, Vinay. "The Politics of Representing AIDS", review of Richard and Rosalind Chirimuuta, *AIDS, Africa and Racism, EPW* 26, 47 (23 Nov. 1991):2687-88.

Marglin, Frederique Apffel. "Smallpox in Two Systems of Knowledge." In *Dominating Knowledge: Development, Culture, and Resistance*, pp. 102-44. Edited by Frederique Apffel Marglin and Stephen A. Marglin. Oxford: Clarendon Press, 1990.

Masani, P. "Humanization as De-Alienation: On the Theological Implications of Modern Science." *Alternatives* 7, 4 (Sept. 1981):265-90.

Mazumdar, Pauline M. H. "Blood and Soil: The Serology of the Aryan Racial State." *Bulletin of the History of Medicine* 64 (1990):187-219.

Nair, Kusum. *In Defense of the Irrational Peasant: Indian Agriculture after the Green Revolution*. Chicago: Univ. of Chicago Press, 1979.

Nandy, Ashis and Visvanathan, Shiv. "Modern Medicine and Its Non-Modern Critics: A Study in Discourse." In *Dominating Knowledge*, pp. 145-84. Edited by Frederique A. and Steve Marglin. Oxford: Clarendon Press, 1990.

Nandy, Ashis, ed. *Science, Hegemony and Violence: A Requiem for Modernity*. Tokyo: United Nations University; New Delhi: Oxford UP, 1988; paperback ed., 1990. [Review by T. G. Vaidyanathan in *Lokayan Bulletin* 7, 1 (Jan.-Feb. 1989):71-76.]

Nandy, Ashis. *Alternative Sciences: Creativity and Authenticity in Two Indian Scientists*. New Delhi: Allied Publishers, 1980; rev. ed. in paperback,

New Delhi: Oxford Univ. Press, forthcoming [1994].

Nandy, Ashis. "Emancipating Science." In *Science and Technology and Future*. Edited by Buchholz and Wolfgang Gmelin. Munchen: K. G. Saur, 1979. Also in *Seminar*, no. 238 (June 1979).

Nandy, Ashis. "Science in Utopia: Equity, Plurality and Openness." In *Social Reality: Perspectives and Understanding*. Edited by Janak Pandey. New Delhi: Concept, 1988. Earlier version in *Indian International Centre Quarterly* 10, 1 (1983).

Rahnema, Majid. "A New Variety of AIDS and its Pathogens: Homo Economicus, Development and Aid." *Alternatives* 13, 1 (January 1988):117-36.

Rajan, Roby. "Pathological Rationality/Rational Pathologies." *Alternatives* 17 (1992):339-70.

Sangwan, Satpal. *Science, Technology and Colonisation: An Indian Experience 1757-1857*. Delhi: Anamika Prakashan, 1991.

Sardar, Ziauddin, ed. *The Revenge of Athena: Science, Exploitation & the Third World*. London & New York: Mansell Publishing, 1988.

Sardar, Ziauddin. "Science and Health: Medicine and Metaphysics." In *The Revenge of Athena*, pp. 106-19. Edited by Z. Sardar. London & New York: Mansell Publishing, 1988.

Sethi, Harsh. "The Politics of Health in India." *National Medical Journal of India* 5, 2 (March-April 1992).

Shiva, Vandana and Bandyopadhyay, Jayanta. "The Large and Fragile Community of Scientists in India." *New Quest*, no. 79 (Jan.-Feb. 1990):5-22.

Srinivas, M. D. "Logical and Methodological Foundations of Indian Science." In *The Revenge of Athena: Science, Exploitation & the Third World*, pp. 261-289. Edited by Ziauddin Sardar. London & New York: Mansell Publishing, 1988.

Srinivasan, Cheenu Raman. "Goods and Gods: Cultures of Technology of India, 1900-1990." Unpublished Ph.D. Dissertation, University of Pennsylvania, 1993.

Srinivasan, Cheenu Raman. "No Free Launch: Designing the Indian National Satellite." Unpublished manuscript, Dept. of History and Sociology of Science, U. of Pennsylvania, 1993.

Uberoi, J. P. Singh. *Science and Culture*. Delhi: Oxford UP, 1978.

Visvanathan, Shiv. "Atomic Physics: The Career of an Imagination." *Alternatives* 10, 2 (June 1984):193-236; reprinted in *Science, Hegemony and Violence*, pp. 257-88. Edited by Ashis Nandy. New Delhi: Oxford UP, 1992 [1988].

Visvanathan, Shiv. "Bhopal: The Imagination of a Disaster." *Alternatives* 11, 1 (Jan. 1986):147-65.

Visvanathan, Shiv. "On the Annals of the Laboratory State." Reprinted in *Science, Hegemony and Violence*, pp. 257-88. Edited by Ashis Nandy. New Delhi: Oxford UP, 1988.

Visvanathan, Shiv. *Organizing for Science: The Making of an Industrial Research Laboratory*. New Delhi: Oxford UP, 1985.

Visvanathan, Shiv. "Reflections on the Technology of Transfer: Notes on the New Panopticon." *Lokayan Bulletin* 6, 1-2 (Jan.-April 1988):147-60.

Visvanathan, Shiv and Sethi, Harsh. "Bhopal: A Report from the Future." *Lokayan Bulletin* 7, 3 (May-June 1989):47-67.

Worboys, Michael. "Science and British Colonial Imperialism: 1895-1940." Unpublished D. Phil. thesis, University of Sussex, 1980.

XVI. SUBALTERN STUDIES AND OTHER INDIAN HISTORIES

Adas, Michael. "South Asian Resistance in Comparative Perspective." In *Contesting Power: Resistance and Everyday Social Relations in South Asia*, pp. 290-316. Edited by Douglas Haynes and Gyan Prakash. Delhi: Oxford UP, 1991.

Advani, Rukun. "Indian History From Above and Below: Two Academic Parodies." Delhi: Don't Press, 1990.

Amin, Shahid. "Approver's Testimony, Judicial Discourse: The Case of Chauri Chaura." In *Subaltern Studies V*, pp. 166-202. Edited by Ranajit Guha. Delhi: Oxford UP, 1987.

Amin, Shahid. "Gandhi as Mahatma." In *Subaltern Studies III*, pp. 1-61. Edited by Ranajit Guha. Delhi: Oxford UP, 1984.

Amin, Shahid. Introduction to *A Glossary of North Indian Peasant Life*, by William Crooke. Edited by Shahid Amin. Delhi: Oxford UP, 1989.

Arnold, David. "Cholera and Colonialism in British India." *Past and Present*, no. 113 (1986):118-51.

Arnold, David. "Gramsci and Peasant Subalternity in India." *Jrl. of Peasant Studies* 11 (1984).

Arnold, David. *Police Power and Colonial Rule: Madras 1859-1947*. Delhi: Oxford UP, 1986.

Arnold, David. "Touching the Body: Perspectives on the Indian Plague, 1896-1900." In *Subaltern Studies V*, pp. 55-90. Edited by Ranajit Guha. Delhi: Oxford UP, 1987.

Bandyopadhyay, Sekhar. "Caste in the Perception of the Raj: A Note on the Evolution of Colonial Sociology of Bengal." *Bengal Past and Present* 104, Pts. 1-2 Nos. 198-99 (Jan.-Dec. 1985):56-80.

Banerjee, Sumanta. *In the Wake of Naxalbari: A History of the Naxalite Movement in India*. Calcutta: Subarnarekha, 1980. Republished as

India's Simmering Revolution: The Naxalite Uprising. London: Zed Books, 1984.

Banerjee, Sumanta. *The Parlour and the Streets: Elite and Popular Culture in Nineteenth Century Calcutta*. Calcutta: Seagull Books, 1990. [Review by Santo Datta, "A Collision of Class Cultures", *Jrl. of Arts and Ideas*, no. 22 (April 1992):57-63.]

Basu, Tapan; Datta, Pradip; Sarkar, Sumit; Sarkar, Tanika; and Sen, Sambuddha. *Khaki Shorts and Saffron Flags: A Critique of the Hindu Right*. Tracts for the Times, no. 1. Delhi: Orient Longman, 1993.

Baxi, Upendra. "The State's Emissary': The Place of Law in Subaltern Studies." In *Subaltern Studies VII: Writings on South Asian History and Society*, pp. 247-64. Edited by Gyanendra Pandey and Dipesh Chakrabarty. Delhi: Oxford UP, 1992.

Bayly, C. A. "Rallying around the subaltern." *Journal of Peasant Studies* 16, 1 (1988):110-20.

Bhabha, Homi. "Signs Taken as Wonder: Questions of Ambivalence and Authority Under a Tree Outside Delhi, May 1817." *Critical Inquiry* 12, 1 (Autumn 1985):144-65; also reprinted in *Europe and Its Others*, ed. Francis Barker et al. Volume I. Colchester: Univ. of Essex, 1985, and in *Race, Writing and Difference*, ed. Henry Louis Gates, Jr. Chicago: Univ. of Chicago Press, 1986.

Bhadra, Gautam. "The Mentality of Subalternity: Kantanama or Rajdharma." In *Subaltern Studies VI*, pp. 54-91. Edited by Ranajit Guha. New Delhi: Oxford UP, 1989. Also published as Occasional Paper, no. 104, Calcutta: CSSS, 1990.

Bhalla, Alok and Chandra, Sudhir, eds. *Indian Responses to Colonialism in the Nineteenth Century*. New Delhi: Sterling, 1993.

Bharucha, Rustom. "Around Ayodhya: Aberrations, Engimas, and Moments of Violence." *Third Text*, no. 24 (Autumn 1993):45-58.

Bharucha, Rustom. *Questions of Faith*. Tracts for the Times, no. 3. Delhi: Orient Longmans, 1993.

Bhattacharya, Sabyasachi. "Colonial Power and Micro-Social Interactions: Nineteenth Century India." *EPW* (1-8 June 1991):1399-1403.

Bhattacharya, Sabyasachi. "Paradigms Lost: Notes on Social History in India." *EPW* 17, 14-16 (Annual Number 1982):689-96.

Breckenridge, Carol A. and van der Veer, Peter, eds. *Orientalism and the Postcolonial Predicament*. Philadelphia: Univ. of Pennsylvania Press, 1993.

Breckenridge, Carol A. "The Politics and Aesthetics of Colonial Collecting: India at World Fairs." *CSSH* 31, 2 (1988):195-216.

Chakrabarty, Dipesh. "Class Consciousness and the Indian Working Class: Dilemmas of Marxist Historiography." *Jrl. of Asian and African Studies* 23, 1-2 (1988):21-31.

Chakrabarty, Dipesh. "History as Critique and Critique(s) of History." *Economic and Political Weekly* 26, 37 (14 Sept. 1991):2162-66. Also published as "Subaltern Studies and Critique of History," *Arena* (Melbourne), no. 96 (Spring 1991):105-120.

Chakrabarty, Dipesh. "Marx after Marxism: A Subaltern Historian's Perspective." *EPW* 28, 22 (29 May 1933):1094-96.

Chakrabarty, Dipesh. "Open Space/Public Space: Garbage, Modernity and India." *South Asia* (New Series) 14, 1 (1991):15-32. Also published as "Of Garbage, Modernity and the Citizen's Gaze." *EPW* 27, 10-11 (7-14 March 1992):541-547.

Chakrabarty, Dipesh. "Rethinking Working-Class History." *EPW* 26, 17 (27 April 1991):1117-19.

Chakrabarty, Dipesh. *Rethinking Working-Class History: Bengal, 1890-1940*. Delhi: Oxford UP, 1989.

Chakrabarty, Dipesh. "Sarir, samaj, o rashtra: Oupanibeshik bharate mahamari o janasangskriti." *Anustup*, 1988. [In Bengali.]

Chakrabarty, Dipesh. "Trade Unions in a Hierarchical Culture: The Jute Workers of Calcutta, 1920-50." In *Subaltern Studies III*, pp. 153-96. Edited by Ranajit Guha. Delhi: Oxford UP, 1984.

Chakravarti, Uma. "Beyond the Altekarian Paradigm: Towards a New Understanding of Gender Relations in Early Indian History." *Social Scientist*, no. 183 (August 1988):44-52.

Chakravarti, Uma. "Women, men and beasts: The Jataka as Popular Tradition." *Studies in History* 9, 1 (Jan.-June 1993):43-70.

Chandra, Bipan. *Communalism in Modern India*. New Delhi: Vikas Publishing House, 1983.

Chandra, Sudhir. "Communal Consciousness in Late Nineteenth Century Hindi Literature." In *Communal and Pan-Islamic Trends in Colonial India*, pp. 180-195. Edited by Mushirul Hasan. New Delhi: Manohar, 1981.

Chatterjee, Partha. "A Religion of Urban Domesticity: Sri Ramakrishna and the Calcutta Middle Class." In *Subaltern Studies 7: Wrtings on South Asian History and Society*, pp. 40-68. Edited by Gyanendra Pandey and Partha Chatterjee. Delhi: Oxford Univ. Press, 1992.

Chatterjee, Partha. *Bengal 1920-1947: Vol. I: The Land Question*. Calcutta: Published for the Centre for the Study of the Social Sciences by K. P. Bagchi, 1984.

Chatterjee, Partha. "Caste and Subaltern Consciousness." In *Subaltern Studies*

VI, pp. 169-209. Edited by Ranajit Guha. Delhi: Oxford UP, 1989; also published as Occasional Paper, no. 111. Calcutta: CSSS, 1989.

Chatterjee, Partha. "For an Indian History of Peasant Struggle." *Social Scientist*, no. 186 (November 1988):3-17.

Chatterjee, Partha. "Gandhi and the Critique of Civil Society." In *Subaltern Studies III*, pp. 153-95. Edited by Ranajit Guha. Delhi: Oxford UP, 1984.

Chatterjee, Partha. "History and the Nationalization of Hinduism." *Social Research* 59, 1 (Spring 1992):111-150.

Chatterjee, Partha. "More on Modes of Power and the Peasantry." In *Subaltern Studies II*, pp. 311-349. Edited by Ranajit Guha. Delhi: Oxford UP, 1983.

Chatterjee, Partha. *Nationalist Thought and the Colonial World: A Derivative Discourse?* London: Zed Books, 1986; reprint paperback ed., Minneapolis: Univ. of Minnesota Press, 1992.

Chatterjee, Partha. *The Nation and Its Fragments: Colonial and Post-Colonial Histories*. Princeton: Princeton UP, 1993.

Chatterjee, Partha. *The Nationalist Resolution of the Women's Question*. Occasional Paper, no. 94. Calcutta: CSSS, 1988. Also published in *Recasting Women: Essays in Colonial History*, pp. 233-53. Edited by Kumkum Sangari and Sudesh Vaid. New Delhi: Kali for Women, 1989; New Brunswick, New Jersey: Rutgers UP, 1990; paperback ed., Delhi: Oxford UP, 1992.

Chatterjee, Partha. "Their Own Words? An Essay for Edward Said." In *Edward Said: A Critical Reader*, pp. 194-220. Edited by Michael Sprinker. Oxford: Basil Blackwell, 1992.

Chatterjee, Partha. "Transferring a Political Theory: Early Nationalist Thought in India." *EPW* 221, 3 (1986).

Chatterjee, Partha and Pandey, Gyanendra, eds. *Subaltern Studies VII: Writings on South Asian History and Society*. New Delhi: Oxford UP, 1992.

Chaudhury, Ajit K. "In Search of a Subaltern Lenin." In *Subaltern Studies V*, pp. 236-51. Edited by Ranajit Guha. Delhi: Oxford UP, 1987.

Cheran, R. "Cultural Politics of Tamil Nationalism." *South Asia Bulletin* 12, 1 (1992):42-56.

Cohn, Bernard S. *An Anthropologist among the Historians and Other Essays*. Delhi: Oxford UP, 1987.

Cohn, Bernard S. "Cloth, Clothes, and Colonialism: India in the Nineteenth Century." In *Cloth and the Human Experience*, pp. 303-353. Edited by Annette B. Wiener and Jane Schneider. Washington, D.C.: Smithsonian Institution Press, 1989.

Cohn, Bernard S. "Law and the Colonial State in India." In *History and Power: The Study of Law*, pp. 131-52. Edited by Jean Starr and Jane Collier. Ithaca, New York: Cornell UP, 1989.

Cohn, Bernard S. "Representing Authority in Victorian India." In *The Invention of Tradition*, pp. 165-210. Edited by Eric Hobsbawm and Terence Ranger. Cambridge: Cambridge UP, 1983; paperback ed., 1984.

Cohn, Bernard S. "The Census, Social Structure and Objectification in South Asia." *Folk* 26 (1984):25-49.

Cohn, Bernard S. "The Command of Language and the Language of Command." In *Subaltern Studies IV*, pp. 276-329. Edited by Ranajit Guha. New Delhi: Oxford UP, 1985.

Cohn, Bernard S and Dirks, Nicholas B. "Beyond the Fringe: The Nation State, Colonialism and the Technologies of Power." *Jrl. of Historical Sociology* 1, 2 (June 1988):224-29.

Contursi, Janet A. "Political Theology: Text and Practice in a Dalit Panther Community." *JAS* 52, 2 (May 1993):320-339.

Copley, Antony. "Indian secularism reconsidered: from Gandhi to Ayodhya." *Contemporary South Asia* 2, 1 (1993):47-66.

Das, Veena. "Subaltern as Perspective." In *Subaltern Studies VI*, pp. 310-324. Edited by Ranajit Guha. Delhi: Oxford UP, 1989.

Das, Veena, ed. *Mirrors of Violence: Communities, Riots and Survivors in South Asia*. Delhi: Oxford UP, 1990.

Datta, P. K. "'Dying Hindus': Production of Hindu Communal Common Sense in Early 20th Century Bengal." *EPW* 28, 25 (19 June 1993):1305-19.

Datta, P. K. "VHP's Ram at Ayodhya: Reincarnation through Ideology and Organisation." *EPW* 26, 44 (2 Nov. 1991):2517-2525.

Datta, P. K. "War Over Music: The Riots of 1926 in Bengal." *Social Scientist*, nos. 205-6 (June-July 1990):38-48.

Datta, P.; Pati, B; Sarkar, S.; Sarkar, T.; and Sen, S. "Understanding communal violence: Nizamuddin Riots." *EPW* 22, 45 (Nov. 1990):2487-2495.

De, Barun. *Problems of the Study of Indian History*. Occasional Paper, no. 116. Calcutta: CSSS, 1990.

Devalle, Susana B. C. *Discourses of Ethnicity: Culture and Protest in Jharkhand*. New Delhi: Sage, 1992.

Devji, Faisal F. "Hindu/Muslim/Indian." *Public Culture* 5, 1 (Fall 1992):1-18.

Dhanagaare, D. N. "Subaltern Consciousness and Populism: Two Approaches in the Study of Social Movements." *Social Scientist*, no. 186 (Nov. 1988):18-35.

Dharampal. "A Note on the Disruption and Disorganisation of Indian Society in the Last Two Centuries." *PPST Bulletin* 3, 2 (Nov. 1983):18-47.

Dirks, Nicholas B. "Castes of Mind." *Representations*, no. 37 (Winter 1992): 56-78.

Dirks, Nicholas B. "Colonial Histories and Native Informants: Biography of an Archive." In *Orientalism and the Postcolonial Predicament*. Edited by Carol Breckenridge and Peter van der Veer. Philadelphia: Univ. of Pennsylvania Press, 1993.

Dirks, Nicholas B. "Colonialism and Culture." Introduction to *Colonialism and Culture*, pp. 1-25. Edited by Nicholas Dirks. Ann Arbor, Michigan: Univ. of Michigan Press, 1992.

Dirks, Nicholas B. "From Little King to Landlord: Property, Law, and the Gift Under the Madras Permanent Settlement." *CSSH* 28, 2 (1986):307-333; also published in revised form as "From Little King to Landlord: Colonial Discourse and Colonial Rule." In *Colonialism and Culture*, pp. 175-208. Edited by Nicholas Dirks. Ann Arbor, Michigan: Univ. of Michigan Press, 1992.

Dirks, Nicholas B. "History as a Sign of the Modern." *Public Culture* 2, 2 (Spring 1990):25-33.

Dirks, Nicholas B. "Ritual and Resistance: Subversion as a Social Fact." In *Contesting Power: Resistance and Everday Social Relations in South Asia*, pp. 213-238. Edited by Douglas Haynes and Gyan Prakash. Delhi: Oxford UP, 1991.

Dirks, Nicholas B. *The Hollow Crown: Ethnohistory of an Indian Kingdom*. Cambridge: Cambridge Univ. Press, 1987; 2nd edition, paperback, Ann Arbor: Univ. of Michigan Press, 1992.

Dirks, Nicholas B. "The Invention of Caste: Civil Society in Colonial India." *Social Analysis* 25 (1989):42-52.

Dirks, Nicholas B. "Is Vice Versa? Historical Anthropologies and Anthropological Histories." In *The Historic Turn in the Human Sciences*. Edited by Terence McDonald. Forthcoming, 1995.

Dirks, Nicholas B, ed. *Colonialism and Culture*. Ann Arbor, Michigan: Univ. of Michigan Press, 1992.

Duara, Prasenjit. "Rescuing History from the Nation-State." *Working Papers and Proceedings of the Center for Psychosocial Studies*, no. 48. Chicago: Center for Psychosocial Studies, 1992.

Engels, Dagmar. "The Age of Consent Act of 1891: Colonial Ideology in Bengal." *South Asia Research* 3, 2 (November 1983).

Engels, Dagmar. "The Limits of Gender Ideology: Bengali Women, the Colonial State, and the Private Sphere, 1890-1930." *Women's Studies International Forum* 12, 4 (1989):425-437.

Ernst, Waltraud. *Mad Tales from the Raj: The European Insane in British India,*

1800-1858. Wellcome Institute Series in the History of Medicine. London: Routledge, 1991.

Fox, Richard G. *Gandhian Utopia*: *Experiments with Culture*. Boston: Beacon Press, 1989. [Review by Vinay Lal in *Gandhi Marg* 12, 2 (July-September, 1990):236-240.]

Freitag, Sandria. *Collective Action and Community*. Berkeley: Univ. of California Press, 1989.

Freitag, Sandria. "Crime in the Social Order of Colonial North India." *MAS* 25, 2 (1991):227-61.

Freitag, Sandria. *Culture and Power in Banaras: Community, Performance and Environment 1800-1980*. Delhi: Oxford UP, 1990.

Freitag, Sandria. "Enactments of Ram's Story and the Changing Nature of 'the Public' in British India." *South Asia* (New Series) 14, 1 (1991):65-90.

Ghosh, Amitav. *In an Antique Land*. London: Granta; New Delhi: Ravi Dayal Publisher, 1992; New York: Knopf, 1993.

Ghosh, Amitav. "The Slave of Ms. H.6." In *Subaltern Studies 7: Writings on South Asian History and Society*, pp. 159-220. Edited by Partha Chatterjee and Gyanendra Pandey. Delhi: Oxford UP, 1992.

Ghosh, Amitav. "The Slave of Ms. H.6." Occasional Paper, no. 126. Calcutta: CSSS, 1990.

Gidwani, Vinay Krishin. "'Waste' and the Permanent Settlement in Bengal." *EPW* 27, 4 (25 January 1992):PE39-46.

Gohain, Hiren. *The Idea of Popular Culture in the Early Nineteenth Century Bengal*. Calcutta: CSSS, 1991.

Gopal, Sarvepalli, *et al.* "The Political Abuse of History." *Social Scientist*, nos. 200-201 (Jan.-Feb. 1990):76-81.

Gopal, Sarvepalli, ed. *Anatomy of a Confrontation*: *The Babri Masjid-Ram Janmabhumi Issue*. New Delhi: Viking, 1991; Penguin paperback ed., 1991.

Grewal, Inderpal. "The guidebook and the museum: imperialism, education and nationalism in the British Museum." *Bucknell Review* (1990): 195-217.

Guha, Ramachandra. "Forestry and Social Protest in British Kumaon, c. 1893-1921." In *Subaltern Studies IV*. Edited by Ranajit Guha. Delhi: Oxford UP, 1985.

Guha, Ramachandra. "Scientific Forestry and Social Change in Uttarakhand." *EPW* (Special Number, November 1985):1939-52.

Guha, Ramachandra. *The Unquiet Woods*: *Ecological Change and Peasant Resistance in the Himalaya*. Delhi: Oxford UP; Berkeley: Univ. of Califorinia Press, 1989. [Reviewed by Amitava Kumar, "The Double

Failure: Modernity in the Postcolonial Context", *Socialist Review* 22, 2 (April-June 1992):147-151; see also Rashmi Pant, "Man and Nature in the Himalayas", *Times of India Review of Books* 1, 1 (August-Sept. 1990):30-31.]

Guha, Ramachandra and Gadgil, Madhav. "State Forestry and Social Conflict in British India." *Past and Present*, no. 123 (1989):141-177.

Guha, Ranajit. *An Indian Historiography of India: A Nineteenth-Century Agenda and Its Implications*. Calcutta and New Delhi: K. P. Bagchi, for Centre for Studies in Social Sciences, 1988.

Guha, Ranajit. "Chandra's Death." In *Subaltern Studies V*, pp. 166-202. Edited by Ranajit Guha. Delhi: Oxford UP, 1987.

Guha, Ranajit. "Discipline and Mobilize." In *Subaltern Studies* VII, pp. 69-120. Edited by Partha Chatterjee and Gyanendra Pandey. Delhi: Oxford UP, 1992.

Guha, Ranajit. "Dominance Without Hegemony and Its Historiography." In *Subaltern Studies VI*, pp. 169-209. Edited by Ranajit Guha. Delhi: Oxford UP, 1989.

Guha, Ranajit. *Elementary Aspects of Peasant Insurgency in Colonial India*. Delhi: Oxford UP, 1983.

Guha, Ranajit. "Nationalism Reduced to 'Official Nationalism.'" *AAAS Review* 9, 1(July 1985):103-8. [Review of Benedict Anderson's *Imagined Communities*.]

Guha, Ranajit. "On Some Aspects of the Historiography of Colonial India." In *Subaltern Studies I*, pp. 1-8. Edited by Ranajit Guha. Delhi: Oxford UP, 1982.

Guha, Ranajit. "The Career of an Anti-God in Heaven and on Earth." In *The Truth Unites: Essays in Tribute to Samar Sen*. Edited by Asok Mitra. Calcutta: Subarnarekha, 1985.

Guha, Ranajit. "The Prose of Counter-Insurgency." In *Subaltern Studies II*, pp. 1-42. Edited by Ranajit Guha. Delhi: Oxford UP, 1983.

Guha, Ranajit, ed. *Subaltern Studies: Writings on South Asian History and Society*. 6 vols. Delhi: Oxford UP, 1982-89. [Volume I reviewed in *Social Scientist* 10, 8 (August 1982):55-63; *EPW* 19, 24-25 (16-23 June 1984): 942-45.]

Guha, Ranajit and Spivak, Gayatri Chakravorty, eds. *Selected Subaltern Studies*. With foreword by Edward W. Said. New York: Oxford UP, 1988.

Gupta, Dipankar. "Between general and particular 'others': Some observations on fundamentalism." *Contributions to Indian Sociology* (New Series) 27, 1 (Jan.-June 1993):119-37.

Gupta, Dipankar. "Continuous Hierarchies and Discrete Castes." *EPW* 19, 46-48 (17-24 Nov. and 1 Dec. 1984):1955-8, 2003-5, 2049-53.

Gupta, Dipankar. "From Varna to Jati: The Indian Caste System, from the Asiatic to the Feudal Mode of Production." *Jrl. of Contemporary Asia* 10, 3 (1980):249-71.

Guru, Gopal. "Hinduisation of Ambedkar in Maharashtra." *EPW* 26, 7 (16 Feb. 1991):339-41.

Habib, Irfan. *Interpreting Indian History*. Shillong: North-Eastern Univ. Publications, 1987.

Habib, Irfan. "Peasant and Artisan Resistance in Mughal India." *McGill Studies in International Development*, no. 34, Toronto: McGill University, Center for Developing Area Studies, 1984.

Habib, Irfan. "Studying a Colonial Economy — Without Perceiving Colonialism." *Modern Asian Studies* 19, 4 (1985):355-81.

Hardiman, David. Adivasi Assertion in South Gujarat: The Devi Movement of 1922-3." In *Subaltern Studies III*, pp. 231-70. Edited by Ranajit Guha. Delhi: Oxford UP, 1984.

Hardiman, David. "From Custom to Crime: The Politics of Drinking in Colonial South Gujarat." In *Subaltern Studies IV*. Edited by Ranajit Guha. Delhi: Oxford UP, 1985.

Hardiman, David. *Peasant Nationalists of Gujarat: Kheda District 1917-1934*. Delhi: Oxford UP, 1981.

Hardiman, David, ed. *Peasant Resistance in India, 1858-1914: Themes in Indian History*. Delhi: Oxford UP, 1992.

Harlow, Barbara. "Drawing the Line: Cultural Politics and the Legacy of Partition." *Polygraph*, no. 5 (1992):84-112.

Haynes, Douglas. *Rhetoric and Ritual in Colonial India: The Shaping of a Public Culture in Surat City, 1852-1928*. Berkeley: Univ. of California Press, 1991. [Review by Vinay Lal, "Surat under the Raj", *EPW* 28, 18 (1 May 1993):863-5.]

Haynes, Douglas and Prakash, Gyan, eds. *Contesting Power: Resistance and Everyday Social Relations in South Asia*. Delhi: Oxford UP, 1991; Berkeley: University of California Press, 1992.

Heuze, Gerard. "Shiv Sena and 'National' Hindusim." In 2 parts. *EPW* 27, 40 (3 Oct. 1992):2189-95; Pt. II: 27, 41 (10 Oct. 1992):2253-63.

Hill, Christopher V. "Philosophy and Reality in Riparian South Asia: British Famine Policy and Migration in Colonial North India." *Modern Asian Studies* 25, 2 (May 1991):263-79.

Hore, Somnath. *Tebhaga: An Artist's Diary and Sketchbook*. Calcutta: Seagull Books, 1990.

Hume, John Chandler Jr. "Colonialism and Sanitary Medicine: The Development of Preventive Health Policy in the Punjab, 1860 to 1900." *MAS* 20, 4 (1986):703-724.

Inden, Ronald. *Imagining India*. Oxford: Basil Blackwell, 1990. [Reviewed by Declan Quigley, "The Power of Imagination", *MAS* 25, 2 (1991): 403-6.]

Inden, Ronald. "Orientalist Constructions of India." *MAS* 20, 3 (1986):401-446.

Kanwar, Pamela. *Imperial Simla: The Political Culture of the Raj*. Delhi: Oxford UP, 1990.

Kanwar, Pamela. "The Changing Profile of the Summer Capital of British India: Simla 1864-1947." *Modern Asian Studies* 18, 2 (1984):215-36.

Katrak, Ketu. "Indian Nationalism, Gandhian 'Satyagraha', and Representation of Female Sexuality." In *Nationalisms and Sexualities*, pp. 395-406. Edited by Andrew Parker, Mary Russo, Doris Sommer, and Patricia Yaeger. New York: Routledge, 1992.

Kaviraj, Sudipta. "Imaginary History." Occasional Papers on History and Society, 2nd series, no. 7. New Delhi: NMML, 1989.

Kennedy, Dane. "Guardians of Edenic Sanctuaries: Paharis, Lepchas, and Todas in the British Mind." *South Asia* (New Series) 14, 2 (Dec. 1991):57-78.

Korom, Frank J. "Inventing Traditions: Folklore and Nationalism as Historical Process in Bengal." In *Folklore and Historical Process,* pp. 57-83. Edited by D. Rihtman-Augustin and M. Povrzanovic. Zagreb: Institute of Folklore Research, 1989.

Kowlowski, Greg. "The Power of Language and the Language of Power: A Study of Mawlana Muhammad Ali's Political Rhetoric." *South Asia* 5, 1 (1982):29-41.

Kumar, Kapil. *Peasants in Revolt: Tenants, Landlords, Congress and the Raj in Oudh 1886-1922*. Delhi: Manohar, 1984.

Kumar, Kapil. "Peasants' Perception of Gandhi and his Programme, Oudh 1920-22." *Social Scientist* 11, 2 (February 1983).

Kumar, Kapil. "Rural Women in Oudh 1917-47: Baba Ramachandra and the Women's Question." In *Recasting Women*, pp. 337-69. Edited by Sudesh Vaid and Kumkum Sangari. New Delhi: Kali for Women, 1989.

Kumar, Kapil. "Using the Ramcharitmanas as a Radical Text: Baba Ram Chandra in Oudh, 1920-50." In *Social Transformation and Creative Imagination*, pp. 311-34. Edited by Sudhir Chandra. Delhi: Allied, 1984. Also published as Occasional Papers on History and Society, no. 4. New Delhi: NMML, 1986.

Kumar, Kapil, ed. *Congress and Classes: Nationalism, Workers and Peasants*. Delhi: Manohar Publications, 1984.

Kumar, Krishna. "Colonial Citizen as an Educational Ideal." Occasional Papers on History and Society, 2nd series, no. 13. New Delhi: NMML, 1990.

Kumar, Krishna. "Origins of India's 'Textbook Culture.'" Occasional Papers on History and Society, no. 47. New Delhi: NMML, 1988.

Kumar, Krishna. *Political Agenda of Education: A Study of Colonialist and Nationalist Ideas*. Newbury Park, Calif.: Sage Publications, 1991.

Kumar, Krishna. *Social Character of Learning*. New Delhi: Sage Publications, 1989.

Kumar, Krishna. "The Problem of Curriculum." Occasional Papers on History and Society. New Delhi: NMML, 1988.

Kumar, Nita. "Widows, Education and Social Change in Twentieth Century Banaras." *EPW* 26, 17 (27 April 1991):WS19-25.

Kumar, Ravinder. "Chance and Determinism in History." Occasional Papers on History and Society, 2nd Series, no. 24. New Delhi: NMML, 1990.

Kumar, Ravinder. *Essays in the Social History of Modern India*. Delhi: Oxford UP, 1983.

Kumar, Ravinder. "Exploring the Historical Conjuncture." *Social Scientist*, nos. 221-22 (Oct.-Nov. 1991):5-18.

Kumar, Ravinder. Introduction to *Myth and Reality: The Struggle for Freedom in India (1945-47)*. Edited by A. K. Gupta. New Delhi: Manohar Publications, 1987.

Kumar, Ravinder. *The Emergence of Modern India: Retrospect*. Delhi: Manohar, 1990.

Kumar, Ravinder. "The Past and the Present: An Indian Dialogue." *Daedalus* (Fall 1989):27-49.

Kumar, Ravinder. "The Role of Urban Society in Nationalist Politics." Occasional Papers on History and Society. New Delhi: NMML, 1988.

Lal, Vinay. "Committees of Inquiry and Discourses of 'Law and Order' in Twentieth-Century British India." 2 vols. Unpublished Ph.D. Dissertation, The University of Chicago, 1992.

Lal, Vinay. "Literature from Below." *Indian Literature* 34, 3 (May-June 1991):111-18.

Lal, Vinay. "The Incident of the Crawling Lane: Women in the Punjab Disturbances of 1919." *Genders* , no. 16 (Spring 1993):35-60.

Lelyveld, David. *Aligarh's First Generation: Muslim Solidarity in British India*. Princeton, New Jersey: Princeton UP, 1978.

Lelyveld, David. "The Fate of Hindustani: Colonial Knowledge and the Project of a National Language." In *Orientalism and the Postcolonial Predicament*. Edited by Carol A. Breckenridge and Peter van der Veer. Philadelphia: Univ. of Pennsylvania Press, 1993.

Lelyveld, David. "Transmitters and Culture: The Colonial Roots of India Broadcasting." *South Asia Research* 10, 1 (Spring 1990).

Ludden, David. "Historians and Nation States." In *Perspectives, The American Historical Association Newsletter* 24, 4 (1986):12-14.

Ludden, David. "India's Development Regime." In *Colonialism and Culture*, pp. 247-87. Edited by Nicholas Dirks. Ann Arbor, Michigan: The Univ. of Michigan Press, 1992. A Comparative Studies in Society and History Book.

Majeed, Javed. *Ungoverned Imaginings: James Mill's 'The History of British India' and Orientalism.* Oxford English Monographs. Oxford: Oxford UP, 1992.

Mani, Lata. *Contentious Traditions: The Debate on Sati in Colonial India, 1780-1833.* Berkeley, California: University of California Press, forthcoming [1994].

Masselos, Jim. "The Dis/Appearance of Subalterns: A Reading of a Decade of Subaltern Studies." *South Asia* (New Series) 15, 1 (June 1992):105-25.

Menon, Parvathi. "Ayodhya and all that : Communalism and the discipline of history." *Frontline* (11-24 May 1991):47-48.

Murshid, Ghulam. *Reluctant Debutante: Response of Bengali Women to Modernisation, 1849-1905.* Rajshahi, Bangladesh: Sahitya Samsad, Rajshahi University, 1983.

Musselwhite, David. "The Trial of Warren Hastings." In *Literature, Politics and Theory: Papers from the Essex Conference 1976-84*, pp. 77-103. Edited by Francis Barker, Peter Hulme, Margaret Iversen, and Diana Loxley. London & New York: Methuen, 1986.

Nandy, Ashis. "An anti-secularist manifesto." *Seminar*, no. 314 (October 1985):1-12.

Nandy, Ashis. *The Illegitimacy of Nationalism: Rabindranath Tagore and the Politics of Self.* New Delhi: Oxford UP, 1994.

Nandy, Ashis and Trivedi, Shikha, and others. *The Emergence of Nationalities and the Creation of Minorities in India: The Ramjanmabhumi Movement and the Fear of Self.* Forthcoming, 1995.

Nandy, Moti. "Football and Nationalism." Translated by Shampa Banerjee. In *The Calcutta Psyche*, pp. 241-54. Edited by Geeti Sen. New Delhi: Rupa & Co. and India International Centre, 1990-91.

Narasimhan, Sakuntala. *Sati: Widow Burning in India.* New York and New Delhi: Viking, 1990.

Nigam, Sanjay. "Disciplining and Policing the 'Criminals by Birth', Part 2: The Development of a Disciplinary System, 1871-1900," *IESHR* 27, 3 (July-Sept. 1990):257-88.

Nigam, Sanjay. "Disciplining and Policing the 'Criminals by Birth', Part I: The Making of a Colonial Stereotype — The Criminal Tribes and Castes of North India", *IESHR* 27, 2 (April-June 1990):131-64.

Nirajana, Tejaswini. "Translation, Colonialism and the Rise of English." *EPW* 25, 15 (14 April 1990):773-79.

O'Hanlon, Rosalind. *Caste, Conflict and Ideology: Mahatma Jotirao Phule and Low-Caste Protest in Nineteenth-Century Western India.* New York: Cambridge University Press, 1985.

O'Hanlon, Rosalind. "Cultures of Rule, Communities of Resistance: Gender, Discourse and Tradition in Recent South Asian Historiographies." *Social Analysis* 25 (1989).

O'Hanlon, Rosalind. "Issues of Widowhood: Gender and Resistance in Colonial Western India." In *Contesting Power: Resistance and Everday Social Relations in South Asia*, pp. 62-108. Edited by Douglas Haynes and Gyan Prakash. Delhi: Oxford UP, 1991.

O'Hanlon, Rosalind. "Recovering the Subject: Subaltern Studies and Histories of Resistance in Colonial South Asia." *Modern Asian Studies* 22, 1 (1988):189-224.

O'Hanlon, Rosalind and Washbrook, David. "After Orientalism: Culture, Criticism, and Politics in the Third World." *CSSH* 34, 1 (Jan. 1992): 141-67.

Oldenburg, Veena. "Lifestyle as Resistance: The Case of the Courtesans of Lucknow, India." *Feminist Studies* 16, 2 (Summer, 1990):259-87; slightly different version also published in *Contesting Power: Resistance and Everday Social Relations in South Asia*, pp. 23-61. Edited by Douglas Haynes and Gyan Prakash. Delhi: Oxford UP, 1991.

Oldenburg, Veena Talwar. *The Making of Colonial Lucknow 1856-1877.* Princeton: Princeton UP, 1984; paperback ed., Delhi: Oxford UP, 1989.

Ostor, Akos. *Culture and Power: Legend, Ritual, Trade and Revolution in a Bengali Society*. Beverly Hill and New Delhi: Sage Publications, 1984.

Pandey, Gyanendra. "Hindus and Others: The Militant Hindu Construction." *EPW* 26, 52 (28 Dece. 1991):2997-3005, 3008-9.

Pandey, Gyanendra. "In Defense of the Fragment: Writing About Hindu-Muslim Riots in India Today." *Representations*, no. 37 (Winter 1992): 27-55; also in *EPW* (Annual Number) 26, 11-12 (March 1991):559-72.

Pandey, Gyanendra. *The Construction of Communalism in Colonial North India.* Delhi: Oxford UP, 1990. [collects essays first published in *Subaltern Studies* and *EPW*].

Pandey, Gyanendra. "The Masjid and the Mandir: On the Horns of a Dilemma." *The India Magazine* (February 1990).

Parasher, Aloka. "Attitudes towards the Mleccha in Early Northern India — up to ca. A.D. 600." *The Indian Historical Review* 9, 1-2 (1983):1-30.

Parasher, Aloka. *Mlecchas in Early India*. Delhi: Munshiram Manoharlal, 1991.

Po'dar, Preym K. and Subba, Tanka B. "Demystifying Some Ethnographic Texts on the Himalayas." *Social Scientist*, nos. 219-20 (Aug.-Sept. 1991):78-84.

Pollock, Sheldon. "Ramayana and Political Imagination in India." *Jrl. of Asian Studies* 52, 2 (May 1993):261-97.

Powers, David S. "Orientalism, Colonialism, and Legal History: The Attack on Muslim Family Endowments in Algeria and India." *CSSH* 31, 3 (1989):535-571.

Prakash, Gyan. *Bonded Histories: Genealogies of Labor Servitude in Colonial India*. Cambridge: Cambridge UP, 1990.

Prakash, Gyan. "Can the 'Subaltern' Ride? A Reply to O'Hanlon and Washbrook." *CSSH* 34, 1 (Jan. 1992):168-85.

Prakash, Gyan. "Science 'Gone Native' in Colonial India." *Representations*, no. 40 (Fall 1992):153-178.

Prakash, Gyan. "Writing Post-Orientalist Histories of the Third World: Perspectives from Indian Historiography." *CSSH* 32, 2 (April 1990):383-408; also published in revised form as "Writing Post-Orientalist Histories of the Third World: Indian Historiography Is Good to Think", in *Colonialism and Culture*, pp. 353-88. Edited by Nicholas Dirks. Ann Arbor, Michigan: Univ. of Michigan Press, 1992.

Prakash, Gyan, ed. *The World of the Rural Labourer in Colonial India*. New Delhi: Oxford UP, 1992.

Raychaudhuri, Tapan. "Indian Nationalism as Animal Politics." *Historical Journal* 22 (1979):747-63.

Robb, Peter. "New Directions in South Asian History." *South Asia Research* 7, 2 (1979):123-42.

Sabin, Margery. "The Suttee Romance." *Raritan* 11, 2 (Fall 1991):1-24.

Sanyal, Hitesranjan. "Trends of Change in the Bhakti Movement in Bengal." Occasional Paper, no. 76. Calcutta: CSSS, 1985.

Sarkar, Sumit. *'Popular Movements' and 'Middle Class' Leadership in Late Colonial India: Problems and Perspectives of a 'History from Below.'* Calcutta: K. P. Bagchi, for CSSS, 1983.

Sarkar, Sumit. *A Critique of Colonial India*. Calcutta: Papyrus, 1985.

Sarkar, Sumit. *Marxian Approaches to the History of Indian Nationalism*. Presidency College Historical Pamphlets, no. 1. New Delhi & Calcutta: K. P. Bagchi, 1990. Reprinted in *The Book Review* 15, 4 (July-Aug. 1991):17-20.

Sarkar, Sumit. *Modern India, 1885-1947*. Delhi: Macmillan, 1983.

Sarkar, Sumit. "Ramakrishna and the Calcutta of His Times." In *The Calcutta Psyche*, pp. 99-121. Edited by Geeti Sen. New Delhi: Rupa & Co. and India International Centre, 1990-91.

Sarkar, Sumit. "Social History: Predicament and Possibilities." In *Fresh Perspectives on India and Pakistan: Essays on Economics, Politics, and Culture*, pp. 256-74. Edited by Iqbal Khan. Oxford, 1985.

Sarkar, Sumit. "The Conditions and Nature of Subaltern Militancy: Bengal from Swadeshi to Non-Co-operation, c. 1905-22." In *Subaltern Studies III*, pp. 271-320. Edited by Ranajit Guha. Delhi: Oxford UP, 1984.

Sarkar, Sumit. "The Kalki-Avatar of Bikrampur: A Village Scandal in Early Twentieth Century Bengal." In *Subaltern Studies VI*, pp. 1-53. Edited by Ranajit Guha. Delhi: Oxford UP, 1989.

Sarkar, Sumit. "The *Kathamrita* as a Text." Occasional Papers on History and Society, no. 22. New Delhi: NMML, 1986.

Sarkar, Tanika. *Bengal, 1928-1934: The Politics of Protest*. Delhi: Oxford UP, 1987.

Sarkar, Tanika. "The Woman as Communal Subject: Rashtrasevika Samiti and Ram Janmabhoomi Movement." *EPW* (31 August 1991):2057-62.

Sarkar, Tanika and Butalia, Urvashi, eds. *Women of the Hindu Right: A Collection of Essays*. New Delhi: Kali for Women, forthcoming [1995].

Sayer, Derek. "British Reaction to the Amritsar Massacre, 1919-1920." In *Crossing Cultures: Essays in the Displacement of Western Civilization*, pp. 142-81. Edited by Daniel Segal. Tuscon and London: Univ. of Arizona Press, 1992. A slightly different version published in *Past and Present* 131 (1991).

Sen, Asok. "'Subaltern Studies': Tinti ba Du-ti prashna ja ami karte pari" [in Bengali]. *Anustup* (Autumn 1985).

Sen, Asok. "Subaltern Studies: Capital, Class and Community." In *Subaltern Studies* V, pp. 203-35. Edited by Ranajit Guha. Delhi: Oxford UP, 1987.

Shaikh, Farzana. "The language of representation: towards a Muslim political order in nineteenth-century India." In *Language, History and Class*, pp. 204-226. Edited by Penelope J. Corfield. Oxford: Basil Blackwell, 1991.

Sharpe, Jennifer. "Scenes of an Encounter: A Double Discourse of Colonialism and Nationalism." Ph. D. Dissertation, 1988. Abstracted in *Dissertation Abstracts Intl.* 48, 10 (April 1988):2623A.

Sharpe, Jenny. *Allegories of Empire: The Figure of Woman in the Colonial Text*. Minneapolis: Univ. of Minnesota Press, 1993.

Sharpe, Jenny. "The Unspeakable Limits of Rape: Colonial Violence and Counter-Insurgency." *Genders*, no. 10 (Spring 1991):24-46.

Sharpe, Jenny. "The Violence of Light in the Land of Desire; or, How William Jones Discovered India." *boundary 2* 20, 2 (Summer 1993):26-46.

Siddiqi, Majid Hayat. "Bluff, Doubt and Fear: The Kheiri Brothers and the Colonial State, 1904-45." *IESHR* 24, 3 (July-Sept. 1987):233-63.

Siddiqi, Majid Hayat. "History and Society in a Popular Rebellion: Mewat, 1920-1933." *CSSH* (1986):442-67.

Simeon, Dilip. "Communalism in Modern India: A Theoretical Examination." *Social Science Probings* 4, 1 (March 1987).

Singha, Radhika. "'Providential' Circumstances: The Thuggee Campaign of the 1830's and Legal Innovation." *Modern Asian Studies* 27, 1 (Feb. 1993):83-146.

Singha, Radhika. "A 'despotism of law': British criminal justice and public authority in North India, 1772-1837." Unpublished Ph.D. Dissertation, Cambridge University, 1990.

Smith, Richard Saumarez. "Rule-by-Records and Rule-by-Reports: Complementary Aspects of the British Imperial Rule of Law." *CIS* 19, 1 (1985):153-76.

Spivak, Gayatri Chakravorty. "Can the Subaltern Speak? Speculations on Widow Sacrifice." *Wedge*, nos. 7/8 (Winter/Spring 1985):120-30. Also in *Marxism and the Interpretation of Culture*, pp. 271-313. Edited by Gary Nelson and Lawrence Gorssberg. Urbana: Univ. of Illinois Press, 1988.

Spivak, Gayatri Chakravorty. "The Rani of Sirmur." In *Europe and Its Others*. Edited by Francis Barker *et al.* Colchester: Univ. of Essex, 1985.

Steedman, Carolyn. *The Radical Soldier's Tale*. London: Routledge, 1988.

Stein, Dorothy K. "Women to Burn: Suttee as a Normative Institution." *Signs* 4, 2 (Winter 1978):253-68.

Stephens, Julie. "Feminist Fictions: A Critique of the Category 'Non-Western Woman' in Feminist Writings on India." In *Subaltern Studies VI*, pp. 92-125. Edited by Ranajit Guha. Delhi: Oxford UP, 1989. And see response by Susie Tharu, pp. 126-31 in same volume.

Stree Shakti Sangathana. *We Were Making History: Women and the Telengana Uprising*. London: Zed Press; Delhi: Kali for Women, 1990.

Subramaniam, V. "Karmayoga and the Rise of the Indian Middle Class." *Jrl. of Arts and Ideas*, nos. 14-15 (July-Dec. 1987).

Thapar, Romila. "Communalism and the Historical Legacy: Some Facts." *Social Scientist*, nos. 205-6 (June-July 1990):4-20.

Thapar, Romila. "Epic and History: Tradition, Dissent and Politics in India." *Past and Present*, no. 125 (1989):3-26.

Thapar, Romila. "Imagined Religious Communities? Ancient History and the Modern Search for a Hindu Identity." *Modern Asian Studies* 23, 2 (May 1989):209-31.

Thapar, Romila. "Interpretations of Indian History." In converation with Kunal Chakrabarti and Geeti Sen. *IICQ* 20, 1-2 (Spring-Summer 1993): 115-35.

Thapar, Romila. *Interpreting Early India*. Delhi: Oxford UP, 1992; Oxford India paperback, 1993.

van der Veer, Peter. "Ayodhya and Somnath: Eternal Shrines, Contested Histories." *Social Research* 59, 1 (Spring 1992):85-110.

van der Veer, Peter. "Hindu 'Nationalism' and the discourse of 'modernity': The Vishva Hindu Parishad." In *The Dynamics of Fundamentalist Movements*. Edited by Martin Marty and S. Appleby. Chicago: Univ. of Chicago Press, 1991.

Vicziany, Marika. "Imperialism, Botany, and Statistics in Early Nineteenth-Century India: The Surveys of Francis Buchanan (1762-1829)." *Modern Asian Studies* 20 (1986):625-50.

Visweswaran, Kamala. "Family Subjects: An Ethnography of the 'Women's Question' in Indian Nationalism." Unpublished Ph.D. Dissertation, Stanford University, 1990.

Washbrook, D. A. "Ethnicity and Racialism in Colonial Indian Society." In *Racism and Colonialism: Essays on Ideology and Social Structure*. Edited by R. Ross. The Hague: Nijhoff, 1982.

Yang, Anand, ed. *Crime and Criminality in British India*. Tuscon, Arizona: Published for the Association for Asian Studies by the Univ. of Arizona Press, 1985.

Yang, Anand. "Disciplining 'Natives': Prisons and Prisoners in Early Nineteenth Century India." *South Asia* 10, 2 (1987):29-46.

Yang, Anand. "Whose Sati? Widow Burning in English Nineteenth Century India." *Journal of Women's History* 1, 2 (1989):8-33.

XVII. Theatre, Dance, and Performance Studies

Adarkar, Neera. "In Seach of Women in History of Marathi Theatre 1843 to 1933." *EPW* 26, 43 (26 Oct. 1991):WS-87 ff.

Akshara, K. V. "Western Responses to Traditional Indian Theatre." *Journal of Arts and Ideas*, no. 8 (July-September 1984):43-55.

Ashley, Wayne and Regina Holloman. "From Ritual to Theater in Kerala." *The Drama Review* 26, 2 (Summer 1982):59-72.

Banerjee, Sumanta. "Having the Last Laugh: Women in the Nineteenth Century Bengali Farces." *Manushi*, no. 59 (July-August 1990):15-20.

Banerji, Himani. *Representation and Class Politics in the Theatre of Utpal Dutt*. Occasional Paper, no. 106. Calcutta: CSSS, 1990.

Bharucha, Rustom. "A Collision of Cultues: Some Western Interpretations of the Indian Theatre." *IICQ* 11, 3 (Sept. 1984):287-307.

Bharucha, Rustom. "Politics of Indigenous Theatre: Kanhailal in Manipur." *EPW* (Annual Number) 26, 11-12 (March 1991):747-54.

Bharucha, Rustom. *Rehearsals of Revolution: The Political Theatre of Bengal*. Calcutta: Seagull Books, 1983.

Bharucha, Rustom. *Theatre and the World: Essays on Theatre and Politics of Culture*. Delhi: Manohar, 1990.

Bhattacharya, Rimli. "'Public Women': Early Actresses of the Bengali Stage — Role and Reality." In *The Calcutta Psyche*, pp. 143-69. Edited by Geeti Sen. New Delhi: Rupa & Co. and India International Centre, 1990-91.

Chatterjee, Sekhar. "The Colonial Theatre in India." *Theatre Research International* 8, 3 (Autumn 1983):233-34.

Deshpande, G. P. "Dialectics of Defeat: Some Reflections on Literature, Theatre and Music: Colonial India." *EPW* 22, 50 (12 Dec. 1982):2170-76.

Guha, Probir; Meduri, Avanthi; Neff, Deborah; and Zarrilli, Phillip. "The Aftermath: When Peter Brook Came to India" and "More Aftermath After Peter Brook", both in *The Drama Review* 30, 1 (1986):92-99 and 32 (Summer 1988):14-20.

Hansen, Kathryn. *Grounds for Play: The Nautanki Theatre of North India*. Berkeley: University of California Press, 1992.

Kapur, Anuradha. "Actors, Pilgrims, Kings and Gods: The Ramlila at Ramnagar." *Contributions to Indian Sociology* (New Series) 19, 1 (1985).

Kapur, Anuradha. *Actors, Pilgrims, Kings and Gods: The Ramlila at Ramnagar*. Calcutta: Seagull Books, 1990. [Reviewed by Avanthi Meduri, "Studies in Performance: Performance Studies", *Jrl. of Arts and Ideas*, no. 22 (April 1992):45-49.]

Kapur, Anuradha. "Notions of the Authentic." *Jrl. of Arts and Ideas*, nos. 20-21 (March 1991):7-19.

Kapur, Anuradha. "The Representation of Gods and Heroes: Parsi Mythological Drama of the Early Nineteenth Century." *Journal of Arts and Ideas*, nos. 23-24 (Jan. 1993):85-107.

Karnad, Girish. "Theatre in India." *Architecture and Design* 7, 4 (July-August 1990):87-99.

Martin, Carol. "Feminist Analysis across Cultures: Performing Gender in India." *Women and Performance* 3, 2 (1987-88):32-40.

Meduri, Avanthi. "*Bharatha Natyam*—What Are You?" *Asian Theatre Journal* 5, 1 (Spring 1988):1-23; briefly excerpted as "Dancing for gods — and men", in *Economic Times* (22 April 1992), p. 10.

Meduri, Avanthi. "History as an Image: Mimesis and Parody in Bharatnatyam." In *Proceedings of the Fifth Hongkong International Dance Performance*, Vol. 2, pp. 107-23. Hongkong: Hongkong Academy for the Performing Arts, 1990.

Meduri, Avanthi. "Western Feminist Theory, Asian Indian Performance, and a Notion of Agency." *Women and Performance* 5, 2 (Spring 1992): 90-103.

Schechner, Richard. "Magnitudes of Performance." In *Performance Theory*. London & New York: Routledge, 1988.

Schechner, Richard. *Performative Circumstances from the Avant Garde to Ramlila*. Calcutta: Seagull Books, 1990.

Schechner, Richard. "The Ramlila of Ramnagar"; "Perfomer Training Interculturally"; and "Performers and Spectators Transported and Transformed", all in *Between Theater and Anthropology*. Philadelphia: Univ. of Pennsylvania Press, 1985.

Schechner, Richard. "Wayang Kulit in the Colonial Margin", and "Striding Through the Cosmos", in *The Future of Ritual: Writings on Culture and Performance*. London & New York: Routledge, 1993.

van Erven, Eugene. "The Theatre of Liberation of India, Indonesia, and the Philippines." *Australasian Drama Studies* 10 (April 1987):5-18.

Wade, Bonnie C. and Pescatello, Ann M. "The Status of Women in the Performing Arts of India and Iberia: Cross-Cultural Perspectives from Historical Accounts and Field." In *The Performing Arts: Music and Dance*, pp. 119-37. Edited by John Blacking and Joann W. Kealiinohomoku. The Hague: Mouton, 1979.

Williams, Sylvia. "Marguerite Duras' India Song — Texte Threate Film." *Australian Journal of French Studies* 23, 3 (Sept.-Dec. 1986):277-89.

BIBLIOGRAPHY OF CONTEMPORARY SOUTH ASIAN CULTURAL STUDIES, ARRANGED BY AREA FOR BANGLADESH, PAKISTAN, AND SRI LANKA

I. Bangladesh

Ahmed, Rafiuddin, ed. *Bangladesh: Society Religion and Politics*. Chittagong: South Asia Studies Group, Univ. of Chittagong, 1985.

Ahmed, Rafiuddin, ed. *Religion, Nationalism and Politics in Bangladesh*. Delhi: South Asian Publishers, 1990.

Ahmed, Rehnuma. "Women's Movement in Bangladesh and the Left's Understanding of the Women Question." *Jrl. of Social Studies*, no. 30 (1985):27-56.

Blair, Harry W. "Ideology, Foreign Aid and Rural Poverty in Bangladesh: Emergence of the Like-Minded Group." *Jrl. of Social Studies* 34 (1986):1-27.

Blanchet, Therese. *Meanings and Rituals of Birth in Rural Bangladesh*. Dhaka: Univ. Press Ltd., 1984.

Guhathakura. "Gender Violence in Bangladesh: The Role of the State." *Jrl. of Social Studies* 30 (1985):77-90.

Jahangir, B. K. *Problematics of Nationalism in Bangladesh*. Dhaka: Centre for Social Studies, 1986.

Jahangir, B. K. *Violence and Consent in a Peasant Society and Other Essays*. Calcutta: Centre for Social Studies, 1990.

Kabeer, Naila. "Subordination and Struggle: Women in Bangladesh." *New Left Review*, No. 168 (April/May 1988).

Kabeer, Naila. "The Quest for National Identity: Women, Islam and the State of Bangladesh." In *Women, Islam and the State*, pp.115-43. Edited by Deniz Kandiyoti. Philadelphia: Temple UP, 1991.

Rahim, Amin-ur. "After the Last Journey: Some Reflections on Bangladeshi Community Life in Ontario." *Polyphony: The Bulletin of the Multicultural Society of Ontario* 12 (1990):8-11.

White, Sarah C. *Arguing with the Crocodile: Gender and Class in Bangladesh*. London: Zed Books, 1992.

Zene, Cosimo. "The Authority of the Face: Missionary Representations in

South-West Bangladesh." *History and Anthropology* 6, 2-3 (1993): 125-55.

II. PAKISTAN

Ali, Tariq. *Can Pakistan Survive? The Death of a State*. Harmondsworth: Penguin Books; London: Verso Books, 1983.

Hashmi, Alamgir. "Pakistani Literature in English: Past, Present, and Future." *South Asia Bulletin* 10, 2 (Fall 1990):48-53.

Hashmi, Taj Ul-Islam. *Pakistan as a Peasant Utopia: The Communalization of Class Politics in East Bengal, 1920-1947*. Boulder, Colorado: Westview Press, 1992.

Jalal, Ayesha. "The Convenience of Subservience: Women and the State of Pakistan." In *Women, Islam and the State*, pp. 77-114. Edited by Deniz Kandiyoti. Philadelphia: Temple UP, 1991.

Mumtaz, Khawar and Shaheed, Farida. *Women of Pakistan: Two Steps Forward, One Step Back*. London: Zed Press, 1987.

Shaheed, Farida. "Legal Systems, Islam and Women in Pakistan." *Ethnic Studies Report* 3, 1 (1985).

III. SRI LANKA

Brow, James. "Nationalist Rhetoric and Local Practice: The Fate of the Village Community in Kukulewa." In *Sri Lanka: History and the Roots of Conflict*. Edited by Jonathan Spence. London: Routledge, 1990.

Framework, no. 37. Special Issue on Sri Lanka Cinema. Guest Editors: Robert Crusz and Ashley Ratnavibhushana.

Hellmann-Rajanayagam, D. "The Concept of a 'Tamil Homeland' in Sri Lanka: Its Meaning and Development." *South Asia* 13, 2 (1988):79-110.

Ismail, Qadri. "Boys Will Be Boys: Gender and National Agency in Frantz Fanon and the Liberation Tigers of Tamil Eelam." *South Asia Bulletin* 11, 1-2 (1991):79-83.

Jayamanne, Laleen. "Hunger for Images, Myths of Femininity in the Sri Lankan Cinema, 1947-1989." *South Asia Bulletin* 12, 1 (1992):57-75.

Jayamanne, Laleen. "Speaking of 'Ceylon', a Clash of Cultures." In *Questions of Third Cinema*, pp. 150-69. Edited by Jim Pines and Paul Willemen. London: British Film Institute Publishing, 1989.

Kapferer, Bruce. *A Celebration of Demons: Exorcism and the Aesthetics of Healing in Sri Lanka*. Bloomington: Indiana UP, 1983.

Kapferer, Bruce. *Legends of People, Myths of State: Violence, Intolerance, and Political Culture in Sri Lanka and Australia*. Washington: Smithsonian Institution Press, 1988.

Kemper, Steven. *The Presence of the Past: Chronicles, Politics and Culture in Sinhala Life*. Ithaca, New York: Cornell UP, 1991.

Manogavan, Chelvadurai. *Ethnic Conflict and Reconciliation in Sri Lanka*. Honolulu: Univ. of Hawaii Press, 1987.

Obeyesekere, Ranjini and Fernando, Chitra, eds. *An Anthology of Modern Writing from Sri Lanka*. Tuscon: University of Arizona Press, 1981.

Obeyesekere, Ranjini. "The Problem of Language in the Sinhala Theater." In *Ediriweera Sarachchandra: Festschrift 1988*. Colombo, 1988.

Obeyesekere, Ranjini. "The Sinhala Literary Tradition: Polemics and Debate." *South Asia Bulletin* 12, 1 (Spring 1992):34-41.

Peebles, Patrick. "Colonization and Ethnic Conflict in the Dry Zone of Sri Lanka." *Journal of Asian Studies* 49, 1 (1990):30-55.

Risseeuw, Carla. *Gender Transformation, Power and Resistance among Women in Sri Lanka: The Fish Don't Talk about the Water*. Leiden: Brill, 1988; Delhi: Manohar, 1991.

Risseeuw, Carla. "Gender, Kinship and State Formation: Case of Sri Lanka Under Colonial Rule." *EPW* 27, 43-44 (24-31 Oct. 1992):WS46-54.

Roberts, Michael. "'Our Duty to Act': Brown Sahibs in Universal Suits: A Review Article on the Abortive 1962 Coup in Sri Lanka." *South Asia* 6, 2 (1983):62-77.

Roberts, Michael. "Ethnicity in Riposte at a Cricket Match: The Past for the Present." *CSSH* 27 (1985):401-29.

Roberts, Michael. "From Southern India to Lanka: The Traffic in Commodities, Bodies and Myths from the Thirteenth Century Onwards." *South Asia* 3, 1 (1980):36-47.

Rogers, John D. *Crime, Justice and Society in Colonial Sri Lanka*. London: Curzon; Maryland: Riverdale Press, 1987.

Rogers, John D. "Cultural Nationalism and Social Reform: The 1904 Temperance Movement in Sri Lanka." *IESHR* 26 (1989):319-41.

Rogers, John D. "Culture and Social Resistance: Gambling in Colonial Sri Lanka." In *Contesting Power: Resistance and Everyday Social Relations in South Asia*, pp. 175-212. Edited by Douglas Haynes & Gyan Prakash. Oxford: Oxford UP, 1991; Berkeley: University of California Press, 1992.

Samaraweera, Vijaya. "The 'Village Community' and Reform in Colonial Sri Lanka." *Ceylon J. of Historical and Social Studies* (New Series) 8 (1980):68-75.

Scott, David. "Conversion and Demonism: Colonial Christian Discourse and Religion in Sri Lanka." *CSSH* 34, 2 (April 1992):331-365.

Scott, David. *Formations of Ritual: Colonial and Anthropological Discourses on the Sinhala Yaktovil*. Minneapolis: Univ. of Minnesota Press, 1994.

Scott, David. "The Cultural Poetics of Eyesight in Sri Lanka: Composure, Vulnerability, and the Sinhala Concept of *Distiya*." *Dialetical Anthropology* 16, 1 (1991):85-102.

Scott, David. "The Demonology of Nationalism: On the Anthropology of Ethnicity and Violence in Sri Lanka." *Economy and Society* 19, 4 (1990):491-510.

Sivanandan, A. "Sri Lanka: Racism and the Politics of Underdevelopment." *Race and Class* 25, 1 (Summer 1984):1-38.

Stirrat, R. L. *Power and Religiosity in a Post-Colonial Setting: Sinhala Catholics in Contemporary Sri Lanka*. Cambridge: Cambridge UP, 1992.

Wickremeratne, Ananda. *The Genesis of an Orientalist: Thomas Williams Rhys Davids and Buddhism in Sri Lanka*. Delhi: Motilal Banarsidass, 1984.

APPENDIX ONE

JOURNALS MENTIONED IN THE BIBLIOGRAPHY

Alternatives (Delhi & New York)
American Ethnologist
Annual Review of Anthropology
Anthropological Quarterly
Antiquity
Anustup (Bengali; Calcutta)
Architecture and Design (Delhi)
Architectural Review
Arena (Melbourne)
Ariel, a Review of International English Literature
Art·History
Artrage (London)
Asian Culture
Asian Folklore
Asian Music (Cornell)
Asian Theatre Journal
Australasian Drama Studies
Australian Association of Asian Studies (AAAS) Review
Australian Historical Association Bulletin
Australian Journal of French Studies
Bahuvachan (Bhopal; only one issue)
Bansuri (Canada)
Bengal Past and Present (Calcutta)
Berkshire Review
The Book Review (Delhi)
boundary 2 (Duke University Press, Durham, North Carolina)
Bucknell Review
Bulletin of Concerned Asian Scholars
Bulletin of the History of Medicine
Calcutta Historical Journal (Calcutta)
Callaloo (Univ. of Virginia; Johns Hopkins Univ.)
Cambridge Anthropology (Cambridge, U.K.)

Ceylon Journal of Historical and Social Studies
Cinema in India
Cinema India International
Cineaste
College Literature
Comparative Education Review
Comparative Studies in Society and History
Contemporary South Asia (Abingdon, Oxfordshire, U.K.)
Contention (Los Angeles)
Continuum (Australia)
Contributions to Indian Sociology (Delhi)
Copyright
Critical Inquiry (Chicago)
Critical Quarterly
Criticism
Cultural Anthropology
Cultural Critique
Cultural Studies
Cultural Survival Quarterly
Current Anthropology
Current Science
Daedalus (Washington, D.C.)
Deep Focus (Bangalore)
Diacritics
Dialectical Anthropology
Diaspora
Differences
The Drama Review (known as TDR; New York)
Dutch Quarterly Rv. of Anglo-American Letters
East-West Film Journal (Honolulu)
Eastern Anthropologist
Economic and Political Weekly (Bombay)
Economy and Society
Emergences (UCLA)
Environmental Ethics
Environmentalist
Ethnic and Racial Studies
Ethnology (Trivandrum)
Ethnomusicology

Ethos
Feminist Review
Feminist Studies
Film Quarterly (Berkeley)
Focus on Law Studies (Chicago)
Folk
Framework
Frontline (Madras)
Futures
Gandhi Marg (New Delhi)
Genders (Boulder, Colorado)
Geographical Review
Granta
Historical Journal
History and Anthropology
History of Photography
History of Religions
History Workshop Journal
IDS (Institute for Development Studies) Bulletin
IUMDA Bulletin (Delhi)
Illustrated Weekly of India (Delhi)
Immigrants and Minorities
Impact of Science on Society
In the Wake of Marx (Calcutta)
India International Centre Quarterly (Delhi)
The India Magazine (Bombay)
Indian Economic & Social History Review (Delhi)
Indian Historical Review (Delhi)
Indian Institute Magazine
Indian Literature (Delhi)
Indological Taurinensia
Inscriptions (Univ. of California, Santa Cruz)
Interculture (Montreal)
International History Review
International Journal of Popular Culture
International Review of the Aesthetics and Sociology of Music
International Social Science Journal
Itinerario (Leiden)
J. of American Folklore

J. of Anthropological Research
J. of Arts and Ideas (Delhi)
J. of Asian Studies
J. of Asian and African Studies
J. of Commonwealth Literature
J. of Commonwealth and Comparative Politics
J. of Communication
J. of Communication Inquiry
J. of Conflict Resolution
J. of Contemporary Asia
J. of Contemporary Thought
J. of Cultural Geography
J. of Developing Societies
J. of Ethnic Studies
J. of Film and Video
J. of Historical Geography
J. of Historical Sociology
J. of Homosexuality
J. of Imperial and Commonwealth History
J. of Indian Council of Philosophical Research
J. of Indian Philosophy
J. of Pacific History
J. of Peasant Studies
J. of Popular Culture
J. of Public Culture
J. of Ritual Studies
J. of Social Studies
J. of the American Oriental Society (Philadelphia)
J. of the Anthropological Society of Oxford
J. of the British Astronomical Association
J. of the Royal Society of Arts (London)
J. of the Society for the Anthropology of Consciousness
J. of the Society of Architectural Historians
J. of Women's History
J. of World History
Jump Cut
Kunapipi (Aarhus, Denmark)
Left Curve
Literary Criterion

Lokayan Bulletin (Delhi)
Mainstream (Delhi)
Man
Manushi (Delhi)
Massachusetts Review
Media, Culture and Society
Melus
Middle East Report (known as MERIP; Washington, D.C.)
Mississippi Review
Modern Asian Studies (Cambridge)
Modern Fiction Studies
Mountain Research and Development
National Medical Journal of India
New Formations
New Ideas in Psychology
New Left Review (London)
New Literary History (Baltimore)
New Quest (Poona)
Nineteenth-Century Prose
North Dakota Quarterly
October (M.I.T.)
Oxford Literary Review (Oxford)
Pacific Viewpoint
Past and Present (Cambridge)
Patriotic People's Science and Technology (PPST) Group Bulletin
Philosophy East and West (Honolulu)
Photographic Collector
Political Geography
Politics and Society
Polygraph (Duke Univ.)
Polyphony: The Bulletin of the Multicultural Society of Ontario
Popular Music
Public Culture (Chicago)
Qtly. Jrl. of Speech
Qtly. Rv. of Film and Video
Qtly. Rv. of Film Studies
Quest
Qui Parle
Race and Class (London)

Raritan (Rutgers Univ.)
Representations (Berkeley)
Rethinking Marxism (New York)
Review Fernand Braudel Center (Binghamton, New York)
Samya Shakti: A Journal of Women in Society (Delhi)
Sangarsh (Bangalore)
Science as Critique
Screen (London)
Seminar (Delhi)
Signs (Chicago)
Social Analysis
Social and Economic Studies
Social Research (New York)
Social Science Probings
Social Scientist (Delhi)
Social Text
South Asia
South Asia Bulletin
South Asia Research
South Atlantic Quarterly
Southwest Review
Soviet Literature
Splice (Calcutta)
Stanford Literary Review
Strategies (UCLA, Los Angeles)
Studies in History (Delhi)
Studies in Romanticism
Subaltern Studies (Delhi)
Sunday (Calcutta)
Sunday Observer Colour Magazine (Delhi and Bombay)
Sunday Statesman Miscellany (Calcutta)
Ten.8 [Photographic Magazine]
Textual Practice (U. of Wales; London)
Theatre Research International
Theory and Society
Third Text (London)
Times of India Review of Books (only one issue; Delhi)
Toronto South Asian Review (Toronto)
Transition

Victorian Studies (Bloomington, Indiana)
Vistas in Astronomy
Visual Anthropology
Voice Literary Supplement (New York)
Wasafiri
Wedge
Western Folklore
Wide Angle
Women and Performance
Women, Take One
Women's Review of Books
Women's Studies International Forum
Women's Studies Quarterly
Word and Image
Works and Days
World Literature Written in English
Yale J. of Criticism (New Haven, Conn.)
Yale J. of Law and the Humanities (New Haven, Conn.)
Yale Review (New Haven, Conn.)

Appendix Two

SELECT BIBLIOGRAPHY OF CULTURAL STUDIES IN GENERAL

Cultural Studies, as I have described it in the brief introductory essay to this volume, and as it is generally understood, has spawned an enormous literature. A far more comprehensive bibliography, by no means identical with this one, will be found in *Cultural Studies*, ed. Lawrence Grossberg, Cary Nelson, and Paula A. Treichler (New York and London: Routledge, 1992), pp. 731-770. But in the three years that have elapsed since the volume by Grossberg went to press, the literature has grown enormously, and indeed today it would be impossible to compile a bibliography of that sort, particularly if the periodical literature were taken into account. Scores of journals are devoted to cultural studies, including *Critical Inquiry*, *Cultural Studies*, *Cultural Critique*, *New Formations*, *Arena*, *Representations*, *Polygraph*, *Diaspora*, *Differences*, *boundary 2*, *Genders*, *October*, *Oxford Literary Review*, *Public Culture*, *Social Text*, *Stanford Literary Review*, *Emergences*, and *Third Text*. The selection that follows, which does not take account of literature published after 1991, is very much a personal one, but it provides more than an adequate illustration of the range of literature that has emerged over the years, and of the nature of the politics of knowledge in the academy, and to a lesser degree outside it.

Anderson, Benedict. *Imagined Communities: Reflections on the Origin and Spread of Nationalism*. London: Verso, 1983; new ed., 1990.

Angus, Ian and Jhally, Sut. *Cultural Politics in Contemporary America*. New York: Routledge, 1989.

Ashcroft, Bill; Griffiths, Gareth; and Tiffin, Helen. *The Empire Writes Back: Theory and Practice in Post-colonial Literature*. London: Routledge, 1991.

Benjamin, Jessica. *The Bonds of Love: Psychoanalysis, Feminism, and the Problem of Domination*. New York: Pantheon, 1988.

Bennett, Tony. "The Exhibitionary Complex." *New Formations* 4 (1988): 73-102.

________. *Outside Literature*. London: Routledge, 1990.

Bennett, Tony; Mercer, Colin; and Woollacott, Janet. *Popular Culture and Social Relations*. Milton Keynes: Open UP, 1986.

Bennett, Tony and Woollacott, Janet. *Bond and Beyond: The Political Career of a Popular Hero*. New York and Methuen, 1984.

Bhabha, Homi K., ed. *Nation and Narration*. London: Routledge, 1990.

Botsman, Peter. *Theoretical Strategies*. Sydney: Local Consumption Publications, 1982. Nos.2/3.

Bradley, Stuart. "Introduction to the Cultural Study of Music." CCCS Stenciled Paper No. 61. Birmingham: CCCS, n.d.

Brantlinger, Patrick. *Crusoe's Footprints: Cultural Studies in Britain and America*. New York and London: Routledge, 1990.

Butler, Judith. *Gender Trouble: Feminism and the Subversion of Identity*. London and New York: Routledge, 1990.

Bynum, Caroline. *Holy Feast and Holy Fast: The Religious Significance of Food to Medieval Women*. Berkeley: Univ. of California Press, 1987.

Carby, Hazel V. "'On the Threshold of Woman's Era': Lynching, Empire, and Sexuality in Black Feminist Theory." In Gates, ed., *'Race', Writing, and Difference*, pp. 301-16.

Carter, Erica and Watney, Simon, eds. *Taking Liberties: AIDS and Cultural Politics*. London: Institute for Contemporary Arts, 1989.

Carter, Paul. *The Road to Botany Bay*. London and Boston: Faber and Faber, 1987; reprint ed., Chicago: Univ. of Chicago Press, 1990.

Centre for Contemporary Cultural Studies, Birmingham. *The Empire Strikes Back: Race and Racism in 70s Britain*. London: Hutchinson, 1982.

Clifford, James. *The Predicament of Culture: Twentieth-Century Ethnography, Literature, and Art*. Cambridge, Mass.: Harvard UP, 1988.

Clifford, James and Marcus, George, eds. *Writing Culture: The Poetics and Politics of Ethnography*. Berkeley: Univ. of California Press, 1986.

Corrigan, Philip and Sayer, Derek. *The Great Arch: English State Formation as Cultural Revolution*. Oxford: Basil Blackwell, 1985.

Cowling, Mary. *The Artist as Anthropologist: The Representation of Type and Character in Victorian Art*. Cambridge: Cambridge UP, 1989.

Crimp, Douglas, ed. *AIDS: Cultural Analysis/Cultural Activism*. Cambridge, Mass.: MIT Press, 1988.

de Lauretis, Teresa. "The Violence of Rhetoric: Considerations on Representation and Gender." *Semiotica* 54, 1-2 (1985):11-31.

________, ed. *Feminist Studies/Critical Studies*. Bloomington: Indiana UP, 1986.

Dijkstra, Bram. *Idols of Perversity — Fantasies of Feminine Evil in Fin-de-Siecle Culture*. New York: Oxford UP, 1986.

Dollimore, Jonathan and Sinfield, Alan, eds. *Political Shakespeare: New Essays in Cultural Materialism*. Manchester: Manchester UP, 1985.

Dorfman, Ariel. *The Empire's Old Clothes: What the Lone Ranger, Babar, and Other Innocent Heroes Do to Our Minds*. New York: Pantheon Books, 1983.

Dyer, Richard. *Heavenly Bodies: Film Stars and Society*. New York: St. Martin's Press, 1986.

Easthope, Anthony. *British Post-Structuralism*. London: Routledge, 1988.

________. *What a Man's Gotta Do: The Masculine Myth in Popular Culture*. Boston: Unwin Hyman, 1990.

________. *Literary into Cultural Studies*. London: Routledge, 1991.

Easthope, Anthony and McGowan, Kate, eds. *A Cultural Studies Reader: Texts and Textuality*. Toronto: Univ. of Toronto Press, 1992.

Fiske, John. "British Cultural Studies and Television." In *Channels of Discourse: Television and Contemporary Criticism*. Edited by R. Allen. Chapel Hill, North Carolina: Univ. of North Carolina Press, 1987.

________. *Television Culture*. New York: Routledge, 1987.

________. *Reading the Popular*. Boston: Unwin Hyman, 1989.

________. *Understanding Popular Culture*. Boston: Unwin Hyman, 1989.

________. *Introduction to Communication Studies*. 2nd ed. London: Routledge, 1990.

Frith, Simon. *Music for Pleasure: Essays in the Sociology of Pop*. New York: Routledge, 1988.

Gallop, Jane. *The Daughter's Seduction: Feminism and Psychoanalysis*. Ithaca, New York: Cornell UP, 1982, paperback ed., 1984.

________. *Reading Lacan*. Ithaca, New York: Cornell UP, 1985, paperback ed., 1987.

Gates, Henry Louis, Jr., ed. *'Race', Writing and Difference*. Chicago: Univ. of Chicago Press, 1986.

Gilroy, Paul. *There Ain't No Black in the Union Jack: The Cultural Politics of Race and Nation*. London: Hutchinson, 1987; new ed., with foreword by Houston A. Baker, Jr., Chicago: Univ. of Chicago Press, 1991.

Giroux, Henry; Shumway, David; Smith, Paul; and Sosnoski, James. "The Need for Cultural Studies: Resisting Intellectuals and Oppositional Public Spheres." *Dalhousie Review* 64 (1985):472-86.

Gless, Darryl J. and Smith, Barbara Herrnstein, eds. *The Politics of Liberal Education*. Durham, North Carolina: Duke UP, 1992.

Gravdal, Kathryn. *Ravishing Maidens: Writing Rape in Medieval French Literature and Law*. New Cultural Studies Series. Philadelphia: Univ. of Pennsylvania Press, 1991.

Grossberg, Lawrence; Nelson, Cary; and Treichler, Paula, eds. *Cultural Studies*. New York and London: Routledge, 1992.

Hall, Lesley A. *Hidden Anxieties: Male Sexuality, 1900-1950*. Oxford: Basil Blackwell, 1991.

Hall, Stuart. "Cultural Studies: Two Paradigms." *Media, Culture and Society* 2 (1980).

________. "The Emergence of Cultural Studies and the Crisis of the Humanities." *October*, no. 53 (Summer 1990):11-90.

Hall, Stuart; Hobson, Dorothy; Lowe, Andrew; and Willis, Paul, eds. *Culture, Media, Language: Working Papers in Cultural Studies, 1972-79*. London: Unwin Hyman, in association with Centre for Contemporary Cultural Studies, 1980.

Haraway, Donna. "Situated Knowledge." *Feminist Studies* 14, 3 (1988): 575-599.

________. *Primate Visions: Gender, Race, and Nature in the World of Modern Science*. New York: Routledge, 1989.

________. *Simians, Cyborgs, and Women: The Reinvention of Nature*. New York: Routledge, 1991.

Harlow, Barbara. *Resistance Literature*. New York & London: Methuen, 1987.

Hebdige, Dick. *Subculture: The Meaning of Style*. London: Methuen, 1979; reprint ed., London: Routledge, 1987.

________. *Hiding in the Light: On Images and Things*. London and New York: Routledge, 1988.

Hobsbawm, Eric and Ranger, Terence, eds. *The Invention of Tradition*. Cambridge: Cambridge UP, 1983, paperback ed., 1984.

Hoggart, Richard. *The Uses of Literacy: Changing Patterns in English Mass Culture*. Boston: Beacon Press, 1961.

Hunt, Lynn, ed. *The New Cultural History*. Berkeley: Univ. of California Press, 1989.

Hutcheon, Linda. "Circling the downspout of empire: post-colonialism and post-modernism." *Ariel* 20, 4 (October 1989).

Huyssen, Andreas. *After the Great Divide: Modernism, Mass Culture, Postmodernism*. Bloomington: Indiana UP, 1986.

________. "Mass Culture as Woman: Modernism's Other." In Tania Modleski, ed., *Studies in Entertainment: Critical Approaches to Mass Culture*. Bloomington: Indiana UP, 1986.

Johnson, Richard. "What is Cultural Studies Anyway?" *Social Text* 6, 1 (1987):38-80.

Johnson, Richard, *et al*, eds. *Making Histories*. London: Hutchinson, 1982.

Jones, Gareth Stedman. *Languages of Class: Studies in English Working Class History 1832-1982*. Cambridge: Cambridge UP, 1983.

Kaye, Harvey J. *The British Marxist Historians*. Oxford: Polity Press, 1984.

Keller, Evelyn Fox. *Reflections on Gender and Science*. New Haven: Yale UP, 1985.

Kerber, Linda K. "Separate Spheres, Female Worlds, Woman's Place: The Rhetoric of Women's History." *Journal of American History* 75, 1 (June 1988):9-39.

Kruger, Barbara and Mariani, Phil, eds. *Remaking History*. Dia Art Foundation Discussions in Contemporary Culture No. 4. Seattle: Bay Press, 1989.

LaCapra, Dominick. *History and Criticism.* Ithaca, New York: Cornell UP, 1985.

Louvre, Alf and Walsh, Jeffrey, eds. *Tell Me Lies About Vietnam: Cultural Battles for the Meaning of the War.* Milton Keynes: Open University Press, 1988.

Martin, Emily. *The Woman in the Body: A Cultural Analysis of Reproduction.* Milton Keynes: Open UP, 1987.

Mattelant, Armand. *Advertising International: The Privatisation of Public Space.* Translated by M. Chanan. London: Routledge, 1991.

Minh-ha, Trinh. *Woman, Native, Other: Writing Post-Coloniality and Feminism.* Bloomington: Indiana UP, 1989.

Mitchell, Timothy. *Colonising Egypt.* Cambridge: Cambridge UP, 1988; paperback ed., Cairo: The American University in Cairo Press, 1989.

________. "Everyday Metaphors of Power." *Theory and Society* 19, 5 (October, 1990): 545-77.

Modleski, Tania. *Loving with a Vengeance: Mass Produced Fantasies for Women.* London: Methuen, 1984.

________. *Studies in Entertainment: Critical Approaches to Mass Culture.* Bloomington: Indiana UP, 1986.

Moi, Toril. *Sexual/Textual Politics: Feminist Literary Theory.* London and New York: Routledge, 1985.

Morris, Meaghan. "Banality in Cultural Studies." *Discourse* 10, 2 (Spring/ Summer 1988):3-29.

Mudimbe, V.Y. *The Invention of Africa: Gnosis, Philosophy, and the Order of Knowledge.* Bloomington: Indiana UP; London: James Currey, 1988.

Mukerji, Chandra and Schudson, Michael. *Rethinking Popular Culture: Contemporary Perspectives in Cultural Studies.* Berkeley: Univ. of California Press, 1991.

Nairn, Tom. *The Break Up of Britain.* London: New Left Books, 1977.

Norris, Christopher, ed. *Music and the Politics of Culture*. London: Lawrence & Wishart, 1989.

Pagden, Anthony. *Spanish Imperialism and the Political Imagination*. New Haven: Yale UP, 1990.

Phizacklea, Annie. *Unpacking the Fashion Industry: Gender, Racism and Class in Production*. London: Routledge, 1990.

Pletsch, Carl E. "The Three Worlds, or the Division of Social Scientific Labor, circa 1950-1975." *CSSH* 23, 4 (Oct. 1981):565-90.

Punter, David, ed. *Introduction to Contemporary Cultural Studies*. London: Longman, 1986.

Ranciere, Jacques. *Nights of Labour: The Worker's Dream in Nineteenth-Century France*. Philadelphia: Temple UP, 1989; paperback ed., 1991.

Ross, Andrew. *No Respect: Intellectuals and Popular Culture*. London: Routledge, 1989.

________. *Strange Weather: Culture, Science and Technology in the Age of Limits*. London: Verso, 1991.

________, ed. *Universal Abandon? The Politics of Post-modernism*. Minneapolis: Univ. of Minnesota Press, 1988.

Said, Edward. *Orientalism*. New York: Vintage Books, 1979.

________. "In the Shadow of the West." *Wedge*, nos. 7/8 (Winter/Spring, 1985):4-11.

________. "Orientalism Reconsidered." *Race and Class* 27, 2 (1985):1-15.

________. "Representing the Colonized: Anthropology's Interlocutors." *Critical Inquiry* 15, 2 (Winter, 1989):205-25.

________. "Figures, Configurations, Transfigurations." *Polygraph*, no. 4 (1991):9-34.

Samuel, Raphael and Thompson, Paul. *The Myths We Live By*. London: Routledge, 1990.

Samuel, Raphael, ed. *Patriotism: The Making and Unmaking of British National Identity*. 3 vols. Vol. 1: *History and Politics*; Vol. 2: *Minorities and Outsiders*; Vol. 3: *National Fictions*. London: Routledge, 1989.

Slemon, Stephen. "Modernism's last post." *Ariel* 20, 4 (October 1989):3-17.

Scott, James C. *Weapons of the Weak: Everyday Forms of Peasant Resistance*. New Haven and London: Yale UP, 1985.

Scott, Joan. *Gender and the Politics of History*. New York: Columbia UP, 1988; paperback ed., 1991.

Showalter, Elaine. *The Female Malady: Women, Madness and English Culture*. London: Virago, 1987.

Stoler, Ann L. "Making Empire Respectable: The Politics of Race and Sexual Morality in Twentieth-Century Colonial Cultures." *American Ethnologist* (Nov. 1989):634-60.

Tiffin, Helen. "Post-colonialism, post-modernism and the rehabilitation of post-colonial history." *Jrl. of Commonwealth Literature* 21, 1 (1988): 169-81.

Turner, Graeme. *British Cultural Studies: An Introduction*. Media and Popular Culture, No. 7. Boston: Unwin Hyman, 1990.

Veeser, H. Aram, ed. *The New Historicism*. New York & London: Routledge, 1989.

Walsh, Jeffrey and Aulich, James. *Vietnam Images: War and Representation*. London: Macmillan, 1989.

Watney, Simon. *Policing Desire: Pornography, AIDS, and the Media*. Minneapolis: Univ. of Minnesota Press, 1987.

Weeks, Jeffrey. *Sexuality*. London: Tavistock, 1986.

________. *Against Nature: Essays on History, Sexuality and Identity*. London: Rivers Oram Press, 1991.

Williams, Raymond. *Culture and Society 1780-1950*. London: Chatto and Windus, 1958; reprint ed., Penguin, 1963.

________. *The Long Revolution*. London: Chatto and Windus, 1961; reprint ed., New York: Harper & Row/Harper Torchbook, 1965.

________. *Keywords: A Vocabulary of Culture and Society*. 2nd ed. New York: Oxford UP, 1983.

Worsley, Peter. *The Three Worlds: Culture and World Development*. London: George Weidenfeld & Nicolson, 1984; Chicago: Univ. of Chicago Press, 1990.

Young, Robert. *White Mythologies: Writing History and the West*. London: Routledge, 1990.